Working the Difference

∴

Working
the Difference

∵

SCIENCE, SPIRIT, AND THE SPREAD
OF MOTIVATIONAL INTERVIEWING

E. Summerson Carr

THE UNIVERSITY OF CHICAGO PRESS
CHICAGO AND LONDON

The University of Chicago Press, Chicago 60637
The University of Chicago Press, Ltd., London
© 2023 by The University of Chicago
Published 2023
Printed in the United States of America

32 31 30 29 28 27 26 25 24 23   1 2 3 4 5

ISBN-13: 978-0-226-82760-5 (cloth)
ISBN-13: 978-0-226-82762-9 (paper)
ISBN-13: 978-0-226-82761-2 (e-book)
DOI: https://doi.org/10.7208/chicago/9780226827612.001.0001

Library of Congress Cataloging-in-Publication Data

Names: Carr, E. Summerson, 1969– author.
Title: Working the difference : science, spirit, and the spread of
motivational interviewing / E. Summerson Carr.
Other titles: Science, spirit, and the spread of motivational
interviewing
Description: Chicago ; London : The University of Chicago Press,
2023. | Includes bibliographical references and index.
Identifiers: LCCN 2023001750 | ISBN 9780226827605 (cloth) | ISBN
9780226827629 (paperback) | ISBN 9780226827612 (e-book)
Subjects: LCSH: Motivational interviewing—United States. | United
States—Civilization.
Classification: LCC BF637.I5 C377 2023 | DDC 158.3/90973—dc23/
eng/20230222
LC record available at https://lccn.loc.gov/2023001750

For Daniel

Contents

Illustrations

FIGURES

TABLES

Prologue

Imagine you and your co-workers have been sent into a bleak, windowless room. Each of you is armed with a cardboard box containing a half-dozen emptied Campbell's soup cans, assorted wires of different sizes and colors, recycled binders filled with arcane operation manuals, and a long list of websites to consult. Your task is to build a perfect communication device. The device should assure that all who use it feel clearly heard and therefore recognized when they speak—so that any difference between what speakers mean and what listeners understand from their speech is eliminated. Moreover, at least during acts of communication, the device should help flatten out power imbalances that typically disrupt face-to-face interactions.

In addition to guaranteeing that speakers' already established feelings, ideas, and thoughts are transparently revealed, your device must help its users generate new feelings, ideas, and thoughts when they speak. In other words, it should help people talk themselves into feeling and thinking things. As if that were not enough, your communication device must inspire people to transform the things they talk about into other kinds of behavior, but only if that behavior is normatively acceptable. For instance, when they speak of taking better care of themselves or getting rid of bad habits, the device should assure that those things actually come to be.

Needless to say, this is a tall order, especially given the incessant calls about various crises outside the room that demand your attention. Your stress is compounded by the fact that your primary task is urgent; some even say it's a matter of life or death given that existing technologies of talk are failing to allay pressing social and psychological problems. Outsiders doubt that you and your colleagues are up to the challenge. This is despite the fact that almost everyone in the room has at least two years of post-graduate training, even if their salaries and work conditions hardly reflect that. And while you all have ample experience with communication and its breakdowns on which to draw, you also realize that more resource-rich experiments to perfect communication—even those designed by comparatively well-known experts and subjected to extensive scientific study—have produced far from ideal results.

And so the doubt is contagious despite the wealth of knowhow in the room. You've all pored over available instructions, and the task still seems impossible. More troubling, you and your colleagues continuously debate the problem you are trying to solve. For example, there are disagreements about whether the problem at hand is fundamentally technical or philosophical. Those in the latter camp pose questions like: What counts as communication? What do you do when a problem has no solution? Why does this always happen to us? The more technically inclined ask: What happens if the device facilitates antisocial talk, and how will we shut it down if that occurs? These arguments quickly grow divisive, and most of your co-workers take sides. Others studiously avoid the conflict and grimly set to work alone, desperately connecting and reconnecting parts, hoping for some signal.

If there is one point of agreement, it is this: there is just no way to build the perfect communication device, especially with the piss-poor box of materials you've been handed. And even those may soon be taken away due to state and agency budget cuts, which augur layoffs, potentially cutting your team in half. The more time you spend in the room, the more alienated you feel, if not about the impossible nature of your charge, then about your lack of progress. You don't make enough money for this shit; you just want to help people; you are burning out fast.

Just then, when all are ready to give up and some are contemplating a new line of work altogether, a dashing "trainer" enters the room. The trainer tells you, gently but firmly, to put down all the cans and wires, close the manuals, and turn off the computers. With a remarkable blend of confidence, humility, and sympathy, he assures that if you are willing to devote yourself to continuous practice, you already possess the capacity to vastly improve, if not perfect, communication because you—as a sentient human being—can learn to speak and listen in new ways. He knows this, he says, because he himself was once enclosed in a room and situation like the one you are in now, until he discovered and devoted himself to the method that he will now teach you: a "conversational style" that he describes as both technical and spiritual.

Some of your weary colleagues roll their eyes at the latter descriptor, but others soon begin to feel revitalized in that very same bleak, windowless room where the trainer is now leading a series of highly interactive exercises. You all begin to stage and rehearse professional conversations, following a seemingly straightforward set of rhetorical rules and straining to enact less specifiable but still palpable sensibilities that the trainer models for you. It's deceptively hard work, and mistakes abound. Not everyone is into it. But, before long, this technology of conversation starts to feel like an art to you; the method becomes simpler, and at the same time more elegant. More importantly, your once overwhelming work begins to feel more manageable and significantly more rewarding as you focus on the minutiae of dyadic communication. You feel the exhilaration of learning, as the "conversation style" seems to require so much skill and finesse, and as you improve, you seem to acquire the qualities you so admire in your trainer. Although you are tested repeatedly in this new style of speaking, it doesn't feel perfunctory, but rather born of dedication to professional growth and striving.

As the trainer promised, you come to realize that achieving perfect communication requires no materials or equipment other than your own, untapped human capacities. Rather than being overwhelmed by impossibility, and drained by collegial division, you refocus your attention on the means rather than the ends of your work, feeling a sense of achievement regardless of outcome. You begin to see why, as your trainer said, you can practice this conversation style in any kind of professional work and with any population. The tension-filled differences that you encounter in your work—between people's positions, problems, and ways of seeing the world—seem not to matter nearly as much as they once did, almost as if they had simply dissipated.

As the months and years go by, you and several of your colleagues become so dedicated to this method that you want not only to practice it with your own clients, but also to teach it to other professionals trapped in windowless rooms, ensnared in division, and tasked with impossibility. You also learn that this new line of work is lucrative, as evidenced by your well-heeled, widely traveled trainer, who attends conferences regularly with other trainers in exotic locales far from the depressing terrain of your current everyday work. Perhaps, most amazingly, you feel personally and profoundly, as well as professionally, transformed by the method. As your training continues, you feel the spirit of the technique and you want to live as well as work with it. And while now fully acknowledging that devising a perfect communication device is simply not possible, you feel you have come as close as you can to fulfilling your original charge.

You have discovered motivational interviewing. And, maybe more importantly, it has discovered you.

Motivating Americans, Defusing Difference

Picture a cramped, dully lit room in an unidentifiable building, in an un-identifiable office park in a semi-identifiable region of the United States, given the pastel rendition of a Navajo weaving hanging on the wall. Here, wedged between a faux fireplace and a fake plant, two middle-aged white men's swiveling office chairs are pulled so close together that their lower limbs threaten to entwine. But ultimately, it is a special kind of conversation that entwines them. This conversation will mysteriously align what they say and even, perhaps, eventually what they otherwise do.

The exchange begins when one of the men—who sports a tidy, blond ponytail along with his business-casual garb—curtly confirms that he has been sent to this room because he recently failed a drug test, admin-istered by the company where he works long and hard as a middle man-ager. The second man, who wears a neatly trimmed beard, expresses sym-pathy with the first man's predicament. He uses the colloquial expression "you got snagged" to refer to the random, company-issued drug test, add-ing, "I would imagine you're pretty angry about that." This statement elic-its a lengthy, animated account from the ponytailed man, who frames the drug test as a violation of his privacy and autonomy, qualifies his drug use as strictly recreational, and betrays irritation to have landed in such con-strained therapeutic quarters. Nevertheless, the bearded man continues to respond in surprisingly sympathetic terms. He repeats—or "reflects"—the ponytailed man's complaints about his company and defenses of his drug use with little probing and no outward signs of objection. As if in commis-eration, the bearded man comments: "It happens in your private life and really, the company has no reason to be concerned about this" and "it's none of their business really, in a way." The ponytail man nods along, ap-parently put at ease by his new, agreeable companion.

The ponytailed man begins talking more—and seemingly more delib-erately—offering up new strands of the quickly developing conversation: the tedium and burdens of work, the worker's right to a private life, the re-

Figure 0.1. William Miller demonstrating motivational interviewing with "Ponytail John." Still from *Motivational Interviewing Professional Training VHS Videotape Series* (Miller, Rollnick & Moyers 1998).

laxation offered by "smok[ing] a joint," the irritation of wives who press to have babies and complain about their husbands partying with the boys. As the conversation proceeds, there seems to be total agreement between the two men about each topic raised. At the very least, the bearded man appears strikingly nonjudgmental about what he learns about the ponytailed man's habits. It's as if he is a friend or neighbor rather than a professional therapist (or, certainly, a well-known expert of addiction treatment!).

Gradually, something unexpected happens, at least from the perspective of the ponytailed man. Despite all the bearded man's seeming support to the contrary, the once resistant ponytailed man concedes that he uses drugs far more regularly than he initially let on, that he uses not just marijuana, but also cocaine and even heroin, and that his habits have "caused [him] a little internal conflict," as they have for his wife and boss, whose concerns he actually understands. As the ponytailed man details the formidable stresses of his job, he mentions, almost in passing, that "there's a need to really blow off steam sometimes I guess," adding that he is uncertain how he would "function" without drugs—statements quite out of line with his initial account. Just as he had done earlier in their conversation, the bearded man apparently agrees with everything the ponytailed man says.

He also noticeably hedges and pauses along the way, as if searching for just the right way to summarize all he has heard:

> So you have a *lot* of responsi*bility*. The, the *job* you have ya-, you're *working* with a lot of people; you're *overseeing* a lot of people. You've got . . . na- not . . . a *family* yet but you've got uh, also a *marriage* and you're *responsible* there, and in some ways this is a pull to . . . feel, feel *free* of that at least for a little while; to feel free of that responsibility. And that's . . . I hear there's a little more than just partying or having a good time. As you've said: *need*; that there's a sense of it might be hard to deal with all that if you didn't have these drugs to use; that in a way, you need these to break the tension, to get away from the stress and responsibility.

In the bearded man's re-renderings, new meanings have been subtly layered into the ponytailed man's preceding statements. Drugs are no longer signs of fun, freedom, and relaxation; instead, they index need, dependency, and escape from responsibility. Through a series of "complex reflections," combined with "affirmations," "open questions," and "summaries" issued by his companion, the ponytailed man's predictable indignation at violations of privacy dissipate into admissions of concern about his own behavior. Rather than defending his initial position, the ponytailed man, with no apparent anger or alarm, nods along through this now deeply critical, if still sympathetically delivered, recasting of his past behavior.

By the end of the twenty-one-minute interview, an air of sobriety fills the room that was once charged with drug-related camaraderie. Almost like magic, the ponytailed man's verbal descriptions of his drug use—and perhaps by extension his drug-using behavior—have *changed*.

. .

At first blush, the method demonstrated by the bearded man seems deceptively facile. A layperson might reasonably conclude that he simply repeats everything that his interlocutor says. One might also note, perhaps with some puzzlement, that these repetitions are consistently offered, whether faced with spirited defenses of party-making and stress-relieving drug use or expressions of regret and concern about it. However, the bearded man— American clinical psychologist, prolific social scientist, and Christian spiritualist, Dr. William R. Miller—is demonstrating a behavioral method, called *motivational interviewing* (MI), that consists of rhetorical techniques and sensibilities that typically take years to master.[1] Despite the commitment involved, thousands of North American professionals who have viewed this training film have embraced motivational interviewing in the hope that they, like Miller, will be able to get clients to "talk *themselves* into change"— that is, without obvious professional prodding (Miller & Rollnick 2013, 159; see also Miller & Rollnick 2002, 8–9, 76). Through this special way of speaking, motivational interviewers work to effectively, if subtly, close the gap between differing views of normatively problematic behavior.

Professionals who delve more deeply into the study of training film vignettes like "Ponytail John" (see figure 0.1)—named after the client-actor whom Miller interviews—learn that what sound like simple repetitions are instead elegantly deployed "reflections."[2] Over the course of their training, they also begin to understand that reflections come in many varieties, which, if properly performed in the course of what could otherwise be a tense and loaded professional exchange, can yield amazing results. When combined with other rhetorical techniques and poetic devices—such as unusually lengthy pauses, copious false starts, and pronounced hedging— reflections can help *motivate* client-interviewees to articulate a statement like "[my drug use] has caused me a little internal conflict, I guess," which the once blasé Ponytail John concedes about eighteen minutes into the filmed exchange. Such a statement is an instance of what MI insiders call "change talk"—that is, an utterance that *animates* professional/normative goals even if it is concertedly *framed* and ideally *experienced as* the client's own.[3] The film's leitmotif, like the method it demonstrates, is that men like Ponytail John strongly prefer to think that their talk and other behavior is wholly self-motivated.[4]

In MI, as in the Anglo-American speech act theory of J. L. Austin (1962) and John Searle (1969), statements are considered behavior in their own right, and are thought to stimulate other referenced behaviors.[5] Invested in these ideas about the forces and effects of language, motivational interviewers work to elicit statements like "maybe it's time to cut back a little" from conflicted clients like Ponytail John, believing that those clients are indeed more likely to curtail their drug use once they say that they "will" (or even that they "might").[6] And, considering the devolution of the US mental and behavioral health system, in which it has become increasingly unlikely that any given professional and client will meet on multiple occasions, it is understandable that one or both of the parties involved in the motivational interview may hang onto the promissory power of words.

Learning to conduct a motivational interview isn't easy. It involves habituation to intricate rules, techniques, and principles of dyadic communication, some of which are explicitly delineated as "skills" while others are acquired more osmotically as "spirit" over a continuous course of practice, supervised by experienced trainers and coaches. By way of this supervision, MI trainers promise their growing audience that when "skills" and "spirit" are properly combined, professionals will be relieved of some ethical and practical quandaries that characterize their routine work, not in the least because their clients will feel more befriended than bossed into behavioral change.

MI may now seem rather fantastical, if not quite as facile to my readers. People can't *really* talk themselves out of heroin habits, even when in the charming presence of highly skilled psychologist-rhetoricians like William Miller . . . *right*?! Rather than providing a clinical response, I consider this question culturally and historically, reissuing it alongside an explanation for the remarkable spread of MI across professional fields. Readers will discover, as I did, that MI's dissemination has been fueled by technocratic *science* as much as by adherents' deep investments in the *spirit* of the method. Through the ethnography of MI training, we will learn about the multifaceted labor required to scale an innovation—in this case, one that is intriguingly packaged and taught as a "conversation style" that transcends the bounds of any one (speech) community (Miller & Rollnick 2013, 12).[7]

Motivational interviewing (MI) was first developed in the early 1980s as a method for engaging problem drinkers in the United States. With the help of scores of MI-specific books, several thousand research articles, the enviable status as an evidence-based practice, and a virtual army of devoted trainers, MI is now common practice in a wide variety of professional fields, including counseling psychology, child welfare, corrections, dentistry, education, nursing, nutrition and weight control, primary care medicine, safe water interventions, and social work. Across these varied domains, MI promises professionals the requisite skills for "addressing the common problem of ambivalence about change" (Miller & Rollnick 2013, 29, 410). Indeed, MI is designed to resolve troubling differences in the ways people see and behave in the world wherever and whenever they might arise.

MI proponents are generally sparing in their ontological claims. However, from the beginning, their official thesis statement has been that *ambivalence*, or "simultaneously wanting and not wanting something, or wanting both of two incompatible things," has been "human nature since the dawn of time" (Miller & Rollnick 2013, 6; see also Miller & Rollnick 2002, 19).[8] As a conversation style for resolving this putatively universal struggle, MI trains professional attention squarely on the dynamics of dyadic communication (i.e., "interviewing") regardless of the qualities of the person or problem at hand. Thus, unlike standalone treatments grounded in an elaborated theory of human psychology, such as psychodynamic or cognitive behavioral therapy (CBT), MI is concertedly plastic and pragmatic.[9]

This means that whatever competing behavioral impulses or habits are in focus—drinking alcohol or cutting back; taking prescribed medications or avoiding their unpleasant side-effects; eating balanced meals or hitting the drive-through—professionals of various stripes and orientations can use MI once trained to do so.

While aimed most directly at resolving competing behavioral impulses within client-interviewees (i.e., ambivalence), MI also works to mitigate challenging differences *between* subject-positions, including of course the differences in perspective between the professional-interviewer and the client-interviewee. Significantly, these perspectival differences are frequently correlated with other socially salient distinctions, distinctions that have long been separate and unequal—though you'd hardly know that from watching Miller and Ponytail John. After all, in the North American institutions where MI is taught and practiced, the motivational interview does not simply convene "the expert" and "the layperson." The living legacy of the United States means that experts are overwhelmingly white, male, and born to class statuses that give them ready access to formal education and other means of advancement. Clients of helping professions are typically people who do not enjoy these positions and means. As we will see, MI explicitly disavows expertise, but has little to say about its sociological entailments.

MI's relative silence around race, gender, class, and linguistic difference, as I understand it, is part and parcel of its effort to be a universally applicable practice, one that transcends the cultural history that so profoundly shapes it. Understandably, readers may find this ironic in a method that presents itself not simply as a way to equalize dyadic exchange, but sometimes also as salve for ideological and institutional divisions. Accordingly, in their focus on MI's central themes and organizing logics, the following chapters attend to the myriad ways that difference is managed in the scaling of cultural forms, and how professional actors are involved in this complex work.

In this book, I bracket the question of whether MI is therapeutically productive for clients, and their experience of the method more generally, which has already been the subject of copious research.[10] Empirically, I turn instead to the world of MI training to explore how the method is *professionally* productive, having revitalized thousands of North American practitioners. For example, at "U-Haven"—a sprawling, urban social service agency where I studied a yearlong advanced training in MI—I tracked how a group of experienced social workers began to rethink and reengage the sundry challenges that characterize their everyday practice. This might include persuading an elderly person with schizophrenia to take a much needed shower, urging an inveterate heroin user to save enough money for rent, or rallying residents in an assisted living facility to take the necessary steps to rid their quarters of bedbugs.

U-Haven's twelve MI trainees inevitably found that the method was not always successful in achieving these ends. Nevertheless, they invested in the training and were especially captivated by Miller's filmed demonstrations of MI, even though their clients have little in common with Ponytail John, save his professed drug habit. U-Haven clients are uniformly poor, almost always unemployed, and unstably housed or homeless; they typically have chronic health and mental health problems, histories of trauma, and active drug habits; disproportionately, they are people of color. During their MI training, professionals were dissuaded from typologizing clients and their problems, and following prescriptive courses of action. Instead, they were trained to treat client engagements abductively, taking each client statement as a sign of what to do and say next. And while some of the U-Haven trainees eventually reverted to diagnostic logics, blaming professional failure on the severity of clients' problems, others read clients' recalcitrance as a sign that they themselves were not yet skillful enough, and accordingly reinvested in the practice of MI.

In some cases, MI became a professional's ticket out of the grim, overpopulated offices of U-Haven. For instance, soon after the yearlong training ended, Austin—a newly minted LCSW—left the impossible caseloads of U-Haven behind to set up a private practice in a tony downtown highrise. His website now attests what issues he treats: "Alcohol Abuse, Anger Management, Anxiety, Codependency, Depression, Drug Abuse—Heroin, Cocaine, Meth, Prescriptions Pills, Gambling, Infidelity, Sexual Addiction, Trauma and PTSD and Video Game Addiction." Austin also teaches MI to professional students as an adjunct professor at a well-regarded university.

Since the early 1990s, MI has become increasingly widely recognized and therefore reimbursed as an "evidence-based practice" (see chapter 4). This, in turn, has meant a growing number of lucrative professional opportunities for those equipped to train the method to others. That said, when Susan—a clinical psychologist and longtime member of the Motivational Interviewing Network of Trainers (MINT)—described learning MI as "opening a door that I didn't know that I needed to step through," she was not referring to the well-paying contracts she landed to train MI in community mental health programs, child welfare agencies, correctional settings, and addiction treatment programs. For Susan, the metaphorical "door" MI opened was one *inside* herself. Like many of the MINT members and trainers whom I met, interviewed, and sometimes followed across the United States—such as Bob, Lois, Lynette, Melony, Norman, Travis, and Wyatt[11]— Susan emphasized how MI spirit profoundly transformed her very way of being and relating in the world. And while some trainees see relatively little worth in MI—like some young dieticians who greeted talk of MI spirit with dramatic eye-rolls and unabashed sighs—others feel so revived that they make the training of the method their *vocation*.[12]

As my research continued well beyond U-Haven, eventually including a training conducted by William Miller himself, I came to believe that the training industry I was studying offered the chance to revisit the spirit of American capitalism, which Max Weber identified long ago. Accounts such as Susan's led me to ask: What are the differently registered if deeply felt investments and gains of training MI? What about MI resonates with and even revives so many burned-out professionals, so much so that they themselves feel compelled to spread the word? What does it take for a conversation style, with specific technical features, to be adopted as a spirit, an ethic, and a powerful way of being with people? What accounts for MI's resonance across widely divergent fields of practice? And why does MI seem so familiar, for some, even like an internal door? With these questions in mind, I focus on MI as a means of disseminating what I came to understand—and this book elaborates—as a normatively American innovation.[13]

TRAINING THAT MAKES A DIFFERENCE

For those interested in the constitution and circulation of expertise, professional training is a ripe subject of study.[14] Most apparently, training is a transactional event wherein trainers impart specific principles, perspectives, methods, skills, and/or sensibilities to apprentices, some of whom go on to train others. Professional training is therefore also a scalar endeavor (see Carr & Lempert 2016; see also Latour 2007; Philips 2016), whether the most pressing goal is to produce more practitioners, more sophisticated practice, better or broader implementation, increased professional stature, and/or wider public recognition. As if that were not interesting enough, training is also a ritual that processes people from one socially salient category to another, tethering them to technical, ethical, and even spiritual ways of knowing along the way (see Carr 2021).

Training takes on additional weight for practitioners in the US "helping professions" where work conditions are typically bleak, draining, and particularly demanding.[15] Despite postgraduate education and the ongoing training required to keep their licenses, social workers—for instance—do not enjoy widespread public regard and respect. They also populate a field so variegated and are faced with a charge so diffuse that professional boundaries, and therefore status, are notoriously difficult to delimit (Abbott 1995). At the same time, helping professionals are charged with resolving highly complex problems that require elaborate skillsets, with necessary resources to do so rarely at hand. The "continuing education" that licensure typically requires—and the training industry that purveys it—substitutes promised skills for dwindling resources, as if the former can compensate for the latter.[16]

While training is inherently interesting for an anthropology of expertise, my focus on the professional training of MI is ethnographically motivated. This is because "helping professionals" are MI's primary clients, the most proximate and significant target of the intervention. As I learned over years of studying those who disseminate the method—from its founders and lead developers to seasoned trainers, as well as those working to join the training ranks—MI is first and foremost focused on changing the way these professionals communicate.

Thus, MI training is not simply about imparting MI; MI training *is* MI—an intervention in and of itself. And while they may only convince a portion of their professional apprentices to change the way they communicate in any given setting, these trainers have dedicated themselves to scaling MI across professional and institutional borders, and have enjoyed tremendous success in doing so. Indeed, if you are an American who has made more than fifteen cumulative visits to a doctor, nurse practitioner, counseling psychologist, dentist or dental hygienist, parole officer, nutritionist, school counselor, or social worker over the past five years or so, the chances are very good that you have been motivationally interviewed, and probably more than once. This is not to say, of course, that you were the recipient of a version nearly as elegant as what Miller demonstrates in his interview with Ponytail John.

At this point, readers may understandably object: "But I've never even heard of motivational interviewing! How could I have been party to it?" Recall that MI is a method of speaking, adaptable by design to varying goals, theoretical orientations, and models of intervention. This means that professionals who have been trained to use MI, and who do so regularly, rarely brand their practice accordingly. Therefore, while you might readily find a "psychodynamic" or "trauma-informed" psychotherapist by searching the web, you would be hard pressed to find a professional who advertises themselves *as* a "motivational interviewer" even if they make prolific use of the method. By contrast, should you be a clinical supervisor of an understaffed nursing unit, the manager of a harm-reduction program for homeless drug users, or the chair of an OB-GYN clinic at a university hospital, looking to train your staff in an "evidence-based practice," a simple web search will yield many clearly branded MI *trainers*, frequently in your immediate vicinity and almost always willing to travel.

What is more, to the untrained ear, MI is very difficult to "hear," even though it is a very specific style of speaking. Quite unlike the pronounced and stilted routines of psychoanalysis, the mantra-filled self-talk associated with CBT, or even the confessional speech rituals of American "self-help," MI consists of highly conventional principles and practices of communication, making it sound only "natural" to many North American interviewees. So when your dental hygienist is motivationally interviewing you to floss your teeth, or when your corrections officer is motivationally interviewing you to adhere to the terms of your parole, it should sound as if they are engaging in a normal conversation—unusual only in the sense that they don't sound nearly as directive or authoritative as you might normally expect, while they do sound far more understanding. Thus, if you happened to recognize that you were being motivationally interviewed, the practitioner surely would be doing it incorrectly.[17]

Like other mainstream American counseling methods, MI aims at normative attitudinal and behavioral changes. As you might imagine, whether or not they use MI, your dental hygienist still wants you to floss and your parole officer will be some kind of angry if you violate the terms of your parole! Accordingly, and as masterfully diagrammed in MI training films, the motivational interviewer must steer the course of the conversation while seeming to follow the client's lead. In actual practice, this entails the disciplined deployment of specific speech acts, carefully calibrated to what the client says, which cannot be predicted in advance. Yet while MI trainers work to make professionals keenly conscious of the way that they communicate with clients, the conversation style is invisible to those clients by design.

While it is likely that many readers of this book will have been at one time motivational interviewees, whether knowingly or not, *who* participates, *how*, and *where* in MI is markedly stratified (see figure 0.2). The vast majority of MI's *leading proponents* are like Miller: white, highly educated professionals; they are also mostly men, with some prominent exceptions. While more than three-quarters of MI *trainers* are also white professionals, a slight majority of whom are women, the *helping professionals* whom they train are far more diverse in terms of race, class, and educational attainment than the trainers are. The labor force in fields where MI has the strongest foothold—addiction treatment, behavioral health, social work, and corrections—has an overrepresentation of women and people of color. Furthermore, the *client base* with which these helping professionals typically work is significantly less economically advantaged, less educated, and far more likely to be nonwhite compared to the overall US population. It is therefore particularly striking that the method is so often officially demon-

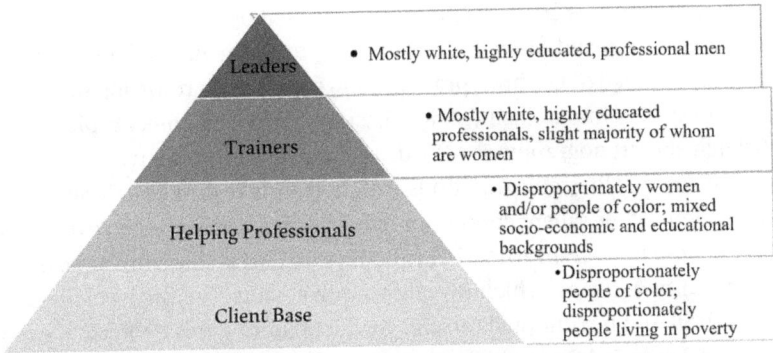

Figure 0.2. The demographics of MI's North American dissemination.
Prepared by Katie Gibson.

strated on film in dyads purged of racial, ethnic, or linguistic difference, as well as observable economic disparity.[18]

MI is also widely trained outside the United States, especially in the United Kingdom and Scandinavia. In the chapters that follow, I argue that despite MI's universalist claims and significant international spread it is a culturally saturated, even quintessentially American practice. This does not mean that MI fulsomely or evenly reflects a national population and a uniform way of seeing the world, as figure 0.2 clearly illustrates. Rather, MI shows us how and why *particular* ideas, perspectives, and people gain traction and establish footholds. In this sense, the question of what is "American" about some practice demands that we examine the ideals and logics that are institutionally organized and formally replicated by elite actors, if sometimes innovatively so.

ORIGINS AND DESTINATIONS: THE REMARKABLE TRAVELOGUES OF MOTIVATIONAL INTERVIEWING

By my reading, motivational interviewing is a prototypically *American* method. Although its transnational spread is almost as impressive as its transinstitutional reach, MI is saturated with conventionally Anglo-American sensibilities and orientations. That is, MI trades in, works with, and responds to a set of ideals that have been institutionalized and therefore historically empowered in the United States.

The story of MI also reveals important lessons about how and why particular interventions travel not just within the United States, but also beyond it, though this book is empirically focused on MI's US terrain. It is all too tempting, and often quite justifiable, to begin and end an explanation of the spread of US-born practices and products by resorting to the familiar terms of "imperialism," "globalization," and "millennial capitalism." Through the ethnography of MI's dissemination, I instead work to track how historically locatable traditions are laboriously reworked *as* innovation and to identify the salient conditions that empower innovation to extend its reach (compare to Irani 2019). In my book, then, MI is an exemplary case of scaling cultural forms, which reveals how professional actors level divided ideological and institutional terrain. By documenting this dedicated, even devoted, labor, I elaborate the creativity and conservatism involved in *motivating Americans* and *managing difference*.

By Dr. William R. Miller's telling, and in contrast to my own, the remarkable rise and spread of motivational interviewing is a decidedly *international* tale, shot through with uncanny coincidences and good—perhaps even divine—fortune. According to Miller, MI began rather provincially in the early 1970s in Milwaukee, where he, as a freshly minted psychologist, discovered how to listen to and learn from alcoholics in the VA hospital where he was interning. Before long, MI would become an adventure. Traveling overseas, Miller arrived at a "barbershop in Norway" (see figure 0.3a), which—if you pay close attention to his account—was located on the thickly forested premises of a psychiatric hospital for alcoholics and was vacated for the visiting Miller to use as an office. In this pastoral/institutional setting, Miller taught courses on CBT and provided group supervision for the young psychologists in residence who, having been schooled in Europe, were "very analytic."[19]

The Norwegian interns wanted to role-play with the American psychologist, asking Miller to demonstrate the techniques he used in his practice.[20] Miller responded in an unusually nonconfrontational, nonauthoritative, and even nonclinical way to the alcoholic clients they were enacting, almost as if he were simply making friendly conversation with a new neighbor, peer, or colleague. He asked few questions, listened intently, and consistently offered what sounded like platitudes. Yet Miller still somehow managed to direct the course of the conversation until those with whom he conversed expressed resolution. The puzzled interns accordingly upped the ante: they role-played exaggerated versions of their most confounding and frustrating patients—as if saying (as Miller recounts), "Okay, smart guy, show us what you would do with *this*." Eventually, like the legions who followed them, the interns found that the placid Miller could not be rattled and continued modeling his method with a decided uninterest in the post-hoc explanations they offered of their clients' role-played behavior.

The young Norwegian psychologists frequently interrupted the American Miller during these dramatic reenactments, sensing there was something subtly effective about his mysterious style of conversation, asking him what he was thinking and why he was doing what he was doing. Miller replied that he was simply practicing what his "clients in Milwaukee had taught him." But exactly *what* those Milwaukeeans had taught him wasn't quite clear to Miller himself at that point. As Miller now tells it, "I began to verbalize some decision rules that I was using and that I was not conscious of and that were embarrassingly different from the [CBT] lectures I was giving in the next room [at the teaching hospital]." For Miller, these are the rules for operationalizing nonhierarchical exchange and projecting sincere interest, as if the client is at least as much of an expert as the professional interviewing them. These are also the rules for cultivating the sense that one's clients talked *themselves* into behavioral change. As Miller's later writings clarified: "If [the professional is] arguing for change, and your client against it, you've got it exactly backward" (Miller & Rollnick 2013, 9).[21] One might imagine that this is what seemed most exotic, if ultimately attractive, to the Norwegians in that barbershop.

Miller also began considering names for his increasingly conscious method. As he told me in his Albuquerque living room many years later, "interviewing" derived from his desire for a term that would be "ambiguous," while still evoking the idea that the client/interviewee had knowledge, even expertise, that the professional/interviewer was trying to garner. Nevertheless, to Miller, "interviewing" sounded "more professional" than the term "conversation," which he also considered. As for "motivational," this was a "logical" choice, according to Miller, not because there was "any theory it came from" (and indeed there is no use trying to pin down Miller on the ontology of motivation, as we will see below). Rather, it simply "came to [him] that [his method] was about evoking motivation," suggesting there was something intuitive as well as logical about this lexical choice. By 1983, he wrote up these decision rules in a "crummy little paper," entitled "Motivational Interviewing with Problem Drinkers," which he circulated among friends, surprised when one of them offered to publish it (Miller 1983).

After his inspiring stint in Norway and back in the United States, Miller set to work developing and testing variations of this method of conversation, which he first conceived as a way to engage alcoholics in treatment. To his amazement, his evaluation studies—conducted with a growing number of students and colleagues, first at the University of Oregon and then at the University of New Mexico, where he is today an emeritus professor— showed that, rather than acting as mere entry point to treatment of another

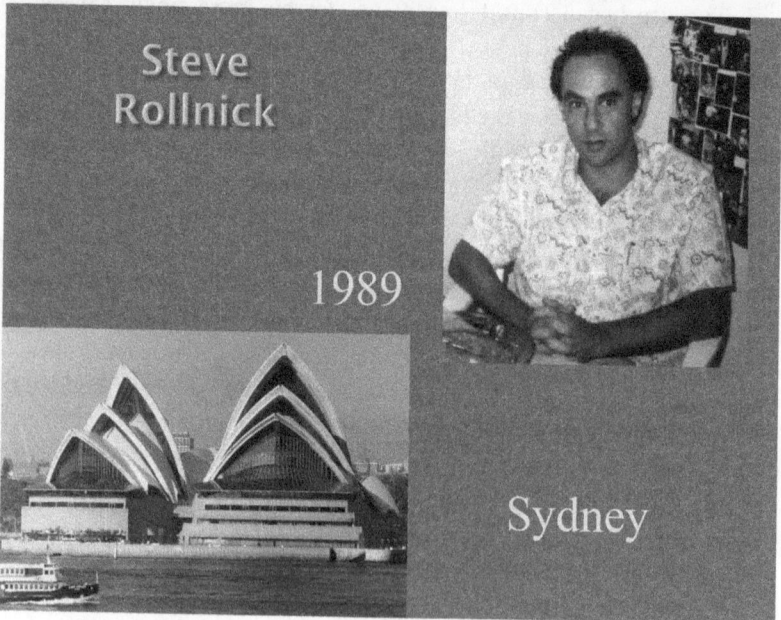

Figure 0.3a and b. William Miller's PowerPoint Slides, presented during his public lecture, "Motivational Interviewing and Quantum Change," at the University of Chicago, September 14, 2014. Slides, with original photography, courtesy of William R. Miller.

kind, MI inspired people to "get better on their own" with no need for further intervention. Yet, it was not until the next leg of MI's journey, in the late 1980s, that Miller recognized that MI had grown in a way that he "could have hardly imagined." At a public lecture I attended, Miller told it this way:

> Then I went off on another sabbatical. This time to Australia. And in the office next to mine there was this South African *bushman*, uh, who was at the time living in Cardiff, Wales but working in Australia. So, he's a man of the world. And his name was Steve Rollnick. And he said to me: "Miller? You, you're that guy who wrote that article on motivational interviewing?" And I said: "You read it? I'm impressed that someone read it!" And he said, "Read it? No! I'm *teaching* MI all up and down the UK. It has become the preferred treatment for addiction and I don't even know if I'm doing it right!"

So, Miller asked the "bushman/man of the world" to show him what he did—that is, to role-play MI as Miller himself had once done in the Norwegian psychiatric hospital, 15,000 kilometers away. An astonished Miller observed: "What [Rollnick] did had exactly the same *heart*. Exactly the same *dance*. And exactly the same rhythm in working with patients."

It is worth noting that Western mythology is laden with stories of relatively ordinary men leaving their home countries, having epiphanies when confronted with different ways of seeing and being in the world, realizing that there was something fundamentally the same in these differences, and returning home to amass admirers and followers. That said, and as he explained to me, the last thing that Miller wants to be known as is a "guru," the Hindi loan term that, in the United States, tends to pejoratively index a decidedly un-American leader who persuades and initiates by way of charismatic authority. Thus, when some in Scandinavia, where there is an unusually high density of MI trainers per capita, have muttered that *they* are the ones who originally developed the method, Miller hardly takes offense. Nor would he likely be offended by his closer-to-home colleague's suggestion, offered during an interview with me, that Miller developed MI in conversation *with her*, though he was the one who so masterfully and cogently "packaged" it. To be sure, the more others claim an authorial connection to MI, the more proof there is for Miller that what *he did* was to recognize something that is always already there, something transcendent. Miller, therefore, prefers to think of himself not as MI's originator, but rather as its "scribe."

According to Miller, the similarities that he recognized between Roll-

nick's practice and his own are signs of what both men came to call "spirit"—
or "the underlying set of mind and heart within which MI is practiced, including partnership, acceptance, compassion, and evocation" (Miller &
Rollnick 2013, 413). And while Miller readily concedes that there are technical aspects of the motivational interview that can and should be consci-
entiously practiced with the assistance of an experienced MI trainer, and
even a more personalized MI coach, he is clear that it is the *spirit* of MI that
permeates the method wherever it is consciously practiced.

US-based MI trainers frequently echo Miller's awe, as if they had tapped
into something both deeply familiar and also transcendent when they first
encountered MI. More commonly and much more mundanely, professionals attending MI trainings claim that MI is familiar precisely because it so
closely approximates what most American psychotherapists have been
taught since the 1970s: that is, the client-centered principles of therapeutic communication popularized by mid-twentieth-century American psychologist Carl Rogers. As these relatively unimpressed professionals commonly report to their trainers, MI seems very similar to what they already
learned as, simply, "good practice."[22] In other words, they struggle to see
what's new in what they experience as already established ways of engaging
in therapeutic exchange.

The pages that follow detail MI's response to the charge that there is
"nothing new" about the method. Along the way, I ask readers to consider
how the process of innovation necessarily involves creatively repackaging
institutionalized traditions, and—more particularly—resolving differences
that tradition harbors. I will further offer that while MI has concertedly
framed itself as international, universal, and even transcendental, and has
in fact enjoyed significant uptake outside the United States, the ideas that it
repackages and revives are ones that have long been entrenched in US institutions, and not just clinical ones.

Indeed, in recombining fundamental ideas in competing schools of
American psychotherapy, MI also draws on American democratic ideals (chapter 1). If insiders sometimes claim that MI is a "natural language"
(Miller & Rollnick 2013, 4), they teach it as a speech style, one that is clearly
grounded in historically specific traditions of Anglo-American rhetoric
(chapter 2). MI is deeply, if never explicitly, Protestant in its ethical commitments, including its construal of (spiritual) labor (chapter 3). Some European MI proponents, including Rollnick, worry that MI's growing status
as an "evidence-based practice," not to mention a "brief" and "cost effective" one, blends intervention science with neoliberal and neo-Keynesian
economics, again revealing its American character (chapter 4). At the same
time, MI draws on Anglo-American strands of spirituality, humanism, and

political philosophy and dissent. This includes the way MI enlivens core principles of American pragmatism, offering US-based helping professions an abductive way to approach their work (chapter 5).

The study of innovations, of the crafting of new forms out of culturally recognizable material, reminds us that culture is never given, but always made. This is hardly a new insight in anthropology, nor is the corollary point that cultural reproduction of any sort should never be thought apart from the history of just which parties gain authority and which practices find institutional haven.[23] After all, if I am right in saying that innovation is creatively repackaged tradition, we should never take for granted what practices count as tradition from the start.

As Miller's origin story demonstrates, it can be quite counterproductive for innovations to declare their context-specific roots. That said, MI does not rest on the claim that the method is universally applicable. Instead, ideological *difference* is MI's fodder, that which it seeks out so as to resolve. As we will see, moving the method radically depends on the continual questioning of the boundaries conventionally used to demarcate institutions and their ideals, including the normative division of science and spirituality.

AMERICAN SCIENCE, AMERICAN SPIRIT (OR, THE MOVEMENT IN THE METHOD)

If MI all started with "one crummy paper" about communicative decision rules, the diversity and sheer volume of Miller's own writings on MI are now nothing short of extraordinary, contributing to his distinction as one of the world's most frequently cited social scientists, according to the Institute for Scientific Information (ISI). Miller's initial encounter with Rollnick in Australia soon morphed into a decades-long collaboration between the two men, beginning with their decision to disseminate the method through a textbook they would write together. Among those who train and coach other professionals in MI, that first edition (1992) came to be known, half-jokingly, as the "MI Bible."

By the time Miller and Rollnick were at work on the second edition of their textbook, an intervention research industry had developed to assess MI (as well as other behavioral methods) relative to a growing number of populations and fields of application, including substance abuse treatment, mental health counseling, primary care medicine, corrections and parole, HIV risk prevention, diet and weight control, smoking cessation, domestic violence treatment and prevention, and safe water interventions.[24] Over the next thirty years, the number of peer-reviewed papers on MI multiplied, including hundreds of randomized controlled trials (RCTs) and meta-analyses, some of which were authored by Miller, his students, and other MI proponents. Thus, in addition to further elaborating MI "spirit," Miller and Rollnick were able to lace user-friendly, scientizing references to the ballooning MI research through the next editions of the MI Bible.

This scientific production was a necessary, if hardly sufficient condition of MI's dissemination in the United States. As elaborated in chapter 4, RCT research on MI qualified the method for consideration by the federal and state bureaucracies that baptize, list, and legitimate "evidence-based practices" (see also Carr & Norwood 2022). Gutted by devolution, North American health and human service organizations are under intense pressure to demonstrate that the methods and programs they adopt are "evidence based" in order to secure public funding and/or reimbursement. While the designation of MI as an "evidence-based practice" has created a demand for MI training in an array of professional fields, offering a wealth of entrepreneurial opportunities for MI trainers, these trainers face the formidable challenge of meeting the expectations of an increasingly heterodox professional audience.

One could rightly credit any number of texts—from translated MI textbooks to the "doubling" number of published studies—for fueling MI's impressive dissemination, as Miller often does. In public lectures, Miller tellingly touts the power of these texts, and therefore the method they represent, with PowerPoint slides listing the number of MI publications, the rate at which they are "doubling," and the two dozen languages (so far) into which MI books have been translated. And, indeed, alongside the three editions of Miller and Rollnick's textbook (with a fourth edition in production), an ongoing stream of population- and field-specific books on motivational interviewing has been published, including textbooks on MI in health care, education, mental health counseling, diet and nutrition, intimate partner violence, and corrections. In recent years, more and more MI "workbooks" have appeared as well, suggesting that one might brush up on one's MI skills and spirit with a click on Amazon and in the comfort of one's own home. However, it remains the case that, unlike competing interventions, MI has never been officially manualized, which would allow individuals and institutions to learn the approach via text, without the need for an in vivo human trainer.[25]

Thus, MI's scaling heavily depends on the boots-on-the-ground labor of several thousand professional trainers, who are members of the Motivational Interviewing Network of Trainers (MINT).[26] Active members, about two-thirds of whom are North Americans and most of whom are white, middle-class, mid-career professionals with graduate degrees, call them-

selves "MINTies." They typically enjoy a wide range of professional perqui-
sites and opportunities that they could only have imagined in their previous
careers as helping professionals, including an official status that is increasingly recognized by potential contractors for their services.[27] Whether
contracted by state governments (as with California's statewide MI training of parole officers), conducting trainings with medical practitioners in a
large hospital or social service staff in a small agency, launching advanced
trainings that attract hundreds of professionals, offering online trainings
from their own family rooms, or "coaching" advanced MI practitioners via
Skype and now Zoom, these trainers help move the method as they themselves move, traveling across the country and sometimes the world.[28] And
although MINTies are generally appreciative of MI's status as an evidence-
based practice, which has driven the demand for their labor, they focus
their trainees' attention on the spirit as much as the science of the method.

Miller has been directly involved in training many MINTies and is a generous and eager interlocutor with the countless admirers who email him
with questions and kudos. He is also an engaged participant in MINT's
annual Training New Trainers (TNT), a three-day event generally held in
posh locations around the globe and typically attended by hundreds of established members as well as new initiates. Though the event culminates in
MINT membership, it is strikingly devoid of ritual: "It's just more training,
really," one new MINTie told me plainly, if cheerfully, when I participated
in and observed the TNT in 2014. (When I was invited to give a talk about
this book to the MINT Forum in October 2022, it appeared that these qualities of the gathering had not much changed.)

That said, MINT clearly has a plan for the dissemination of MI. In the
very same small journal in which Miller had introduced MI a quarter of a
century earlier, he and Rollnick laid out an unmistakably pyramidic design
to disseminate MI:

> Within the Motivational Interviewing Network of Trainers (MINT)
> alone, more than 1,500 people have completed training as MI trainers. If
> each of them has trained 100 clinicians, and each clinician has practiced
> MI with 100 people, then at least 15 million people have already been
> intended recipients of MI as a result of MINT alone. (Miller & Rollnick
> 2009, 129)[29]

If the essential role of MINT trainers in the scaling of MI is quite explicit in
this account, more frequently Miller downplays and even abstracts the sys-
tematicity and human labor involved in MI's dissemination.[30] Along with
his fellow proponents, he suggests instead that forces that quite exceed any

plan or design, and even elude post-hoc empirical explanation, are at work in moving MI through the world. For instance, in the very year he wrote of MINT's design to reach 15 million "intended recipients," he gave an interview to the academic journal *Addiction*, in which he offered:

> The response [to MI] really is amazing, and it has spread into corrections and health care and many other areas. I am not sure I understand it. The verb that I use is that people seem to "recognize" it. When they hear MI described, it is not as if they are hearing it for the first time. The people who take to it sort of recognize it . . . We have not done that much to disseminate it. It just seems to flow naturally. (Miller 2009, 890)

First, note that in this formulation of recognition-by-MI, Miller is referring to professionals rather than clients when he references those who "hear MI described" and accordingly, even almost automatically, "take to it." As both Miller and Rollnick have told me, MI is as much about changing professionals' behavior as it is about changing clients' behavior, and that the latter depends on the former. However, MINT's efforts are nowhere in sight in the suggestion that MI "flow[s] naturally"—if also rather wondrously—to the extent that professionals "recognize it."

"Recognition" is a pregnant term in American political and religious discourse alike, as it is in MI. Recognition-by-MI casts the method as democratic (chapter 1), while also more implicitly connecting it to the experience of Protestant conversion (chapter 3). Indeed, many MINTies—whatever their religious upbringing and affiliation—speak of their relationship to MI in a recognizably Protestant American register. And while the MINTies I came to know sometimes revealed the laborious nature of their training work—including recalcitrant trainees, unreceptive institutions, and unpaid contracts—they just as often erased that labor in claiming, like Miller, that MI "flows" thanks to its spirit.

In American Protestantism, an experience of spiritual connection and conversion is typically completed by a commitment, or covenant, to share that experience with others. And like many spiritually revived Americans before them, some MINTies report that they feel compelled to transmit the spirit of their method to others, almost as if they were spreading the Word. And while their work is both contractual and profitable, MINTies frequently cite an inspiration to "pay it forward"—a culturally resonant phrase that smooths out the potential disjuncture between spiritual labor and profit-driven work. When coupled with my own observations of the social organization of MI training, these insider accounts suggest that the labor of moving MI has distinct revivalist qualities. More particularly, and as I elaborate in chapter 3, the movement of MI in many ways resembles American religious revivals, whose practitioners likewise traveled the country, setting up (tent) meetings so as to transmit a spirit in and through an especially potent method of oratory.

Religious revivals, including American variants, are often said to be born when traditional values come into contact with troubling new ideals, inspiring devotees to defend those values even while reforming and restabilizing stressed institutions. With the case of MI in mind, I will argue that revivals can also be fueled when contemporaneous principles, which historically recur as ideological oppositions and institutional impasses, are effectively leveled by spiritually motivated, charismatic actors. And while revivalists' faith need not be shared by all those whom they encounter, the success of a revival can be measured by the degree to which its messages spread into new fields of practice.

From MI's lead proponents to the thousands of trainers who teach, coach, and cultivate the method, MI's disseminators challenge us to see the spirit in the calculus of a pyramid, the passion in positivist science, and the presencing of oneself in a professional skillset. As we will see, the trainers who move MI in the world are also, by their own accounts, profoundly *moved by* it, requiring a consideration of the affective and spiritual dimensions of their scalar work, alongside the economic and political conditions that make it possible and rewarding.

THE DIFFERENCE IN DISSEMINATION

Why do certain ideas, practices, and projects travel and enjoy widespread uptake? What does it take for a cultural product to transcend the situation of its birth and baptism, leaving its more parochial brethren behind? Given its acuity in finding established paths on which to travel, its ingenuity in leveling ground that might otherwise hinder its spread, and its ability to inspire a cadre of professionals devoted to dissemination, MI offers a tantalizing opportunity to revisit these perennial questions. Accordingly, this book participates in a lively cross-disciplinary discussion, joining the works of other scholars interested in movement, whether in terms of circulation, citation, commoditization, diffusion, entextualization, globalization, imperialism, liquidation, missionization, (post)colonialism, scale, standardization, translation, or worlding.

Among those in the applied sciences, including Miller and many of his colleagues, the most familiar and influential of these accounts probably remains Everett Rogers's 1962 *The Diffusion of Innovations*, now in its fifth edition (Rogers 2003).[31] A rural sociologist who studied the dissemination of seed technologies, Rogers loosely defined "innovation" as ideas, things, practices, or methods recognized as "new." His influential account of innovations, so defined, relied heavily on the presumption of rational actors in rational organizations who make rational decisions, calibrated by the amount of information available to them and other technical capacities. Furthermore, Rogers was clearly more interested in determining the characteristics of innovation "adopters," whom he categorized in a taxonomy ranging from "early adopters" to "laggards," than in examining the qualities of disseminators. He also tended to assume that an innovation remains quite stable in its transmission, with his central question being the conditions that lead economically driven people to adopt it or not.

Though using different terms and driven by distinctive sensibilities, anthropologists have long shared Rogers's interest in the dynamics of diffusion.[32] Linguistic anthropologists have shown that what appears to simply "flow" across contexts is actually the effect of translation and other citational practices, practices that require significant labor by the various parties involved.[33] Similarly, Science and Technology Studies (STS) scholars have demonstrated how human and nonhuman actors work together to create a sense of constancy through transformations, so that things on the move may be discovered again and again—from context to context—as *the same* (see, for instance, Latour 1999, 58). This book examines the question of movement from a complementary angle. I show how innovative methods like MI move by actively managing *difference* in perspectives, affiliations, disciplinary ideals and identifications, and professional locations.

Indeed, just as the MI session is devoted to the resolution of competing ideas and ideals, so too is MI as a project and product. As MI proponents know all too well, fierce ideological opposition lurks within the institutions where helping professionals work and train no matter how much a single position may be structurally enforced. Some professionals come to see MI as helping them manage the myriad conflicts of their everyday work, within and beyond the clinical encounter. Thus, Marcus, a devout Alcoholics Anonymous (AA) member and paraprofessional at U-Haven, finds that MI allows him to "hold people accountable" for the addictions they deny *and* to seriously engage those very people's accounts of their problems as equally valid to his own.[34] Vernon, a lead psychologist at a northeastern Veterans Affairs (VA) hospital, thanks MI for helping him couch his humanist tendencies in the language of evidence-based practice and thereby evade the scrutiny of bureaucratic management. And Amber, a disciplined adherent of Medicare's eight-minute rule, credits MI for allowing her to "really," if quickly, "connect" with her patients and to train other nurse practitioners to do so.[35]

The chapters in this book track the ingenious ways that MI proponents work with socially salient distinctions and, in doing so, move the method. As we will see, *working the difference* sometimes means dismissing marked difference from the start, as in claims that MI is globally applicable or when white male client-actors are left unmarked, standing as universal subjects. More often, it entails drawing attention to difference so as to overcome it, such as when some opposition is rendered irrelevant and thereby drained of potential force. Perhaps most intriguingly, in an age when so many Americans bemoan partisanship while actively participating in it, MI shows us how a wide array of partisan positions—including ostensibly apolitical ones—can be transformed into generative paradox.

As we follow MI's dissemination, we will learn how the method productively exploits normative distinctions in prominent lines of North American thought. For instance, when faced with the question of whether the motivational interview is an expertly driven, directive intervention *or* a method that fully recognizes and accommodates client autonomy, MI says yes. To the question of whether motivational interviewers are performing an elaborate speech style *or* authentically presencing themselves to their clients, MI says yes. To the question of whether MI trainers are driven by a divine calling *or* by the promise of profits, MI says yes. And to the question of whether motivational interviewing is scientific, endowed with an authoritative evidence base, *or* mystical, graced with transpersonal spirit, MI says yes. In these ways and others, MI concertedly eschews partisan propositions; yet it also revives tired oppositions by recombining them, effectively assuring its growing professional audience that there is no need to take sides.

In anthropology, one of the most influential approaches to questions of difference is that of Anna Lowenhaupt Tsing. In her 2004 book, *Friction*, Tsing urges anthropologists to study universals, including the kind of liberal universal claims Miller makes. She argues that universals are always the result of friction, or the qualities of interconnection across difference and diversity. In her more recent account of a global commodity—the matsutake mushroom—she warns against the "banish[ing] of meaningful diversity" (2015, 38) as well as the silencing effects of universals. Yet as Susan Gal and Judith Irvine (2019) remind us, differentiation—or the distinctions drawn between kinds of people, positions, projects, signs, sign activities, and species—is also ideological from the start, with potential to be violent and even destructive. Moreover, as Scott MacLochlainn (2022) has recently argued, the nonspecific (or generic) can be highly productive, serving a wide range of social actors, institutions, and projects. The question, then, is how, why, and to what ends some forms are identified *as different* and managed as such. This, we will see, is a highly selective and laborious process, one that propels the method across fields of professional practice. And while MI scales itself by working the difference in various ways, its cultivation of paradox is particularly revealing.

Indeed, MI shows us that paradox acts as symbolic twine, binding together otherwise unresolvable oppositions. Paradox manages differences by allowing the ideas that people normatively hold apart to orbit each other in practice. Whereas other antinomies insist upon "either/or," paradox answers "both/and" to the question of how two opposing ideas can be true at once. Paradox thereby provides the opportunity to reconsider normative distinctions, without demanding compromise or even reconciliation. Because paradox accommodates, even entertains, difference, it can also stimulate reflection, asking us why we set up the world the way we do. In this sense, paradox is productive precisely because it allows us to retain valuable ideals while refusing the tired distinctions in which they are typically ensnared. Because paradox reconfigures problems paralyzed by either/or formulations, those able to capitalize on this potency, and keen to do so, can employ paradox as a resource, enjoying the bounty of having it both ways.

As a primer, let us briefly consider a pregnant example: the paradoxical formulation of *motivation* by MI's lead proponents. If you crack open the MI Bible, you'll find ample reference to motivation as an *internal* property, over which the person has ownership. Though there may be more or less of it, and it may be more or less apparent, motivation is framed repeatedly as a psychological possession of the client-interviewee. Passages such as those found in the lefthand column of table 0.1 (A1–3) reflect an epistemology found in many North American interventions: motivation can be found inside the client and called forth by the professional, if only—in this case—by way of a particular "conversation style." This is all the more familiar because this definition of motivation has deep roots in liberal conceptions of selfhood, and—as many have argued—has been rejuvenated in neoliberal ones.

Yes, *and*: in other passages of the very same book, Miller and Rollnick explicitly *disavow* the idea that motivation is internal, residing within the individual as a personal state or trait—in one case, a mere nineteen pages after strongly suggesting precisely that. Consider the MI Bible's definitive statement that motivation is "an interpersonal process, the product of an interaction between people." In this second and very different definition of motivation, interaction takes precedence over interiority, with motivation defined as a semidurable *social product* manufactured by the motivational interview (table 0.1, B1–3).

Motivation originates both inside *and* outside of people? A psychological property *and* a social product? A preexisting state *and* an interactional dynamic? "This method seems to want to have it *both ways*—and relative

Table 0.1. The "motivation" in motivational interviewing

BOTH...	AND
A1. "Motivational interviewing: A collaborative conversation style for strengthening a person's own motivation for change." (Miller & Rollnick 2013, 12)	B1. [MI departs from] "the idea that motivation is internal, residing within the individual as a personal state or trait." (Miller & Rollnick 2013, 44)
A2. "Motivation for change is not installed, but is evoked. It's already there and just needs to be called forth." (Miller & Rollnick 2013, 23)	B2. "Motivation is in many ways an interpersonal process, the product of an interaction between people." (Miller & Rollnick 2002, 22)
A3. Motivation is a psychic property of a person, evoked by a particular kind of conversation (i.e., the motivational interview).	B3. Motivation is a social product, generated out of a particular kind of conversation (i.e., the motivational interview).

to its definitional terms at that!" I murmured to myself when I first encountered these passages. I vacillated on what to make of these confounding pages in MI's foundational textbook, and once sitting across from their author, I took the opportunity to pin him down on his definition of motivation, only to find that what I viewed as conceptual contradictions at the heart of MI, he celebrated as precisely what makes his method productive and unique.[36] A clearly amused Miller underscored the plenitude of paradox:

> ESC: So am I right in thinking that *you're* thinking that motivation is *both* inside and outside of people?
> WRM: Yeah ... I love paradoxes. Yeah.
> ESC: Yeah?
> WRM: Is it inside or outside? The answer is yes. [*broadly smiling*]
> ESC: [*laughs*] Okay ... good.

Note here how swiftly Miller enervates my implicit critique. The master communicator had turned the tables, leaving me with a number of questions for *myself*. Why was *I* expecting theoretical purity? Why was *my thinking* not flexible enough to see that some quality—like motivation—could be both inside *and* outside? Why did less than airtight definitions make me suspicious, as if fuzzy thinking or chicanery were probably to blame?

Admittedly, mine were the queries of a disciplinarian, if one who has been trained to seriously engage others' ways of thinking and organizing their conceptual worlds. Over the course of my study, I heard many other disciplined professionals, when first encountering MI, ask similar questions, as if forcing their trainers to pick sides, only to find the proposed opposition devitalized in elegant response. As we will learn in chapter 1, the question of whether psychic interiority is the proper target of intervention, the site where motivation among other drives and affects is located, has long divided schools of American psychology, schools that MI, not surprisingly, claims to reconcile. In answering both/and to charges of either/or, MI deflates the differences that can partition professionals, giving MI's proponents every reason to "love" paradox. Indeed, a method that rarely says "no" is one that allows ready and wide adoption. What could stand in the way of a method that always finds a way to agree?

Just as paradox abounds in MI texts, it also infuses MI trainings. It is possible, MI trainers suggest to their weary apprentices, to lead and follow a client at the same time, to be expert and inexpert, to perform and presence oneself within a single interaction. Some trainees find this freeing and deeply rewarding.[37] Yet, in tracking MI's travels, we will also learn that the generative work of leveling difference can be frustrating, even troubling, for the more partisan among us. After all, we just got a glimpse of how both/and formulations of motivation drain a potentially productive debate about where human action originates—a debate whose implications resonate far beyond therapeutic encounters.

While MI's "love" of paradox can stimulate inquiry and action, it also tends toward conservatism, enervating what might otherwise be productive ideological conflict, including partisan efforts to prove the supremacy of some ideal relative to another (see Weiner 1993, 5).[38] Furthermore, while paradox affirms difference in the present, it can also disguise difference in the past (Weiner 1993, 10; see also Roitman 2013, 38; Kierkegaard 1985; Žižek 2006). This includes how people and practices have been historically partitioned, often unequally so, in ways that demand recognition and redress. For all these reasons, moving MI is fraught and risky work, demanding that we carefully analyze just what MI defuses and who and what it revives, at what costs and to what ends.

[CHAPTER 1]

American Democracy

(Or, How to Direct Autonomous Subjects)

It was a sweltering summer morning on a bleak corner of a mid-sized, postindustrial American city. I pulled into a half-empty parking lot and gathered the recording equipment splayed across the front seat of my rental car—a mess caused by an earlier audit during the drive from Chicago. Scanning the silent parking lot for signs of life, I approached the nondescript, four-story office building where I had been invited to gather with ten helping professionals, praying it was air-conditioned. "I'M HERE FOR THE MO-TIVATIONAL INTERVIEWING TRAINING," I awkwardly announced in response to the enervated "yyyessss" at the other end of the intercom. After a long pause, a barely audible buzz granted me passage though the heavy glass door. Surmising that the voice was uninterested in providing further assistance and wondering which way to head in the linoleum-floored hallways, I happened upon two middle-aged, white women who looked as if they had only recently gained their bearings. "You here for the training, too? We think it's up this way." I happily followed along, eager to record the first MI training that I ever attended.

By the time we finished a disturbingly slow elevator ride and found the right room, I gathered that the women had driven from the state capital to attend their fourth group training session. I also learned that both women had recently completed their first "tapes," a standard practice in advanced MI training, which was clearly the focus of their conversation before I'd bumped into them. This meant that they each audio-recorded themselves conducting a motivational interview, turned the recordings over to their trainer, and were now anxious to receive their "scores." "Mine is *awful.* I *know* it is," one of the women lamented; the other rolled her eyes in reply: "I'm *sure* it isn't *awful.* You're getting the hang of it!" They were still thick in commiseration when we entered the training room. Norman, the trainer who had invited me, offered a warm welcome and began introducing me as "the linguist" to the trainees I had yet to meet, all of whom hailed from social service agencies around the city and its suburban outskirts.[1]

As the trainees took turns explaining where they worked—a homeless shelter, a child welfare program, a youth center, a private psychotherapy practice focusing on addictions—I couldn't help but wonder what percentage of their salaries they were sacrificing toward their training in MI. Camilla, the youngest and only nonwhite member in the group, was being sponsored by the agency where she worked as a youth counselor, thanks to a supervisor who saw the training as valuable "professional development." From what I could gather, the remaining trainees were paying out of pocket to deepen their skills in and knowledge of this increasingly popular method, if perhaps on a sliding scale. Over lunchtime chatter and follow-up interviews, I learned more about why Norman's trainees saw MI as a worthy if somewhat risky investment. Once she was seated beside me, and speaking under her breath, one of the women from the elevator asked me if *I* knew how one "got into the MINT"—the Motivational Interviewing Network of Trainers, an international organization then numbering about 1,350 active members, all of whom had gone through extensive training in MI as well as tutelage in how to train MI to others. This training includes MINT's annual Training New Trainers (TNT), which I would observe years later.

By the end of that summer day, it was clear that at least half of Norman's trainees were intent to join MINT so as to make their work more lucrative, flexible, and independent, *and* that they found the steps for doing so far from transparent, even with longtime MINT member Norman's warm and generous tutelage. Eventually, one of them succeeded. Years after I first met him, Glenn was "MINTed," leaving the understaffed social service agency he managed (and whose offices he'd lent to Norman for the training session I attended). Soon thereafter, Glenn established his very own training firm, with six trainers in his employ, ample state and private training contracts, and a sophisticated website.

Norman is not nearly as polished as his successful apprentice, though he remains a sought-after member of MINT. When I first met him in 2009, he had long since quit his job as a parole officer to travel the country, and the world, to train others in MI. His work included crisscrossing the United States to conduct MI coding, holding regular Skype coaching sessions with a psychologist in Bulgaria, and even traveling to Singapore to train doctors in the method. For his trainees, the ever affable, globe-trotting Norman is living proof that if they devoted themselves to rigorous, ongoing MI training, they could escape the frustrations of frontline human service work and pursue a more rewarding professional path, while still fulfilling their mission to help others.

Norman also provided ample evidence that there is no contradiction between being "an old guy" who is "slow" and "apologizes for everything"—

as one trainee affectionately described him—and being a successful MI trainer. Though Norman is an MI pioneer in the field of corrections, author of several papers and a book on the topic, and an experienced trainer, he repeatedly questioned himself aloud, asked trainees how he was doing, and if they needed something he hadn't managed to give. When his PowerPoint slides included technical points, he readily attributed them to others, at one point even saying that he "didn't really understand it all." When I returned home to Chicago, I was greeted with voicemail that continued in this vein. Norman reiterated his request that I send him my recordings of the training, asked me what I thought about it, and relayed that he was "uncertain" about so many aspects of his work. He added that when it comes to MI, "there's always so much to learn."[2]

It is not just Norman who exudes this endearing, if initially puzzling, sensibility when he trains—a professional repertoire that I now understand as MI's signature *(in)expertise* (see also Carr 2023). As my fieldwork went on, and I observed MI trainers in action, I continued to marvel at emphatic displays of uncertainty, disavowals of authority, and the continual downplaying of otherwise impressive credentials. Most of the trainees, who were depending on trainers to learn the method, hardly seemed to mind. In fact, when I returned to interview some of Norman's trainees not long after the first session I attended, they explained that this pronounced humility is a large part of what makes Norman an effective MI trainer, a "real model," as one of them put it, even a "*guide.*" After all, MI centrally involves openly eliciting direction from the (lay)people—whether clients or trainees—whom one is ostensibly charged with directing. And, as party to this practice over the course of many trainings, I ultimately concluded that, just as expertise is enacted (Carr 2010a), so is its seeming antithesis.

I even found (in)expertise at the very "top" (or, as MI proponents would surely prefer, "center") of the MI training community. Consider my observations of the founder and lead developer of MI at a university-sponsored lecture I attended along with 240 others. William Miller, sporting his signature bolo tie, casually leaned against the podium throughout his talk and fumbled with the remote for his PowerPoint presentation almost as if he were at home, clicking through stations to find the local evening news. During the lecture, Miller fluidly shifted between explanations of information-packed slides displaying the latest research on MI—which boasts hundreds of randomized controlled trials (RCTs)—and humility-laced anecdotes of the method's origin story. At one point, he bent down to pull a book he had authored from a worn cloth bag resting on the floor near the podium, reading passages aloud in the register of a town librarian. The talk seemed to transform large swaths of the university audience into grownup grandchildren, who recognized the wisdom of the speaker without feeling bound by paternalistic adage. One lecture evaluation read, "I was deeply engaged and moved"; another commented on Miller's "captivating vocal tone"; still another remarked that "Dr. Miller is such a pleasant and humble person, a pleasure to learn from and listen to." (In)expertise, it appears, has highly appealing, even *charismatic* qualities.

The next day, during a training that Miller was conducting at the same university, a highly educated audience of professionals eager to advance their MI knowledge were satiated by the founder's (in)expertise. He greeted new trainees as if they were old friends, with his hands in his pockets, head cocked and slowly nodding, glistening eyes fixed, intently listening to their questions and comments, all the while modeling his method. Five hours, 141 PowerPoint slides, and several application exercises later, Miller leaned back in his chair and whimsically broke into a folk song about the dangers of motorcycle riding, a topic broached by a trainee for a demonstrated (or "role-played") MI session he had engaged in minutes earlier. While the audience marveled at how effortlessly Miller had eased the motorcycle rider into taking safety precautions, Miller himself offered a far more critical self-review, pointing out several ways that his interview could be improved. Miller—like Norman—insisted that, when it comes to MI, he is not the expert.

Miller not only refuses the moniker "expert" himself; in his writings, lectures, and published interviews, he also explicitly warns his professional audience against expert hubris. Condemning the "diagnostic method" by which clinical knowledge is typically accrued, Miller suggests that "question-answer routines" are not just ineffective, failing to ascertain the complexities of behavioral change, but are also unethical, reinforcing the authority of the party who directs the inquiry and decides what counts as knowledge.[3] By contrast, Miller frames MI as a "collaborative conversation style" and a "way of being with people" that involves the practiced presentation of the professional self as a receptive, nonjudgmental listener.

MI's foundational textbook underscores these points, further asserting that the rejection of expertise is fundamental to the very constitution of the method. For instance, Miller and Rollnick write: "Many professionals during post-graduate education were taught and expected to come up with the right answer and provide it promptly. Willing suspension of this reflex to dispense expertise is a key element in the collaborative spirit of MI" (2013, 16). Expertise is also repeatedly framed as a "trap," ensnaring because its "most common effect is to edge [clients] into a passive role, which is inconsistent with the basic goals of motivational interviewing" (2002, 60). And in case readers somehow missed the prominent warnings scattered throughout the text (2013, 42, 136, 142), the book's glossary of MI-specific terms includes this:

> **Expert Trap:** The clinical error of assuming and communicating that the counselor has the best answers to the client's problems. (Miller & Rollnick 2013, 409)

By contrast, Miller and Rollnick insist: "within motivational interviewing, in a real sense it is the client who is expert" (2002, 60).

William Miller is hardly the first US-born, PhD-educated, white man to grapple with the paradox of expertise. On the one hand, Miller surely knows that expertise authorizes the individuals and collectives who accrue it—not just by providing an institutionalized repertoire of seeing and interacting, but also by naturalizing that repertoire *as knowledge* and, more particularly, as the cognitive property of experts (Carr 2010a). On the other hand, Miller came of age during an era in which there was widespread concern, even among experts themselves, that expertise is at odds with the "American character"—that is, individuated open-mindedness as opposed to the rigid conformity of Cold War rivals (Cohen-Cole 2014). This general, if selective skepticism about experts goes above and beyond the partisan wrangling in which some stoke distrust for expertise while others harness it, as we have seen in recent years. For while American experts have long enjoyed substantial institutional authority, they have also faced significant public mistrust precisely to the extent that they appear disengaged from the people and problems that they presume to know.

This chapter argues that by examining MI's signature (in)expertise, we discover a modal if broadly overlooked way to defuse deep tensions in American governance, tensions that extend far beyond the institutional sites where MI is trained and practiced. I further propose that the "expert trap" is not simply a warning against a "clinical error," as MI's glossary entry defines it; it is a caution against *political error* as well. More specifically, the performance and projection of (in)expertise is a way that MI—as a behavioral intervention with directive elements—manages culturally saturated anxieties about the external direction of and authority over ostensibly autonomous, self-governing subjects.[4] Whether enacted in an interview with a client or modeled by a trainer like Norman, MI's pronounced (in)expertise invites the participation of equal parties with equally valid knowledge who feel free to choose and pursue their own ends. In this way, MI presents itself as a microform of participatory democracy: a method that recognizes autonomous individuals, hosts their free speech, and equalizes the interactional terms of once hierarchical relations, one dyad at a time.[5]

Freedom, equality, participation, recognition, autonomy are powerful key-words in MI precisely because they are what Nancy Fraser (2003) calls "folk paradigms of justice"—that is, influential ways in which social relations are imagined, understood, and evaluated *as* democratic ones.[6] In the United States, these folk paradigms enjoy a diverse range of advocates, animators, and institutional hosts who, in evoking their constitutive terms, transform putatively apolitical arrangements into potential events of democratic expression and reflection. MI training incorporates these democratic paradigms into a disciplined set of professional practices that circumvents the public mistrust of authority and, more particularly, of the authority of expertise.

However, and as we will see, MI's democratic aspirations are significantly complicated by the fact that motivational interviewers are also *intent on directing* the client toward normative, professionally supported behavioral change goals—whether quitting smoking, sanitizing water, losing weight, or taking prescribed medications. It is not unusual for those at an early stage in these trainings to find this quite confusing. In Norman's and Miller's workshops alike, the ostensibly contradictory aims to recognize clients as equal and fulsome participants *and* to direct them are translated into a recipe for professional action. In this sense, MI training not only enlightens a problem with which American democrats of many stripes have long grappled—that is, how to (non)authoritatively/(in)expertly direct rightfully self-governing subjects—it also reveals some innovative ways this problem is managed and ideologically resolved.

Norman and his fellow trainers are hardly alone in addressing conundrums such as how to square the force of rhetoric with the demand that individual speech be free; how to exert influence without appearing to do so authoritatively; and how to recognize others as equals without an equitable redistribution of knowledge and power (see Fraser 2008). In fact, these challenges have haunted and divided psychologists in the United States, among others, well before the development of MI.[7] Thus, before entering further into MI training rooms, we must account for MI's rapprochement of two long-opposed schools of American psychology: the client-centered tradition founded by Carl Rogers and the "directive" approach associated with B. F. Skinner.

A BRIEF AMERICAN HISTORY OF (THERAPEUTIC) RECOGNITION

In the late summer of 2010, I made my first trip to Albuquerque to record a series of interviews with William Miller. I was taking him up on an unprompted invitation he had sent a year earlier, when I was just beginning to consider studying MI. Uncannily, Miller had already heard of my nascent interests (presumably from a local trainer with whom I had spoken just a few days before). Imagine my surprise when I received an email, with no subject line, from MI's founder:

> My friend told me that you may be interested in ethnographic study of how motivational interviewing is disseminating. If I can be helpful to you in this regard, feel free to contact me. When I wrote the original article in 1983, *I certainly had no idea* how it was going to flower. (emphasis added)

By the time I came face to face with this welcoming host—first in a University of New Mexico office and then in a tidy suburban ranch home—I was nine months into my study of a yearlong MI training, conducted by one of Miller's former apprentices, and had already completed much briefer studies of MI trainings, including Norman's. By that point, I had also interviewed more than a dozen MI trainers, had spent significant time poring over the MI literature, including interviews others had conducted with Miller, and had viewed his online talks and lectures. Given this work, I understood that "I certainly had no idea" is not a throwaway line in an email missive; it is, instead, a common refrain in Miller's framings of MI, in which he marvels at how far the method has come from its, and *his*, professional origins.

I had also learned that MI, as a conversation style, is characterized by disciplined naïveté and accordingly offers its practitioners a range of rhetorical devices that project uncertainty and invite the respondent to offer their own explanations of whatever phenomenon is in focus—in this case, the "flower[ing]" of MI. Inexpert statements also foster the sense that both parties' explanations are equally valid, apparently demoting the party who is anticipated and authorized to hold that knowledge. In the email above, the very founder of the method marks my interest in MI's dissemination and welcomes exchange, while "certainly" expressing his uncertainty about the topic of discussion. Thus, as I prepared to ethnographically interview Miller, I was keen to the possibility that he was already motivationally interviewing *me*.

Before I reached Albuquerque, I had also learned that Miller began his postgraduate career counseling alcoholics in the early 1970s at a VA hospital in Milwaukee, a 1,000-bed facility that I slowly circled one fall afternoon when I was first contemplating this project (see figure 1.1). I had become fascinated with Miller's reformulations of mainstream American ideas about addiction, having myself just completed a book on the topic (see Carr 2011). Yet, by his own account, when Miller first took the position at the VA, he knew next to nothing about the field he would later revolutionize. This is

Figure 1.1. Milwaukee VA Medical Center. Public domain.

what he told historian of addiction treatment and recovery William White, who characterized Miller as "one of the most influential voices in the modern treatment of alcohol and other drug problems":

> [When] I went on internship to Milwaukee, I mainly just put on my *Carl Rogers' hat* and with reflective listening essentially asked these people— mostly men—to teach me about their experience: "How did you get to this place in your life?" "What's been happening in your life?" and "Where are you going from here?" I didn't have any therapeutic advice for them, so I just listened, and they seemed to appreciate that, to respond well. I learned an awful lot from *these folk's own stories . . . I have always loved stories*. And, there was *chemistry* also. Then I began to read the literature and it said, "Alcoholics are liars and they have this immature personality that is so defended that you can never get through it. You've just got to hit them with a brick to get anywhere, and you can't trust them." *It puzzled me because those weren't the same people I'd been talking to. It didn't seem right*. (Miller 2009, emphasis added)[8]

Here, Miller plainly disavows expertise, claiming that he "didn't have any therapeutic advice" for the men at the VA, and therefore "just listened" to them, at least after asking them a series of open questions. He portrays his approach as narrative and humanistic, circumventing attempts to diagnose problems or provide prescriptive advice. Moreover, in saying that he "learned an awful lot from these folk's own stories," Miller retrospectively positions his clients as knowledgeable subjects, if not experts in their own right, providing an early iteration of what would later become a mantra, repeated in MI texts and trainings alike: "we learn from our clients."

In characterizing his approach as a fledgling practitioner, Miller underscores that he *recognized* the men that so many others misrecognized. Confronted with the pathological characterizations of alcoholics that were rife in American addiction scholarship and practice at the time—that is, alcoholics are untrustworthy, immature liars and should be approached as such—the defiant young Miller (as animated by the older and wiser, if ever humble Miller) states his opposition to the authority of the literature: "Those weren't the same people I'd been talking to. It didn't seem right." Whereas clinical authorities caricatured "alcoholics" in a way that justified and perpetuated their lack of engagement with them, Miller enjoyed conversations with "people," finding them to be a source of learning. MI's founder makes clear that scientific and institutional authorities—those publicly recognized as experts—had not fully recognized alcoholics as people from the start.

As a master conversation stylist, William Miller is surely aware that the term "recognition" enjoys multiple resonances and registers in North American English.[9] As touched upon in my introduction, and expanded upon in chapter 3, *recognition* is a pregnant term in Protestant American discourse, suggesting a relatively unmediated relationship with the spirit(ual) and a capacity for sacred empathy. In this register, if sometimes in more secularized ways, trainers often count themselves as those who have been powerfully recognized by MI and train the method as a way to recognize others. "Recognition" is also a resonant political term, which—contemporaneous with Miller's time at the VA—served as philosophical hinge for group demands for civil rights and equal treatment.[10] Recognition, in both of these senses, is shot through with—sometimes even tied together by—humanist ideals, which we hear in Miller's account of recognition of clients *as people*. Consider, for example, the mid-century work of philosopher and psychologist Frantz Fanon (1963, 1967). Fanon's exploration of the wounded self-perception of colonial subjects, whose humanity was unrecognized by white colonizers, was highly influential in liberation movements in the United States and beyond.[11]

Some have argued that recognition has been a prominent scaling heuristic of late liberalism, which seeks the incorporation of others, offering accommodation in exchange for absolution (Povinelli 1998, 582; Povinelli 2002; see also Markell 2003). As Charles Taylor put it in an influential essay, "a number of strands in contemporary politics turn on the need, sometimes the demand, for recognition" (1994, 25), suggesting that to recognize is to resist the authoritarian state and to realize democracy. And while many have periodized recognition, as a folk paradigm of justice, to identitarian social movements (e.g., Taylor 1994; Young 1990; see also Fraser 2008; Honneth 2003, 122–24) and the rise of the multicultural state (e.g., Povinelli 1998, 2002), the history of MI reveals additional veins in genealogies of recognition. In fact, a discourse of recognition infuses, even organizes, Carl Rogers's framing of his highly influential mid-twentieth-century therapeutic program, which he had unequivocally staked against behaviorist psychology, the tradition in which Miller was trained. It is therefore particularly telling that the young Miller (as narrated by the older Miller) entered his first postgraduate clinical position wearing a "Carl Rogers's hat." This indicates that, despite his own decidedly behaviorist training, Miller appreciated that since the mid-twentieth century, Rogerian therapy—otherwise known as "humanist" or "client-centered" therapy—has been virtually synonymous with ethically sound and politically progressive psychotherapeutic practice.

Rogers staked his therapeutic program on the premise that clients will "self-actualize" as long as professionals abstain from overtly evaluating and directing them—the most apparent excesses of expertise (for example, Rogers 1946, 1951, 1961). "Unconditional positive regard" for those in the process of self-actualization, despite intervening behavior that may be destructive or dysfunctional, became the centerpiece of Rogers's highly influential approach. Its central technology was "reflective listening"—an ostensibly passive process of verbally echoing client statements that effectively cast the client-centered therapist as supportive witness to the client who is so-centered. Much like Miller would do a few decades later, Rogers cast diagnosis as profoundly antidemocratic, claiming that it simultaneously props up expert authority and fails to recognize its subject.

Developing his approach in postwar America, Rogers was originally interested in creating the therapeutic conditions that allowed clients to see themselves as free and to act accordingly. By the late 1950s and early 1960s, in line with growing anti-authoritarian sentiment, he sought opportunities to frame his therapeutic program in overtly political terms. For instance, on a public stage in 1962 Rogers asserted:

> Man has long felt himself to be a puppet in life, molded by world forces, by economic forces. He has been enslaved by persons, by institutions,

and, more recently, by aspects of modern science. But he is firmly setting forth a new declaration of independence. He is discarding the alibis of "unfreedom." He is choosing himself, endeavoring to become himself: not a puppet, not a slave, not a copy of some model, but his own unique self. I find myself very sympathetic to this trend because it is so deeply in line with the experience I have had working with clients in therapy. (Kirschenbaum & Henderson 1989, 83)

We can see here how Rogers's critique is scaled from the clinical to the political by way of recognizably democratic ideals. We can also hear Hegelian echoes of Fanon, if in less elegant and deracialized terms, as Rogers avers that "man" has been "enslaved by persons, by institutions, and . . . by modern science," uniformly cast as "alibis of unfreedom." The paradigmatically democratic premise of Rogers's antidote is unmistakable: once clients' natural struggle to self-realize is recognized and positively regarded, they can be set free. No longer "slaves" or "puppets," "unique selves" set forth from the Rogerian therapeutic encounter psychically prepared to newly declare their independence as autonomous Americans.[12]

This portrait of the therapeutic encounter as democracy writ small reappears in official framings of MI. Like Rogers, Miller portrays MI as a method that equips professionals to recognize the individual clients they engage as equal and autonomous parties, just as he once recognized the men at the Milwaukee VA. For instance, the preface of *Motivational Interviewing* reads: "We continue to emphasize that MI involves a collaborative partnership with clients, a respectful evoking of their own motivation and wisdom, and a radical acceptance recognizing that ultimately whatever change happens is each person's own choice, an autonomy that cannot be taken away no matter how much one might wish to at times" (Miller & Rollnick 2013, viii).

In turn, thousands of American professionals—across a wide range of fields—have embraced MI as an exemplary means of recognizing and engaging otherwise overlooked clients as autonomous equals. Yet as Nancy Fraser (2008) has beautifully elaborated, recognition does not imply redistribution, and may even be a hindrance to it. The political limits of recognition *cum* unconditional positive regard may eventually be laid bare as MI makes further inroads into fields like corrections and child welfare, which are especially poorly equipped to realize democratic premises and promises. Or, could it be that MI's clients are recognized as equal parties no matter their *actual* ability to freely participate or collaborate?[13]

This was one of the many puzzles I had come to discuss with Miller, who later that evening extended a more phenomenological account of recognition-by-MI into an explicit political framing of his method as anti-dote to authoritarianism, a point to which I return below. In doing so, he both marked deep ideological tensions in American conceptions of recognition *and* indicated that MI had a way to defuse these divides. From (at least) the mid-twentieth century to this day, behaviorism—while enjoying all sorts of institutional hosts and inspiring many "third wave" therapies—has been a favorite target of North American critics.[14] Indeed, Rogers himself publicly attacked behaviorism as profoundly antidemocratic and was especially critical of Skinner's focus on the environmental correlates of human behavior, his attendant rejection of mentalist explanations, and his unapologetic insistence that therapeutic interventions should stimulate and reinforce ethical, socially adaptive behavior. In fact, it was to Skinner that Rogers addressed his 1962 comments, quoted above, in a debate before a university audience who—like an increasing proportion of the Cold War American public—found behaviorism suspicious if not down-right politically problematic. Thus, to take flight from 1980s Milwaukee, MI arguably *had* to translate its behavioral elements into a client-centered framework.

COLD WAR THERAPIES, MI REMEDIES: THE POLITICAL HISTORY OF (THERAPEUTIC) (IN)EXPERTISE

In mid-twentieth-century America, political questions were commonly couched in psychological terms, with many Americans viewing the Cold War as a battle between the safeguarding of freedom of thought and the active suppression of it. B. F. Skinner's radical behaviorism was widely associated with the latter tendency, not just by the FBI, which assembled an ample file on the social scientist (Wyatt 2000), but also by scholarly colleagues who increasingly regarded Skinner's scholarly program as narrow and rigid (Cohen-Cole 2014, 124–25; Hull 2010, 258).

Although American historians argue that skepticism of experts reached new heights in the postwar period, the public's critique of expert authority was in fact quite selective. At the same time that readers were lapping up Dr. Spock's now infamous child-rearing advice, they chafed at the *Ladies Home Journal* article in which Skinner described the "air crib" that he de-signed for his baby daughter and his wife, whose maternal labor he was in-tent to help save.[15] Skinner's 1948 utopian novel, *Walden Two*—which imag-ined a community where punishment had no place, sexual equality reigned, and positive reinforcement began at birth with the aim of fostering self-control and cooperation, and eliminating competitive individualism—was

Figure 1.2a. B. F. Skinner. Science History Images / Alamy Stock Photo.

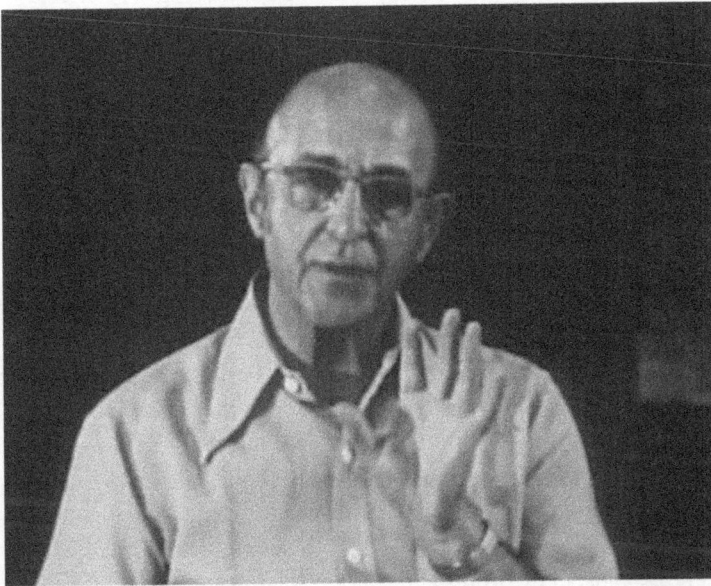

Figure 1.2b. Carl Rogers. Screenshot from his 1974 lecture on empathy,
American Personnel & Guidance Association.

met with similar reactions. By the time Skinner summarized his scientific work and philosophy for a popular audience with the 1971 publication of *Beyond Freedom and Dignity*, prominent critics had definitively cast Skinner's unapologetic behaviorism not just as antidemocratic, but as distinctly un-American as well (Nye 1992; Richelle 1993; Rutherford 2009). More particularly, Skinner's central thesis of *operant conditioning*—that is, the ongoing shaping of behavior relative to its environmental consequences (see, for example, Skinner 1953, 65–67; Skinner 1971, 26)—was perceived as an attack on the cherished ideal that American individuals are authors of their own acts, whose participation in public life is unmediated by external authorities.[16] Operant conditioning was even translated as "another word for Nazism" (Michel Lancelot, as cited in Richelle 1993, 4).[17]

Indeed, a tellingly broad range of well-known political figures expressed outrage over Skinner's rejection of the ideal of the sovereign will and the free-thinking subject, as well as his interest in designing environments to stimulate and direct prosocial human behavior. For instance, within months of Noam Chomsky's scathing review of Skinner's *Beyond Freedom and Dignity* in *The New York Review of Books*, which compared a Skinnerian world to "a well-run [if punishment free] concentration camp" (1971, 22),[18] Nixon's vice president, Spiro Agnew, issued a warning to the American public that "Skinner attacks the very precepts on which our society is based" and seeks to perform "radical surgery on the national psyche" (1972, 22)—a psyche that the Cold War American public increasingly insisted should be recognized, not directed.[19]

Skinner came face to face with one of his fiercest critics when he joined Carl Rogers for the first of two public debates in 1962. The debate was charged, in part because neither man was the least bit shy in embracing the "real world" implications of their disciplinary concerns.[20] If they agreed on little else, both conceded that the psychological was political, if with some notable caveats.[21] Claiming that his own brand of therapeutic encounter facilitated Americans who were ready to redeclare their independence, Rogers suggested that the survival of American democracy was at stake in the choice between client-centered therapy and the behaviorism of his opponent.[22] Take, for instance, this unsparing charge:

Here are some of the words and concepts that I have used which are almost totally without meaning in the behaviorist frame of reference: *freedom* is a term with no meaning; *choice*, in the sense I have used it, has no meaning...*Purpose, self-direction, value* or *choice*—none of these has any meaning; *personal responsibility* as a concept has no meaning. (Kirschenbaum & Henderson 1989, 85)

In his appeal to the university audience, Rogers underscored that clinical direction *is* political direction, and that behaviorism *is* totalitarianism, if on a smaller scale. Homing in on Skinner's foundational premise that "man . . . [is] the product of past elements and forces and the determined cause of future events and behaviors" (Kirschenbaum & Henderson 1989, 85)—a notion that Rogers associated with Freud as much as with Skinner—the animated Rogers went on to offer a familiar formula, positing that the realization of democratic ideals hinges on the self-actualization of the American individual, unfettered by external control.

Throughout the debate, Rogers repeatedly returned to the idea that "minimizing the significance of the subjective" (Kirschenbaum & Henderson 1989, 86) is as much of an anathema in politics as it is in psychotherapy. Rogers's therapeutic program, after all, depended on the idea that people should be authors of their own acts, and that their behavior traceable to sources within themselves. Therefore, to overtly offer expert direction is to interfere with the process of self-actualization and, by extension, to violate the principle of individual freedom. Skinner, for his part, was keenly alert to how Rogers's critical characterization of behaviorism reflected the "national tendency . . . to suppose that the individual . . . has something inside himself which is very important" (Kirschenbaum & Henderson 1989, 118). He nevertheless maintained that "the inner events which seem so important to us are not essential to action and probably do not, in any important case, precede action" (Kirschenbaum & Henderson 1989, 101).[23] Whereas Rogers insisted that therapists accept the "principle that the individual is basically responsible for himself" (1946, 416), Skinner believed that the goal of interventions is precisely to direct, or positively "condition," people to act in responsible ways (Skinner 1953, 382–83). Thus, for Skinner, the pressing question was not *whether* to direct people, but how to do so positively, productively, and nonpunitively.[24]

Skinner (1957) extended these principles to his theory of *verbal behavior*, which he argued is always shaped by the environment, past and present, including one's immediate interlocutors. Whereas Rogers idealized as unencumbered self-expression—once even claiming that the "[verbal] material from client-centered interviews comes closer to being a 'pure' expression of attitude than has yet been achieved by other means" (1947, 358)—Skinner maintained that ethical professionals should help craft conditions, or positively reinforce, speech and other behavior, and should do so transparently.[25]

At an especially critical juncture of the debate, Skinner emphasized his conviction that no human intervention—whether directive or client-centered—should have surreptitious elements. Skinner also subtly raised the question of just what his opponent might be hiding, suggesting that even the most putatively unmediated "ways of being with people" have directive elements, whether the practitioner admits it or not. Interestingly, Rogers's own students transcribed and analyzed their teacher's psychotherapy sessions, showing the subtly directive ways that the founder of client-centered therapy selectively reinforced particular client statements, while remaining silent in the face of others (Traux 1966; Traux & Carkhuff 1967; see also Smith 2005).[26] Interestingly, Miller frequently cites this research, including in my interviews with him. "Rogers was not happy with that finding," he once told me with just a hint of glee. As I later came to understand, MI's signature (in)expertise is rooted in this alleged dissatisfaction, as well as in an adept understanding of how one might direct speech while assuring it is heard as free.

DRAINING THE DIFFERENCE: GUIDING FREE SPEECH AND CLIENT-CENTERED DIRECTIVENESS

Given the divisive debates about psychological approaches and their political correlates, one can readily imagine why the young Miller donned a Rogerian hat rather than a Skinnerian lab coat upon entering an urban VA hospital, especially after having registered with his local draft board as a conscientious objector. That said, Miller's doctoral training in behavioral psychology is arguably at least as important to the development of MI, if less prominent in its self-description, as MI's more overt affiliation with Rogers's client-centered approach. For one thing, the behaviorist in Miller sees people in terms of their acts rather than their essences (or, as he once put it to me, "my training was behavioral and so it's natural for me to think in terms of what people do and not who they *are*"). Accordingly, MI trainers discourage their apprentices from explaining clients' behavior by way of presumed internal states, and they concertedly resist intervention agendas that are not behaviorally targeted.[27] In lieu of the mentalist explanations that Rogers favored, MI training refocuses professional attention on readily evident behavior—that is, what clients do and how, with particular attention to the context of the interview itself.[28] More specifically, and as we will see below, MI trainers provide guidelines for how to set up communicative events to produce speech from clients, speech that—significantly—is understood as behavior in its own right.

Nowhere are MI's behaviorist leanings more apparent than in its working understanding of language, and its formulation of the interview as a speech act.[29] A careful read of MI's foundational textbook reveals the influence of psychologist Daryl Bem (1967, 1972), who is widely credited for applying Skinner's ideas about verbal behavior to self-perception theory, and who accordingly insisted that meaning is not contained in an utterance or in the person who emits that utterance, but rather emerges in the act of the utterance in the context of interaction (see Wright 1987, 86).[30] In this view, central to MI's understanding of how interviews can motivate, speech produces rather than simply refers to psychic states (table 1.1, A1). More specifically, from Bem, Miller and Rollnick derive their central thesis that *people tend to believe what they hear themselves say, understanding* verbal expression as a kind of behavior that can also precipitate other behavior (table 1.1, A2). In other words, as Miller and Rollnick catchily put it: "We can literally talk ourselves into (or out of) things" (2013, 86). Accordingly, the motivational interview is designed to produce speech that *shapes* what the client thinks, believes, or feels—that is, "change talk"—and therefore what they do. And if often showing up more subtly, MI's behaviorism is unmistakable in statements such as this: "from an operant perspective, the MI counselor responds to client speech in a way that differentially reinforces change talk" (table 1.1, A3).

Yes, and . . . Consider now that in the very same article (and even on the same page!), Miller and Moyers make a dramatic pivot from the idea of co-produced, differentially reinforced change talk, claiming that the motivational interview also "*evok[es]* [clients'] own intrinsic motivations for change" (table 1.1, B3). Furthermore, across editions of *Motivational Interviewing*, there are numerous passages that figure speech as a means of inner reference, as in Miller and Rollnick's plain statement: "before a person speaks, he or she has a certain meaning to communicate" (table 1.1, B2). Thus, in MI, speech is *both* a behavioral instrument for generating thoughts, feelings, and other behaviors, *and* a conduit for tapping and revealing the preexisting inner states of speakers (table 1.1, B1). Note that in reconciling these antithetical ideas about language, MI works the political differences of opposing American therapeutic approaches as well. More specifically, MI promises its adherents that speech can be a way of persuading others to speak and act in certain (pro-social) ways, while still maintaining speech's and speakers' status as free.

Indeed, if Rogers concluded late in his career that the "basic difference between a behaviorist and a humanistic approach to human beings is a philosophical choice" (1980, 56), Miller seized upon that disjuncture as an opportunity for professional innovation. In line with the general tendency of MI to defuse ideological difference, the first book-length description of the method accordingly presents MI as both "client-centered" *and* "directive" at one and the same time (Miller & Rollnick 1992). Sixteen years later, the method was intriguingly cast as "client-centered . . . with a twist" (Arkowitz

Table 1.1. The "interview" in motivational interviewing

BOTH...	AND
A1. Speech produces psychic and social states. (see Miller & Rollnick 2013, 3)	B1. Speech refers to preexisting psychic states. (see Miller & Rollnick 2013, 21–22, 28)
A2. People tend to believe what they hear themselves say. (Miller & Rollnick 2013, 9, 13; see also Bem 1967, 1972)	B2. "Before a person speaks, he or she has a certain meaning to communicate." (Miller & Rollnick 2002, 69)
A3. "From an operant perspective, the MI counselor responds to client speech in a way that differentially reinforces change talk." (Miller & Moyers 2006, 7; see also Skinner 1963)	B3. The interview "*evok[es]* [*clients'*] *own intrinsic motivations* for change." (Miller & Moyers 2006, 7; see also Miller & Rollnick 2002, 34)

& Miller 2008, 4), "the twist" being that the motivational interviewer is always working *to direct* the client toward a specific behavioral change goal.

MI's *client-centered directiveness* (see Carr & Smith 2014) is puzzling enough on paper; it is far more difficult to cultivate in practice. Consider that trainees must proceed through "eight stages in learning motivational interviewing" (Miller & Moyers 2006)—an article that is compulsory reading in almost every advanced MI training I have studied. In it, they learn that their first task is to develop "an openness to collaboration with clients' own expertise" (2006, 3)—that is, enact client-centeredness. A few paragraphs later, professionals are reminded that they are also to be "consciously and strategically goal-directed" (7), and steer the client to some behavioral change goal while keeping the initial charge in mind. Although these instructions may, understandably, befuddle outsiders and are a tall order for apprentices, MI trainers maintain that the motivational interview is simultaneously a site where clients can freely express and direct themselves in accordance with their "own expertise" and an opportunity for professionals to "strategically goal-direct" clients to change what they say and do.

That said, in order attract people to training, and retain them once they are there, MI must carefully frame its reconciliation of two opposed philosophies of therapeutic practice that have historically influenced if not organized their potential audiences. To this end, MI's client-centered directiveness is now commonly presented as a "middle ground," with the "directing

BOX 1.2. Some Verbs Associated with Each Communication Style

Directing style	Guiding style	Following style
Administer	Accompany	Allow
Authorize	Arouse	Attend
Command	Assist	Be responsive
Conduct	Awaken	Be with
Decide	Collaborate	Comprehend
Determine	Elicit	Go along with
Govern	Encourage	Grasp
Lead	Enlighten	Have faith in
Manage	Inspire	Listen
Order	Kindle	Observe
Prescribe	Lay before	Permit
Preside	Look after	Shadow
Rule	Motivate	Stay with
Steer	Offer	Stick to
Run	Point	Take in
Take charge	Show	Take interest in
Take command	Support	Understand
Tell	Take along	Value

Figure 1.3. MI in between. From *Motivational Interviewing: Helping People Change*, 3rd ed. (Miller & Rollnick 2013). Used with permission of Guilford Publications Inc.; permission conveyed through Copyright Clearance Center Inc.

style" (read: behaviorist approach) and the "following style" (read: client-centered approach) cast as unnecessary extremes (Miller & Rollnick 2013, 4–5). It is also portrayed as a sensible amalgam, incorporating aspects of each (figure 1.3), with the *interviewer* characterized as a "guide," rather than an expert who directs or a blind adherent to the authority of others. In these resonant, even folksy, terms, Miller and Rollnick explain, "It is not the guide's job to order you when to arrive, where to go, and what to see or do. Neither does a good guide simply follow you around wherever you happen to wander" (2013, 4–5). The MI guide is a person who *both* knows a terrain *and* is deeply attuned to—indeed, *recognizes*—where others want to go, deftly circumventing (expert) traps.

Here, we should recall that "guide" was a term that appreciative trainees applied to Norman, who managed to "collaborate . . . encourage . . . lay before . . . look after . . . support" (2013, 5; see figure 1.3), all the while administering a specialized instrument to evaluate their practice. And while Norman assigned numerical scores, gave unsparing if not unwelcome feedback, and served a significant gatekeeping role into MINT membership, he managed to do so without seeming to "administer," "authorize," "decide," or "tell," thanks to his mastery of (in)expertise. A closer look at the list of associations in figure 1.3 suggests that although both directing and following are presented as undesirable extremes, the latter is thought more palatable than the former. After all, to therapeutically direct is to "command . . . determine . . . govern . . . order . . . prescribe . . . preside" and even to "rule" (Miller & Rollnick 2013, 5)—apparent affronts to democratic paradigms of justice.

Considering these political resonances, we see why MI often euphemizes its directive elements in its most public framings. For instance, note how signs of professional direction are differentially indexed in the title of each edition of MI's foundational text:

Motivational Interviewing: Preparing People to Change Addictive Behaviors (1992)
Motivational Interviewing: Preparing People for Change (2002)
Motivational Interviewing: Helping People Change (2013)

In reading MI's most recent textbook packaging, a newcomer to MI would reasonably conclude that professionals are trained to "help" rather than "prepare," to "guide" rather than "direct," and to hold authoritative prescriptions for behavior change at bay. These euphemisms suggest that MI is attentive to a familiar pressure, once staged in the debate between Rogers and Skinner: that is, to recognize (clients as) democratic subjects who are free to speak and therefore choose their own ends.

Of course, in practice, tolerance for directiveness is all too commonly calibrated to the class status of those so directed (not to mention the professional status of those issuing directions).[31] After all, however normatively offensive, directiveness is commonplace in many institutional settings in which MI is currently practiced, including primary health care, corrections, and addiction, whether because clients are mandated or are thought to pose threats to themselves or others, and/or professionals are working under performance quotas and time constraints, which demand the rapid production of behavioral change. This is all the more reason to split the difference, as MI is especially adept at doing. So, as MI has spread across professional fields over the last forty years, encountering new practitioners and attendant modes of practice, it finds that client-centeredness and directiveness sometimes must be juggled, depending on the needs and expectations of different professional audiences. This was a primary challenge in preparing the third edition of the MI textbook, as Miller explained it:

WRM: [Steve Rollnick and I] had thought more and written more about the ethics of motivational interviewing in relation to questions that were coming up in workshops of: "isn't this just manipulating people?" from one side, and from the other side, "Shouldn't you be doing something? You're just kind of sitting there." And so, we had both extremes of concern. [T]o the very directive person this looks pretty slow [. . .]

ESC: Right.

WRM: Or, on the other hand, "Are you doing something to people without really being honest with them about what you're doing?" Soooo . . .

ESC: Hmm.

WRM: So that continues to be an interesting dialogue.

Taking a familiar position between "extremes of concern," Miller animates an "interesting dialogue" between well-worn ideological lines (that is, the client-centered practitioner, accused of being "slow" and passive by the directive person, who in turn is charged with "manipulat[ion]").[32] Yet note that a *third* troubling term arises in MI's efforts to be both/and—*honesty*. And while Miller casts the question of "are you doing something to people without really being honest with them about what you're doing?" as "ethical," it is also implicitly political. After all, *transparency* is also a folk paradigm of justice, which poses challenges for American democrats far beyond the helping professions.

Several years after this living room conversation, I observed the founder of MI dealing in real time with the "interesting dialogue" he had presaged for me, as he co-led an advanced MI training. Miller's efforts to get MI to speak to "both sides" of the audience, while quelling concerns about the method's transparency to its clients, offer important lessons about what it takes to direct autonomous subjects and orchestrate free speech. In MI training, I argue, we discover not only an elemental puzzle of American democracy, but also an especially revealing way to "solve" it.

DIRECTION, DETECTION, AND DEMOCRATIC REFLECTION

When Miller arrived on an ivy-covered campus in the summer of 2014 to conduct an advanced MI training with his former trainee Ki, MI had just celebrated its thirty-first birthday. Famous among helping professionals, Miller effortlessly attracted dozens of applications for the daylong training, from which he and Ki selected a highly educated group of seventy participants, including clinical researchers from around the university, clinicians of various stripes, and social service providers from all over the city.[33] These professionals, or the organizations that employed them, paid $250 apiece and relinquished a full day's work to brush up on their MI knowledge, and to do so in Miller's presence. Unbeknownst to some of the university training participants, Miller had recently completed the third edition of *Motivational Interviewing* and, with it, launched what insiders were already calling "MI-3."[34]

Early in the morning on the day of the training, Ki darted through hallways, assuring that participants' folders were in order, double-checking the audio-visual setup, and periodically pausing to greet arriving participants with characteristic warmth. Having observed Ki train MI apprentices in another setting, I received an admission along with a greeting: training alongside Miller was especially nerve-wracking, a pinnacle moment in Ki's career to date. By contrast to the sweating Ki, Miller had already settled in the training room and appeared remarkably relaxed, laying his crossed hands placidly on one knee and somehow managing to drape his slender frame on an institutional stacking chair, as if reclining. The training commenced with the chime of a miniature Tibetan-style bell, which would be used throughout the day to mark transitions between practice exercises and didactic presentation. Ki welcomed the participants, who had picked up flavorless Danishes and bitter coffee, settled themselves at one of the ten preset tables, and turned toward the front of the room with what appeared to be great expectations. I could not help but think of Norman as Ki did little to hide his nerves—another masterful enactment of (in)expertise.

As if demonstrating MI's readiness to, professionally and democratically, level the playing field for master and apprentice, Ki took the reins of the training early on, introducing the definitional changes in MI's key terms with the help of an elaborate PowerPoint presentation, endowed with a signature aesthetic (figure 1.4).[35] In describing the "evolution of MI from MI-2 to MI-3," Ki began—not surprisingly—with the paradigm of recognition. Specifically, he focused the audience on MI-3's "new language of *partnership*," which he described as "the evolution of *collaboration*." Audience members, in line with MI-2 and the second edition of Miller & Rollnick's textbook (2002, 34), had long used the latter term to indicate their "client-centered" readiness to abdicate professional authority and recognize clients as equally (in)expert. And while some may have wondered why the shift in nomenclature was necessary, Ki's explanation suggested to me that MI-3's new take on (in)expertise was the offspring of the "interesting dialogue" that Miller had laid out for me in Albuquerque.

There really is a *shared* expertise when we are working with those we serve. Really recognizing that while I certainly have expertise to bring to bear, that ultimately the person or the people with whom I am working are *truly* the experts in their own experience. And acknowledging that not only further *engages* people in their process of change, but in fact can save a lot of time. If we find out what people already know, we can include that right up front in the process of change.

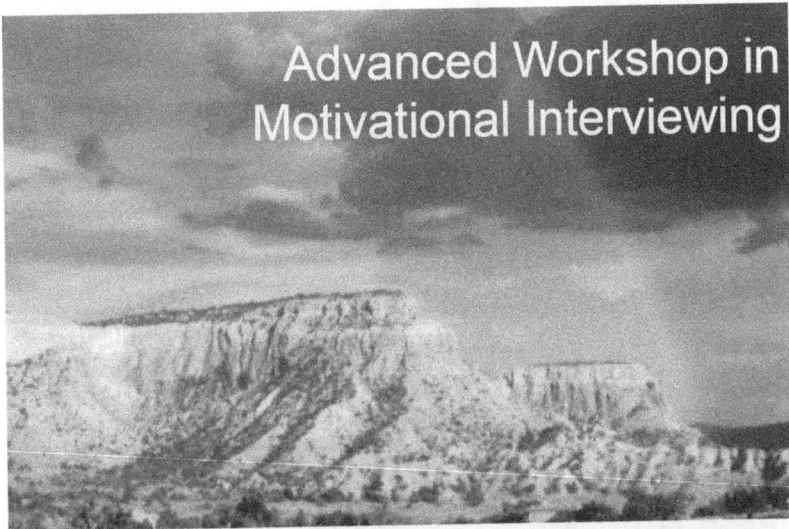

Figure 1.4a and b. Two of 141 slides from William R. Miller's advanced training, September 15, 2014. Slides, with original photography, courtesy of William R. Miller.

Here, we see that professional expertise is neither entirely negated nor framed as a "trap." Rather, expertise is redistributed, or "shared" with (lay)people/clients, who are "truly the experts" when it comes to their "own experience." While we hear the familiar democratic ideals of participation, equality, and recognition that characterized earlier iterations of MI, the introduction of utilitarian terms is striking. Namely, MI-3, as Ki describes it, *economizes* client-centeredness, presenting "partnership" as more efficient than "collaboration," engaging people in a way that can "save a lot of time" (see also Miller & Rollnick 2013, 56). Whether audience members were bound to fee schedules, or simply working in high-demand, resource-strapped service organizations, we can imagine their various interests in the economy of MI-3's (in)expertise.

If Ki's account of efficient client-centeredness appeared to satisfy the audience, who raised no immediate questions or concerns, he was soon to face a familiar challenge. His next task was to explain why MI-3 had abandoned the term *directive*—which had coded the method's behaviorist "goal-orientation" for more than thirty years—in favor of "directional" (see figure 1.4b). With his tall, slim figure casting a long shadow on the purple projection of the slide he stumbled to parse, Ki took a deep breath, saying: "I will give this a try and then I may . . . so . . . so there is *direction* and there is *directing* and there is *being directional* . . . and, versus *being directive*." Flashing a self-deprecating smile as the audience began to titter, Ki continued: "And [by] that I mean there . . . there was a time when being directive was a part of the MI definition. Right? It was a *directive* style. I think there is an effort to move a bit away from that because it can, there is, it's, it's not too far from being directive to, 'Here's what you need to do; here's what you are going to do.'"

Voicing the commands of a baldly "directive" professional, Ki's stumbling indicates concern with how authoritarian the method might appear to others, whether practitioners or clients.[36] As if issuing a warning, or perhaps an apology, Ki continued: "It has been said that MI is *negative reinforcement*." Pausing, as if to let that comment sink in with the audience, he then offered, "there is something *aspirational* potentially" about MI's rebranded behaviorism. Evoking the image of the "guide," Ki added that when it comes to MI's new brand of behavior change, "we are moving away from something and ideally we are always moving towards something."

Despite Ki's efforts, questions from some puzzled members began to arise. Whether they were doctors encountering chronically overweight patients, psychologists dealing with functional alcoholics, or social workers struggling to engage self-harming teens, those gathered before Ki understood that clients seldom share professionals' behavioral goals and commitments from the start, significantly complicating attempts to serve as guide. A skeptical psychologist in the room raised one such example, referencing those who have been court-mandated to treatment. Particularly, she questioned Ki's reframing of "direction" as "aspiration," implying that there might be something disingenuous at play, a point that seemed to gain traction judging from the half dozen nodding heads around the room. At stake in this discussion was not only (or even primarily) the more or less directive nature of MI-3, but how *transparent* that direction is.

There it was: the troubling thorn in the "interesting dialogue" as Miller had described it to me in his living room several years earlier. Before the now flustered Ki could respond, Miller rose from his sideline repose to take center stage. Rather than sidestepping the question of transparency, he shared an inside secret with the soon-to-be-recaptivated audience, hinting at the need to keep it under further wraps.

> I say sometimes about 80 percent of what we do comes right out of Carl Rogers . . . but having a direction in which to move in motivational interviewing, you need to know where you are trying to go, otherwise you are doing just client-centered counseling, which is fine. But MI is *directional.* "I want to get over *there*; *that* is where we are going."

Note the pronouns Miller employs, voicing the professional "I" who should be steering the interview. Significantly, this "I" has a conversation *with herself*, rather than with her client, about which way the intervention is headed. What is more, having resituated the 80 percent Rogerian interviewer in the proverbial driver's seat, Miller reminds his trainees that their vehicle is language. Reorienting the question of transparency from what the client knows to the *professional's awareness* of their own behavioral goals, Miller added, with emphasis: "The way you get over there is with the evoking process of using *particular forms of language.*"

In so saying, Miller makes a striking pedagogical U-turn. In addition to assuming that the interviewer *evokes* the "motivations and reasons and ideas for change" from the client, as Ki had earlier implied, Miller advised trainees that they can "influence the amount of change talk that you are going to hear rather dramatically" through the strategic directing of the interview as a kind of conversation (see also Miller & Moyers, 2006). Perhaps in a canny read of his diverse professional audience, Miller promptly stripped away any impression that his method—in practice—had become any less directive, whatever the change in terminology. In emphasizing the directive side of motivational interviewing over the client-centered side, Miller demonstrates yet another productive pleasure of paradox: in those moments when one can't have it both ways at once, there is always a well-established side in which to take temporary shelter.

With the central rhetorical principle of MI effectively underscored, Miller and Ki began preparing apprentices for their first practice exercise, providing a pithy reminder of the interview's constituent speech acts—open questions, reflections, affirmations, and summaries (OARS)—all borrowed from client-centered therapy. Yet, as Miller reminded his apprentices, motivational interviews only succeed to the extent that they make "*selective* use of Rogerian tools to create direction." As he put it at the training:

> Motivational interviewing gets directional [because] we ask particular questions and not others; there is guidance about which things to re-flect. *Where* you ask for elaboration. There are particular guidelines [in MI] that I never ran across in client-centered counseling that are kind of *nudging* people in certain direction. (Miller's emphasis)

Implied in Miller's explanation is that the "certain" direction in which clients are "nudged" is toward cultural and professional norms of healthy behavior, if not to a more specific set of institutional mandates. In so suggesting, Miller had both answered and, arguably, set aside the audience member's earlier question about the ethics of more or less explicit direction. For here, according to Miller, the issue is not that the content of professional directives is necessarily ethically misguided; nor is directing problematic, in and of itself. The issue is rather that transparent attempts to persuade or direct are *practically* ineffective, for, as he warned apprentices, "the truth is you can't tell somebody what to do." As those who continued their training in MI would discover, effective MI practitioners are effective rhetoricians, who can influence or "nudge" people to do certain things as long as their efforts are under their clients' radar.

This is not to say that this training, or the others that I studied, circumvented or obscured all ethical aspects of directing client behavior. In fact, later that day, the co-trainers devoted significant time to discussing the kinds of situations in which taking a neutral stance would be professionally irresponsible, such as drunk driving or suicidal ideation, as opposed to other situations, like divorcing a spouse or taking a new job, when professional direction could unnecessarily impinge on client autonomy. And while reminding trainees that "MI was developed to . . . strategically guide behavior in a particular direction," they offered no prescriptions about healthy and unhealthy behavior that could apply across all cases. Instead, they highlighted the idea of "equipoise"—defined as a "conscious clinical decision" about whether and when to remain neutral (see also Miller & Rollnick 2013, 232–37).[37]

To be sure, motivational interviewers are trained to be highly conscious about their clinical decisions and rigorously reflexive about the ways they seek to realize them throughout any given interview. It is all the more striking, then, that their professional decisions and directions are designed to be opaque to client interviewees, who are "nudged" rather than baldly directed toward particular behavioral goals. Indeed, there was a glaring ethical quandary that was never plainly addressed by the co-trainers: what to make of the opacity of the motivational interview to client-interviewees? For if MI proponents are dedicated to recognizing clients, whether as collaborators or as partners, whose knowledge and expertise generally equals that of the professional, their intervention generates a radically *unequal* distribution of knowledge about the terms and dynamics of professional-client engagement.

Given their democratic aspirations, MI proponents are particularly sensitive to this critique and certainly will not enjoy reading it here. In an article titled "Ten Things That MI Is Not," which is commonly cited and distributed in MI trainings, Miller and Rollnick are adamant that "MI is not a way of tricking people into doing things they don't want to do" (2009, 131). Of course, the *point* is not to trick the client. Rather, from MI proponents' perspective, professional direction is disguised *in order to* generate the client's experience of being recognized as an equal co-participant (see also Zhang 2020). More specifically, the motivational interview is designed so that clients are the ones who articulate professional objectives and who, in turn, hear *themselves* as experts and feel recognized as such.

In this way, MI simply enlightens a particularly stubborn problem with which American democrats have long grappled: that is, how to authoritatively direct subjects recognized to be self-governing and who feel they participate on their own terms.[38] It also offers telling resolution by rhetorically masking rather than abolishing expert authority and disguising rather than avoiding professional direction, alerting us to the possibility that expertise in democracies, more generally, may regularly rely on subterfuge. Indeed, if some adherents see in MI a recipe for participatory democracy writ small, it may be precisely because, as Miller put it to that room full of captivated apprentices, "Motivational interviewing is a kind of non-authoritarian way of trying to move in a particular direction where you [the professional] want to go."

CONCLUSION: MI, (IN)EXPERTISE, AND
THE AUTHORITY OF AMERICAN DEMOCRACY

In that stunningly paradoxical statement, I heard an echo of my first MI training, back on that sweltering summer day with Norman and his trainees. Specifically, I remembered a post-lunch round of "real-plays," a common exercise in MI trainings. Unlike role-plays, in which the parties involved assume roles based on a scenario derived from an actual or fictitious encounter with clients, in real-plays trainees present problems with which they themselves are grappling—temporarily becoming clients of the method they are being trained in.[39]

In this case, the topical focus of the real-play was trainees' hesitancy to record practice MI sessions for Norman to evaluate, the very topic that preoccupied the women with whom I shared the elevator that morning. Before beginning the exercise, Norman reminded those playing the interviewer to "roll with resistance"—that is, to affirm all the articulated reasons their client/colleague resists audio-recording, while subtly stimulating them do so—or at least to say that they will do so.[40] And while such a "change statement" would be part product of rhetorical direction, it should feel as though the interviewee came up with it spontaneously, on their own.

Uncannily, Mary, who had been fretting aloud over her practice recordings when I first met her, was paired with her consoling friend, who was now enlisted as the "observer." The trio was rounded out by the real-playing Camilla—a Black woman, approximately thirty years younger than the other two, with relatively little professional experience and no advanced degree. Given that the trio reflected the stratification typical of real-world social service provision, I promptly abandoned my plan to circulate among the real-playing trios. I was instead fixated on whether Mary's trio could realize MI's foundational charge. In this case, that would entail Mary directing Camilla toward a change statement, all while recognizing her and equalizing the terms of exchange.

The play began. From the outset, Camilla was adamant that she would not be recording a session, first offering, "I can't stand the sound of my own voice," with which Mary effusively sympathized. Moments later, Camilla's explanation shifted, as she said that she didn't relish being "judged"—even by "sweet Norman"—that she was so young compared to everyone else, and that she didn't want to feel like she was "back in high school." Mary slipped, telling Camilla that she was obviously "extremely accomplished" and "just as good at this as everyone else." Camilla dug her heels in, relisting all the ways she felt unprepared for the unpleasant task. Taking in the raised

eyebrow of her observing friend, Mary got back on a "roll," summarizing—
in ever so slightly exaggerated terms—why Camilla wasn't going to produce
a tape, indeed even why she shouldn't or perhaps even *couldn't* produce
a tape.

Suddenly, everything changed: Camilla announced that it was time to
"quit [her] whining" and record a "damn practice tape!" As if they had surprised themselves, the women grew wide-eyed and, for a moment, fell silent. The real-play ended with a round of high-fives and smiling astonishment that MI had "worked." "I'm gonna do it," Camilla kept repeating as
she helped pull dispersed chairs across the linoleum floor back to the long,
cloth-covered table.

Per usual, the entire group gathered to discuss the exercise. Mary and
Camilla, both still aglow with accomplishment, were itching to report
on the fruits of their dyadic labor. Camilla began, explaining how she had
"changed her mind, totally," but only after a temporary hitch:

> CAMILLA: And the thing is, is that when [Mary was] goin' there [about my
> accomplishments relative to my youth], that was what really made
> me want to resist a lot.
> NORMAN: You could kind of *feel* that direction.
> CAMILLA: Yeah. But then, like [Mary] was saying, when it comes down to it,
> I have to just suck it up, do it, and quit whining [recording a practice
> tape].
> NORMAN: But in the end, *she* didn't say it to you.
> CAMILLA: No, she did *not* say that to me.
> NORMAN: Right. In the end, *you* said it.
> CAMILLA: *I* did.
> NORMAN: *That's* motivational interviewing.

As Norman points out, even though Mary momentarily erred by allowing Camilla to "feel the direction" early in the interview, she recovered in
the end, achieving her professional goals without betraying them as her
own. This reveals that the motivational interview falters when professional
authority—and by extension white, middle-aged authority—allows itself
to be seen, opening itself up to any number of responses (such as shutting
down, refusing to respond or participate, or making empty promises).[41]
That, Norman underscores, is *not* MI.

As Miller explained to his university audience, and as Norman suggested
to his real-players, MI is a method of exchange that shrouds its own directive elements, allowing practitioners to steer the conversation while ap-

pearing to simply respond to the client whom they have recognized and "centered." As Norman declared in response to his apprentices' post–real-play report: "*That's* motivational interviewing."

Rather than singling out Miller or Norman, or even the method they train, let us recall what we learned from the Skinner-Rogers debate. In particular, while Rogers insisted that the American client be free from expert direction altogether, Skinner underscored that people should be able to *know and see* how they are being directed, and not simply so that they can blindly follow it, but so they can determine how to respond. The longstanding embrace of client-centered approaches as most ethical, if not necessarily most effective, suggests that much of the American public is ready and willing to sacrifice transparency, and be recognized as autonomous and equal without actually redistributing knowledge or power (see Fraser 2008). In this sense, Miller's nod to "nonauthoritative direction" arguably refines a paradigmatic way of doing American democracy, if in this case, in the context of a dyadic professional exchange.

If this seems far-fetched, consider that Miller himself first prompted me to think of MI in terms of American democracy, while we were seated together in his Albuquerque living room. Returning from his kitchen, having done some dinner menu planning with his wife, Miller was apparently pondering my central question of why MI had spread so dramatically. Signaling for me to turn on my recorder, he offered one more characteristically tentative, if provocative response:

WRM: I've wondered sometimes if there's something about the state of the culture where [MI] is a complementary idea whose time has come.
ESC: Hm, mm, hm.
WRM: I mean America's become a very polarized, binary, authoritarian place in a way. And [MI] is the—radically different from that. You know, radically different from trying to figure out who are the good guys and who are the bad guys and who's gonna make somebody else do what, you know. And it's not unique to this country, I mean. This is—but it may be that you know [MI] particularly takes in countries that have swung a little bit far in the expert authoritarian direction.
ESC: Hm!
WRM: And it's kind of a complement that people recognize, say, "Yeah, there's another, there's a different way to do this," you know, "than the way we're living."

Miller went on to substantiate the claim that MI is an antidote to authoritarianism, explaining that the method had been adopted with particular enthusiasm in professional fields with pronounced directive tendencies. He specified that practitioners in addiction treatment, corrections, and health care—where "doctors have a long history of godlikeness"—were especially eager to disengage themselves from the "expert trap" and did so by way of MI.

That said, in 2010, it is unlikely that Miller anticipated just how "polarized, binary, and authoritarian" the United States would become with the election of Donald Trump. Under current conditions, while some pour gasoline on the flames of a longstanding mistrust of expertise, associating it with elitism, others have tried to harness it as a salve for growing authoritarianism, proposing that expertise is precisely what a now faltering American democracy needs (see Nichols 2017; see also Cohen-Cole 2014).

These historical contingencies notwithstanding, American expertise and American democracy—as cultural idioms—have some rather profound differences, suggesting why the latter remains the more attractive choice for framing institutional and professional practices in the United States. Expertise divides expert and lay, claiming ownership over some domain of knowledge and the responsibility to wield that knowledge wisely relative to those who do not share it. Democracy consistently promises that unevenly weighted ways of knowing, which are differentially reinforced by any number of social institutions and ideologies, can nevertheless be equalized, including within face-to-face encounters. No wonder Miller, his colleagues, and his apprentices emphatically choose to recognize clients as individuals and equal partners, and to disavow rather than assert expertise, in order to figure and forge a democratic practice.

Yet, while the terms of democracy remain a more appealing frame for professional practice in the United States, we would do well to recognize that whereas expertise tends to acknowledge its authority, small-d American democrats remain inclined to deny and obscure it. In the end, how MI explains itself, whether in textual representations or during the course of in vivo training, is a reflection of how it understands the ideological proclivities of its audience. The rise and spread of MI suggests that (in)expertise is a form of American democratic governance that far exceeds the motivational interview, even if it finds particularly exquisite expression there.

CHAPTER 2

American Rhetoric

Therapeutic Performance and the Poetics of Behavior Change

On the morning of the first day of Ki's advanced training at U-Haven, twelve urbanite apprentices entered and circled the 400-square-foot train-ing room.[1] Cheerful if clipped greetings provided the soundtrack for what looked like an awkward, slow-motion square dance. Apprentices' eyes darted nervously between fellow participants and the folding chairs tucked under the adjoined tables, as if one seat might offer more comfort, or per-haps a better view, than the next. The two video cameras that I had placed in the room's corners, with the help of a technically savvy research assistant, surely heightened the sense of an encompassing audience ready to evaluate apprentices' performance. That said, participant-observation is part and parcel of every MI training, whether or not an anthropologist, her assis-tants, and recording equipment are involved. In vivid and often amusing terms, veteran MI practitioners recount the discomforts of having their re-hearsals of MI continuously examined by colleagues, trainers, and coaches, while appreciating that ongoing evaluation is critical to the cultivation of their method.

U-Haven is one of the largest social service organizations in a major American city and is strikingly diverse in the services it offers (among them: residential care, drop-in programs, counseling services, medication management, refugee resettlement, shelter, outreach services, needle ex-change, and medical care and referrals). Accordingly, its staff is profession-ally diverse, ranging from psychiatrists, nurses, and social workers—some with master's degrees from elite institutions, others with BSWs or equiva-lent bachelor's degrees—to paraprofessional staff who were once clients of U-Haven's services. Some U-Haven staff members administer complex pro-grams, writing grant proposals and hiring staff to keep them afloat, while others provide direct services, such as counseling or case management. Yet, despite this professional diversity, U-Haven staff are uniformly charged with treating highly complex and pressing problems that require elaborate skillsets, and the resources with which to do so are rarely at hand. For the apprentices in the MI training, this typically included assuring that people have a safe place to live, receive SSI or VA benefits, use clean needles, access mental health care, stay out of prison, visit doctors, take prescribed medications, and/or stay alive.

Ki—whom we observed train alongside Miller in a much different setting—was intimately familiar with the challenges of apprentices' work. As a senior clinical supervisor at U-Haven, he ran weekly supervision meetings wherein direct line staff regularly recounted failed or faltering strategies of engagement and a concomitant sense of inefficacy. Beholden to the principles of harm reduction, U-Haven prides itself on serving clients that other city programs reject because of the complexity of their problems, though this commitment weighs on staff. In contrast to contingency-based programs—which require drug users to abstain from drugs and attend drug treatment while receiving case management, shelter, or ancillary services—harm reduction programs, like U-Haven, focus on providing such resources to all participants in need of them, regardless of whether or not they abstain from drugs. Practically, this means that U-Haven professionals regularly interact with participants who are high, inebriated, in withdrawal, or otherwise suffering effects of drug and alcohol use. It also means that, relative to professionals in more traditional service settings, they have comparatively little leverage in getting their clients to address what the staff deem to be the behavioral correlates of clients' circumstances. Without formal contingencies for service provision, U-Haven professionals depend on their powers of persuasion in fulfilling their charge to reduce harm and are frequently frustrated by stalemates with clients.

Ki designed the advanced training in MI with these kinds of issues in mind, intent to test his faith that MI works in even the most challenging settings. At the training's outset, Ki traced in slow steps an otherwise invisible 10-foot arc at the front of the room, resting his ocean-blue eyes on each apprentice in turn as he spoke, making the elegant, almost balletic gestures with his hands that were central to his self-presentation. His speech was punctuated by unusually long pauses, almost as if speaking in verse, as well as by stutters, hedges, and false starts, which suggested he was searching for just the right words. Ki nevertheless provided a remarkably clear and compelling outline of his plan for the year, all in five minutes flat. (I later marveled at time-stamped transcripts, wondering how much practice had been devoted to producing such an efficient, if seemingly unrehearsed, inauguration.)

As Ki explained it on that October morning, after a full-day inauguration, the training group would meet once a month from 9:00 to 11:00 a.m. over the course of a year. Between sessions, there would be homework: chapters to read from the then hot-off-the-press third edition of Miller and

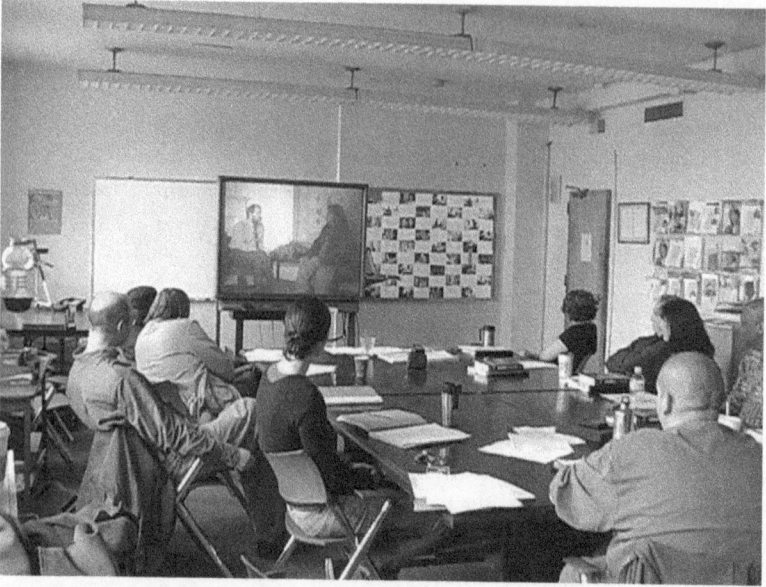

Figure 2.1. U-Haven apprentices watch as William Miller demonstrates MI with "Silent Man," in *Motivational Interviewing Professional Training VHS Videotape Series* (Miller, Rollnick & Moyers 1998). Photograph by author.

Rollnick's textbook and the thick binder of articles on MI, and exercises to practice with clients. Six months into the training, apprentices would start to audio-record a total of three MI sessions with clients, which—once scored—would serve as the basis of individualized coaching. Monthly sessions would include short, didactic PowerPoint presentations, a host of role-playing application exercises, and occasional film study.

As we learned in the introduction, the client-actors in the most widely circulating demonstration films tend to be white males; the films also tend to portray problems that are fairly discrete, rather than multiple and overlapping, and include class markers and other subtle signs that the resources to address those problems are well within reach —quite unlike the circumstances of U-Haven's clientele. Perhaps this is why Ki began his apprentices' film study with "Silent Man," a noticeably disheveled client-actor who appears to be of Indigenous descent and apparently earns his nickname for saying next to nothing and speaking very softly, at least until the end of Miller's interview (see figure 2.1). Struggling to habituate themselves to the delicacies of the conversation style, U-Haven trainees would marvel at how "easily" and "naturally" Miller deployed the powerful rhetorical techniques that they themselves so laboriously practiced during their training when watching this and other filmed demonstrations.

The filmic Miller also clearly impressed U-Haven trainees because the *way* he talks is so subtly and gently persuasive—a quality that apprentices also saw in their own trainer, Ki. Both Miller and Ki seemed so attuned to and allied with the client in front of them, almost as if they were dancing rather than talking, while still managing to get clients to engage in normatively and professionally desired behaviors. So even though U-Haven professionals were more likely to conduct MI sessions on a traffic-filled street or in the elevator of a single-room occupancy (SRO) residence than in an air-conditioned office adorned with faux plants and wall-hangings, they nevertheless came to believe, like their trainer, that the rhetorical techniques deployed in the demonstration films, once mastered, could revive their own practice.

·.·

Focusing on an advanced MI training at U-Haven, this chapter asks: *What happens when a rapidly growing community of helping professionals are retrained as rhetoricians?* For, as we will see, apprentices to MI learn to approach behavior change as an aesthetic as well as a clinical endeavor. At a minimum, this means they are trained to refocus attention from their clients' psychic states to the qualities and effects of their own speech. At U-Haven, as well as all the other sites I studied, MI training cultivates rhetoricians who can develop and subtly deploy persuasive lines of reasoning attuned to specific circumstances (*inventio*), organize what is said when (*dispositio*), speak in a style that resonates with a particular interlocutor (*elocutio*), track the course of the exchange and recall specific rhetorical devices on an as-needed basis (*memoria*), and attend to the pace, pitch, and volume of speech as well as gesture and bodily comportment (*actio*).[2] Thus, if attention to sociological difference is abstracted in MI training, attention to rhetorical difference is very carefully honed.

Over the course of their training in MI, apprentices learn that it is not only, or even primarily, *what* Miller says during filmed demonstration interviews that is so compelling; *how* he says what he does is at least as important. Through their ongoing practice of the method, apprentices come to understand how challenging it is to grasp MI's signature *poetics*—that is, the intonation, meter, and pronunciation that distinguish Miller's and MINTies' speech. Notably, while there is elegance in MI's poetics, the register is also distinguished by marked disfluency, including the unusually long, mid-statement pauses Miller deploys in his model interviews (see table 2.1). And although MINTies systematically use specific poetic devices, they seldom explicate them, leaving apprentices to acquire MI's rhetorical style via imitation. This chapter explains why MI's pause-filled poetics is an

Table 2.1. The poetics of Miller's reflections (line breaks demarcate pauses)

---

so you have a *lot* of responsi*bility*

the the
job you have you
ya you're
working with a lot of people you're *overseeing* a lot of people
you've got
na not
a *family* yet but you've got uh also a *marriage* an
you're
responsible there an in some ways this is a pull to

feel
feel *free* of that at least for a little while to feel free of that responsibility

---

Source: Created by author. Based on William Miller's demonstration with "Ponytail John" (see introduction, p. 2).

"active ingredient" in MI's art of persuasion: in realizing MI's behavioral goals; in convening and cohering a professional community; and ultimately in disseminating (or scaling) the practice.[3] (For this reason, pauses in MI trainers' and proponents' speech will be marked parenthetically in seconds and tenths of seconds in this chapter. The significance of the length and placement of these pauses will be discussed later in the chapter.)

Extending the discussion in chapter 1, I demonstrate here that the realization of MI's signature "client-centered directiveness," "non-authoritarian direction," and (in)expertise depends on the use of a highly stylized way of speaking, which works to ensure that interlocutors feel fully "heard" and therefore feel respected as autonomous individuals even when persuaded to speak and act as directed, as in the case of Ponytail John. With the help of training films, role-playing, and evaluated audio-recorded practice sessions, apprentices learn how to manage the delivery of a professional message so that the interview seems like a natural exchange between neutralized equals—in which expertise and authority, as well as sociohistorically marked, institutionalized forms of difference, play no part—all the while persuading interviewees to change their behavior. In this sense, MI rhetoric is American rhetoric par excellence.

Since the establishment of the republic by of white colonial settlers, speakers on US soil have contended with the widespread ideal that one should speak from the heart, and attendant suspicions of institutionally culti-vated and stylized speech. It is not surprising, then, that MI trainees grapple with the longstanding cultural denigration of rhetoric as a substantively empty, insincere mode of communication. Thus, as rhetoricians in train-ing, they must learn to *perform naturally*, as if MI were language acquired by birth and not a style that had been rigorously studied or acquired by im-itation. In highlighting the tensions that arise in learning how to conduct a motivational interview, the pages that follow demonstrate the challenging business of becoming American rhetoricians, charged with the paradoxical goals of *directing* while *collaborating, co-producing* motivation and *eliciting* it as if it was already the client's own, and *performing* a highly stylized way of speaking while striving to authentically *presence* themselves in a thera-peutic exchange.

These ideological tensions are addressed, if not fully resolved, through the aestheticization of professional speech, with trainers focusing appren-tices' attention on the immediate effects of their words on the here and now of the dyadic exchange. Indeed, in line with trainers' frequent remind-ers that "clients are the best teachers," professionals who use the MI reg-ister learn to carefully calibrate not just *what* they say, but *how* and *when* they say it, in accordance with the speech of the individual who sits before them. Thus, in MI, the task of behavior change is undertaken as an ethical as well as aesthetic one, with one's speech explicitly understood to radi-cally depend on another's (see Bakhtin 1990; Rosaldo 1982). In document-ing what happens when a therapeutic endeavor is taught and taken up as an aesthetic, rhetorical, and thereby ethical one, I suggest that MI prompts us to consider two institutionalized, widespread, and interrelated assump-tions: (1) therapy is an unadorned, if not unmediated, channel for sincere self-expression; (2) rhetoric is comparatively empty, devoid of speakers' ethical commitments. Along the way, we will consider how traditions of American persuasion selectively erase differences between persuaders and those whom they seek to persuade.

RHETORIC, ROLE-PLAY, AND REFLEXABILITY (OR, RELEARNING HOW TO SPEAK AT U-HAVEN)

It was no accident that Ki picked exactly twelve apprentices from the pool of applicants to his training. That number allowed him to evenly break the group into pairs, triads, or foursomes for various exercises that allowed trainees to practice the techniques he taught during the didactic portion of monthly training sessions. As a member of MINT, Ki had access to and had himself practiced scores of MI-specific exercises, including "Out of the

Woods," "Dr. Clark's Referral," "Drumming for Change Talk," and "Calling the CATS." Many of these exercises, as U-Haven trainees had anxiously anticipated, involved closely evaluated, highly improvisational public performance.

Much like improv actors, U-Haven's MI apprentices had to be at the ready.[4] Sometimes, in the course of a PowerPoint presentation, Ki would suddenly turn to an unsuspecting apprentice and animate a random statement that a U-Haven client might make (such as, "I blew my check. I need an advance"; "I can't stand these meds anymore"; "It took me forever to get here"). Betraying varying levels of apprehension, the targeted trainee would then venture an MI-consistent response. Ki inevitably followed these surprise improvisations with thanks and praise, finding the "gems" in apprentices' frequently fumbling responses.

This kind of role-playing is an indispensable part of MI training, and not because it allows apprentices to put theory into practice. Practice is undertaken for practice's sake, with the idea that one will continuously learn from each role one takes up in every role-play. As we will explore in chapter 5, MI training is concertedly pragmatic, in that apprentices are trained to be rigorously attentive to the effects of their own actions, to avoid preemptive conclusions about the nature of the problem and person immediately before them, and to appreciate that what works in one conversation may not work in the next.[5] Through role-plays, MI trainees come to appreciate that there are no stock responses or scripts for motivational interviews, in large part because there is no operating theory of personhood or pathology that might serve as a basis.

Since the content of what to say therefore cannot (and should not) be determined in advance, role-plays provide opportunities to experiment with MI-specific methods of managing unpredictable conversations to come. Just as important, however, role-plays are opportunities for professionals to analyze *themselves*, and particularly their way of speaking, rehearsing the various roles they may come to play in the mercurial, real-life drama of behavior change.

For these reasons, advanced MI training sessions, including those at U-Haven, typically devote substantial time to role-plays. Usually, U-Haven apprentices rehearsed motivational interviews in triads: one playing the part of the practitioner, another the role of a problem-plagued client, and the third serving as enlisted observer. During these exercises, Ki circulated among role-playing groups, squatting so as to listen (as much as watch), nodding ever so slightly and sometimes emphatically as the interview progressed, exchanging pregnant glances with assigned observers, working to discern if they heard the nuances of the role-play as he did (figure 2.2).

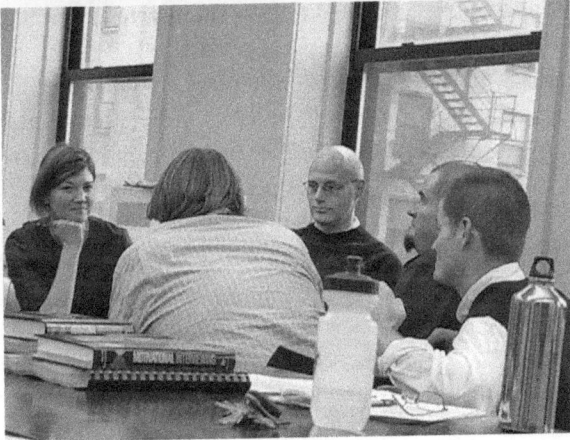

Figure 2.2a, b, and c. Role-playing exercises at U-Haven.
Photographs by author.

Early in MI training, role-play exercises typically focus on practicing the four primary speech acts or "strategies" that constitute the motivational interview—Open Questions, Affirmations, Reflections, and Summaries—better known by the acronym OARS (see table 2.2). As Ki explained to his apprentices: "Everything and anything that we do . . . relies very heavily on the OARS. As I've heard many people in the MINT say, if you're gonna invest time and energy into [learning MI] time [is] well spent with OARS."[6]

Although the apprentices were familiar with OARS as counseling skills that—as even MI's lead proponents recognize—are not unique to MI, and already used them in their daily work with clients, they invariably experienced the *MI-specific performance* of these speech acts to be deceptively difficult to pull off during training. Indeed, once the person playing the client broached a topic he or she wished to address, those practicing the role of interviewer came to appreciate that there is no rhetorical formula that can be adopted across interviews, but only more or less strategic improvisations using OARS.

If MI training is similar to improv training, it does not necessarily attract those with a penchant for dramatic performance. U-Haven trainees squirmed when their affirmations sounded canned; they winced after asking a closed question (which invited unproductive yes-or-no responses) when they realized they could have asked open ones (that would have induced more talk from clients); they sighed, chortled, and threw up their hands to hide their faces when they found themselves lost about what to summarize at the end of a role-played session, as if their mouths had failed them as much as their memories. And while Ki was always nearby chiming in with encouragement during role-plays—"beautiful," "that's right," "*exactly*"—apprentices continued to hear themselves sounding decidedly less fluent than their trainer and colleagues did.

The feedback sessions following role-plays are at least as important in MI training as the performances themselves. After all, role-plays are fractal recursions of the performer/audience participation framework that characterizes MI training and allows performing apprentices to get direct feedback from those cast as observers (see Irvine & Gal 2000).[7] Assigned observers typically use worksheets to assure they are assessing the right things. They sometimes report their findings on an "OARS Tracking Sheet," which requires them to tally how many times the role-playing interviewer uses one of the four rhetorical strategies (see figure 2.3). The worksheet also asks for a count of "other" (that is, MI-*inconsistent*) conversational strategies that are used, such as asking "closed questions," "providing opinions or advice," or "teaching"—all glosses for projecting potentially off-putting expertise.

In this sense, the post–role-play evaluation session is not just an op-

Table 2.2. The four fundamental speech acts or "strategies" of the motivational interview

"Four Strategies"	As Defined in the Glossary of *Motivational Interviewing* (Miller & Rollnick 2013)	As Explicated in the Course of Ki's Training
Open Question	· "A question that offers the client broad latitude and choice for how to respond." (411)	· Cannot be answered with a "yes" or "no" or with one or two words · Nonrhetorical; seeks information from the client in an ostensibly neutral way · Encourages the client to talk
Affirmation	· "An interviewer's statement valuing a positive client attribute or behavior." (405)	· Supports clients' sense of efficacy, strength, and power · Acknowledges challenges and difficulties · Validates feelings
Reflection	· "An interviewer statement intended to mirror meaning (explicit or implicit) of preceding client speech." (412)	· Rephrasing what you think you heard · Making a guess at what the client means; a hypothesis · Adjusting hypotheses about client behavior at various levels of complexity
Summary	· "A reflection that draws together content from two or more prior client statements." (413)	· Strategically "distilling" what the client has said and offering it back to them

portunity for the interviewer, who receives structured feedback about OARS counts and qualitative comments on how well they produced and responded to change talk; evaluations are also a chance for the observer to objectify the role they would soon inhabit and to imagine how they might strategically manage the improvised expressions of the role-played client. Trainers therefore insist on frequently switching so as to give all apprentices the opportunity to evaluate *their own* performance, as heard in the dramatized present as well as the projected, actual future (see Bakhtin 1981).

Over the course of these exercises, apprentices developed increasing re-

Observer Sheet 5: OARS

Listen for examples of the counselor's use of each of the OARS responses. As you hear them, place a hash mark (/) in the appropriate row. Make notes of good examples of each type of OARS response that you heard.

Counselor Response	Count (hash marks)	Good Example(s)
Open Question		
Affirm		
Reflect		
Summary		

Figure 2.3. Reflecting role-plays: An OARS tracking sheet.

flexivity about their own speech. Take Marcus, a middle-aged Black program manager, who had just received what he thought was a soft-pedaled evaluation from an OARS-counting colleague. In debriefing the role-play with Ki, with the other eleven apprentices listening in, Marcus ruefully recounted:

> The other thing is, is . . . I think two of us struggled with this: the opinion and advice piece. Uh, I ended up towards the end giving my opinion and advice, and I knew I was doin' it, but I couldn't stop myself from doin' it. But once I realized I was doin' it, I did turn it around at the end, but I, I just could not stop. I, I had to tell him what I thought my opinion, my advice was, but I couldn't stop, even if I knew it. Even I knew it. I I saw myself . . . doin' it; I still did it.

While Marcus was troubled by his MI-inconsistent speech acts, Ki took the otherwise problematic "giving of opinion and advice" as a victory, precisely because Marcus *had heard himself doing it*, which he readily pointed out to his fretting apprentice. Trained as analysts of themselves as speakers, MI trainees are not only expected to track, in real time, precisely what they are saying and doing when they engage in a motivational interview; they are also trained to adjust their speech in studied relation to how each client responds in the here and now of the interview.

Indeed, the primary purpose of role-plays is to make apprentices more reflexive about the immediate effects as well as the constituents of their speech. Not surprisingly, then, as the U-Haven training continued, apprentices provided increasingly incisive and sometimes scathing commentary about their own performance, much as Marcus did. In the meantime, their trainers assuaged their guilt and explained that there was really no rhetorical mistake from which one could not recover. As Ki put it when responding to Marcus's comment during the training:

> If that's [i.e., giving opinions and advice, in MI-inconsistent ways] something that (1.2) you feel pretty tuned into, you're good. Right? I think ideally, what we're doing is we're tracking it, though. OK? So I'm starting to feel the inclination to give some advice (1.1) or to render an opinion. Or to provide some information. And to give yourself a *pause*. "Is that what's really needed here?"

Note that Ki again praises Marcus precisely because he is "tuned into" his mistakes, which suggests a mode of knowledge known as *reflexivity*. Yet, in MI training, reflexivity is not about knowing who one is but rather about continually watching what one is doing and saying; it is therefore also a way of learning sensitized to the built-in uncertainties of social and discursive interaction. Accordingly, Ki asks Marcus and his colleagues to discern their own conversational "inclination(s)" before they act. The trainer soon added that there are "no hard and fast rules in MI," only (rhetorical) techniques designed to cope with the vagaries of loaded "conversations." Significantly, Ki wrapped up his response by urging Marcus to *pause*, reminding him that he can slow down the interview to ask himself anticipatory questions, like whether giving advice is "really what is needed here."

As Ki's comments indicate, MI training cultivates a kind of reflexivity that is better described as *reflexability*, in which one collects and considers evidence from the immediate past in the present to chart a knowable, if yet unknown, future. In this sense, *reflexability* is not simply a matter of being present to one's actions; it also demands anticipation of what one *will be* doing and saying relative to the emerging demands of unfolding encounters with clients. Significantly, then, *reflexability* is not a stable state of self-knowledge that one can simply inhabit. As Ki clarifies, the goal is not to become the kind of person or professional who never gives advice because of some ideological principle or identitarian stance. Rather, *reflexability* is a highly adaptive knowhow that is designed to cope with and adjust to the unfolding of social life, and particularly verbal interaction, the trajectory of which can never be fully known or knowable in advance.[8]

No matter how harsh or soft-pedaled their criticism of interviewing colleagues—how many checks they had placed on their tracking sheet— those who observed and those who played clients invariably sympathized with the excruciatingly heightened sense of self-consciousness that role-plays inspired for interviewers, knowing it would soon be their turn to play that role again. Nevertheless, there was always something restorative about the feedback sessions following role-plays, even when that feedback was critical. Post-hoc critiques folded what the role-playing interviewer invariably experienced as too practiced or inauthentic—no matter how skillful their performance was—back into the realm of the "real." Alongside the expected feedback from the assigned observer, those who played the role of the client reported how "heard" they felt, how willing or unwilling they were to share more with those who played the role of the professional. For instance, Ki asked Marcus's "client"—his fellow trainee Peter—how "it felt" when Marcus offered advice. When Peter responded, after a pregnant pause, "it didn't feel unnatural," Marcus's "struggle" as well as the artifice of the exercise, seemed to evaporate.

Importantly, such feedback blurred the lines between the role-played client and the professional who played that client, and therefore between the role-play and actual practice. Thus, in addition to tracking emerging technical skills, role-playing helped apprentices anticipate and inhabit the professional roles they actually played and would continue to play long after they left the training room. If MI training succeeded, trainees would continue to be reflexable professionals, primed to see and carefully speak relative to what future clients actually *say* and *do* rather than to who clients and professionals are presumed to stably *be*.

AMERICAN REFLECTIONS: THE PROFESSIONAL CRAFTING OF BEHAVIOR-CHANGING TALK

As highlighted in chapter 1, directing others can be a thorny business in the United States, given the construal of personhood in terms of autonomy and attendant ideologies of speech as free individual expression. Thus, for their method to be maximally palatable, motivational interviewers must not only project attunement to and alignment with clients so that they feel recognized and simply understood as individuals; interviewers must also conceal signs of persuasion from their own speech.

In striving to achieve these complex rhetorical feats, those participating in advanced MI training, like the apprentices at U-Haven, realize that there is much more nuance to the deployment of MI's signature speech acts than they initially realized. They begin experimenting with algorithms of OARS—for example, offering at least two reflections for every open question. They concentrate on the ordering of their speech acts, so that they culminate in motivating "summaries." And, over the course of their training, apprentices grow to appreciate that MI's constitutive speech acts are not created equally, and that some pose interactional risks that can outweigh potential rewards.

For instance, just as soon as U-Haven apprentices began feeling comfortable with the O of OARS, Ki explained that no matter how elegantly they are posed, open questions can appear diagnostic, as if one is simply mining the client for data needed to come to expert conclusions. In another training I studied, the trainer was especially adamant on this point, attributing a shaky role-playing session to an overreliance on questions, telling his apprentices that: "Questions do not communicate empathy. They do not (0.2) communicate interest, curiosity. 'How do you feel about that?' This is . . . this is a traditional question in therapy that (0.7) is almost *verboten* in MI." Miller and Rollnick indeed warn that open questions can ensnare unwitting practitioners in the dreaded "expert trap," writing in the third edition of their foundational text: "asking a run of questions not only communicates that 'I'm in control here,' but also sets up an implicit expectation that once you have enough information you will have the answer" (2013, 42).[9]

As all MI trainers know, plainly warning against the "expert trap" is less than half the battle. Their apprentices must master an *(in)expert register* that projects professional uncertainty rather than authoritative knowledge in engagements with clients. In lieu of questions that risk projecting expertise, MI trainers enthusiastically tout *reflections*, defined as "an interviewer statement intended to mirror meaning (explicit or implicit) of preceding client speech" (Miller & Rollnick 2013, 412) and as "one of the most important and challenging skills for motivational interviewing" (Miller & Rollnick 2002, 67). Accordingly, across trainings I studied, much effort is devoted to perfecting reflections. Typically, apprentices first learn to use reflections like denotative checkpoints, opportunities to assess "whether [their] understanding of the client's inner world is correct"—as the forebear of the MI reflection, Carl Rogers, once put it (1986, 375). In strikingly consistent terms, Ki once told U-Haven apprentices:

> The reflection (0.5) relates it back to the person to whom we're listening (0.4) as a way to (0.7) among many other things check in with them around to what extent am (0.5) am I getting this am I understanding what's going on with you?

Note that in Ki's explanation, the properly performed reflection appears to discursively distribute knowledge, projecting an image of a professional whose understanding is wholly dependent on their client's ongoing verbalizations. Thus, like Rogers, Ki indicates that reflections can produce the sense that the practitioner presently lacks definitive knowledge of the client's inner world, as well as keen interest in accruing that knowledge from the client-as-expert. In this way, the realization of client-centeredness, the experience of recognition, and the projection of (in)expertise hinge on the performance of the reflection.

As their training proceeded, Ki taught apprentices that quite aside from the definitional claim to serve as a "mirror" of client speech, "there's a lot [more] one can do with a skillful reflection." If deployed in an MI-consistent way, the reflection can achieve what a question is normatively designed to do—yield responses—and do so in far more productive ways. Along these lines and midway through the U-Haven training, Ki proposed to his increasingly sophisticated apprentices: "The idea here is a reflection states a *hypothesis*. It's making a *guess* about what the person means." Clearly demoting the denotative function of the reflection, and suggesting what it might—as a professional performative—produce, he elaborated:

> And there's no penalty for missing, so one thing about this exercise is (1.9) is that we get caught up in (1.6) you know (0.8) wanting to get it right. And I think sometimes the fear of getting it wrong is what might, um, (1.9) uh, (3.1) make me more reluctant to try a reflection. I don't want to get it wrong. It's okay to get it wrong. Right? Because, again, the idea is (1.1) what happens next. We learn motivational interviewing from our participants. Right? So as, as long as the reflection, right or wrong, leads us further down the path, then (1.0) that's okay. Sometimes getting it wrong gives us as much information as it does to get it right. Okay?

According to Ki—and quite contrary to Rogers's stated goal to accurately reflect clients' "inner world(s)"—the denotative fidelity of a reflection is neither necessary, nor even especially desirable in motivational interviewing. Instead, the trainer emphasizes the yields of *inaccurate* reflections, clearly stating that, in MI, there is no reward for "getting [a reflection] right" in relation to what the interviewee means. After all, an accurate reflection would effectively erase the opportunity for the client to correct or elaborate, and in turn potentially truncate the conversational "path" and bounty of "information" one might gather along the way.[10]

In other words, the reflection pragmatically produces what an open question aspires to, but often cannot achieve because of its conventional associations with professional authority. As Ki put it in another training session, "The idea is (1.5) it doesn't matter if it's right or wrong. The grade isn't how accurate are your reflections. The measure is (2.3) what are the *results* of your reflections."[11] The MI reflection directs, as well as reflects, prompting the client to elaborate, revise, and potentially talk themselves into change. In other words, reflections should help produce the difference between ways of thinking and feeling so that professionals can resolve it.

Through their ongoing rehearsals, apprentices discovered that reflections are particularly tricky precisely because they are, in essence, clinical questions in tonal disguise (see Miller & Rollnick 2002, 69). That is, the yield of the MI reflection depends on one's ability to *intonationally masquerade* questions as declaratives. Ki therefore reminded apprentices to control the inflection of their voice at the end of their statements. "It's not: 'You're feeling angry about that?'" Ki explained, using exaggerated falsetto to mark that he was asking a question, and perhaps make it seem particularly cartoonish to do so. Demonstrating the more productive alternative, Ki deployed a markedly flat, almost robotic rendition of the very same sentence—now performed as a reflection—that still exuded the interest, curiosity, and empathy that open questions purportedly lack. With this in mind, MI apprentices spend hours working to transform interrogative statements into declarative ones—or open questions into reflections—by reflexively (or *reflexably*) attending to and transforming their intonational habits.

Further still into their training, U-Haven apprentices began to grasp that the more *inaccurate* a reflection is in a denotative sense, the more potentially productive it can be in a performative one. Herein lies the power of what apprentices came to know and practice as an especially important variation on the MI reflection: the "amplified reflection," which "turns up the volume a bit on the client's statement" (Miller & Rollnick 2013, 199; see table 2.3). Based on MI's understanding of ambivalence as more a potentiality of interaction than a state of mind, the goal of the amplified reflection is not to decipher the "implicit or explicit meaning" of clients' state-

Table 2.3. The types, functions, technicalities, and effects of MI reflections

Types of MI Reflections	Rhetorical Function	Technicalities	Rhetorical Effect
Simple or Straight Reflection	· "A *reflection* that contains little or no additional content beyond what the client has said." (Miller & Rollnick 2013, 413)	· Flat intonation · Rewording of statement *without* adding meaning	· Client feelings of being recognized or heard · Client elaborations of the statement (and potentially change talk)
Amplified Reflection	· "A response in which the interviewer reflects back the client's content with greater intensity than the client has expressed; one form of response to client *sustain talk* or *discord*." (Miller & Rollnick 2013, 406) · "an overstatement." (199) · "a guess." (395)	· Flat intonation · Rewording of client statement *with* added meaning	· "The other side of ambivalence: change talk." (Miller & Rollnick 2013, 199) · Protest of the reflected statement leads to change talk which equals and leads to changed behaviors.
Double-Sided Reflection	· "An interviewer reflection that includes both client sustain talk and change talk, usually with the conjunction 'and.'" (Miller & Rollnick 2013, 408)	· Flat intonation · "And" rather than "but" so as to give them equal (and unbearable) weight · The "recency rule": state the pro-change side of the reflection last for subtle lingering effect	· Increased ambivalence · Discomfort with the status quo · Change talk

ments (412). It is rather to "evoke the other side of ambivalence: change talk" (199). Miller and Rollnick offer this example:

CLIENT: I think things are just fine in our marriage the way they are.
INTERVIEWER: **There's really no room for improvement.**
CLIENT: Well, I mean things aren't *perfect*, but I'm happy enough as it is.

INTERVIWER: Things just couldn't possibly be any better in your marriage than they are right now.

CLIENT: I'm pretty satisfied, but I guess both of us aren't.[12]

Marital strife would usually be very low on the list of pressing problems that
most U-Haven clients generally suffer and may therefore not readily resonate at U-Haven in terms of the kinds of persons and problems the example
depicts. Nevertheless, Ki repeatedly riffed on the example to underscore
that the point and effect of amplified reflections remain the same no matter
where and with whom they are practiced. So whereas he once praised his
apprentices' "simple reflections" as accurate "mirrors" of a sample client
statement like, "I blew my SSI check. I need an advance," he later characterized these very same reflections as being of "the lowest risk" as well as the
lowest reward, "because they're not quite as (1.3) well, strategic and (0.5)
directive" as amplified ones.

With this warning in mind, Ki's apprentices began rehearsing during
role-playing sessions how to *inaccurately reflect*—or "amplify"—various
statements their clients might make. Consider the following example. In
one spring training session at U-Haven, a round-robin exercise focused on
amplified reflections was cued up when an apprentice named Elaine answered Ki's call to "throw something out that you've heard a [client] say in
the last couple days." Animating one of her clients at the residential program
she supervised, Elaine announced: "I want to quit Suboxone!"[13] Without
further explanation of the client or case at hand, the exercise commenced.
Apprentices struggled to "turn up the volume" by offering reflections that
they now half-recognized to be too simple: "You don't like taking Suboxone
anymore"; "You feel it's really time to stop." Some even resorted to asking
questions, such as: "Do you mean that you're ready to be drug free?" with
Ki gently reminding that if the intonation was flat and the first four words
of the sentence were cut, a lovely (if still simple) reflection would result
(i.e., "You're ready to be drug free."). After a few more tries, Ki intervened,
modeling a startlingly amplified reflection. Offering his "guess" at what the
fictitious client meant, Ki reflected: "You're thinking that (1.2) you may go
back to using [heroin]."

The room suddenly grew silent. Apprentices cocked their heads, furrowed their brows, and flashed inquisitive if uncomfortable smiles. In response to their evident puzzlement, Ki explained that by amplifying the
statement in the way he did, the client might be prompted to offer objections to the behavior Ki referenced and, in so doing, talk *themself* into staying away from heroin, whether or not they quit their prescribed Suboxone.
While Ki equivocated at some length about the particular circumstances in

which this amplified reflection might work, as well as how it might fail, he also underscored the rewards at stake: "You know, an amplified is a (0.6) risk as far as overstepping. And getting some pushback. Actually, you *want* some pushback." In this case, "pushback" would entail the client responding something to the effect of: "I am *never* going back to using [heroin] again"—an unequivocal change statement rhetorically produced by the interviewer if actually uttered by the client. As in the Socratic method, the client/student articulates the answer that the practitioner/teacher has had in mind all along.

Impressed heads began nodding around the training table as the practical potential—if not the long philosophical legacy—of Ki's rhetorical reflection sank in. Difference with which to work had been rhetorically manufactured. In addition to showing them how to amplify a reflection, Ki had also provided an example of what is called, in MI, "developing" or "instilling discrepancy"—that is, creating ambivalence in clients when "they are not truly ambivalent, at least not yet" (Miller & Rollnick 2013, 247; see also 243–54).

Now, several months into their training, U-Haven apprentices appreciated that Ki's provocative amplification had a much greater chance of working—that is, eliciting change talk—because of the *way* he said it. There was nothing confrontational about his tone. He sounded thoughtful. Nonjudgmental. Earnest. Sincere. Like he was trying to understand and was ready to support whatever the client decided to do. Apprentices now understood that "overstepping" is unlikely when these are the qualities of one's speech. Accordingly, they set about fine-tuning not just *what* they might say in the course of a real-time therapeutic exchange, but also—and more concertedly—*how* they would productively say it. Now, distributing their reflexive attention between the semantics and poetics of their own speech acts, they practiced how to control the tone of affirmations so as to sound sincere rather than saccharine, how to punctuate open questions with unconventionally long pauses, and how to rearrange and recharge clients' relatively banal statements in motivational summaries.

As apprentices delved deeper into this rhetorical work, they were faced with yet another paradox. As they strove to become "fluent" in MI, they found that the poetry of MI centrally entails *dis*fluency, including the unusually long pauses, hedges, and stutters that characterized their own trainer's speech. In the meantime, I was learning that traits that at first appeared to be idiosyncratic tics in Ki's speech are widely shared among experienced MI trainers and, most certainly, MI's lead proponents. These register-specific disfluencies help project uncertainty, deflect authority, and thereby entice interviewees to "talk themselves into change."

MOTIVATING DISFLUENCY: THE POETICS
AND PRAGMATICS OF PAUSE

He learned from Socrates not only how to speak, but also how to be silent.
AESCHINES, in Stobaeus, *Anthology* 3.34.10

They heard, in every pause, the cry of liberty or death. They became impatient of speech—their souls were on fire for action.
WILLIAM WIRT on the public response to Patrick Henry's
renowned speech (1816)

Pauses play a prominent if quotidian role in conversation between North American speakers of Standard American English (SAE): they are a way for a speaker to mark that their turn at making meaning has been temporarily satisfied and that their interlocutor may proceed.[14] Yet, as poets, rhetoricians, and others who devote themselves to the arts of speaking appreciate, the metrical and rhythmic features of a statement—including caesura, or pauses inserted in the midst of a line or sentence—can add substantially to that statement's effect, sending messages that inflect, enforce, and exceed the bare denotational weight of the words contained therein.

The power of pause is precisely why influential European rhetoricians— like the eighteenth-century Irish actor and author, Thomas Sheridan— promoted the use of intra-turn pauses to draw attention to and heighten the impact of the words that follow them. The notoriously shy Thomas Jefferson, who purchased Sheridan's 1762 book, *A Course of Lectures on Elocution* (1968), apparently took note. Jefferson's elaborate markings on his personal drafts of the Declaration of Independence, which was written to be read aloud, display careful attention to the "rhythmical pauses of emphatical stress that divide the piece into units comparable to musical bars or poetic lines," as Jay Fliegelman points out (1993, 10). Lengthy and "riveting" pauses were also prolifically deployed by Jefferson's contemporary, rival, and renowned orator, Patrick Henry (14).[15] As unequally talented participants in the elocutionary revolution of the mid-eighteenth century, both men nevertheless understood that the pauses in one's speech can focus a public's attention on the words they punctuate, and can accordingly motivate those newly attuned listeners, even lighting their "souls . . . on fire for action" (Wirt 1816).[16]

Although MI rhetoricians certainly do not consult elocutionary manuals, they nevertheless appreciate that intermittent silence has profound effects on a professional utterance, and by extension upon those who hear it.[17] Thus, once U-Haven trainees had a good handle on how and when to speak using OARS, Ki turned their attention to how and when *not to speak* by building pauses into their open questions, affirmations, reflections, and summaries. For instance, while championing the most powerful of MI speech acts, Ki suggested that reflections could be rendered even more effective when stylized with silence. Specifically, he advised:

> And sometimes following a reflection (1.2) we need to allow a little bit of time (0.9) right, for it to sit [. . .] That's sometimes what I do is I put out a reflection you know two or three seconds goes by which feels like two or three minutes—and then I [*snaps finger*] I jump in and say, "well did I get that right?" So the idea is to *allow* for that *silence* a little bit to (2.6) sort of allow it to percolate.

In modeling an interchange that includes the tag question, "Did I get that right?" Ki violates a rhetorical principle of MI: that is, to avoid closed-ended questions, which by inviting simple yes-or-no responses, can unnecessarily truncate the therapeutic dialogue.[18] Yet, as Ki clarifies, the tag question has an overriding value in this case: that is, to project uncertainty that the professional has accrued a full understanding of the client and to affirm the desire to do just that.

The pause-laced reflection that Ki models also projects client-centeredness and does so even more powerfully. As the trainer underscores, the reflection's potential power derives not only nor even primarily from its semantic content, but rather from its stylization with lengthy and loaded silence. As apprentices would later learn, what "percolates" in the well-timed silence is the idea that the professional is carefully considering what the client has said and the resulting experience of having been heard or "centered." In this sense, Ki's lesson suggests that the poetics of pause help manage clients' perception of professionals' client-centeredness (see table 2.4, col. A).

Deeper still into the U-Haven training, Ki underscored that pause-filled reflections have a *directive* potential as well in that they can help steer the interview toward particular areas of focus (see table 2.4, col. B). Whereas questions can betray expert formulas by obviously seeking certain kinds of information, reflections can generate the very same information in a way that is unlikely to be recognized and resisted, as clients jump in to fill the discomfiting semantic gaps left open by professionals' pauses. As Ki explained:

KI: The other way in which a reflection can be a bit like an open-ended question (2.6) and I think we might have touched on this last time is (0.6) we allow it to (0.2) linger for a moment. Right? The temptation

(1.0) when we reflect something and we don't get an immediate response (0.9) is to what?

T: Ask another question.

KI: Right. We fill the space. Right? "Oh my god, what did I just say?"
Right? Um (0.7) allow some space. Right? Just take a, and I know,
like, two seconds can feel like (1.4) right? It can feel like forever.
Often. Just allow a few seconds, a three-count. Right? And just see
what happens.

Strikingly, Ki's example is one in which the practitioner worries that he
or she has reflected something that is semantically misaligned with the client's intended meaning, prompting an imagined "Oh my god!" Instruct-
ing his apprentices to let their reflections—whether right or wrong in their
meaning—"linger" in silence, Ki also prepares them to capitalize on the
discomfort that this awkward, seemingly unnatural, poetic device might
initially stimulate. After all, "two seconds" can "seem like forever" to clients and professionals alike, considering the silence-avoidant conventions
of SAE speakers.[19]

To cope with the discomfort, Ki offers a metric mnemonic device, tell-

Table 2.4. The potential of pauses in MI

	Project Client-Centeredness	Direct	Produce Change Talk
Pauses can index speaker's thoughtfulness, especially in relation to their interlocutor, and therefore can:	X		
Pauses can index lack of speaker's knowledge/expertise (as if hedging) and therefore can:	X	X	X
Pauses can focalize, drawing attention to the words that follow, and therefore can:		X	X
Pauses, when not in turn-relevant places, can allow speakers to hold the floor and therefore can:		X	
Pauses, in turn-relevant places, can exploit conventional distaste for prolonged silence in dyadic conversation, prompting others to speak, and therefore can:			X

ing trainees to "allow a few seconds, a three count" before verbally intervening in what he proposes could be a productive therapeutic moment.
Advising apprentices to "just see what happens" after a three-count pause,
he indicates that it may be *the silence in the reflection*, relative to the off-
base denotational content, that prompts the client to "fill in" the awkward
conversational gap left open by the practitioner (i.e., "I'll never go back to
using heroin!"). Ki thereby implies that by strategically *saying nothing*, the
practitioner is nevertheless *doing something*, something quite significant at
that: spurring the client to talk and (hopefully) talk themselves into change
(see table 2.4, col. C).

With these lessons in mind, apprentices grew to more fully appreciate
that, as Ki had once told them, reflections take "an especially long time to
become proficient in," precisely because their potential depends on certain rhythms of their delivery, including the pauses, hedges, and stutters
that characterized their own trainer's speech. And while it is difficult to determine the degree to which their learned (dis)fluency derived from their
trainer's explications of the powers of pause, there is no doubt that Ki was
always at work *modeling* the pause-filled poetics he explained during his
lessons. Indeed, throughout the training sessions, Ki punctuated his own
speech in striking and unconventional ways, resulting in a rhythmic pattern that was mimicked by his most attentive apprentices. Note that these
pauses occur *within* Ki's turns of talk and are extremely lengthy relative
to the conventions of Standard American English. These intra-turn pauses
differ functionally from the turn-ending ones that—as Ki explained to
his apprentices—can "percolate" and produce client speech. Specifically,
intra-turn pauses guard against interruption, allowing the motivational interviewer to subtly hold the floor and direct the conversation (table 2.4,
col. B).

Some listeners might infer from Ki's pauses that he is trying to organize his lessons before he verbalizes them, and indeed some of his pauses
occur at what psycholinguists call "planning junctures."[20] However, there
is a regularity—even a pattern—to Ki's intra-turn pauses which he carries
over into his modeling of MI sessions and even into his everyday speech,
indicating an awareness that the rhythm of his speech can produce certain
interactional effects (see table 2.5). What is more, the very same pattern
of pause is found among other experienced MI trainers, most notably the
method's lead proponents, who punctuate their speech with the very same
lengthy and idiosyncratic pauses when they demonstrate the method. In
fact, it was not long into my study before I could fairly reliably if not infalli-
bly approximate how long the practitioners I interviewed and/or observed
had been practicing MI by attuning my ear to the rhythm of their speech.

Table 2.5. A technical transcription of Ki's intra-turn pauses

---

A. So the idea is to *allow* for that *silence* a little bit to (2.6) sort of allow it to percolate.

B. The idea is (1.5) it doesn't matter if it's right or wrong. The grade isn't how accurate are your reflections. The measure is (2.3) what are the *results* of your reflections.

C. The other way in which a reflection can be a bit like an open-ended question (2.6) and I think we might have touched on this last time is (0.6) we allow it to (0.2) linger for a moment. Right?

D. If that's something that (1.2) you feel pretty tuned into, you're good.

E. [Simple reflections] are not quite as (1.3) well, strategic and (0.5) directive.

The systematic study of MI demonstrations substantiated these intuitions, ultimately explaining why MINTies—following generations of American rhetoricians—empower their speech with well-timed silences.

With this in mind, let us briefly revisit the MI demonstration films, which, after all, play an important role in disseminating MI as a register of speaking with distinctive poetic features. (As one apprentice remarked after viewing Miller interview "Soccer Mike": "It's one thing to [0.7] have these things explained to you like [0.2] 'this is how you do an open question. This is how you *reflect*.' It is another thing to [0.5] *hear* people doing it, people way more experienced than we are.") Recall how U-Haven apprentices appreciatively commented on how "fluent" Miller sounds when he demonstrates his method on film. Now consider that whether interviewing Silent Man or Ponytail John, Miller's speech is in fact replete with hedges, stutters, dropped gerunds, and unusually long pauses—the very same pauses that U-Haven apprentices hear in their own trainer's speech (see table 2.1). These disfluencies are found in "Rounder" as well, a training film favorite that features the well-known MI proponent and process researcher, Dr. Theresa M. Moyers, engaged in a virtuoso performance of MI with a man playing a stubborn, hard-drinking cowboy (see figure 2.4; Miller, Rollnick & Moyers 1998). Although the overall pace of Moyers's and Miller's speech varies rather dramatically, with Moyers speaking at a much faster clip, there are key similarities in their poetics, and particularly in their deployment of intra-turn pauses.

Technical transcription of MI demonstration films reveals several prominent patterns of pause, all of which are unconventional relative to Standard American English. Specifically, both Miller and Moyers regularly pause within infinitives, between the word "to" and the remainder of the infinitive phrase (table 2.6, row A); immediately after conjunctions and before subordinate clauses (table 2.6, row B); and after coordinating conjunctions like "and" and "but" (table 2.6, row C). Across the two most popular demon-

Figure 2.4. Screenshot of University of New Mexico psychologist Theresa Moyers performing a reflection with "Rounder." *Motivational Interviewing Professional Training VHS Videotape Series* (Miller, Rollnick & Moyers 1998).

stration films, three-quarters of performed reflections—the most important MI speech acts—are stylized with one of these three unusual patterns of pause.[21]

Note that these intra-turn pauses have a "cliff-hanging" quality, occurring at moments when the practitioner in question clearly has not completed their turn at talk and more speech will follow. Because none of the pauses occurs at conventional "transition-relevance places," when a speaker cedes the floor, it is highly unlikely that another speaker will intervene, quite aside from the social conventions that characterize American pedagogical or psychotherapeutic practices.[22] So if pauses project the sense that the practitioner is searching for just the right way to explain what they mean, and is therefore deflecting their own expertise and centering the client, the pauses also allow them to hold the floor and thereby direct the course of the ensuing conversation. This is precisely, if intuitively, why Ki tells his apprentices to let their statements "percolate" in periodic pauses.

These patterned intra-turn pauses—exemplified in training videos and performed by MINTies like Ki—suggest that MI has developed a recognizable *practice poetics*. Quite aside from the way individual professionals

Table 2.6. Patterns of pause in motivational interviewing

A. Mid-Infinitive Pauses	**Miller:** In some ways this is a pull to (1.2) feel (0.3) feel *free* of that at least for a little while to feel *free* of that responsibility.
	Moyers: So it seems to you that I might try ta (0.2) push you around an make you do a whole bunch of things you don't wanna do.
	Ki: So the idea is to *allow* for that *silence* a little bit to (2.6) sort of allow it to percolate.
B. Post-Conjunction; Pre–Subordinate Clause Pauses	**Miller:** hh, uh(.) an an she has some reason for that as as you can see it but (0.3) it also feels annoying to you that (0.5) that she has that concern.
	Moyers: hm(.) so she's afraid that (0.3) if you take the children (.) with you that you'll be drinking an then you might hurt them an get in an accident.
	Ki: If that's something that (1.2) you feel pretty tuned into, you're good.
C. Post-Conjunction Pauses	**Miller:** so it's kind of unusual an (1.0) an you got snagged.
	Moyers: so drinking kina helps you relax and (0.5) and (0.5) you know (0.5) cope with your life.
	Ki: [Simple reflections] are not quite as (1.3) well, strategic and (0.5) directive.

may develop their own communicative idiosyncrasies, *practice poetics* refers to the way particular stylistic elements are systematically cultivated within a particular school or method, and therefore mark and mobilize a recognizable register of professional practice—as they do in MI (Carr & Smith 2014).

Indeed, MI's practice poetics "estranges" (Shklovsky 2015) the motivational interview from both everyday discourse and competing interventions, thereby distinguishing it as both a register and *a brand* of psychotherapy (see Silverstein 2016). However, MI's poetics is far more than an autotelic stylization—having no function outside itself (see Jakobson 1960); it is an "active ingredient" of the method, helping the professional to achieve the competing demands to be both subtly directive and patently client-centered at once.[23] Similar to the ways Patrick Henry once deployed pauses to stimulate impatience for revolution, setting "souls on fire for action" (Wirt 1816), those who have mastered the pause-filled poetics of MI can stimulate change talk—and perhaps by extension, changed behavior—in client interviewees.

SEMANTICS, POETICS, AND THE REPRODUCTION OF MI

In October 2013, I received a lengthy email from William Miller, on which Stephen Rollnick and Theresa Moyers were copied. Remarkably, if quite characteristically, Miller had tracked down an article I had authored on MI's poetics while it was still in pre-copy.[24] Miller praised the piece as "fascinating" and "offering a fresh perspective." Quoting a few lines from the paper (Carr & Smith 2014), he specifically lauded the idea that "MI practitioners . . . say something in the moments that they say nothing," and that "like most poets, MI practitioners clearly know they must master just how and when to say what they do if they want what they say to be effective." If pleased with the comparison of his apprentices to poets, Miller nevertheless and matter-of-factly observed: "We have never thought or taught much about 'signature pauses' let alone that unconventional patterns of silence may be characteristic, even distinctive of MI."

Initially, I was befuddled by Miller's claim that he had overlooked salient features of the conversation style that he has developed and modeled for more than forty years. Of course, I hardly expected that he or other MI proponents had deciphered the precise pattern and length of their pauses, as I had with my former student, Yvonne Smith, thanks to her technical transcriptions. Yet, the very question of pause had been inspired by observing MI trainers in action, such as Ki, who explained and modeled the powers of well-timed silences to trainees.

Years later, when I presented my research at the annual MINT meeting in Atlanta, the MINTies in attendance revealed significant savvy regarding what intra-turn pauses could project and achieve within the motivational interview. For instance, one well-known MINTie nodded to the rhetorical nature of motivational interviewing, and the importance of pause to professional comportment more particularly, offering: "there is *theater* in the pauses . . . a little bit of show business in MI and a little bit of drama and a little bit of poker face." Others were more specific in their diagnosis, commenting on how pauses can focalize and direct, with another MINTie commenting: "It almost seems as if there's an emphasis . . . as if there's a pause my ears are going to what is going to come after that. What is going to come after I say something? And it's powerful" (see table 2.4, row 3). Making apparent reference to the ability of pauses to help project client-centeredness, still another long-time MINTie suggested that the "pause thing . . . it almost feels as though this is how MI spirit comes to life" (see table 2.4, row 1).

These native insights—insights that linguistic anthropologists call metapragmatic, focused as they are on what some feature of sign activity *does* as well as what it says (see, especially, Silverstein 1993)—indicate that

MINTies have indeed "thought and taught" about the powers of pause. That said, Miller was clearly correct in another regard: while MINTies like Ki may emphasize the poetics of MI, including the powers of pause, in their training, the MI literature that they know so well and otherwise frequently cite offers scant support for their doing so. Save an occasional passing comment, such as Miller and Rollnick's rather vague comment that silence can "generate thoughtfulness" in clients and practitioners alike (2002, 280), there is remarkable *silence about silence* in MI proponents' textual expositions of their method. And while Miller and his co-authors have been intent on describing the method's *semantic* features—such as the content and type of professional speech acts—they have written very little about their register's poetics.

By contrast, since its origination, MI has become increasingly sophisticated in its semantic analyses, thanks in large part to the contributions of psycholinguist Paul Amrhein, who was also copied on the aforementioned email. Largely due to Amrhein's interventions, the third edition of *Motivational Interviewing* features a semantic taxonomy that parses change talk into "subtypes." Accordingly, trainers of MI-3 now elaborate the "strength" of various words out of which to build a summary or reflection, encouraging apprentices to use the mnemonic device DARN-CAT (Desire Statements, Ability Statements, Reason Statements, Need Statements, Commitment Language, Activation Language, and Taking Steps) to read the "degree of commitment" in clients' statements and craft responses in kind.[25]

Amrhein has also drawn fellow MI proponents' attention to the semantic "slope" of the motivational interview—that is, what kinds of speech acts professionals deploy *when*, suggesting that this critically affects how clients will respond.[26] This has led to trainers' emphasis on the "recency rule"—a cognitive-semanticist thesis that the last thing said in a dyadic exchange tends to be the most memorable and potentially moving. In one training I observed, when an apprentice tried to recall the "trick" of summaries, her trainer reviewed the logic of the recency rule: "Yeah, that's Amrhein. That's our linguist guy who says that, um (1.5) most of the time we want to leave the (1.2) person's *thinking* on the positive rather than leave them thinking about the negative." The recency rule also applies to "double-sided reflections" (see table 2.3), which are designed to address clients' verbal vacillations between maintaining and changing their behavior. As the same trainer put it, "When you give double-sided reflections, you give the (0.7) *positive* at *the end*," with the idea that positive behavior may follow. This reminds us that "working the difference," at least in the event of the motivational interview, is guided by behavioral norms as much as is the normatively driven professional.

MI proponents' selective attention to their conversation style's linguistic features carries over into the guidelines for MI-specific fidelity instruments that are used in research, training, and coaching. Recall here Ki's promise to assess his apprentices, as they began recording MI sessions with actual clients. In doing so, he would use the Motivational Interviewing Treatment Integrity (MITI) scale to assess "how well or poorly is a clinician using motivational interviewing" (Moyers et al. 2014, 3).[27] Amrhein has participated in the development of the MITI, which has grown increasingly rigorous over its various editions in offering detailed guidelines for coding speaker semantics, including what is said when.[28] By contrast, the poetics of MI is still left unspecified, treated only by an abstract "gestalt score" for "spirit."[29] So while MITI coders I have studied frequently comment on the "tone" of interviewers they evaluate, even suggesting that what might have been a semantic misstep (like a closed question) can be mitigated by *the style* in which it was delivered, the MITI guidelines offer little assistance in making such determinations.

This striking disjuncture between MI proponents' self-conscious labeling of MI as a "conversation style" and Miller's pointed remark that he and his colleagues have not "thought about" their signature pauses initially appears to confirm a prominent and longstanding thesis, which posits that the less presuppositional and more context-creating some feature of language is, the more it evades speaker awareness (see Silverstein 1993, 2001; Lucy 1993; Mannheim 1986; Pressman 1994; see also and compare to Carr 2011, chapter 6; Zuckerman & Enfield n.d.). By this account, since the semantic aspects of language tend to presuppose rather than create their reference points—that is, the socially agreed upon meaning of a word—they are more easily accessible to speakers' awareness than the equally meaningful way speech is styled with particular tones and rhythms to achieve particular effects. Put more simply, the operating assumption since Michael Silverstein's seminal work is that speakers are more aware of *what* has been said than *how* it has been said and to what social ends.[30] Considering the context creativity of MI's distinctive use of caesura, adherents to this thesis may conclude that even those who are trained to be highly reflexive about their speech, like MI's rhetoricians, may struggle to articulate, or perhaps even appreciate, what pauses achieve.

However, given the difference in the reflexive attention paid to MI's poetics by experienced trainers in the field, like Ki, and by those charged with official, textual accounts of the method, like Miller, we would be wise to consider an additional thesis, one that accounts for the social, political, and economic stakes of metalinguistic awareness. This would begin by differentiating speakers' *awareness* of the qualities of speech and speakers' *explicit commentary* about those very same qualities (see Carr 2011).[31] Conflating what people know and what they report about what they know effectively erases the contingencies of those reports, such as who elicited them, how the reporter anticipated the report would travel and in what form, as well as conventions and proclivities about what is reportable under which circumstances (see Carr 2010b). Once we take this distinction between knowing and reporting seriously, we can explore the possibilities of what might be gained by revealing or overlooking and abstracting or specifying various aspects of a native tongue, especially when that speech is institutionally and professionally registered.

Consider, for instance, the scalability of MI across institutional contexts.[32] Recall that the social and economic organization of MI training relies heavily on devoted and skillful trainers (that is, MINTies) to disseminate the method through in vivo or electronically mediated training. Whereas manualized psychotherapies, such as dialectical behavior therapy (DBT), can be textually disseminated, requiring less labor on the part of human trainers, MI has resisted manualization—which is especially remarkable given the prolific production of articles and textbooks about the principles of the method, which always stop short of a "how to" guide.

MI proponents concertedly chose not to manualize, disseminating their method through text, but established instead a self-reproducing corps of vetted trainers to provide in vivo training. In interviews with me, Miller frames this choice relative to the shared hope of convening and cohering a professional community—one that will actively continue to disseminate the method, taking it into ever expanding directions. Thus, rather than "government [by] paper" (Hull 2012) and the bureaucratic dynamics implied therein, MI's dissemination relies on the skills and style of MI trainers (as well as their charisma and spirit, as elaborated in the following chapter).

There are economic as well as social consequences of this decision, including the continuous reproduction of MI training and the distribution of profits throughout the MI training community. Given that essential elements of MI as a conversation style, such as the poetics of pause, are not circulated through textual artifacts, professionals wishing to master the method must depend on more experienced practitioners (that is, MINTies) to model those elements at cost, whether paid out of pocket or charged to their respective organizations. While the registration fee for the nonprofit MINT's authorizing Training New Trainers (TNT), alone, is now well over $1,000, preparation to apply requires extensive prior training and coaching, which can cost several thousand dollars.[33] Manualization of MI as a conversation style would significantly disrupt, and perhaps obviate, these means of reproduction and capital accumulation. Without having to attribute financial motives to particular parties, we can nevertheless appreciate that there may be good economic reasons not to "think much"—or at least, not to *write much*—about pause or MI's other poetic features if, as some MINTies conceded to me, they are an active ingredient of the method's skills and spirit.[34]

Although Miller is clearly invested in the training of MI and the MINT—where he serves as symbolic figurehead, leaving the increasingly complex operations of the organization to others—such financial concerns seemed furthest from his mind as we continued to converse about MI's poetics of pause. Rather, he raised distinctly *spiritual* concerns, suggesting that MI practitioners' widespread use of signature pauses is a sign that a transcendent force unites them. Challenging my argument that MI's pauses spread because apprentices imitate a style of speaking consistently modeled by more experienced practitioners, whether on film or in vivo, Miller more specifically posited that the poetic features of the register derive not from the conscious intentions of those who convey or adopt the conversation style. The pauses, he proposed instead, are endowments of the method's underlying spirit, which are "intuitively" rather than intentionally adopted by apprentices over the course of their training:

> I think a conscious focus on such elements [as pause] would disrupt the process. So how do practitioners learn and adopt this way of speaking? Obviously, modeling is one possibility, but I suspect it derives more intuitively from the underlying spirit. I think, for example, that it could be counterproductive to instruct interviewers to pause after "to" "that" or "and." These pauses are being produced by some superordinate process.

Here, Miller implicitly underscores a pregnant distinction, emphasized throughout the MI literature and echoed in MI training, between MI skills (the technical aspects of the register that can be accessed and adopted by almost anyone) and MI "spirit" (the ineffable quality of the method that touches and transforms an elect, if not elite, subset of practitioners). Note that while skills and spirit may be normatively opposed, MI requires them both at once. As MI trainers commonly tell their apprentices, you can have all the requisite (rhetorical) skills, but if you don't have the spirit, you are not really practicing *MI*.

However, in this case, Miller proffers that MI's signature pauses are more spiritual than technical, acquired through something transcendent rather than learned products of rhetorical technique. It is with this logic in mind that he warns against reflexive focus on pause as "disruptive" and "counterproductive"—a remark that is especially striking given the reflexability so

concertedly cultivated in MI apprentices. He thereby effectively acknowledges that there is something strategic about "not thinking much" about
MI's signature pauses. This suggests, more generally, that while recognizable registers facilitate the spread of products (Silverstein 2016; 2023; see
also Nakassis 2016), leaving some aspects of that register unspecified helps
control and direct that spread, patterning modes of reproduction and dissemination.

In the next chapter, we will learn more about MI spirit, its projected and
experienced qualities, and its transformative effects, including why Miller
maintains that there is nothing antithetical about the endowment of spirit
and the profits of MI's reproduction and dissemination. In the meantime,
I will simply note that while Miller focuses on spirit rather than profit in
his email to me, I understand that what he calls "consciousness" of MI's
poetics—what linguistic anthropologists call metalinguistic awareness—
is "counterproductive" in both ways at once. That is, reflexive attention
to pause would simultaneously enervate MI spirit by indicating that the
method is merely technical and, *in so doing*, significantly undercut the social and economic vibrancy of the MI training industry, which is designed
to teach things that manuals cannot.

Yet Miller's claim that MI's pauses "are being produced by some superordinate process," as opposed to a practiced rhetorical one, suggests that
there is still something else about recognizing the poetics of the conversation that is "counterproductive" to the training of his method. To conclude,
we must understand that laying bare the rhetorical nature of motivational
interviewing—whether to apprentices, clients, or the general public—has
special risks given the negative cultural associations with rhetoric and the
art of verbal performance, which are hardly MI's own.

Such attempts to naturalize or spiritualize highly stylized ways of speaking dates back to the early days of the republic. We need only recall Jefferson's epic struggles to speak a "natural language" to contextualize Miller's
attempt to spiritualize a particular rhetorical technique of his self-described
conversation style. Across mainstream political, religious, therapeutic, and
other institutional settings, speakers in the United States have very subtly
laced their poetics into their semantics, so as to assure that what they say
appears to be the natural and sincere expression of their inner state rather
than an aesthetically managed means of persuasion. For whether "speaking
from the heart," "speaking for the people," or channeling the word of God,
many North American rhetoricians have long gone to great pains to not
"think about"—or *reveal that they think about*—how they speak. Yet, if the
felt difference between the semantics and poetics of speaking is not MI's

own, the innovative means of working that difference is certainly worthy of note.

CONCLUSION: PERFORMANCE AND PRESENCE
IN AMERICAN RHETORIC

On the last day of the training at U-Haven, Ki asked his apprentices to comment on "one thing that [they will] take away from this training."[35] After a brief silence, Jamal replied that he was "thinking all the time" about the way he speaks to clients, adding that while he was ever more conscious of his speech, MI nevertheless "seem[ed] (0.5) more *natural*" to speak than it once had. In content and delivery, this comment implied that, over the course of the training, two types of reflexivity had become one: a fully conscious register had morphed into automatic response.[36] In reply, Ki offered these words of encouragement, and did so as if he were playing a joyful tune:

> And (1.4) you know, motivational interviewing, learning—learning the
> *words* and then (1.1) putting them together with the *music* so that you can
> together dance. And that's (0.7) that seems like you're getting the words,
> starting to listen to the music, and now trying to figure out how to go
> about it. And that's, that's wonderful.

Like the other trainers I studied, Ki often resorted to musical references when explaining the process of learning MI. In doing so, these trainers underscore that the process involves far more than mastering a specialized vocabulary ("learning the *words*"); it also requires perfecting the performance of MI's distinctive tones and rhythms ("listen[ing] to the *music*"). Drawing on Miller's writings, trainers often compare learning MI and learning to play the piano.[37] For instance, early in the U-Haven training, after an especially frustrating round of role-plays, Ki once told his apprentices that they needed to learn "Chopsticks" before moving on to "Beethoven or Rachmaninoff." Ki went on to promise that if apprentices remained devoted to their training, the stilted, hyper-self-consciousness they felt tapping out OARS, as if with one finger, would evaporate into the apparent ease with which experienced musicians play masterpieces.[38] Jamal's parting comments were therefore music to Ki's ears, in that they marked and overcame the normative distinction between conscious performance and sincere presence.

Though Miller worried about an overly conscious focus on rhetorical technique, he would surely appreciate Jamal's comments as well as Ki's response. A musician and composer of choral music, Miller also frequently likens MI to ballroom dancing and, in so doing, reminds his apprentices that the music of MI should always be attuned to another. For example, when he joined Ki to co-conduct the daylong advanced training featured in the previous chapter, Miller suggested that, with continued practice, a motivational interviewer can feel like Fred Astaire, effortlessly dancing up a flight of stairs, leading with keen awareness of how one's partner is moving.

These analogies seemed to especially resonate with a U-Haven trainee named Karl, who now sat before Ki *and* Miller on an elite university campus, wearing an ever-so-faint smile along with his slicked-back silver hair, perhaps imagining gliding alongside his very own Ginger Rogers. Now enrolled in ballroom lessons with the master of MI himself, Karl had come a long way from that awkward square dance on the first day of the U-Haven training. But Karl was still at U-Haven, as he had been for seventeen years, pounding the pavement to find clients at risk of eviction for unpaid rent, working to persuade clients one-third of his age to take their HIV meds, handing out clean socks and toothbrushes to people living in tents, sitting by the bedside of an emaciated, dying, and otherwise alone client.

On one work outing with Karl, while speaking across the aisle of an empty mid-afternoon train car, he told me: "My dad was a well-known doctor before he died of Alzheimer's. My brother is also a doctor, and the other one is a lawyer. My sisters are professionals too." By contrast to Karl, who takes public transportation to work, his family members "all live in the suburbs" and regularly betray what he thought might be racism, or just "fear of poor people, or maybe the city in general." With a barely detectable smirk, he continued, "At Thanksgiving, they all want to hear stories about my work, just to ask me what the hell I am doing."

Karl knew that there was nothing glamorous or easy about his work, but he was dedicated to it for reasons he didn't fully understand. And because working at U-Haven was filled with frustrations—including ongoing stalemates with clients whose self-destructive behavior often baffled him—he wanted to become "fluent" in MI. "It *is* like a dance," he told me after the university training, "It really is. We need to learn to dance like that with our clients."

At the time, I should have asked Karl to elaborate on what exactly he meant by "danc[ing] like that." I would venture that there was something about the type of dance evoked—so markedly bifurcated by gender difference, only to be soothed by Astaire's and Rogers's ability to move as one—that was particularly appealing to Karl. I take it, too, that this is part of why Fred-and-Ginger's iconic dancing, rather than square- or line-dancing, is MI's metaphor of choice: it suggests how the method can rhetorically manage differences of opinion between client and professional, as Miller did with Silent Man, no matter what loaded demographic differences are involved. In this case, rather than erasing the differences of class, race, and professional status faced by those, like Karl, who use MI in their daily practice, an MI vision of Fred-and-Ginger euphemistically analogizes them. (We might also note the marked spontaneity of these iconic American dance routines: they can break out anywhere and anytime, and be woven into endless settings and situations, just as MI aspires to do. Viewers will also recall a sense of a spirit that seems to spark the Astaire-and-Rogers numbers, both moving with and seemingly overtaking the technical prowess of the dancers.)[39]

In substituting musical metaphors for technical explanations of MI's signature poetics, Miller, Ki, and fellow MI proponents liken their method to a performance art that is far more acceptable to and appreciated by North American audiences than the art of rhetoric. Whereas music, and particularly dancing, is known to move the senses and form connections between people, rhetoric is commonly thought to be more artful than aesthetic. And, whereas music and dance are considered forms of self-expression, rhetoric is popularly portrayed as manipulative and insincere. With the help of musical analogies, MI trainers shed these pejorative associations, all the while teaching apprentices to stylize their therapeutic messages, homing in on elements of delivery, much as trained rhetoricians do.

To be sure, in the contemporary United States, to characterize a statement as "rhetoric" is generally to condemn it, to charge it with lack of substance, and to render it suspicious all at once. If the primary function of a statement is not to denote, we wonder what that statement, and its speaker, might otherwise have in mind. For instance, people in the United States commonly disparage the "rhetorical question" as one that offers nothing other than that which is already known. American political rhetoric—in the highly mediated, collective imagination—has no regard for real problems or real people; it persuades not because of its relation to the world that precedes it, not because of any anchor in reason, but because of the way it tethers the audience and the rhetorician (see Fliegelman 1993; Hill 2000; Lempert & Silverstein 2012). More generally, it is assumed that rhetoric "invents" and manipulates reality rather than reflecting it, as so many believe that language should do (if ideally and not in actual practice). Perhaps even worse, some believe that rhetoric, if successful, manipulates people, making us believe, think, or do things we otherwise wouldn't. If American rhetoric is considered an art at all anymore, it is certainly one that many speakers in the United States have been socialized to believe has no substance and no legitimate role in the relations between people. With all of this in mind, there are few reasons for any professional method to explicitly display its rhetorical features.

Once loaded with these pejorative connotations, rhetoric appears directly at odds with what Americans who willingly seek professional guidance tend to expect from therapeutic discourse. Indeed, to baldly highlight the idea that therapeutic speech is *stylized* challenges the ideal that therapy is a site of human authenticity, where client and practitioner alike speak in ways that are unfettered by social stimuli or agendas. After all, however much we appreciate their professional charge to positively alter our thoughts, feelings, and behavior, many also expect therapists to see us for who we really are and to speak with us accordingly. Their questions should be probing ones that pull from us inner thoughts, feelings, and ideas, whether we knew they were there or not. American therapy purportedly reveals our inner truths rather than producing them, even when those truths so often happen to be precisely in line with normative social expectations. Those who enter therapy with an agenda other than truth seeking and revelation, whether professional or client, are radically suspect both for their ethical alignment with other people and for their ontological commitments (Carr 2009, 2011).[40]

If notoriously shy about their rhetorical sophistication, all American psychotherapeutic exchanges are devoted to the production of *moving words*, even if those words are typically conceived as derivative of latent commitments on the part of the client, unearthed by the authentic presence of the professional. In this sense, MI is unique not because it trains its apprentices in specific rhetorical techniques, but rather because it understands and openly describes itself as a "conversation style." This, in and of itself, opens MI up to American critics who are deeply suspicious of stylized speech, perhaps especially when it speaks across historical, institutionally supported, and loaded difference. Not surprisingly, then, MI proponents sometimes euphemize and naturalize the rhetorical nature of their method. And while professionals who train and practice MI are not immune to the cultural expectation that they should be "authentic" and "genuine," rather than performative or instrumental, when they speak, they ultimately embrace the paradoxes of Anglo-American rhetoric, refusing the ideological dichotomy between performance and presence, persuasion and sincerity, spirit and technique.

Furthermore, in the training of MI at sites such as U-Haven, we find an ethical view of verbal performance at play, which fundamentally challenges narrow formulations of American rhetoric. In MI, the art of rhetoric is an ethical exercise of forging sincere relations and producing interpersonal truths. After all, in line with the MI training adage "we learn MI through our clients," the rhetoricians of MI consistently hold themselves to others' standards, reflexably calibrating their way of speaking and acting to the client before them (Carr, 2011 chap. 6; see also Bakhtin 1990). Style is not inimical to what MI proponents call spirit—nor to what I understand as sincerity—but is rather productive of it.[41] This is why, for experienced MI trainers like Ki, there is nothing antithetical about the practice poetics that they demonstrate and cultivate during the course of MI training and the possibility of a therapeutic encounter that is felt by both parties to be genuine, natural, and real. MINTies' work suggests that the performative and poetic dimensions of the motivational interview lay the groundwork for the client and clinician alike to realize and experience authentic *(co)presence.*

CHAPTER 3

American Spirit

Presence, Profit, and Professional Reenchantment

> Without [MI's] underlying spirit, MI becomes a cynical trick, a way of trying to manipulate people into what they don't want to do: the expert magician skillfully steers the hapless client into the right choice.
>
> MILLER & ROLLNICK (2013, 14)

If there was one person at U-Haven who truly dreaded role-plays when the MI training first began, it was Libby. The forty-four-year-old midwesterner had earned an MSW from a top public university and had plenty of experience in particularly challenging human service settings. But her fear was apparently heightened because, unlike her fellow trainees, most of whom had worked at U-Haven for years, Libby was relatively new to the agency. She lamented how, during MI role-plays, "you might be interacting with someone you don't really *know* very well. And maybe you're afraid of being judged by ... by ... by your *comments*." With her round, curl-framed, ever-smiling face slightly reddening, Libby continued: "Maybe they'll think: 'Oh, *that* was a dumb thing to say.' Especially when you're learning things, you're ... I mean, you're afraid of making a *mistake*."

Libby added that she had participated in plenty of role-plays in graduate school and realized that "they *are* really helpful" when trying to put clinical ideas into practice. Furthermore, she'd taken an entire graduate class on MI; reread "the book" when she arrived at U-Haven, after seeing her new boss had it on his shelf; and had acquired some MI-specific pointers from Ki, her clinical supervisor, when talking through how to manage a "particularly difficult client." With all of this, her standout memory of MI was of a fumbling role-play, years before, wherein she realized, with evident embarrassment, how "hard it was, you know ... I don't think I really understood it fully."

Libby's comments, offered during an interview before the U-Haven training commenced, suggest more than a generalized performance anxiety, as a relatively new actor in front of an unfamiliar audience. The social worker was especially daunted by the performance of MI's constitutive *techniques*, which she believed one could either master or "mistake." As we will see in this chapter, her fears were rather radically misplaced.

During the ensuing months of the training, Libby was a quiet but clearly engaged participant. Given her revelation, I tried not to heighten her anxiety and kept my recording devices pointed toward other participants. Still, signs of Libby squirming through role-plays were hard to miss, if decidedly less so as the months passed. I was fascinated to see a very different Libby when I began shadowing her during her outreach work for U-Haven.[1] This work involved going to city shelters, soup kitchens, and homeless encampments with the intent to engage people with severe mental illnesses who—thanks to a federal grant—could get services and resources at U-Haven that were unavailable elsewhere in the city. Watching Libby engage and assess people, and sometimes coach them in how to qualify for U-Haven programs, I marveled at the poise, straightforwardness, and gentleness that characterized these loaded exchanges, no matter how chaotic and makeshift the setting. And though Libby sometimes fumbled when she tried to roll out an MI technique, perhaps for my benefit, she nevertheless seemed to be an especially talented clinician who was consistently empathic and able to remain calm in the face of acute social suffering, inequity, injustice, and uncertainty.[2]

As it turned out, I was not the only one impressed by Libby's way of interacting with clients. In an unexpected twist, Norman—the MINTie we met in chapter 1—was contracted to formally assess and "coach" all the U-Haven trainees toward the end of their training.[3] As a well-known MINT member, Norman was especially highly regarded as a coach and "coder," having received specialized training in how to use the MITI, a fidelity instrument specific to MI. With this training, Norman mostly made his living coding, working with his wife who transcribed practice interviews so he could score them, and meeting with advanced trainees individually to review and improve their work. Norman even ran a listserv for MITI coders, where MINT members discussed coding quandaries and kept up with the latest developments of the instrument, of which there have been many.

Though most of her fellow trainees were rather hesitant to engage in Norman's coaching, in no small part because it required them to find opportunities to record themselves with a willing client in the crunch of their daily work, Libby jumped at the chance.[4] Over a couple of months, she produced three tapes with three different clients and met with Norman, in a cramped and charmless if relatively private office donated by a senior colleague, to pore over his MITI-coded and scored transcripts of her interviews. And though, as is very typically the case, Libby's "technical scores" started off very low, her "spirit" impressed Norman from the start.

Behavior Counts

Category	Definition or Sub-classification	Comments	Count	Your Per-cents	Beginning Proficiency	Competency
Giving Information	Gives info, provides feedback, discloses personal info		0	No standard yet. Generally, less is better.		
MIA MI-Adherent	Asking permission, affirms, emphasizes pers control, support	Good not to have too many, MI recommends some.	0	MIA is what percent of your total adherence counts?		
MIN Non-adherent	Advise, confront, direct		1	0%	90%	100%
Question (subclassify)	Closed Question	MI would recommend a ot less closed questions.	58	Open questions are what percent of your total questions?		
	Open Question		23	28%	50%	70%
Reflect (subclassify)	Simple		17	Complex reflections are what percent of total reflections?		
	Complex	This is both the most difficult and possibly most important MI skill. You demo'd ability--the ratio is the only matter now.	10	37%	40%	50%
Total Reflection to Total Question Ratio		This is possibly the most important ratio.	27/81	0.33	1	2

Scoring Calculation*

Spirit Score (Evocation + Collaboration + Autonomy/3)	60%
Empathy Score	40%
Direction Score	60%
Total Behavior Score	33%
Grand Total (Spirit 30%+Empathy 30%+Direction 10%+Behavior 30%)	46%
Your Overall Score* is:	**46%** *Beginning Proficiency Threshold: 75% • Competency Threshold: 85%*

Figure 3.1. Norman's coding of Libby's recording using an adapted MITI 3.1 coding sheet. From Moyers et al., 2009.

On their first meeting, Norman presented Libby with a MITI-coded transcription of her first interview, which had been conducted with a client struggling with alcohol, and a MITI "Summary Sheet" (see figure 3.1). At the top, the summary noted "Behavior Counts": tallies for how many times Libby performed open questions and reflections, as well as umbrella scores for "MI-Adherent" and "MI-Non-adherent" behaviors. However byzantine these coded documents were, the "Scoring Calculation" at the end of the document was brutally straightforward. In enlarged boldface font, placed alongside the italicized figures for "Beginning Proficiency Threshold" (75%) and "Competency Threshold" (85%), Libby's overall score was listed in enlarged, bright blue font: 46%. Keep in mind that this was nine months into Ki's advanced training, for which she had qualified because of her previous exposure to and knowledge of MI.

Libby's "Global Rating" for "MI Spirit"—based on a "gestalt" or "overall impression" rather than a tally—was another question entirely. As Norman was quick to point out, Libby's "spirit ratings" were "for a first recording . . . pretty amazing." Having digested her scores, Libby began the coaching session much as she had introduced herself to me when we met for our first interview. She reflected that "sometimes it's hard to think on the spot; that's really the hardest part for me is *how* . . . to learn how to incorporate [MI] seamlessly into what I'm doing." Nodding his head rhythmically, with a smile and a twinkle, Norman responded: "How could it be otherwise? What else can you do? It's just going to be clunky until you, until it becomes second nature, which, which for some people comes, you know, after maybe a couple of years of practice and other people—like me—it might take a *lifetime*."

As if to suggest that Libby's life-in-MI was already well underway, Norman launched the coaching session, which, not surprisingly, was laced with role-plays.[5] With my video camera running, I captured the apparent ease with which Libby reenacted the very same interview that had just been scored. Knowing how much the performance-anxious Libby hated role-plays, I was nothing less than gobsmacked. Norman played the client in the transcript, offering Libby new chances to open a question that was closed, seize upon ambivalence, or "request permission" to give advice. The two went back and forth, analyzing the original interview and reenacting it, with mounting enthusiasm. Forty minutes into the session, Norman leaned back in his chair, stared intently at Libby, and after a five-second pause, announced:

> NORMAN: I...I got the feeling you're going to be a champion.
> LIBBY: Uh. I hope so. I think [MI has] given me a really effective tool.
> NORMAN: But, no. I'm talking about...not just with you and your clients. But *other* people noticing: "Hey [Libby]'s got something going for her."

It appeared, for Libby, that role-plays were becoming real, that performance was becoming presence, and rhetorical techniques were becoming a channel for, rather than an encumbrance of, MI spirit. Having secured Libby's promise to produce a second tape that focused on reflections, Norman encouraged her: "Your genuineness comes through already. It's in your *tone*." When the door shut behind her, Norman turned to me, and said: "She's got it. You can *hear* it in her voice." By "it," he meant MI spirit, and I was intent to learn more.

. · .

This chapter delves into what "spirit" is in the eyes (and ears) of MI proponents and details the work of transmitting that spirit to others. This begins with the inculcation of spirit during MI training and coaching—that is, through the ongoing modeling and purposeful rehearsal of the method's constitutive techniques, as we read above. Through this process, trainers, coders, and coaches impress upon apprentices that MI is much more than "an effective tool"—it is also a "mind-set and heart-set" (Miller & Rollnick

2013, 14). And although MI (and, accordingly, the MITI) marks the distinction between *spirit* and *technique*, and warns that technique without spirit is mere "mimicry," it also underscores that achieving "competency" means using MI technique as channel for spirit.[6] Thus, MINTies like Norman assure apprentices like Libby that if they keep rehearsing and role-playing, and do so under trained observation, the rhetorical techniques once stumbled upon and mistaken will eventually allow them to both fully feel MI spirit and transmit that spirit to others.

Proponents make clear that MI spirit cannot be simply "installed," given its immaterial and superordinate qualities. Some insiders also call MI spirit a "gift" that—if not given by nature and/or at birth—can be gradually acquired through a "developmental process" (Dalai Lama & Eckman 2008, as cited by Miller & Rollnick 2013, 23). Outsiders, especially those familiar with Max Weber's famous thesis, may readily translate MI spirit as *charisma*: an aura that, for those not under its spell, regularly invites critical commentary as being crafted rather than gifted. In this chapter, I work with and write between these interpretations of just what is being cultivated and transmitted in MI trainings.[7] To begin, and with the example of Norman and Libby in mind, I propose that just as charisma survives only to the extent that it is recognized by others (Weber 1968), MI spirit manifests in interaction, subject to what others can see, hear, feel, and—when it comes to spiritual guides and gatekeepers like Norman—evaluate and score.

Unlike manualized psychotherapies that can be textually delivered, the transmission of MI spirit, as well as the dissemination of MI, requires the continual co-presence of those, like Norman, who undoubtedly have the spirit and those, like Libby, who hope to acquire it. More important, we will see that the survival of MI spirit depends on its *routine* as well as continual transmission. This means that identifying spirit in a single professional is far less important than propelling the spirit so identified. For instance, note that Norman responds to Libby's comment that she thinks MI is an "effective tool" not just by stating that she has something special—a talent to be valued in and of itself. Rather, Norman emphasizes that "other people," beyond Libby's clients, will recognize that she has "something going on" for her. In later sessions, Norman more pointedly encourages Libby to train MI and thereby transmit MI spirit to other helping professionals just as he has devoted himself to doing. In this faithful encouragement, Norman marks a crucial component of MI's dissemination, which is elaborated in the pages that follow.

Through its focus on MI spirit, this chapter more generally explores the method's relationship to North American Protestantism. While frequently cast and often understood in secular and universal terms, Protestant themes are threaded through my interlocutors' accounts of MI spirit both as an ineffable, deeply felt connection with a greater (if not higher) power and as a motor of a (professional) mission to share that spirit with others. To be sure, it is not just Norman who feels *called* to MI and accordingly understands MI training as *vocation*, in the Weberian sense of the term (1952, 2020). Yet while Weber professed that the Protestant spirit eventually becomes "purely mundane" (1952, 182) once put fully to the task of capital accumulation on colonized North American soil, MINTies tend to describe their profit-generating work as thoroughly enchanted (see Klassen 2011).[8] And although the interviewee may be the most obvious benefactor of a motivational interviewer's manifest spirit, those who feel called to MI—including its most prominent proponents—overwhelmingly make MI *training* their vocation, which helps explain Norman's suggestion to his spirit-filled acolyte. With these dynamics in mind, I demonstrate that MI's dissemination has revivalist qualities, which further fuel its circulation. Indeed, however tempting it is to prematurely resort to MI's status as an "evidence-based practice" to explain its spread (see chapter 4), I propose here that a fulsome analysis seriously considers spirit alongside science, another distinction that MI both highlights and refuses.

The dynamics sketched above and detailed below sometimes lead outsiders to dismiss MI or disparage it as a "cult," a pejorative term that collapses practitioners' spiritual attachments to the method into a grand scheme, or "a cynical trick, a way of trying to manipulate people into what they don't want to do" like an "expert magician" (Miller & Rollnick 2013, 14). As this chapter seeks to show, MI is not a cult. Rather, it is mainstream (or mainline), exhibiting widely recognized and institutionalized white, Anglo-Saxon, Protestant norms, all the while refusing the constitutive antinomies of those norms. MI is *both* enchanted *and* rational, spiritual *and* technical, charismatic *and* bureaucratic. My interlocutors further insist that MI spirit *both* suddenly awakens the converted *and* is realized methodically through (good) work(s). What is gained by refusing these well-established oppositions? By answering this question, we will better understand MI and the ideological difference it exploits, and we might also crack the code of why some American methods travel far and wide, leaving their more partisan and parochial brethren behind.

PLAYING FOR REAL: SPIRIT, TECHNIQUE, AND THE PERFORMANCE OF PRESENCE

The first day of U-Haven training, during a round of introductions initiated when Ki requested names and rationales for joining the yearlong endeavor, Libby laid her cards on the table:

LIBBY: I'm [Libby]. So, I'd like to know, really, how I can kind of move fluently through the process and not just be sitting there stuck for words, you know?

KI: Mmm.

LIBBY: To be able to do it more effectively, more *naturally*.

KI: OK, so a little, may- . . . even more reflexively . . . more automatically.

LIBBY: Yes.

Here again, Libby expresses her desire to become "fluent" in MI, so as to save herself the embarrassment of getting "stuck for words." Fluency, as she first describes it, means to be both effective and *natural*, almost as if speaking a mother tongue. Yet, while Libby's stated concern appears calibrated to an evaluating audience, Ki turns the articulated concern back on Libby herself. Recast (and amplified—see chapter 2) by Ki, Libby's goal is to be more "reflexive" and "automatic." In the end, Libby affirms Ki's suggestion that, if first learned and practiced as a conversation style, with plenty of rules and regulations, MI can and should eventually become "automatic" rather than mechanistic.

Six months into the U-Haven training—thanks to Ki's gentle guidance, film study, and nonstop role-plays—amplified reflections, "decision rulers," and summarizing "bouquets of change talk" were indeed feeling more automatic for Libby and her fellow trainees. A few U-Haven apprentices had even adopted some of the register's subtler poetic features that Ki had modeled, such as keeping their intonation flat when they were seeking information or increasing the dramatic tension of a dialogue by inserting a "three-count" pause (see chapter 2). Given this increasing "fluency," Ki now turned more concertedly to MI spirit. While Ki had discussed the "underlying perspective with which one practices MI" (Miller & Rollnick 2013, 14) from the outset of the training, the task was now to *manifest that spirit* in their performance of MI.

In principle, trainees found that MI spirit—whether explained during Ki's presentations or read about in the MI textbook and articles that they were assigned as homework—was appealing, intuitive, and consistent with what they already understood as good, ethical practice. As trainees understood it, MI spirit meant having a deep, abiding respect for clients as autonomous individuals, whoever they might be and whatever their circumstances, and a desire to collaboratively engage with them as such. Yet trainees found it another matter entirely how to *relay* that spirit, given it seemed to both rely upon and exceed the rhetorical techniques that they had been working so hard to master. As one participant put it, it was now unclear whether the goal was to *learn or unlearn* the lessons to date. Meanwhile, Ki started issuing chilling warnings that suggested that the danger was not "getting stuck for words" but rather being obviously slick with them. For instance, before one exercise, Ki warned: "Reflective listening divorced from genuineness, from the *spirit* of MI: It's awful. You've seen it done. I've probably done it myself. If I'm reflecting, and the person's like: 'Look, man, will you just shut up with that stuff?'"

Here, MI spirit is explicitly linked to genuineness, which—as we learned in chapter 2—is a primary concern not only among MINTies, but for many of their North American brethren as well. The *ideology of inner reference*—in which speech is evaluated relative to how cleanly it apparently channels what speakers already think, feel, and believe, and thereby ostensibly demonstrates who they really are (Carr 2011)—shapes linguistic exchange across a wide variety of US institutions. Speaking sincerely, or revealing one's self plainly in words, has been a near-constant demand among the American electorate (Hill 2000; Lempert & Silverstein 2012; Silverstein 2003).[9] Sincerity is also highly valued in (American) Protestantism, which guards against apparent mediation of divinely inspired will (Bauman 1983; Cannell 2006; Engelke 2007; Harding 2001; Keane 2002; Robbins 2004; Stromberg 1993; Yelle 2012).[10] The cultural expectation that speech is sincere is heightened in American psychotherapy, particularly in the client-centered tradition wherein authenticity is both the means and ostensible goal of the professional exchange (Carr 2006, 2009, 2011, 2013).

It is not surprising, then, that the featured foible of Ki's anecdote is the animated client's recognition that the professional has adopted a register or *conversation style*—phony "stuff" that interferes with what might otherwise be sincere, relatively unmediated communication. The irony is that MI *defines itself* as a conversation style, and training in MI *is* training in rhetoric (see chapter 2). Nevertheless, as Ki makes clear, speaking MI *with spirit* means speaking as if one's speech has no style at all.

Paradoxically, though recognizable rhetorical techniques can interfere with the expression of MI spirit, those techniques are also the means for spirit's development and manifestation (see Miller & Rollnick 2013, 15). After all, and as we saw in Libby's evaluation, the MITI codes for both "spirit" and "technique," and "competency" is only reached through a demonstrated verbal combination of the two. Consider too that, in striking juxtaposition to Ki's warning against discernibly "phony" speech, one dedicated apprentice—having been praised for her "spirit" after months of MI training—reported: "My co-workers now say, 'Your clients really like you.' And I say: 'No, they like the way I *talk* to them.'" This appreciation of how talk can be attuned to others, channel special qualities, and achieve particular effects is also highlighted by Norman's delighted insistence that he heard Libby's spirit in her "voice," and more particularly, in her "tone."

For those undertaking advanced MI training, then, the bind is that stylized speech is both the medium of spirit and its potential encumbrance. What is more, and as Ki readily admitted to his now befuddled apprentices, the qualities (properties) of MI spirit are far more difficult to explain, if easy (for some, including clients!) to decipher. Just as the MITI scores rhetorical techniques as discrete and countable behaviors but treats spirit as "global" and "gestalt," familiar worksheets on which U-Haven trainees could simply tally each other's speech acts were now accompanied by far more ambiguous instructions to "listen for the spirit." Whether enacting the motivational interviewer, the client-interviewee, or the observer, U-Haven trainees were asked after role-plays: how did the interview *feel*? And as the directions became less clear, the stakes seemed to get higher. After all, "making a mistake" or "getting stuck for words" was nothing compared to being told to "shut up" by a client who thinks you're a "phony."

At this disturbing and disorienting juncture of the training, U-Haven trainees took comfort in the trainer they so admired. For if Ki had earlier included himself as one who surely once produced an insincere reflection, there was no sign of that now. And though I could hear the striking similarities among Miller's, Norman's, and Ki's hedges, pauses, and stutters, attuned as I was to the register, the way Ki spoke seemed to trainees to be automatic, as if his performance of MI as a practiced conversation style was simply his sincere self-expression. Thus, however intent they were on using MI in their future work, U-Haven trainees wanted to speak like, and even to *be* like, Ki.

Two centuries of conflating charisma with sincerity, in the terms described here, has made it difficult for North American audiences, however keen and critical, to appreciate the sway of charismatic authority, especially in the everyday throes of seemingly secular labor. Interestingly, before the training began, the chosen participants struggled to articulate just what about Ki was so attractive. For instance, in an interview with my research assistant, Marcus commented: "You're probably familiar with [Ki]? [Ki] is someone that, I mean, I really admire this guy and he . . . he's like someone that I would love to be like my mentor 'cause he . . . he just has so much . . . t-t-I-I just . . . w-wanna know him . . . more so." Months into the training, the apprentices gave more pointed explanations about why their trainer was so engaging: Ki has a presence, called "spirit" in MI, which makes him an especially effective communicator.

. .

As noted above, among many US-based MINTies, MI spirit is experienced and explained as a potential that is easily awakened, even natural, in some, and necessarily more laboriously cultivated in others. Those who train MI further agree that spirit is far more difficult to teach than technique, and they sometimes quietly bemoan those who "just don't have it in them." Nevertheless, MINTies act on the faith that MI spirit can almost always be cultivated with ongoing practice. For Libby, under Norman's tutelage, this did not take long. Indeed, the second time Libby and Norman met, they studied the now coded and scored transcript of a motivational interview regarding her client's unfulfilled hopes to rejoin a Bible study group. Having focused on sharpening her reflections, Libby also remarked that the technique was coming more "naturally" for her. And, in line with Norman's prediction, Libby's MITI score for behavior counts skyrocketed. As Norman put it, "Um, jumping 30 points from one . . . coaching session to the next is . . . um, pretty high." Though Libby was pleased that she had improved in replacing questions with reflections, she remained more concerned with her global ratings—that is, the "spirit" of the interview, which remained high if relatively stable.

In her third and final coaching session with Norman, all doubt disappeared as to whether spirit and technique were working in tandem, and what once bothered Libby as disfluent performance now seemed like effortless presence. Conducted with a long-term client who was apparently deciding whether to divorce her husband, Libby's third interview received a MITI score of 88 percent, exceeding "competency threshold." What is more, Libby's "spirit" was now fully manifest both in the evaluated interview, the twists and turns of which Norman and Libby now discussed with great interest, and in the coaching session itself. As usual, Norman spontaneously initiated a role-play, but this time he cast himself as the interviewer, leaving Libby to play her client. Their focus was how to perfect a spirit-filled "summary." And indeed, Norman's summary oozed MI spirit: it demonstrated collaboration, was evocative, was eloquent if decidedly disfluent, and sounded remarkably sincere. Libby responded, giving a striking rendition of her client's response to Norman's summary, complete with a newly adopted accent. Once breaking role, she evaluated her own performance with remarkable excitement, almost shouting: "That is *exactly* what she would say!" More important still was Libby's reflection on her coach's performance, which had clearly moved her.

LIBBY: That was a great, summary, though . . . wow. Very powerful.
NORMAN: So you *felt* it even just role-playing?
LIBBY: Yes! I did! I was with him! Oh! Yeeeeah. [*nodding*]
NORMAN: You see, that's what MI . . . that's the . . . that's the *power* of reflection.

When Norman asks whether Libby *"felt"* the power of his role-played summary, Libby responds as if she is still the client she performed—*"I was with him,"* she says. This emphatic response suggests that Norman and Libby were not just performing together, but were also co-presencing, feeling a "power" that was both larger than either of them *and* that brought them together. Moreover, for Norman, Libby's seamless movement in and out of the performed and the real was yet another sign that the spirit he had discerned in her tone weeks before was now in full bloom.

Before they parted for the final time, Libby asked for advice about how to focus her continued practice of the method. Norman responded with an MI deflection of expertise, one that both equalized the terms of their engagement and sought more information with which to direct the dialogue. Specifically, Norman told his newly "competent" apprentice: "I would recommend that you keep doing what you are doing. You have made more progress in . . . shorter coaching time than most people I work with. *I'd* like to . . . know what *your* secret is."

Libby laughed. It was the first time I had seen her blush in a very long time. To answer her coach's question, she first acknowledged Ki, calling him a "great teacher." Norman pointed out that Ki had been absent for many months at that point, and could not alone account for the "huge, *huge* leaps" she made. Libby quickly recalibrated, this time giving an explanation that clearly satisfied Norman. Her success, it seems, derived from her firm *belief* in the method.

> LIBBY: Well, one reason I have to say I just . . . really *believe* in MI. I really believe it can . . . help someone make changes and want change. And it does it in a way that [*long pause*] . . .
> NORMAN: So, so MI matches your values.
> LIBBY: Yes. Right. And I think I've been . . . operating on the . . . spirit of MI, you know, long before I did it. So, I think that helps too.
> NORMAN: Already you were collaborative, and honored people's autonomy. It matches your values, and it sounds like you practice it a lot . . . not just for tapes.

After Libby left the room for the final time, Norman turned to me and confided that he wished he worked with more people like Libby. People who learn so fast and work so hard. People who do so *because* they have MI spirit, and have had it within them all along, if not yet awakened.

Libby and Norman's interactions, like many others I witnessed between MI trainer and trainee, suggest that for those guided by the "spirit of MI," the discomfort once felt in rehearsals of a highly stylized way of speaking can pave the way to an encounter that is felt by both parties to be genuine, natural, and real. And, for MINTies like Norman, Libby is living proof that the very same MI techniques that initially seem an obstacle to being genuinely co-present with clients can eventually become spirit's seemingly unmediated channel. But Norman not only invests in Libby as his spirit-filled client, or even simply as a vehicle to transmit that spirit to her clients: it also became clear to me, if not to Libby herself, that the "secret" Norman hoped to unlock was that Libby's manifest MI spirit would compel her to train other professionals.

As (spiritual) gatekeepers armed with the MITI, Norman and his fellow coders are charged with *routinizing* spirit, so it becomes the controlling factor and force of MI's dissemination. Norman much prefers to put this energy into trainees like the spirit-filled Libby, which means transforming her "belief" into "faith," and eventually, "calling" into "covenant"—dynamics to which the following sections turn. Yet, more often than not, Norman is faced with many trainees who have achieved technique without spirit but who are nevertheless intent on becoming MI trainers. Norman is therefore on guard for those who wish to enter MINT not because they are moved by spirit to do so, as he is himself, but rather for patently instrumental purposes.

CALLING AND THE VARIETIES
OF MI SPIRITUAL EXPERIENCE

In the thick of a career that was clearly out of sync with his "underlying set of heart and mind" (Miller & Rollnick 2013, 413), Norman was seriously burning out when he first encountered MI. He had already been training corrections officers, but only in those methods the "state told him to," which, before the late 1990s, were "definitely *not* MI." When MI came along and convinced professionals they could "dance with clients, not wrestle them" (15, 23, 32), "everything changed"—and not just in the field of American corrections, which now considers MI an "evidence-based practice" and trains it prolifically. Everything changed *for Norman* as well. He once told me that finding MI was like "gravity, like coming home again."

Variations of this comment were echoed countless times over the course of my research, during which I traveled across the country collecting interviews with MINT members. Repeatedly, I heard almost evangelical accounts from professionals of various stripes who, upon first encountering MI, found the method to be deeply familiar and strongly felt (like "home" or "gravity"), as well as profoundly transformational. Take Susan (whom we met in the introduction): an active, veteran MINTie in her late fifties who received her training toward her PsyD from a top university. A core faculty member in a clinical psychology program, Susan had been contracted by a psychological rehabilitation center, which had been awarded a federal grant that required counseling staff to receive training in MI. Since Susan would be the trainer, she had to immerse herself in a three-day, intensive training in the method—learning how to both practice and teach MI at breakneck speed.[11] Despite the time crunch involved, and the fact that the method was imposed rather than chosen, Susan said of MI: "I *got* it right away. It came very naturally." She further shared that MI did not just change her professional sensibilities but transformed her life, and even her very being:

> I had it. It was there. It was like sort of opening a door that I didn't know that I needed to step through. It really was. I was like: "Wow!" It was actually a pretty life-changing sort of experience. Now did I do it *right* when I was learning it? No, obviously. It still takes practice, but it was sort of like: "wow, this is really what . . . fits for me."

Like Norman, Susan describes a sense of familiarity—a feeling of "fit" that preceded her actual encounter with MI—as well as a profound, even awe-inspiring transformation once she does. In distinctly enchanted terms, Susan's reported transformation is premised on an insight or epiphany—the "wow" that I repeatedly recorded in my interviews with MINT members—which suggests that finding MI is like an awakening: the necessary "door" Susan opened both is already within her and is a previously unrecognized route to a "life-changing experience." Significantly, Susan notes that while she already "had" the spirit of MI ("It was there"), MI's constitutive techniques eluded her for some time, requiring more practice. In ways that recall Libby's early ordeal, the spirit-filled Susan reports that she wasn't even "do[ing] it right" and more practice of MI's techniques would be required. And remarkably, fifteen years after her first encounter with MI, Susan still believed, when I interviewed her, that her own practice and training of MI is a lifelong endeavor.[12]

Of course, I was eager to share such striking accounts with William Miller, especially since I knew that he grew up in a strict Methodist home; is an ordained minister, former deacon, and current elder in his mainline Presbyterian Church (UCC); and has authored several books on Judeo-Christian spirituality.[13] When we first met in Albuquerque, Miller knowingly nodded as I recounted anonymized snippets from my interviews with MINT members. In response, he first referred to his work on "quantum change"—sudden, irreversible, positive transformation—along with his favorite examples of such: Paul on the road to Damascus, and George Bailey in the classic American film, *It's a Wonderful Life* (Miller & C'de Baca 2001). As Miller continued, he underscored that recognition-by-MI is as much a spiritual encounter as a political one (see chapter 1):

> *Recognize* is the best verb I can come up with for how people often seem to meet MI. Now I don't know what percentage of MI practitioners had that experience. I'm sure there are some who come and [it] sounds kind of interesting, try it. But that "Wow" conversion-like experience . . . the nature of it seems to be recognition. [*long pause*] That when they saw it, they knew it to be true, the second they saw it. "Ohhhh!" [*whispered*] "Whoosh!" [*circling hand in the air*] And it changed their lives.

Note that Miller readily concedes that not everyone enjoys an awakening when they first encounter MI. Nevertheless, consistent with the accounts I shared, he figures MI spirit as both ineffable—an extrapersonal "whoosh" that prompts individual "wow[s]"—and undeniable presence that the spirit-filled "knew . . . to be true." After a contemplative pause, Miller further offered that there is "something transpersonal" about MI spirit, which "is part of what draws people to this, too." In other words, according to Miller, MI spirit can beckon as well as awaken.

As we continued the conversation, Miller drew out a distinction that echoed the MINTies I'd observed and interviewed. On the one hand, Miller stressed that some people "get [the spirit] right away," as Norman and Susan reportedly did. Of this group, Miller sustained a sense of mystery, while conjecturing an existing proclivity for "being loving and accepting of all of humankind—which most of us aren't," if not yet knowing or naming this proclivity *as* MI spirit. On the other hand, Miller said, there are those whose conversion-by-MI occurs well after they have been practicing it for some time. As he put it, MI "is mystical in that it emerges out of the *doing* also.[14] Like spiritual disciplines, somehow the doing of this thing, which can seem pretty mechanical in some ways, does something much larger than that and changes you." In other words, MI spirit can be *both* an innate if not yet awakened gift *and* a potential that can be realized in practice, as long as it is not "mechanically" driven from start to finish (see Weber 1968; 2020).[15]

As Miller was speaking, I recalled Lois, a career nurse who, since earning a PhD, works as a "nursing scientist" and director of an elite university hospital's nursing unit in a major East Coast city. When I spoke with her in a small, impersonal office, well removed from the bustle of the unit, Lois explained that when she was first trained in MI as a practicing nurse, she found talk of MI spirit "fluffy." She went on to describe a slow, methodical acquisition of MI spirit, through not just her continued training, but also her own "ongoing *work*":[16]

> I learned and . . . and became um . . . more entrenched in the *spirit* of MI [. . .]. For a nurse, that was really *hard* for me because that's, not where I came from, that's not the school of thought I came from. And, um, uh . . . my whole life changed. My whole philosophy changed. My practice changed. The way I . . . teach. Everything is changed and . . . I like to base my whole life based on motivational interviewing. [*deeply inhales, long pause*] And, um, once I did that, I found *that*, everything else . . . became simpler.

Here, Lois glosses over what it was about her previous professional training that accounted for her initial skepticism of MI spirit—her impression that it was unrelentingly rational, instrumental, and bureaucratized, as I learned later in our interview. Instead, she emphasizes that MI did not just change her work, but also served as a blueprint on which to base her "whole life," as was the case for Susan and Norman. I found that this spiritual linking of life and labor is remarkably common among North American MINTies, who repeatedly spoke of MI as a *vocation*.

Those who experience the "whoosh" of conversion do not doubt this more methodical and mainline route to MI spirit. After all, Norman's job is to track how MI trainees' scores rise for the spirit he felt immediately himself, as if "coming home again." Working to encourage a group of enervated, spirit-craving trainees, Norman—well before his coaching stint at U-Haven—cited Miller when he shared "a big discussion on the [MINT] listserv about being and doing." According to the coach, coder, and spirit-filled gatekeeper, who frequented the MINT listserv:

> Miller weighed in and said: "we *become* what we *do*." And if you've got the spirit right, you can make technical *errors* that aren't going to . . . you know, that are going to have *way less* significance. I think the last thing that was, was, uh, uh, to quote Frank Sinatra . . . "dobedobedo."

In Norman's evocation of Miller—as part and parcel of his effort to motivate his own local training participants—we can see that a prominent division *within* North American Protestantism is also, if more implicitly, marked and overcome: the difference between spirit as "(do)ing" and spirit as "(be)ing" (i.e, dobedobedo).[17]

Importantly, this kind of framing allows a hard-working apprentice (like

Lois), alongside a gifted apprentice (like Norman or Susan), to all speak as if they have been called to MI and, in turn, understand MI as a *calling*. Now emphasizing spirit-through-work rather than spirit-through-whoosh, Miller reportedly offers up yet another both/and formulation. Specifically, the reported speech now marries a recognizably religious conception of spirit with a patently secular one (this time, Sinatra, rather than Astaire and Rogers), inviting nonbelievers to participate in the transmission of MI spirit as if singing a classic American song.

∴

In *The Protestant Ethic and the Spirit of Capitalism*, Weber famously dispensed with a Lutheran conception of calling as "*the* task set by God" as too irrational to mobilize capitalism in colonial America, "the field of its highest development" (1952, 85, 182). Weber turned instead to the more "rational"—as well as lonelier and decidedly less enchanted—Calvinist to personify the ethic that was eventually realized in American entrepreneurialism (182; see also Appadurai 2016, 41–42). As the story goes, American Calvinists pour themselves into work in order to counteract religious anxiety in the absence of worldly evidence that they have been elected. Indeed, Weber writes of the American Calvinist/colonist, "[work] and [work] alone disperses religious doubts and gives the certainty of grace" (1952, 112). Furthermore, when the calling is not the state one is born into but the enterprise that is chosen, people anxiously strive for visible and material signs of confirmation that the enterprise they have chosen is the right one. When it comes to MI, we might slot Lois (and perhaps Libby) into this category.

However, like many other MINTies I came to know, Norman and Susan share a sense of calling that owes as much to Luther as to Calvin and is more evangelical than mainline in its undertones. They experience sudden conversion, apparently feel little doubt, and give accounts of MI spirit that are thoroughly enchanted. These relatively anxiety-free MINTies experience MI spirit as *presence*, which is felt immediately, and they take up transmitting that spirit to others as a *vocation*, in the sense of a life task, or "definite field in which to work" (Weber 1952, 79). Far more pronouncedly than the average helping professional, US-based MINTies orient the work they were called to do toward others.

For Norman, especially, "labor in a calling appears to him as the outward expression of brotherly love" (Weber 1952, 81). That he sees his MI training work as ongoing, even never-ending, is especially remarkable. Consider that when I first met Norman, in a room full of his trainees, this is how he introduced himself:

I'm [Norman]. Uh ... semi-retired, which means I ... don't have to train what the state tells me to train anymore. I can train what I want and put all my eggs in the motivational interviewing basket. And, um, [I get to] go train this in ... various and sundry, interesting places. It just ... it just continually—it's such a good *fit* for me with my whole philosophy of life, um, that I, uh ... I don't think I could stop doing it. You know, I actually, uh ... when I've had to do the exercise, "How would you like your life to be different in five years?"—we did that last time, didn't we?—it's like: I don't *want* it to be different in five years.

The certainty that Norman has found his "fit" in MI training is unmistakable here. And though the rewards include freedom from the state, semi-retirement, and cross-country and international travels he could only once imagine (not to mention the capital accumulated by continually training his more Calvinist counterparts, who continue *to do* so as *to be*), there is nothing that suggests that Norman takes his work as mundane. Yet while welcoming *both* the spiritually anxious *and* those whose call to MI is more definite and assured, Norman—as a coder and MINT gatekeeper—is constantly on guard for those whose motives are purely instrumental and profit-driven. To preserve, protect, and routinize the spirit of MI as the method moves through the world, he not only seeks people who find spiritual "fit" with the practice, but those who will assist in the work of pairing *calling* and *covenant*.

TRAINING MI: FROM CALLING TO COVENANT

On my first visit to the University of New Mexico to meet William Miller, I also spoke with his former student, close colleague, and co-author, Theresa Moyers, whose work was touched upon in the previous chapter. Moyers is a professor of psychology and a process researcher who has devoted much time to developing and refining MI fidelity instruments like the MITI and training people like Norman how to use them.[18]

Her scientific production notwithstanding, Moyers's account of her work closely aligns with the descriptions above: MI research and training originates in her "core being" and is continuously illuminated by the "light" the method turned on inside her. Moyers has no doubt this work is her calling. "I live for it," she plainly told me. While Moyers helped me better understand the relationship between MI science and MI spirit, to which we will turn in the next chapter, she also focused my attention on an especially important aspect of MI's dissemination. As I had done with other interviewees, I asked Moyers what questions I should be posing to others as I continued with my research. She responded:

TM: Oh gosh. [*long pause, sniffs*] You know, I . . . [*long pause*] Do people feel that they have *special* responsibilities when they—learn MI or when they're *good* at MI, I guess is a better way of saying it. Cause I'm *curious* about that.

ESC: Mmm.

TM: Right. You know, umm, is there something about that therapeutic method *or* being a good therapist *in general* which makes you feel more responsible in a certain way that—being a different kind of therapist doesn't? It's like the 12-Step people. You know, if, if you have recovered using the 12-Step program you *buy* in in a way that umm *explicitly* encourages you to provide service. And there seems to *be* something like that going on in MI and I'm kind of curious, where's that comes from? And how do people *acquire* that and where, you know?

Here, one of MI's best-known empiricists raises what appears to be a strikingly phenomenological, perhaps even mystical, question. She likens those who are "good at MI"—which she equates with being a good therapist more generally—to the "12-Step people" relative to both groups' sense of "responsibility" to "provide service." Yet whereas Alcoholics Anonymous (AA) acolytes, "having had a spiritual awakening as the result of these Steps," are clearly charged with "carry[ing] this message to alcoholics, and to practice these principles in all our affairs" (as AA's final step puts it), MINTies feel similarly responsible in the absence of explicit directives to do so. Notably, Moyers wonders why, how, and from where this sensibility arises in MI, rather than questioning to what extent or even whether it exists.

Moyers also underscores that MI spirit is much more than an individual feeling of being called and/or converted. Being called to MI is being *called on to act*, with work—whether in MI research or MI training—understood as much more than an end in itself. According to Moyers, and corroborated by my own research, MINTies "buy in"—turning responsibility into a kind of reinvestment in the MI enterprise. Repeatedly, MINTies told me that MI spirit compels them to transmit the method to others, almost as if making public the private experience of conversion.[19] Thus, Moyers points to (and MINTies actualize) an idea that Weber arguably glossed over once he dispensed with Lutheran conceptions of calling in his diagnosis of American spirit—that is, calling finds its pinnacle expression in the practice of *covenant*.

Recall that Weber's genealogy of the calling begins with the Reformation, when Catholic monasticism is recast by reformers as selfish withdrawal from the world. For reformers "the valuation of the fulfillment of duty in worldly affairs [became] the highest form which the moral activity of the individual could assume" (1952, 80), until that spiritual duty was thoroughly rationalized in colonial entrepreneurialism, thereby becoming the motor of modern capitalism. Yet while Weber suggests that the idea of "labour in a calling . . . as the outward expression of brotherly love" (81) disappears once the calling crosses the Atlantic, spiritually abandoning American entrepreneurs, MINTies like Moyers think of and feel their work as intimately connected to the good of others. Thus, if there is a sense of *presence* when they first feel MI spirit, MINTies' reinvestment in the method leads to deeply felt experiences of *co-presence*, whether with clients, with each other, or in relation to a transpersonal or "superordinate" force that both brings people together and exceeds them.

In the organization of their spirit-driven labor, as well, North American MINTies arguably have prominent historical precedent to follow. Consider the revivalists of the Second Great Awakening, who traveled the country, using their exceptional oratorical gifts to helm well-organized, protracted "tent" meetings. Whereas earlier itinerant mass evangelists tended to eventually settle into local parishes, the Second Awakening was characterized by a new, professional revivalist class, organized by social engineers like Charles Finney and funded by well-to-do laity, for whom travel became a way of life (McLoughlin 1978, 127–32). And not unlike American MINTies, American Methodists—as inheritors of the "organizational genius" of John Wesley—established "classes" in various localities as a means of participating in and transmitting the method (Klassen 2011, 22–23). For these figures, as for Norman, "conversion was an individual confrontation of the soul" that was sustained by fellowship with brethren who "provided the continuity that routinized and canalized the fervor of the awakening into orderly social institutions" (McLoughlin 1978, 132). Like generations of revivalists before them, MINTies like Norman, Susan, Moyers, Miller, and Lois work as if "individual conversion and external covenant should go together" (Bellah 1975, 18–19). And, as if driven by an agency other than their own, these MINTies unceasingly devote themselves to the generation, demonstration, and transmission of (MI) spirit. As Norman put it in his spirit-filled introduction, not only is he singly focused on training MI for the next five years, he doesn't think he "could stop doing it."

Given his understanding of his MI labor as spiritually motivated, Norman once told me that he, like many other MINTies, faces a pressing problem: how to "share our enthusiasm about MI without being evangelistic." In so saying, Norman certainly did not mean to equate MI with the Gospel, but rather worried that those whom he trained might find any hint of zeal familiarly unattractive. Miller, too, harbored similar concerns. Though, as recounted below, he was eager to talk with me about the relationship between MI and Christian conceptions of brotherly love, he bristled just a bit in response to my suggestion that MINTies—according to their own self-descriptions—seem as though they are driven to "spread the word."

> WRM: [Training MI] is a little different from proselytizing in that way. So it's not going out and say[ing]: "you're doing it wrong, and I've got the right answer." 'Cause that totally misses the point of MI to begin with.
> ESC: Right.
> WRM: But a little more like, "pay it forward."
> ESC: Mm, hm.
> WRM: Or, you know, "[I] might want to make a contribution to making my professional world more positive," or something like that.

Speaking from the perspective of an MI trainer, Miller distinguishes that work from "proselytizing"—an evangelical mode of spiritual conversion that he links to an insistence about "right" and "wrong."[20] This, Miller mentions, "misses the point of MI," presumably both because of the method's distaste for stark and unresolved opposition (that is, "right" and "wrong") and because of the authoritarianism implied by giving such an order. Notably, Miller also provides a much more secular version of MI's dissemination, as he animates a MINTie who simply "might want to make a [positive] contribution" to their "professional world." (Again, note that the "responsibility" is not primarily and directly calibrated to client well-being, but seeks to positively influence, if not transform professional practice.)

Nevertheless, and quite intriguingly, mainline Protestant themes remain subtly woven through this ostensibly secularizing account. For instance, rather than "proselytizing," MINTies "pay it forward." While some say this term was coined by Benjamin Franklin—icon of American entrepreneurialism and personification of the spirit of capitalism according to Weber—it is resonant in American Christian communities as well.[21] As lore has it, Franklin asked his friend to repay a loan by later lending the amount to another person in need; among American Christians it is associated with ongoing loving and giving of oneself to one's proverbial neighbor. In both cases, "paying it forward" means extending oneself out of established webs of reciprocity to less predictable future interactions, with the logic of reinvestment oriented less toward accumulation than toward continual expansion. For MINTies, then, "paying it forward" means working to disseminate MI spirit for the good of others, both proximate and still unknown.

While we will focus on the reconciliation of spirit and profit in MI in the following section, here I ask readers to recall Miller's striking statement—made in a published interview in the journal *Addictions*—that MI just seems to "flow" and "we have not done that much to disseminate it" (Miller 2009, 890; also see the introduction). Although Miller certainly acknowledges to me the labor that this published statement rather radically downplays, a subtle mysticism characterizes both: MI moves through the world because it *moves* people and, only then, because it is *moved* by people. MI never seems to move, according to Miller, by way of technical force.

Finally, it is important to note that Miller's subtle vacillation between a recognizably Protestant ethic and a fully secularized one is also part of the "point of MI" that—from my perspective, if not Miller's—should not be "missed." As someone who periodically attended an Episcopalian congregation in childhood—and as an anthropologist of the United States—I found it hard not to notice that MI's vocabulary is laced with Protestant terminology, such as *spirit, compassion, generosity*, and *acceptance*. Early in my study, I wondered if this was simply symptomatic of the kind of nonsectarian "civil religion" famously described by Robert Bellah. When I mentioned to Miller that MINTies' narratives seemed to be as rich with implicitly Judeo-Christian tenets as Rogerian ones, he excitedly interjected, "Exactly! Yes!" noting that Christianity has been "a real center of my life as a matter of fact." He quickly added these significant qualifications:

> WRM: You certainly don't have to come from a tradition to do this. And I don't want that to be a barrier to people. You know, "Oh, this is a *Christian* thing."
>
> ESC: Mm hm.
>
> WRM: Because, I mean, a Buddhist could do this perfectly well. You know, very compatible with a Buddhist understanding of reality, too. But, I mean, to me, I think always the *heart* of Christianity has been lovingkindness, has been that interest in acting on behalf of the welfare of others, without interest in personal return from that.
>
> ESC: Mm hm.
>
> WRM: And that, to me, is the heart of Jesus's teachings; it's there in Judaism as well; it's a piece of Judaism that he said: this is the real heart of the law. This is what the law is all about. It's loving your neighbor.

In a by now familiar framing, if one that is also representative of the denomination-crossing tendencies of contemporary North American liberal Protestantism, MI is presented as *both* Christian *and* not. According to Miller, this is because "lovingkindness"—or "paying it forward"—is not just found in Jesus's teachings, but in Judaism and Buddhism as well. In addition to this philosophical reconciliation, there is also a hint of a practical impetus: Miller is on high alert for "barriers" that would inhibit MI's "flow." However spiritually motivated they are to pitch a big tent, MI proponents have also disseminated the method in pyramidic fashion. And from the standpoint of strategic marketing, there is little to lose and certainly much to gain in pointing to parallels in other religious traditions from the historically empowered center of American Protestantism/civil religion.[22]

Again, we see the plenty of MI's insistence on both/and. No matter the grounding of Miller's MI and the "heart of Jesus's teachings," a highly ecumenical framing of MI spirit allows for a wide range of interpretations. This too was corroborated by my research. Perhaps due in part to the urban locales of most of the MI trainings I observed, Buddhism, rather than Christianity, was the religious tradition most commonly evoked by MI trainers. For instance, Ki, standing alongside Miller, offered this rendition of MI spirit to a large group of advanced trainees: "*Compassion* is really where we begin to . . . *locate* what is fundamentally important in the practice of MI. As the Dalai Lama described it, it's that fundamental desire that the other be free from suffering—without that, it would be like words without the music."[23]

Consider, too, the time I shared lunch with a MINTie in a small-town, southern restaurant that shared a one-story, pastel-painted building with a fragrance-saturated day spa. As I nibbled on my club sandwich, my lunch companion surprised me by explaining MI spirit by way of an expression that "Hindus use a lot: the light within me recognizes the light within you." He continued: "There's that connection. You can call it higher power, you can call it God, you can call it Oneida, but there *is* something else about two people connecting and it's *greater* than either of those by themselves. *Synergistic*, I guess." As I drove back through the maze of small towns to the motel where I was staying, passing church after church of varying size, physical condition, and apparent stature, I wondered how much my MINTie interlocutor, however goodwilled and generous, knew about the traditions with which he was claiming synergy and how that knowledge aligned with his neighbors.

These recurrent accommodations of non-Christian traditions in MI discourse did not stop me, five years into my research, from sharing my emerging analysis of a Protestant (work) ethic in MI during my invited plenary address at the 2014 MINT Forum. Rex—a psychologist, one of the original members of MINT, and then-chair of its board of directors—was clearly a bit irritated. During an epic and especially fascinating interview a day after my talk, which lasted more than three hours, Rex made sure I understood that he, a veteran MINTie, was "born Jewish," and has long since been an "adamant atheist." Yet Rex also went on to tell me that he is among the "minority" of MINTies who "avoids the language of MI spirit," substituting more secular terms like "empathy" or "compassion," which he associates with Carl Rogers.[24] And when he later described his MI work as a "vocation," he was quick to add: "not a *religious* vocation, but in the sense of a, a *purpose*. That, this is something that I can do that will matter, will [make] my life *meaningful*, that gives me a reason to keep going and to care."

In adamantly disavowing religious terminology while embracing a textbook definition of the Protestant work ethic—that is, work as the path to a "meaningful" and "purpose[ful]" life—Rex reminded me of what Weber called the "thoroughgoing Christianization of the whole of life" (1952, 124). Indeed, to point to the abiding liberal Protestantism of MI is not to imply that everyone who thinks of their work in these terms is a practicing Protestant. In fact, and no doubt largely because MI so concertedly accommodates and deflates traditional difference, Rex has plenty of company in MINT. Nevertheless, and as this chapter shows, MI clearly draws on and reproduces a set of historically dominant, firmly implanted Protestant ideals, including the concept of vocation. And, whether in the coupling of calling and covenant for MINTies like Norman, or in the more secularized terms adopted by Rex, the continued hold and widespread influence of the Protestant ethic provides part of the answer to Moyers's question about the origins of "responsibility."

With this, we can finally turn to the analysis of how MI helps its devoted trainers reconcile spirit and profit, so that the latter is not seen as an impediment to the former. We will see that MI in many ways challenges Weber's chilling prognostication that, in the United States, "the pursuit of wealth" would eventually to be "stripped of its ethical and religious meaning" and take on the "character of sport" (1952, 182). Moreover, while Weber personified the American spirit of capitalism by way of anxious Calvinists, who regarded their riches and size of their networks as (unstable) signs that they had been saved, we find that a different sort of anxiety and means of assuaging it prevails among MINTies. Specifically, to routinize MI means to rigorously work to assure that the profits derived by any one individual from MI training are continually and primarily motivated by MI spirit.

TRAINING AMERICAN SPIRIT AND PROFIT

When I arrived at MINT's 2014 Training New Trainers (TNT), I had engaged in more than five years of observing MI training and interviewing participants. So even as I watched participants collaboratively produce a huge drawing of the fictional character Yoda on large pads of paper, a character who they laughingly agreed exemplified MI spirit, or listen with furrowed brows to a well-known trainer deliver a very long and rather odd lecture on John Searle's speech act theory, there was very little that surprised me.[25]

However, having observed people—like the participants in Norman's coding group—prepare for years to enter MINT, working to get their MITI scores up and to convince an established MINT member to write them a glowing letter of recommendation, I was admittedly taken aback by the relative lack of excitement among TNT participants. I found no dramatic rites of passage, no evident relief among trainees for having made it this far, and a lot less evident collective effervescence than I had expected. In place of the MI spirit talk I was so used to hearing, I listened with interest to copious discussion of MI profits. If almost always in small groups and sometimes in hushed tones, the conference hotel hallways and barstools were filled with conversation about lucrative contracts lost and gained, the costs and profits of entrepreneurial ventures, and calculations about potential co-training gigs. At the end of the week, one newly "MINTed" trainer told me: "[Being a MINT member] doesn't give you any special powers. But you can say, 'I'm MINT trained.' It's getting a little, you know, there's that economic commercial piece of it. It's a *business*."

To that point, I'd found it difficult talking about the profits of MI training with my informants, hesitating to push or pry, having learned it was a sensitive and sometimes even sore subject. Aside from MINTies like Ki, for whom training MI was a built-in aspect of his regular job, many took a much more entrepreneurial route: setting up introductory trainings that cost up to $250 a day and sometimes attracted more than 200 participants; taking contracts at agencies for one-day trainings for which they charged upward of $1,800 plus expenses; hosting online trainings from their basements or living rooms; even taking lucrative contracts with states that had mandated MI training for whole swaths of professionals. By 2010, coding and coaching had come to be known as an especially profitable and stable source of MI-generated income. After all, coding groups, such as the one where I first met Norman, may meet for years, with professionals paying for monthly group sessions, ongoing individual coaching, and, of course, the transcription, coding, and scoring that it took to meet "threshold competency," the green light to apply to MINT.

As a consumer of MI training, having worked in Norman's coding group for well over a year when I met him, Thomas felt these costs in his very own pocket. Having been a Franciscan monk for seventeen years before becoming certified as a family therapist, Thomas had since been struggling to build a private practice, and he believed that becoming a MINT trainer would be the professional kickstart he needed. I later realized that a large part of our interview was devoted to Thomas testing out his wager that the payoff for ongoing coaching with Norman would be worth the investment (see Appadurai 2016). He explained that he had learned from Norman that the Department of Corrections in a neighboring state "had been trying to get people to do MI training and would only look at MINT members. They wanted a MINT because they're '*real*.'" Thomas made quotation marks with his fingers and dramatically raised his eyebrows when uttering the word "real," revealing a sarcastic streak that might have proved problematic within the overwhelmingly, if not uniformly, earnest ranks of MINT, had Thomas ever made it there.

As our conversation continued, it struck me that the former Franciscan was not especially enchanted with, though clearly interested in, the world of MI. However fond he was of his coach, Thomas repeatedly emphasized the rational authority involved in acquiring MINT membership, and his dependency on an established insider conferring legitimacy upon him. For instance, in reference to the state contract, Thomas remarked: "You know, [they wanted] someone that was trained by the 'masters,' that is until they found out those trainees were 'also charging . . . MINT prices' [*laughs*]." Despite the concern with "MINT prices," Thomas understood it was unlikely that the state agency would hire him for a lucrative, long-term contract without his being "MINTed," which, with an eye-roll, he referred to as being "anointed." Thomas concluded: "On one level, they say [being a member of MINT] doesn't mean anything, but in terms of fame and fortune, I think it does."

In so saying, Thomas was apparently echoing his coach, whom I had separately interviewed just hours before. I'd just asked Norman about Mary, one of Thomas's fellow trainees, who was also clearly intent to join MINT. With a hint of uncharacteristic dismissiveness, Norman explained Mary's drive: "It's a prestige thing. The MINT doesn't signify any expertise. But people think it does." Whether "the people" Norman was referring to here were trainees, their potential contractors, or both, the comment stood in contrast to Norman's typically glowing commentary about MINT, a group wherein he clearly found community and even communion. Norman was always eager to attend the annual MINT Forum, was a regular participant on the heavily trafficked MINT listserv, and had an abundance of kind and respectful words for his colleagues. "It's such a fascinating group of people [in MINT]," Norman told me. "I've met so many really smart and kind people." Like Miller, Norman conjectured that MI spirit has the power to convene: "I think, you know what? [MINT] *attracts* . . . kind people. That's part of the . . . *spirit* of MI."

This is a remarkable comment from a MITI coder and coach who works so hard to identify and routinize MI spirit, assuring that MINT remains an organization that attracts "kind" people—that is, people who are moved to join *because of* MI spirit rather than for "fame and fortune," as Thomas cheekily put it. There is some discomfort in this gatekeeping work, the former corrections officer explained, because "MINTies don't like *policing* people." Nevertheless, Norman also believed, as those who trained him in the MITI surely emphasized, that when it comes to MI spirit, "quality control" is necessary. On the frontlines of that effort, Norman is functionally proximate to the corrections work that he had disavowed long ago.

Because coders and coaches are equipped with a tool that is designed to detect subpar skills, as well as "mimicked" skills without spirit, one might initially expect this gatekeeping work to be relatively straightforward. However, Norman and his fellow coders must rely on their own instincts to decipher *economic* instrumentalism—that is, people who pursue the practice of MI simply as a career rather than as a calling. This was likely part of the reason that Norman was so taken with Libby, the U-Haven trainee he predicted would be a "champion." In their last coaching session, Libby apparently knew next to nothing about MINT and was decidedly uninterested in applying when Norman told her, "You're eligible now, if you want to go to the MINT. You'd have that documentation." Thus, what mattered in the end was not simply that Libby had spirit in her "tone" well before she mastered technique; just as importantly, her spirit was confirmed when she professed her "belief" in MI, with no intention to translate that into the "fame and fortune" or prestige and profits that preoccupied Norman's other apprentices.

Preserving the "spirit" of MI within the MINT community has become increasingly urgent as the growing demand for MI training among state and local agencies has created more lucrative opportunities for underemployed, poorly paid helping professionals once they are MINTed. "It might be a business," one MINTie grudgingly admitted, "but you don't want people getting into this *just* for the money. That defeats the whole spirit of MI." So as coach to helping professionals with entrepreneurial ambitions to become MI trainers, like Mary and Thomas, Norman felt obliged to, in his words, "start with the spirit and really spend a lot of time trying to [*long pause*] make that *real* for people."

Despite her drive to join MINT—or perhaps precisely because of the perceived nature of that drive—MI spirit apparently never became "real" for Mary, whose remarkable technical skills I had seen on display during a real-play, focused on a fellow apprentice's hesitancy to produce tapes for Norman to evaluate (see chapter 1). The real-play was conducted with the much younger Camilla, who later remarked, with marked enthusiasm, "that was like therapy you *want* to go to," as Mary beamed appreciatively. As the years passed, and Mary never showed up on the MINT website's world-wide list of trainers, I cautiously asked Norman what had happened, expecting the evasive answer he uncomfortably provided. I came to the tentative conclusion that while Norman recognized how skillful Mary was, he doubted that spirit was what moved her—a conclusion that may be corroborated by the following tense if humorous exchange. It occurred during the very same round of introductions, quoted above, in which Norman made clear his calling to be an MI trainer. When it was Mary's turn to introduce herself, she said: "I was trained, sort of, in [MI] years ago, and what I've since learned from [Norman] is that I have a long way to go in terms of really practicing it." Norman responded with a characteristic quip: "I just said: 'Mary, you have a looooong [*group laughs*] way to go,'" to which Mary somewhat bitingly replied: "You saved all my [MITI] numbers and stuff. *There's* MI spirit. I think you exemplify it."

By the most straightforward reading, Mary's comment indicates an appreciation for Norman's exemplary generosity, an outward sign of his MI spirit, and his patience in coaching her over a long period of time. More specifically, rather than making her start from scratch after a long hiatus between tapes, he "saved her numbers" as she worked toward competency. Others in the group also remarked on Norman's marked generosity. For instance, Thomas told me: "If you meet Miller, or you know [Norman], they are so, so generous about stuff. It's like: 'No, you don't have to buy that; I'll *give* it you. I'll give you my slides.'"[26] Yet another interpretation of Mary's comments is that Norman "exemplifies" MI spirit precisely because he profits from his calling. In other words, however jokingly, Mary indexes the spirit of MI capitalism. After all, the longer it takes for trainees to reach competency and apply to MINT, the more they must pay Norman for coaching and coding. Norman understood fully the potential for frustration, explaining to me: "See, part of the thing with them is they're paying . . . out of their own pocket. So, they don't want to waste their money."

Interestingly, Thomas also came to understand the financial delicacies of MI training, not just as a trainee but as a budding trainer himself. Balking at MINT prices, the Department of Corrections ended up asking the yet-to-be-MINTed Thomas if he would do a "two-day show." Thomas promptly refused unless the department also "committed to taping"—that is, producing recordings that he could code and coach as Norman does. Thomas explained, "Norman really opened my eyes to the tapes, that the *tapes* are the way you learn it." And while Norman surely believed that taping was essential because the MITI could detect requisite spirit, and perhaps also because "commitment" was indicative of calling rather than careerism, "taping" is also far more profitable than a "two-day show." Indeed, the contract with the Department of Corrections never materialized because they thought, as Thomas put it, "I was just trying to make money, 'cause, you know, these tapes are expensive to do."

Concerns about profiteering hardly stop at MINT's gate. *Within* MINT as well, a trainer's financial success can be and sometimes is read as a critical sign that MI has become a revenue-generating sport rather than a spirit-filled calling. This is particularly true when MINTies are working within the same regional "market"—though very few would use that term. A couple of cases of particularly fierce competition and suspicion between MINTies became clear to me when I visited the MINT Forum, and heard the words "self-interested," "self-promotional," and even "profiteering" uttered aloud for the first time among my interlocutors *alongside* the more typical characterizations of the professional community as united by spirit and therefore characterized by compassion, acceptance, and generosity.[27]

Consider the case of Melony, a tall, blond, fifty-something MINTie who describes herself as a "highly spiritual person." When I spoke to Melony at the MINT Forum, she had recently migrated from California to set up an "MI training business" in North Carolina, a state that attracted many MINTies after mandating that primary care physicians receive basic training in the method. Our conversation began when Melony introduced herself as a poet, suggested that the pauses I had identified in the register were a manifestation of MI spirit (see chapter 2), and eagerly volunteered to interview with me the next day. During the first half of our interview, Melony, a former nurse, told a long, riveting story about her spiritual training in India, her epiphanic encounter with MI (and with Miller's "presence" in particular), and the remarkable trail of "bread-crumbs" that led her to take up training MI as her calling.[28] In MI, she said, she found "synchronicities... big picture or 'aha' moments" that were so at odds with the frustrations of the "[traditional] system" in which she used to work.

Though some details certainly differ, Melony's account of being called to MI was quite familiar, echoing those of my other MINTie informants. However, and perhaps because we were in the thick of a professional meeting in an upscale conference hotel lobby, Melony's sanguine MI autobiography abruptly segued into a soap opera, as she described herself at once as a person committed to a "very non-competitive philosophy" and as standing up to fierce competition in one of the most thriving MI markets in the country. Melony explained that she "had been in trouble" with other MINTies for her thriving MI training business. "I'm not shamelessly selling," Melony explained, "but I'm *promoting*, and sometimes that gets criticized within the [MINT] group." She added that because she is not at the "center" of MINT, few came to her defense when hints of her profiteering surfaced.[29]

These accusations were clearly discomfiting for Melony, a person who repeatedly described herself in overtly spiritual terms, almost as if I, too, harbored suspicions.

Later that very same day, without revealing Melony's identity, I broached the concerns she had raised about MI-as-enterprise when speaking with Rex during our marathon interview. He was apparently eager to discuss what he strikingly called, having heard my talk the day before but without my immediate prompting, MI's "conjoining spirit and capital." More specifically, Rex told me about his recent "offline" commiseration with Stephen Rollnick, Miller's UK-based co-author, whom I had interviewed months before. Growing increasingly critical of the discourse of the MINT listserv, they exchanged gripes that those who are "the most vocal about MI spirit" are also those who are "most likely to self-promote their services." Reportedly, Rollnick suggested that the justification of profit in the terms of spirit was a "very American" one, and not nearly as common within the British MINT community.

Though surprised by the candor of Rex's revelation, I already knew that Rollnick harbored concerns about what he repeatedly called, in our conversations, the "productization" of MI, which he associated with the rise of the evidence-based practice movement in the United States (see chapter 4). In the United States, he proffered, the MITI is no longer a tool to assess and assure spirit. Rather than helping to routinize spirit, as it had been intended, Rollnick said the MITI had been "reified" as a vehicle for "marketing" MI and for stimulating the MI training economy more particularly. The MITI and the Americans who wield it for wealth, he continued, are responsible for the unbridled growth of the method that he helped develop alongside Miller, turning a way of helping people into a maximally profitable, packaged, and branded product. And while Rollnick conceded that British MINTies grow "confused" when they realize how much money there is to be made by way of MI training, he insisted that the method is succumbing to the spirit of capitalism rather than adhering to the spirit of MI because of a characteristically American ethos.

Notably, the American Miller responded very differently to the question of MI spirit relative to MI profits when I posed it to him. When I shared informants' concern that the "flow" of MI was becoming more like a capitalist market (which I hardly needed to do, given his steady engagement with MINTies in person, on the listserv, and through his many daily email exchanges), he quickly acknowledged the felt disjuncture: "Whatever it is that draws people to motivational interviewing often is accompanied by at least a suspicion of business, marketing, whatever. It's 'taking advantage of people,' I don't know, whatever it is, which I certainly share some of that myself." Yet as soon as Miller marked the distinction between the enchanted "draw" of MI spirit relative to the generation of profit, he reconciled it in a very MI way, drawing now on a trademark Protestant (American) ethic to justify MI's spirit of capitalism:

> You know, now I just don't have [a] problem with [people making money from training and transmitting MI]. I mean, I don't have a problem with a great ballet dancer or I think baseball players are paid a bit if somebody's really good at what they do. Can command an income for that. And, so I mean, in a way, the *market* will end that if it's not producing results that people *wanted* in the first place. But I don't have a problem with people using their talent to earn a living. I mean that's what . . . *lots* of people do that. So, it just doesn't trouble me and doesn't seem to me inconsistent with motivational interviewing.

Building upon his apparent belief in a self-regulating market, Miller articulates faith in some other classically American ideals, clarifying that he does not see them as "inconsistent with" MI. In comparing a great MI trainer to great athletes or ballet dancers, who similarly "us[e] their talent to earn a living," we find a clear articulation of American professional calling, notably wearing *both* charismatic *and* Calvinist garb. Whereas he begins with sympathetic suspicion of spiritless marketeers, he ends with faith in the superseding force of the American market, which gives a sign of just whose labor is genuinely talented and therefore valuable. In this he seems to confirm Weber's diagnosis that, in colonized North America, "a further, and above all, in practice the most important, criterion is found in private profitableness. For if that God, whose hand the Puritan sees in all occurrences of life, shows one of His elect a chance of profit, he must do it with a purpose" (1952, 162).

As my conversation with MI's founder went on, I noticed for the first time a slightly irritable tinge in my famously generous and personally welcoming interlocutor's explication. Looking back at the transcript, I imagined I had been trying to control my response with a pregnant pause, taking a page out of the master interviewer's book, when he unapologetically continued the exchange by offering, "Probably some of my colleagues would be scandalized if they knew what I charged to go give a talk about motivational interviewing, but I don't feel apologetic about that." I drew from that exchange that Miller certainly feels that he was called and, at the very least, implies that his profits are divine confirmation of that calling, whatever profane gossip and even scandal may ensue.

Years later in my fieldwork, I came upon what Miller had identified as a potentially "scandal[ous]" figure: $10,000 plus all expenses paid, including some fairly luxurious ones. In exchange, Miller spent a full day co-training with Ki, who put in the bulk of the preparatory work in terms of communications and the setup of the day's plan and presentation. He also delivered one of his enchanting talks, almost all of which I—and many others in the packed hall's audience—had already heard elsewhere. Within this immediately enchanted audience, not to mention the North American membership of MINT as I know it, I cannot imagine that anyone would want or expect—at least openly—the apology that Miller says he won't give. This is because, for careerists—whether having slipped through the MITI (as Norman might worry) or having been funneled through the MITI (as Rex and Rollnick contend)—Miller's offered "scandal" has already been predrained by the resolution of American spirit and capital.

·.·

Arguably, unlike the other normative distinctions that MI seizes upon and defuses, this chapter documents a dominant American paradox that is particularly loaded and contemporarily charged, but also has a blueprint to follow. Miller's unusually strained response to me suggests something with which many North American professionals, like many MINTies, are deeply familiar: the need to continually prove that our enterprise amounts to a kind of *covenant*, one that also happens to involve the accumulation of capital. In this sense, when MINT trainers cite an inspiration to "pay it forward," they intimate that any accumulation is simply a side effect of reinvestment in the method. Thus, whether critically resigned to MI's growth as a business or defending it in the name of spirit, the most prominent proponents of motivational interviewing appear to agree that the Protestant Ethic and Spirit of Capitalism are, for better or worse, entwined in their work.

If readers find Miller's and MINTies' talk of spirit foreign, perhaps even a bit alienating, we might ask how many of us share the idea that our work is driven by something greater than we are, eschewing the idea that self-interest plays a role. The number of books we write or studies we publish—perhaps the talks that we are asked to give and the honoraria we collect—become tenuous signs that we have chosen the right vocation. Anxious, we devote ourselves to our work with ever more spiritual fervor and, not infrequently, feel unsatisfied and troubled when signs are not forthcoming. This devotion to and through work is an American condition shared by many in the professional class, including social scientists, and if MINTies are more articulate about how spiritual concerns drive an economy, they are certainly not alone.

CONCLUSION: (DE)SCRIBING MI AND THE PARADOX
OF RATIONAL CHARISMATIC AUTHORITY

I once asked William Miller how he would describe his relationship to the method he founded and to the growing community who take its training as their vocation. The question was inspired, in part, by my observation of how regularly MI trainers not only cite Miller during their trainings, but almost seem to try to channel him.[30] When working to explain a fundamental of the method, for instance, it is not unusual to hear a MINTie use the preface: "If Bill were here, he might say . . ." or to wonder aloud, when faced with an especially difficult question, "What would Bill say?" Even those MINTies who have not personally met Miller seem to be on a first-name basis with him, and—in interviews with me—describe feeling at once a sense of intimacy with and awe of him. For them, "Bill" is the embodiment of MI spirit. In Weber's terms, this means that William Miller also exercises charismatic authority.

Weber (1968) differentiated charismatic authority from traditional authority by the former's dependence on a leader's personal charm as interpreted by their followers. Miller's charismatic sway has been humorously celebrated by MINTies, and not just North American ones, who created a Facebook group called "Bill in My Pocket" in 2015. In the posts, MINTies parodically display keychains, adorned with an image of Miller's face, in the various international locales where they are either training MI or resting from these travels (see figure 3.2). Perhaps for some who post, these may also be read as ways to advertise their success in the calling, including the poster who is "relaxing by the pool on a well-deserved vacation" to the Canary Islands. Others post more domestic scenes, with Miller adorning the near top of a Christmas tree. In this case, the poster ventriloquizes Miller, wishing his followers "Happy Holidays" with a strikingly secular motto.

Yet, as Miller and his co-author Rollnick are well aware, charismatic authority is radically unstable, not only because the legitimacy of the leader must constantly be proven to followers, but also because it has no extra-personal grounding (Weber 1968). As if reading from a page right out of *Economy & Society*, Miller says he and Rollnick have discussed "the danger in being gurus" and more particularly, "the tendency for the method to die when the guru dies." Accordingly, Miller says that both men "have very consciously backed out of that kind of role." They instead adopted a kinship term to describe their relationship to their growing brood of apprentices and the method they have developed together, now laughingly calling themselves the "grandfathers" of MI. It's funny, in part, because the two men were so young when they first met in 1989 in Australia—a chance

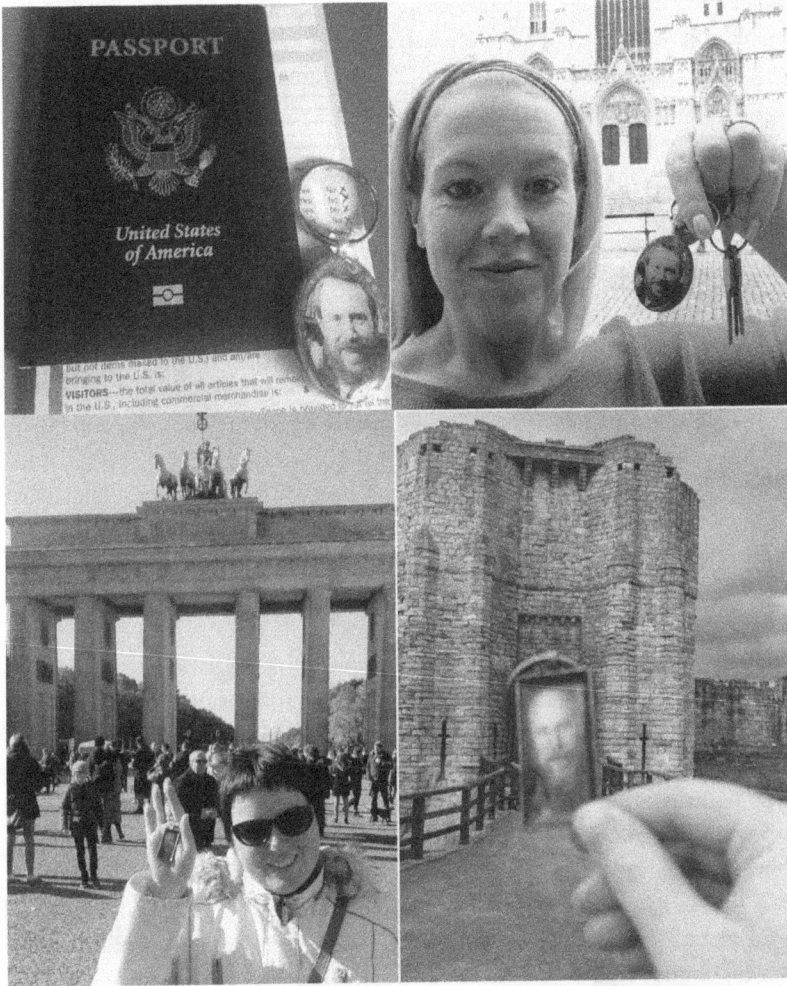

Figure 3.2. Posted photographs from the Facebook group "Bill in My Pocket." Top left, "Crossing the border with Bill," and top right, "Bill and me in Brussels," courtesy of MINT member Kate Watson, PhD. Bottom left, "Brandenburg Bill," and bottom right, "Bill is king of the castle," courtesy of Claire Lane, PhD.

encounter, we should recall from the introduction, that Miller considers evidence not just of his good fortune, but also of the mystical nature of the method.

If seeing himself much more as grandfather than guru, Miller does not hesitate to use enchanted terms. In describing the genealogy of MI, Miller once told me, "I mean, how did motivational interviewing happen? It was *evoked* from me." As for his collaboration with Rollnick, more particularly, he added: "It comes out of the same processes. Kinda mysterious." When I asked him to describe his relationship to MI, he began by swiftly dismissing the idea that he is "the owner of motivational interviewing," distancing himself from the proprietorial connotations of that term. More remarkably, Miller went on to insist that the method, of which he is widely considered the founder, *found him* instead:

> WRM: I don't feel like the creator of motivational interviewing.
> ESC: Really?
> WRM: No. No. Not. No. Definitely. This is something that I have described but I didn't invent it, you know, this. Other people have known this. Discovered it. These are *truths* that have been around for quite a while. In sales, among other places, but to um verbalize and clarify how language works and how that can be used in a *lovingkindness* kind of way, to help other people become free of things holding them back and move their lives forward in a positive way, I mean that's, ya know, it's sort of like—I *channeled* some of that knowledge into these particular applications.

Thickly enchanted with supernatural Protestantism (Klassen 2011), Miller's understanding of his relationship to MI is not unlike those of other MINT-ies, if different in degree: enduring truths—like lovingkindness—found home within him, mobilizing his remarkably fruitful labor (see Miller 2017). The nature of this labor became clearer over the course of our discussion, when Miller landed on what seemed the most accurate self-description of his relationship to MI: that of a *scribe*. If he has some gift, Miller explained, it is that of a clear and cogent communicator; he is someone who happens to have been both equipped with a gift and mysteriously positioned to "describe truths" that have been around for centuries, to "verbalize and clarify" how language can produce co-presence, and to "channel" spirit-filled knowledge. Significantly, MI spirit is understood as a matter of working not for the accumulation of profit (as in "sales"), but for freedom.

Miller was not simply called to MI. Miller's work, along with that of his apprentices, exemplifies the staying power of the ideal of *the calling*—its drawing together of work, spirit, and profit—in contemporary North American professional culture. In this light, the hundreds of studies Miller has published, books he has written, and talks he has given; the thousands of emails from admirers he has so promptly answered; even, perhaps, the sums he charges for lectures are all ongoing fulfillment of an ethical and spiritual obligation that chose him as much as he chose it. It appears, after all, that at least in the case of the growing professional community Miller

helms, the Protestant ethic has hardly shed enchantment as it drives entrepreneurialism and American capital expansion. Indeed, we cannot understand MI's spread without recognizing how American spirit, as experienced
by MINTies, propels it forward.

. .

I think it is safe to say that most contemporary social scientists in the United
States (and elsewhere!) use a very different register to describe our work.
By my experience, our reflexive discourse about what we do and why pre-
dominantly remains on one side of the division Weber drew between rational and charismatic authority as ideal types. Whereas rational authority is
based on rules; is systematized, routinized, and established in bureaucracies; and enjoys longevity precisely because it exceeds the power of any one
person or party, charisma lives only as long as the authority who embodies
it (Weber 1968). As usual, Miller refuses the cultural distinction between
ideal types, combining rational and charismatic authority.[31] The case of MI
raises the question of whether professional practices that blend types of authority are relatively insulated from well-trodden lines of critique.

This is precisely what Miller himself suggested on my return visit to Albuquerque in the fall of 2017. In discussing MI's status as an evidence-based
practice, Miller explained:

> There's something called Solution-Focused Therapy that—unfortunately
> its two progenitors died far too young but, but—in spirit—very similar
> to motivational interviewing. When people ask me: "well what's the dif-
> ference between motivational interviewing and Solution-Focused Ther-
> apy?" I, I somewhat meanly say: "*800 trials.*" There just isn't, isn't that
> much of a scientific emphasis in, and around Solution-Focused Therapy
> its beginning, you know, some, *some* trials but, but not from the very be-
> ginning of the approach, the integration of a pragmatic, evaluative, em-
> pirical approach.

In Miller's rich and revealing statement, we find the conclusion that contemporary American interventions need more than "spirit" to thrive. Specifically, Miller says that Solution-Focused Therapy is "in spirit very similar
to motivational interviewing," and that it is the lack of a scientifically generated "evidence base" ("800 [randomized controlled] trials") that has led
to its relative faltering. Recalling his earlier comments on "the tendency
for the method to die when the guru dies," Miller further offers that any
therapy that rests on charismatic authority alone cannot survive in con-

temporary conditions. Whereas Solution-Focused Therapy's "two progenitors died far too young," the charismatic Miller and Rollnick have not just outlived them, but also have been assured of their method's longevity as it has established—through the work of MI research—a rational ground of authority.

Along these lines, the next chapter explores the co-production of the science and spirit of MI. This includes the way Miller infuses mysticism into his framing of MI's highly productive research industry, repeatedly using terms like "amazing" and "astonishing" to discuss the number of clinical trials of MI. To him, the number of studies is yet another sign of MI's special spirit, which draws in those—whether researchers or practitioners—who make the dissemination of MI their vocation.

CHAPTER 4

American Science

Faith and the Spirited Economy
of Evidence-Based Practice

Aside from co-authoring all three editions of *Motivational Interviewing* with William Miller, clinical psychologist Stephen Rollnick is well known for introducing MI into primary health care delivery, having himself worked for many years in the British National Health Service. He is a prolific trainer of the method he helped develop, and travels widely doing so, including making regular trips to the United States. Given these accomplishments, Rollnick is undoubtedly one of the highest profile proponents of motivational interviewing worldwide, perhaps second only to Miller, and is especially respected in Britain and Scandinavia, where MI is also widely trained. And although Rollnick was originally the one who came up with the term "spirit" to describe the unique endowments of MI, his description of the method is far more down to earth than that of his co-author, who claims the truths of MI were "evoked" from him in a "kinda mysterious" way.

I met with Rollnick for lunch one spring afternoon in Chicago, where he had landed after a busy "period of workshops in different cities." The dynamic psychologist, sporting all-black garb, described himself—with apparent relish—as MI's "delinquent younger brother." Not long into our conversation, Rollnick's "delinquency" manifested in an unabashed critique of MI's rapid growth and dissemination in the United States. More specifically and in no uncertain terms, Rollnick expressed that *evidence-based practice*, as galvanized by American market forces and logics, is dehumanizing MI, draining the method of its signature (if, for him, *secular*) spirit.[1]

Evidence-based practice (EBP) is a technoscientific movement that originated in British medicine and has made significant inroads into North American helping professions since the 1990s.[2] In its early days, EBP defined itself as the practice of using "best evidence" to make clinical decisions and implement interventions.[3] However, by the time I met with Rollnick, EBP had morphed from a model of clinical decision-making grounded in positivist science into a complex system of legitimation that baptizes particular methods *as* "evidence-based."

MI is one such method, in part because it has been the subject of RCTs—otherwise known among EBP proponents as the "gold standard" means of procuring "best evidence." Yet, as both Miller and Rollnick acknowledge, treatment methods are recognized as EBPs not simply, or even primarily, by virtue of their scientific integrity. As we will see, the system of legitimation that rendered MI an EBP is not just complex but also quite populous, involving a wide range of "extrascientific actors," including policymakers, state and federal agencies, academic journals, charitable foundations, registries and clearinghouses, public and private insurers, intervention developers and trainers, health and human service organizations, and helping professionals, themselves.

Evidence-based practice is not only an explicitly scientific discourse; it is a *scientizing* one as well. In the United States, the term "evidence-based" is a powerful performative, producing a wide range of social and economic effects. Most notably, once a practice method is designated as evidence-based in a particular field—like corrections or addiction counseling—the professionals and organizations who adopt that practice are far more likely to receive reimbursement for services. This, in turn, generates a demand for training in the method, a dynamic that occurs in Britain as well as the United States. And while reimbursement for behavioral health and social services is at least as likely to come from public as private insurers, during our lunch, Rollnick was intent on differentiating *American* MI by what he sees as an unholy alliance of scientific ideology and economic interests, with researchers both driving and benefiting from the method's American market.

With little prompting and marked intensity, Rollnick went further to radically question the scientific integrity of the MI research enterprise, not so subtly suggesting that matters of ethics and efficacy have become less valuable than the promise of material gain. For instance, Rollnick told me that clinical researchers—including some within MINT—have defied "thirty-five years" of what has been well established by their academic mentors and colleagues: that is, "common factors" of the therapeutic encounter (like the display of empathy, for instance) are more determinative of treatment outcomes than the defining features of any single therapeutic approach.[4] In the era of EBP, as practice methods vie for recognition, North American MI researchers focus instead on how to attractively package and market their "brand" of helpfulness, or so Rollnick charges. Consider this exchange:

SR: They *productize* the treatment methods because there's no other language that they have for it, for trying to understand helpfulness . . . particularly in North America. Particularly in this country.

ESC: Mm hm.

SR: Um ... if what I'm saying is true, then you would anticipate the treatment method that's viewed as helpful, um, will get, um, reified and *productized.*

ESC: Mm hm.

SR: I dunno if that's the word but, like, you, you know what I mean: gets turned into a product that can be delivered by trainers.

Here, Rollnick leaves no doubt that the problem he identifies is a culturally specific one, given his assertion that "North Americans" have "no other language" except that which is provided by the market. By this account, US-based MI trainers, once driven by humanistic concerns, are at risk of becoming mere couriers with less visible agents controlling and profiting from MI-as-product.

Given the strenuous efforts of contemporary American clinical researchers to cleanse the scientific process of human bias, Rollnick's critique of thoroughly marketized MI may strike EBP advocates and intervention researchers as troubling, misguided, and—yes—even "delinquent." Most remarkably, Rollnick's account stands in fascinating contrast with his American co-author's evident pride in the hundreds of RCTs that he says distinguish MI from its would-be competitors. While MI's American founder sees the remarkable output of MI scientists as yet another sign of the method's (entrepreneurial) spirit, his UK-based counterpart worries that the method they jointly developed has become "productized" in North America, thereby alienating all of those who were once more wholesomely involved in the still unbranded project of "helpfulness." This disjuncture between MI's most prominent transatlantic brothers suggests, once again, the method's remarkable capacity to contain and even thrive on ideological division, including internal critiques.

Despite their obvious differences, Miller and Rollnick both indicate that the story of MI science should account for the politics and economics of contemporary behavioral health and social service interventions in the United States. In accordance, I contend that MI's nomination as an EBP cannot be boiled down to the integrity of clinical evidence generated by disinterested scientists, nor can it be satisfyingly explained by the harnessing of clinical science by free market forces. In fact, evidence-based practices like MI are primarily empowered by state and federal bureaucracies, without which particular methods could hardly be "productized" (see Carr & Norwood 2022). It is within these bureaucracies that MI has been packaged for and advertised to US-based helping professionals and non-profit agencies, if often in marketized terms. Indeed, I argue that the political economy of MI is as neo-Keynesian as it is neoliberal (cf. Carton 2014).

To elaborate these points, this chapter examines the labor involved in the establishment of MI as an "evidence-based practice," including the production of several thousand studies of the method, a substantial proportion of which is conducted by MINT members. The pages below also document how MI spirit infuses MI science, capturing the faith of MI researchers. We caught a glimpse of the melding of science in spirit in the previous chapter, when Dr. Theresa Moyers, just like her training brethren, framed her prolific research as covenant—a mission to preserve MI's spirit rather than "productize" and "package" it. Other North American MI researchers directly challenge Rollnick's cultural critique, if in less enchanted terms. For instance, David, an MI researcher at an Ivy League university, told me: "I have always felt like the purpose of knowledge at this level is not to *brand* yourself. It's to more broadly understand where this fits into the bigger picture of *interacting* with people."

Irrespective of these defenses, the basis of Rollnick's claim is a sound one: there is indeed a growing market for MI training in the United States, a market unimaginable without MI research. That said, once we open the question of who controls the means of production and who profits how from the distribution of MI, some surprises are in store. For instance, we will learn that, rather than feeling diminished and dehumanized by MI science, as Rollnick worries, some American MINTies use the method's scientific status to revive and mobilize their humanistic approach to practice. Moreover, in focusing on MI science, we will see, once again, the method's uncanny ability to manage opposing stances—in this case, amongst MI researchers who insist their work is preservative of MI spirit, internal critics who are concerned about the degradation of the method by way of that very same research, and the trainers who use MI science to signify and disseminate MI spirit.

The world of MI research is especially thick with the method's more general "both/and" sensibility, and not just because it actively defuses the different and typically unequal status of "researcher" and "practitioner." In the industry of North American MI research, the primary efforts are not aimed to purify evidence or the science that produces it, but rather to creatively *hybridize* it (see Latour 1988, 1993).[5] Indeed, while structurally emboldened by the EBP movement, MI science is further vitalized by incorporating precisely what EBP advocates—and positivists more generally—typically strive to leave behind. By engaging with MI research through its advocates and critics, I illustrate how MI science constitutes itself by embracing science's socially constructed antinomies: economics, humanism, politics, practice, perspectivalism, religion, and even mysticism and magic.[6]

THE POWERS OF "THE LIST": EVIDENCE-BASED
PRACTICE AS STATE-SUPPORTED SCIENCE

In September 2009, I navigated bustling, mid-afternoon streets lined with shiny skyscrapers to meet with Susan in her twenty-first-floor office, where she works as a full-time faculty member in a school of professional psychology. She greeted me wearing a prominently shoulder-padded black suit that seemed to swallow her small frame, an equally enveloping smile, and neatly bobbed silver hair. We chatted as I situated myself on one side of her desk, which was topped with student papers, a large flat-screen computer, and now, my own recording equipment.

Susan was one of the very first MINTies whom I interviewed. I was struck by her story of personal and professional transformation by way of MI spirit, unaware that I would collect many such narratives over the subsequent years (see chapter 3). As we talked that afternoon, Susan unabashedly told me that—whether she trains MI to her in-house PsyD students or in "heavy-duty trainings for the state"—her most reticent apprentices make comments such as: "It's like you seem to live [MI]. It just kind of rolls off you." Susan's embodiment of MI spirit is especially interesting considering her graduate studies in an elite psychology department that she called a "hotbed of behaviorism"—a self-description that would have placed her on the latter side of the Rogers-Skinner divide (see chapter 1). Through her training in MI, however, Susan became engrossed in the Rogerian "art of listening to people, being empathic, permitting autonomy" and intent to recognize the "underlying *human* things that go on." And while MI spirit came "very naturally to her," Susan emphasized that many others are not similarly preconditioned. As she put it during our interview: "I think you can teach the *science* of [MI], but the real challenge is how to transmit the *spirit* of the method."

Intrigued by her spirit-filled comments—or my fledgling interpretations of them at the time—I proceeded to ask Susan about the burgeoning science of MI, with a particular interest in what she thought about the method's imbrication in the thriving EBP movement. After all, her remarks seemed to suggest that she might not share EBP's epistemic virtues (Daston & Gallison 2010) about what counts as best evidence and how it should be generated. Reflecting a much broader fetishization of numerical evidence, these virtues are neatly portrayed by the renowned "hierarchy of evidence," which elevates RCTs and meta-analyses, and relegates qualitative studies—including those best equipped to get to the questions in which Susan expressed interest—to its lower rungs. However, when I asked Susan: "Is MI an evidence-based practice?" she responded without the slightest hesitation, equivocation, or hint of critical distance: "Yes . . . yes, it is."

Susan's swift affirmation that MI *is* an EBP turned out to be very telling, though it was quite puzzling to me at the time. For months, I'd been poring over the growing research on MI, including those studies that had stretched my paltry statistical literacy. Luckily for me, ever since EBP advocates realized that it was impractical to ask more or less statistically literate professionals to scan relevant statistical literature to make practice decisions, systematic reviews and meta-analyses had become mediating or "filtering" devices, selectively communicating statistical findings in strict adherence to the aforementioned evidence hierarchy.[7] Having read many of these studies, I was confident in my conclusion that MI only makes a significant difference in treatment outcomes when combined with other interventions. When I interjected this point, naïvely presuming a relationship between the outcomes and MI's status as an EBP, Susan confidently responded: "Um, no, it's actually pretty much a standalone [intervention]." In so saying, she pivoted from the ever expanding grounds of MI research to a very different source of authority.

Revealingly, Susan also physically pivoted toward a large, flat computer screen and clicked her mouse intently, eyes scanning the screen. Seeking confirmation, Susan muttered, momentarily distracted with her task: "It's on my list of Favorites. Yes, it is an evidence-based practice, officially, for about the past eighteen months." With a few more purposeful clicks, Susan's face lit up with rediscovery. She beckoned me and tried to adjust her screen with its freshly loaded display: a webpage for the National Registry of Evidence-Based Practices and Programs (NREPP), a federally contracted list of "scientifically established behavioral health interventions" (see figure 4.1).[8] With her finger now pressed to the screen, she underscored that MI's place on the list was evidence enough. With the matter closed, she now simply added: "MI is listed. Just straight. MI is there."

Although at the time I met with Susan, I knew absolutely nothing about the NREPP, I would later learn how this federal agency became a definitive source in the eyes of US-based professionals, particularly those working in mental health and substance abuse. Through several subsequent conversations with Miller, along with significant background research, I eventually came to see the NREPP as a baptismal site, where particular practices are named and legitimated as "evidence-based" (see Carr & Norwood 2022). Susan was right: while the legitimation of MI as an EBP has involved a wide range of actors—from intervention researchers to those who manage medical, social service and behavioral health organizations—the NREPP played an especially central role precisely because its list was typically read

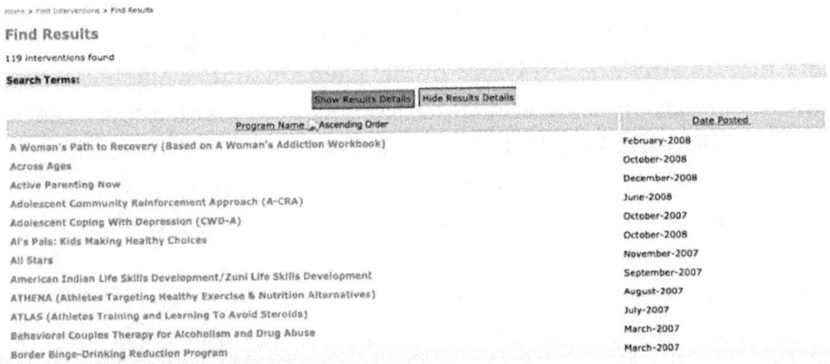
Home > Find Interventions > Find Results

Find Results

119 interventions found

Search Terms:

Show Results Details | Hide Results Details

Program Name Ascending Order	Date Posted
A Woman's Path to Recovery (Based on A Woman's Addiction Workbook)	February-2008
Across Ages	October-2008
Active Parenting Now	December-2008
Adolescent Community Reinforcement Approach (A-CRA)	June-2008
Adolescent Coping With Depression (CWD-A)	October-2007
Al's Pals: Kids Making Healthy Choices	October-2008
All Stars	November-2007
American Indian Life Skills Development/Zuni Life Skills Development	September-2007
ATHENA (Athletes Targeting Healthy Exercise & Nutrition Alternatives)	August-2007
ATLAS (Athletes Training and Learning To Avoid Steroids)	July-2007
Behavioral Couples Therapy for Alcoholism and Drug Abuse	March-2007
Border Binge-Drinking Reduction Program	March-2007

Figure 4.1. The NREPP's alphabetical list of evidence-based programs and practices as it would have appeared on Susan's desktop computer. https://nrepp.samhsa.gov/about.aspx (accessed August 4, 2017).

by practitioners and those who train them as legitimating, *by fiat*, specific inventions *as* evidence-based ones.[9]

Though Susan certainly knew about the NREPP, she was not aware of or especially interested in its inner workings. When I inquired that day in her office, she correctly guessed that to land on NREPP's empowering list, one needed more than "random control stuff"—there also has to be "somebody *championing* it through the system." And while we will learn more about what such championing entails in the following section, here it is important to underscore that the "system" to which Susan refers is a federal bureaucracy rather than a free marketplace of "productized" interventions, as Rollnick unsparingly charged. And although Susan accurately intuits that the NREPP's interpretation of evidence is likely mediated by other (private) parties, it is the federal government that provides Susan with "authoritative" conclusions. As US-based MINTies know all too well, federal and state bureaucracies are the primary parties that package certain intervention methods as "evidence-based" and pave the way for the method's training and dissemination. And once a particular practice, such as MI, is designated as "evidence-based," the professionals and organizations that adopt it are far more likely to receive reimbursement, which means that state and federal funding agencies, as well as private insurance companies, have significant skin in the game.

The emergence of the "fifth branch" of government, composed of scientific advisory committees, is a widely known force in American public health and environmental policy—thanks in part to the pioneering work of Shelia Jasanoff (1990). However, STS scholars have been less attuned to how—in a period of austerity and hostility to public funding of human service and behavioral health organizations—the federal government has increasingly justified social services spending by appealing to science. Consider that, in 2013, the US Office of Management and Budget circulated a memorandum directing agencies to confine their funding to evidence-based practices (Burkhardt et al. 2015). Remarkably, patients are incentivized by EBP too, with the Affordable Care Act waiving copayments when patients seek preventive services supported by "the highest standards of evidence" (McAuley 2015).

Some individual states have followed suit, establishing specific EBP requirements in order to distribute public funding. For instance, in 2003, the Oregon legislature passed SB 267, which mandated that increasing percentages of state funding (up to 75% by 2011) be reserved for human service agencies that implement programs that are "evidence-based" (Oregon Senate Bill 267, 2003). Like the NREPP, the Oregon Health Authority's Behavioral Health Services (n.d.) provides a web-accessible list of such "approved practices." A quick internet search—not unlike the one undertaken by Susan—turns up MI as an "approved practice" on Oregon's list.[10]

Some states do not just respond to established designations of evidence-based practice by federal registries like the NREPP, but actively engage in the definitional process. Interestingly, in these definitions of EBPs, we often find patently economic considerations interwoven with scientific ones. For instance, Oregon's SB 267 (2003) defines an "evidence-based program" as one that: "a) Incorporates significant and relevant practices based on scientifically based research; and b) Is cost effective." When being "cost-effective" becomes as a type of "evidence," EBP becomes far more politically palatable for organizations and the funders on whom they depend. The Oregon case therefore suggests how, at the state level, the term "evidence-based" offers a resonant rhetorical frame to stave off perennial concerns about putatively wasteful public spending on behavioral health and social services.

Not surprisingly then, interventions like MI, which wish to be recognized by the state, tout their ability to effect change with minimal investments of time and money. This may mean supporting—if not enthusiastically encouraging—the use of MI in a single session, or as a "one-shot" addition to other therapies (see Brown & Miller 1993 as cited in Miller & Rollnick 2013, 336). More frequently, MI proponents underscore that the method is an *inherently* efficient approach to the complex task of behavior change. For instance, in a callout box entitled "Listening Saves Time," Miller and Rollnick remark: "If you only have a few minutes to talk and your hope is for behavior change, you don't have time *not* to use MI" (2013, 56; figure 4.2). If such statements are directly aimed at professionals who are

BOX 5.2. Listening Saves Time

The psychiatrist apologized for arriving late at the ongoing afternoon workshop on motivational interviewing. "I'm sorry for being late. I saw 20 patients this morning."

The trainer paused to welcome the newcomer and asked, "Are you able to use MI in your work with such a busy schedule?"

"Do you think that I could actually see 20 patients if I *didn't* use MI?" the psychiatrist replied.

*　　*　　*

"I don't have *time* to do this," busy practitioners sometimes say about reflective listening in particular and MI in general. "I already have too much to do in the time that I have with patients, and if I open up this door of listening, I'll never get anything done! I just need to tell them and move on."

Yet a few well-chosen words can save many mouthfuls of busy talk, none more so than in the use of a reflective listening statement that captures the essence of what the person is feeling and saying. When you hit the nail on the head with an accurate reflection the person feels understood and there may be little need to explore further. People also tend to repeat themselves when they sense (correctly or not) that they are not being heard, and a good reflection can save time.

Just "telling" people what they need to know or do can feel like having done one's job, and there surely are times when conveying facts is efficient. This is particularly so when the person needs and wants information. When what is needed is behavior change, however, telling and warning often don't help. If you only have a few minutes to talk and your hope is for behavior change, you don't have time *not* to use MI!

Figure 4.2. "Listening Saves Time." From *Motivational Interviewing: Helping People Change*, 3rd ed. (Miller & Rollnick 2013). Used with permission of Guilford Publications Inc.; permission conveyed through Copyright Clearance Center Inc.

burdened by the everyday demand for their services, they are also indexes of a political and economic climate in which state support of mental health, behavioral, and social services requires significant rhetorical finesse, including the neoliberal framing of services as efficient and economically advantageous as well as scientifically sound.

The state-specific authorization of behavioral interventions as EBPs led to the migration of many MI trainers, particularly in the immediate wake of the 2007–8 economic crisis, during which fewer American MI trainers enjoyed the stability of full-time positions like Susan's professorship. During these years, many helping professionals realized that their most reliable professional lifelines were entwined with the increased call for methods to be evidence-based, explaining why Oregon is now home to a dispro-portionate number of MINT members and MI trainers. One might argue that these trainers effectively became the professional migrants of state-supported science—and not just in Oregon.

Consider Melony, the MINTie we met in chapter 3, who left California to resettle in North Carolina in 2010 once significant funding became available for MI training—thanks to the state's Behavioral Health Initiative (BHI). The BHI integrated various behavioral health services into 1,400 primary care clinics (North Carolina Department of Health and Human Services 2016). It also mandated MI webinars and trainings, a full day of MI training for all new hires, and long-term MI coaching for individual physicians and staff (Community Care of North Carolina 2017; Dickens et al. 2012). Melony referred to this complex of incentives as "easy pots of money." It appears, then, that US-based MI trainers like Melony are moved by state policies more than by free market economics.[11]

We might recall that Melony went to some pains to describe her MI work as motored by MI spirit. We should also remember Rollnick's reported sus-picions about the rhetoric of spirit as a typically (Protestant) American cover for capital accumulation (see chapter 3). Yet even if we temporarily set aside the tendency of American MINTies to find spirit in all their en-deavors, including scientific ones, migrants like Melony expose the limits of an analysis that reduces MI's spread to the bare economic self-interest of in-dividual actors set free on the American market, on the one hand, or those prone to scientific fetishism, on the other. Given the dependence on gov-ernment bureaucrats who list, legislate, program, fund, and define, rather than on free marketeers who "brand" and "package," US-based MINTies like Melony are best understood as the beneficiaries of state regulation. And while terms like "efficiency" and "cost effectiveness" certainly infuse EBP discourse, MI training is vitalized and motored by state-supported science. Thus, as it turns out, North Americans indeed have *multiple* languages with which to conceptualize their socioeconomic conditions, one of which is the language of John Maynard Keynes.

American progressives saw the 2007–8 economic crisis as an opportu-nity to resurrect what Geoff Mann calls "modern liberalism's most persua-sive internal critique": Keynesianism. According to Mann, Keynes refused to think of politics and economics as naturally different orders of things, and worried moreover that this antinomy simply fueled uncertainty, scar-city, and poverty (2017, 11). Keynes was not simply interested in creating a hybrid or mixed economy through the state regulation of markets, or through the collective regulation of individual entrepreneurialism. Instead, he worked between the normative opposition of economic ideals with the intent "to propose something novel" (49), an approach to economy that could stabilize the chaotic conditions of modern life. In this sense, the neo-Keynesianism of evidence-based practice, which reroutes state support for social services by way of science, is philosophically compatible with, as well as economically lucrative for, US-based MINTies.

With these points in mind, let us briefly revisit Susan in her office, her index finger pressed against her computer screen. Some might mistake Susan's resolute appeal to the NREPP as an act of self-interest, undertaken by a mercenary ready to capitalize on state-supported science. Others might mischaracterize Susan as a blind adherent to state authority, trusting it to vet what counts as science. Both interpretations fail to find the significance in Susan's remarkable and very accurate closing statement about the NREPP: "This is the *federal* [list]. This is . . . I mean, to me, it's sort of like if you get . . . if it's on the federal list, that means they'll *pay* for it [that is, MI training], which means they [that is, government actors] actually do believe it works." What becomes clear, then, is that Susan takes the government's belief in MI as "actual" because it is another source of evidence for what she, herself, already believes, having deeply felt and spiritual as well as pecuniary investments in the method. And while we will further examine the imbrication of MI spirit and science below, for now we can say that, like good Keynesians, Susan and her fellow US-based MINTies trust in state authority *insofar* as it affirms and regulates their own beliefs and practices.

"JUST ONE": FAITH AND DOUBT IN MI SCIENCE

Rollnick and I were just digging into our matching niçoise salads when he started in again on the dangers of EBP, this time foregrounding a slightly different, if related concern. "The whole evidence-based treatment movement is largely a grand illusion," Rollnick groused, that "over-concretizes helpfulness." Helping professionals, he further opined, "cling" to the certainty of science in the face of clinical "chaos." More generally, they face particularly "tough" working conditions with far too little support. Rollnick explained that MI is first and foremost a method designed to help the helping professionals in these challenging circumstances as much as their clients; of the former group, Rollnick vowed, "my heart is with them."

Having studied helping professionals myself for most of my academic career—including, of course, those I encountered during this study—I felt a kinship growing well past our choice of the same lunch menu items. At the same time, although I had witnessed plenty of chaos, I just didn't recognize the "clinginess" that so concerned Rollnick. In fact, I could hardly think of a single US-based MINTie with whom I had spoken—including, most remarkably, MI researchers—who fetishized MI science, as if its findings exerted a power of their own. Instead, and like Susan, they readily believed that MI could and would be recognized as science because the research apparatus, if not the research itself, affirmed what they already knew and felt as something real and true, including MI "spirit."

As Stanley Tambiah once pointed out, science and magic share a similar burden: that is, how to explain action at a distance. More specifically, although the authority of science is grounded in empirical observation and the rigor of method, while magic depends on the persuasive capacities and effects of signs and speakers, both endeavors seek to explain how some "property is imperatively transferred to a recipient object or person on an analogical basis" (1973, 199; also see Tambiah 1990).[12] In other words, both science and magic are fundamentally analogical forms of reasoning. Tambiah insisted that much as scientists reject the existence of causeless effects, people charged with solving problems by way of magic refuse to believe in the inherent potency of medicines or spells. They look instead toward the "analogical transfer of their qualities" (1973, 199), which requires the authority of the human and nonhuman agents involved, if sometimes invisibly so.

Tambiah, who was intent on challenging the classical distinction between science and magic, would surely find the nature of Susan's engagement with the NREPP list particularly edifying. Under no illusions, Susan plainly told me after turning away from the computer, "I'm not a believer in the magic of an evidence-base." By way of analogical reasoning, she instead believed in and promoted MI science and/as MI spirit, while circumventing epistemic questions about the quality or even existence of evidence. Thus, for many US-based MINTies, while there is nothing magical about an evidence-base per se, there is much magic in MI.

Even MI's researchers simultaneously entertain faith and skepticism with regard to the kind of scientific production demanded by the government bureaucracies that make the fateful decisions about which practice methods will be recognized as EBPs. This is certainly true of one of MI's most productive researchers, William R. Miller, who is, not surprisingly, the "champion" that Susan correctly guessed the NREPP requires. Miller has conducted and co-authored several dozen MI studies, and has trained and mentored many other MI researchers. He also fastidiously tracks the number of RCT (or "gold standard") studies of MI, displaying the latest count on updated PowerPoint slides during his speaking engagements or dropping it into more informal professional exchanges. For example, on a return trip to Albuquerque in 2016, when I underestimated the current number of RCTs of MI, he was quick if gentle with a correction: not 800, he said, but "*840*."

Miller is far too ecumenical to keep such count because he believes that, since they are designed to eliminate bias and error through randomization, RCTs are "objective" and, by extension, apolitical, as some people assume (Craciun 2018; de Souza Leão & Eyal 2019). Nor would he be likely to ideologically align himself with EBP's aforementioned hierarchy, and accordingly consider the RCT an inherently superior means of gathering evidence.[13] After all, Miller's own scholarly work ranges from RCTs to published meditations on the relationship between MI and horse-whispering. He once even told me that, of all his studies, he is proudest of his short, co-authored book on "quantum change," which is based on a small set of qualitative interviews. Instead, Miller keeps such a careful count of RCTs because, as the Coalition for Evidence-Based Policy unequivocally puts it, "evidence of effectiveness cannot be considered definitive without ultimate confirmation in well-conducted randomized controlled trials" (n.d.). In other words, as the lead proponent of MI and the applicant to the NREPP, Miller also knows that adhering to EBP's bureaucratic and scientific virtues is economically as well as scientifically consequential for MI's dissemination. Echoing Susan, Miller explained to me: "you have to be on the NREPP list to get paid to do [MI] in some states."

That said, Miller is keen to the fact that the quality and quantity of scientific input is only tangentially related to MI's official designation as "evidence-based." And while he continues to count the number of gold standard studies, he does so with the full awareness that the NREPP *does not*. When I asked how many studies it took to become an EBP, Miller matter-of-factly replied:

WRM: One.

ESC: Just *one*?

WRM: In the addiction field, yeah. NREPP, yeah. The National Register [*sic*] of Evidence Based Programs and Practices, I think it is. I don't know if you've ever looked it up. Um, but, basically if you have one controlled trial, you can get on the list of evidence-based treatments.

It was with incredulity that I digested the information that "you can get on the list of evidence-based treatments" by way of "just *one*" study—that is, if it is of the variety that the NREPP considers "gold." Yet, with the help of a doctoral research assistant, I soon found that the NREPP's own guidelines confirm Miller's account (see Carr & Norwood 2022). The 2017 NREPP guidelines indicate that there must be "at least one" published evaluation study in order for a practice to be considered for inclusion on the list as long as that study: (1) "assesses" a substance use, behavioral health, or mental health outcome of an intervention aimed at a "mental health or substance-

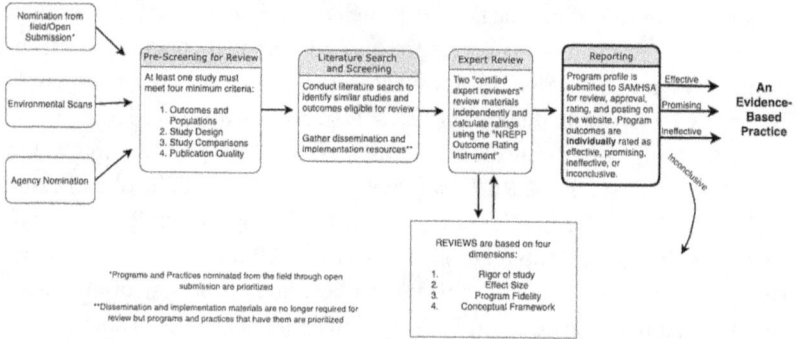

Figure 4.3. NREPP submission diagram, as reconstructed from NREPP guidelines between 2015 and 2018. Prepared by Hannah Obertino Norwood.

using population"; (2) has a "quasi-experimental or experimental design"; (3) compares the intervention to an inactive control (or placebo) or comparison group; and (4) was published after 1995 in a peer-reviewed journal (NREPP 2017). Furthermore, and quite notably, the research seen as meeting the "gold standard" by the NREPP rarely tests one intervention against another and typically compares an intervention to a placebo. As Miller explained it, the intervention science necessary for inclusion on the list "doesn't ask questions like . . . is this [intervention] really any better than something else that you could do?"[14]

If quantity of scholarly output is not the NREPP's primary concern for inclusion, neither is the quality of the tested method's effects. When MI was reviewed, the registry did require applicants to provide evidence of at least one "positive behavioral outcome" to be considered for review (Results First Clearinghouse Database 2020). By 2015 this requirement vanished. As applicants like Miller know from reading these guidelines, the NREPP's primary inclusion criterion was *not* that studies show evidence of efficacy per se, but rather that the evidence was gathered in what the registry considers the most epistemically virtuous way, through at least one "gold standard"/RCT study (see figure 4.3). As the NREPP states quite clearly:

> [Our] definition [of EBP] does not require a "positive effect," just an "observed effect." This means that evidence-based programs on NREPP may be effective or "work." But they may also make no impact or even make a negative impact on the target outcome. (NREPP 2017)

Although registries like the NREPP may adhere to an earlier definition of EBP, listing practices regardless of whether individual outcomes are effective so long as there is vetted evidence worthy of consultation, those registries' users (like Susan) may understandably interpret listed practices to be authorized as "effective," in the more colloquial sense of the term. And while registries may plainly state that they are neither offering evidence of "what works," in the sense of producing particular behavioral goals, nor more generally advocating for particular interventions they list as "evidence-based," professionals, organizations, and insurers can hardly be blamed for thinking otherwise. After all, registry titles like "Effective Child Therapy," "Crime.Solutions.gov," "Social Programs that Work," or "Results First Clearinghouse" clearly suggest a relationship to effectiveness, results, or what works. Those who consult these registries would have to read the proverbial fine print of these websites to find admissions that "evidence-based programs don't necessarily have a positive impact. Instead, they can have no impact or even a negative impact . . . which differs from how many in the field define evidence-based" (Results First Clearinghouse Database 2020).[15]

· ·

If Miller was an applicant to the NREPP, he was hardly a supplicant. As he readily conceded to his slack-jawed anthropological companion, "what constitutes evidence, and how much evidence, are important questions and it's a very, very low bar for NREPP." Furthermore, the fact that MI crossed that "low bar" without much evidence of its efficacy, despite the hundreds of RCTs, was not lost on Miller, who volunteered that outcome data were lacking even in MI's original sphere of addiction treatment, citing a high-profile RCT that showed "no effect on drug use" among research subjects dually diagnosed with a mental illness and substance abuse disorder. Miller also openly acknowledges that in a series of MI studies conducted by the Clinical Trials Network, "basically none of them showed a main effect of motivational interviewing."[16] The most recent edition of MI's primary textbook (MI-3), softens this assessment a bit, stating: "the general conclusions to date have been that MI is associated with small to medium effect sizes across a variety of behavioral outcomes, with the strongest body of evidence being on addictive behaviors" (Miller & Rollnick 2013, 379). The authors, however, reveal that "a number of clinical trials, including some of our own, have reported no meaningful effect of MI on a priori measures" (380), and accordingly provide a list of corroborating citations.[17]

In these candid assessments, the American founder and figurehead of MI effectively agrees with the most trenchant critics of the EBP movement who charge that "the number and types of EBPs on such lists vary widely for reasons apart from the quality of evidence" (Glasner-Edwards & Rawson 2010, 7). Remarkably, however, neither the NREPP's "very, very low bar" nor the failure of MI research to establish definitive evidence of the intervention's efficacy diminishes Miller's faith in MI science. Miller accepts that cost-effectiveness may be more important than scientific integrity when it comes to MI's status as an EBP. He also concedes that state bureaucracies play at least as important a role in MI's scientific status as the researchers he has trained, collaborated with, and respects. For whatever his reasonable quibbles and criticisms, the sheer volume of MI scientific production is—in Miller's eyes—yet another spectacular sign of MI spirit.

Thus, just as he does when he learns of a novel application of MI in practice, he marvels aloud about MI research, describing himself as "amazed" and "astonished" with the publication of more and more studies. ("It's gone so far beyond anything I ever imagined already that I'm just happy to curiously watch where it goes next you know," Miller once told me). For Miller, then, although the growing number of RCTs cannot demonstrate the behavioral outcomes for clients that he hopes for and believes in, they nevertheless are evidence of MI's transformative effect on research professionals who, like their practitioner brethren, take MI as vocation.

Miller's faith in MI is indeed bolstered by these research professionals—including his spirit-filled former student and current collaborator, Dr. Theresa Moyers—who share his sense of awe and go further to transform that awe into scientific action. For her part, Moyers could "care *less*" about questions like, "Is CBT [cognitive behavioral therapy] better than DBT [dialectical behavior therapy]?" that drive those who conduct RCTs. As a process researcher, she instead asks, "When you *have* an efficacious treatment like MI or like CBT or like 12-step, *why* does it work?" Moyers's sheer devotion to this question is clear by her own description: "One contribution I think I make to the world of MI is a focus on *process* and answering questions about *why* things work. [I'm] *very* interested in causal mechanism like *what* makes this treatment work. I just *live* for that." Note that what the RCTs have failed to definitely show, Moyers does not question—that MI *works*. She has faith, if not proof, that it does. Her question, one that she is devoted to and indeed *"lives for,"* is *how*, not whether or to what extent, MI works.

As a member of the same proverbial congregation as Moyers, Miller wagers that there is much more MI research to come, telling me: "I wish there were studies on this or that or the other thing. It's probably gonna happen." (In a recent email exchange, he reported that the number of RCTs has grown to a remarkable 1,969.) Miller will undoubtedly keep counting trials and closely tracking new ways to study MI, taking the NREPP's nomination of MI as an "evidence-based practice" not as an end, but only the beginning. After all, for the kind of MI science Moyers does, *the very lack* of definitive evidence of the method's efficacy is less a threat to continued research on MI than a condition of possibility. As Miller also tactfully points out, "gold standard" studies tend to be "black-boxed," requiring other researchers to open them. That is, RCTs are singularly intent on producing certain conclusions without adequate investment in the intricacies of how and why a method is more or less efficacious. Pointing to these limitations, with no sign of disdain, Miller summed up this scientific ethos as, "We did MI and here's the outcome," while critically adding, "But you never quite know what you're looking at because, without fidelity measures, you don't know if MI was really done." This is another important aspect of Moyers's work, which will be detailed below.

···

As historian of religion Christopher Grasso (2002; 2018) argues, skepticism has been integral to American Protestantism since the Revolution, as adherents strained to show that they arrived at their faith not by way of blind adherence to doctrine, but rather through continual questioning and doubt. This skepticism rendered their faith both rational and genuine in the eyes of others. Just as doubt plays a constitutive role in Protestant faith, so too is it integral to the production of science, as other scholars have shown (for instance, Latour 1999). It is no wonder, then, that, rather than making excuses for intervention scientists' failure to produce evidence of MI's efficacy across hundreds of RCTs, Miller carefully stokes skepticism. He does so not only by "wishing for" more studies of the same kind, but also by pointing to gaps and unanswered questions. By his own description, he takes these research questions to be both mystical and empirical, as do the many researchers who "live to" answer them. Thus, if state bureaucrats with less than rigorous politico-scientific standards are the ones who issue passports, it is the faithful work of MINTies—researchers as much as trainers— that keeps the method moving.

MI SCIENCE: THE GIFT THAT KEEPS GIVING

In the world of MI, an "open question" is as productive in research as it is in practice (see chapter 2) in that it never fails to be taken up as an invitation to investigate further. The hundreds of MINT members who are active researchers are not only intent to produce more and more RCTs, which test MI in an ever widening range of applications in search of a definitive outcome variable; they are also highly motivated and well equipped to investigate questions that RCTs are not designed to answer. This includes the kind of questions Moyers details above, questions about the "active ingredients" of MI. Furthermore, RCTs themselves necessitate fidelity research to assure that professionals enrolled have requisite MI "skills" and "spirit"—that is, whether the MI being tested in RCTs is in fact *genuine* MI. Hence Moyers's complementary line of research, developing and testing MI-specific fidelity instruments, work she has been doing for over twenty years.

As we learned in chapter 3, fidelity instruments like the Motivational Interviewing Treatment Integrity Code (MITI) are used prolifically *in practice* to assess practitioners MI "skills" and "spirit," and to coach them accordingly. These very same instruments are central technologies for evaluating MI practitioners enrolled in research studies. Fidelity research is fed back into the continual refinement of the MITI, which is now in its fourth edition (Moyers, Manuel & Ernst 2014). The evolving MITI itself is the subject of ongoing scientific study.[18] And as if Moyers and her fellow MI researchers did not already have their hands full, the MITI is hardly the only MI-specific fidelity instrument used in research that has itself become a subject of research. For instance, the Motivational Interviewing Skills Code (Miller & Mount 2001) is a fidelity instrument that more comprehensively and exhaustively assesses MI sessions by examining client and interviewer behavior in tandem and has itself been subject to evaluation.[19] All told, MINT recognizes nine fidelity instruments designed to evaluate specific applications of MI, including the two already mentioned, and makes them available on the organization's website.[20]

Note the propagating quality of MI research: it is not simply that the number of RCTs continues to grow, or even that this growth necessitates the study of therapists enrolled in those trials. It is also that a single study spawns many new studies, some of which retroactively evaluate the original study's integrity, while others seek to test if not duplicate results with another set of variables; others still aggregate their findings in meta-analyses. And all of them proliferate into even more MI science. In this sense, each MI study—with its built-in limitations and ever open questions—is like a gift that keeps on giving.

In addition to begetting more scholarly labor, MI research also concertedly reinvests in and works to reinvigorate MI practice. This is particularly true for process research, which ferrets out *which qualities* of MI matter in its delivery: how often or in what order particular speech acts are deployed, the length of the session, the ratio of client to practitioner speech, the perceived tone in which the interviewer speaks, or something else. Since the time of Carl Rogers, isolating and evaluating component parts and qualities is considered of utmost importance to process researchers, particularly in the early stages of a therapy's life. As Miller put it, any counseling method is "bound to include some superstitious stuff that doesn't really matter," leaving it to researchers to decipher "what are the pieces [that do] really matter." For Moyers, this not only means identifying the key qualities of MI, but also "trying to find ways to quantify" them so as to "reliably *decide* whether people are doing MI or not and whether they're hitting quality markers." And, while this is easier for MI "skills" (such as open questions or amplified reflections) that are easily countable, it is far more challenging with respect to MI spirit, although this has hardly stopped Moyers, her colleagues, and her students from trying.

Indeed, spirit appears to be the most satisfying subject of Moyers's voracious scientific appetite, as illustrated by the sample questions she rattled off as we talked in her lab office:

> OK, how does [spirit] translate into practice? What is different about what you do? And if there is something different, umm, do you keep that? Do you consistently use it across different situations? When is it easy for you; when is it hard? And once you get it, do you hang onto it? Or does it *decay*? And if it does decay, how can we keep it from decaying? And what do you need? What do clinicians really need to be able to acquire and keep and consistently use better psychotherapy skills, you know, in general, but MI in particular?

By this account, MI spirit can be kept, transported, rendered easier or harder to use; it can even "*decay*." And, as it turns out, MI's perishability is of increasing concern to Moyers as the method's distribution channels continue to widen. As she admitted to me, "I worry that MI—and I *see* it all the time. [MI] becomes watered down and it . . . and it *loses* its, uh . . . *essence*."

For this reason, Moyers is especially dedicated to feeding her findings back into *MI training*, the means of delivering fresh and wholesome MI. As she explains it, to the extent that researchers can identify which elements of the method are critical, they also decipher what must be emphasized by trainers. Moyers's research has therefore gone further, studying the best ways to train practitioners in MI. The overarching goal that continually drives her multifaceted MI research program is, as she puts it, "improving people's acquisition of MI." Moyers therefore conducts trainings for MI trainers on a regular basis. This includes being centrally involved in the MINT Forum and the annual Training New Trainers (TNT), where she and her fellow researchers give plenary talks and circulate in smaller sessions, updating trainers on the latest developments in fidelity instruments. Moyers realizes that she needs to work closely with trainers not only to preserve the quality of MI, but also to potentially improve it.

Simmel (1978) famously argued that commodities do not circulate because they are inherently valuable, but rather gain value over the course of their travels—an idea that inspired many anthropological studies of circulation (for instance, Appadurai 1986). This may help explain the "costs" Moyers associates with MI's distribution, as well as her ongoing efforts to distill and preserve the very best qualities of the method:

> I would rather spend my time on focusing on: how do I increase quality and how do I *distill* the active ingredients of this treatment; how do I find that out? As opposed to *concerning* myself or censoring or trying to *limit* what I consider bad practice from other people because, even though I would like to, the *cost* of that is too high.

The economic register of Moyers's description seems, in some ways, to confirm Rollnick's worries that American scientists have turned MI into a product. And although Moyers also admits that she "would like to"—if she could—"limit" what she considers "bad [MI] practice," she chooses freedom, if not a free market itself, intimating instead that imposing limits would amount to "censor[ship]." True to MI form, Moyers refuses to try to partition politics, economics, and MI science, framing MI in such a way that it can be seen as *valuable* in all of these ways at once.

If MI's most devoted American daughter might rankle her delinquent UK-based brother by speaking of the method as a product, she insists that she and her scientific colleagues reap no profit. As Moyers underscored, she readily *gives away* the products of her labor: "Somebody will come to me and they'll say: 'Well, can I have your [PowerPoint] slides?' Or 'can I have your videos or can I use your . . . whatever?' And I will say: '*Yes*, of course you can.'" She also pointed me toward the coding instruments and training materials she and her colleagues have developed that are open source, even if MI training films—many starring Moyers herself—are on sale for $275 on the very same site. The substantial costs of MI training notwithstanding, Moyers maintained that MI spreads not because of its profit potential, but rather because of an economic ethos that disregards that potential. As she put it: "A *lot* of why MI is the way it is in the world is because it's gotten given away and people haven't hoarded it. They've been intellectually *free* with it."

The qualifier of "freedom" here is notable, suggesting that Moyers thinks of her own and others' MI research as *a gift*, not because of the actual terms and effects of MI's exchange, but because of the spirit in which it is "given away" (see Mauss 2016). Thus, while we learned in chapter 3 how spirit and profit are reconciled in MI, here we see how the labor of science contributes to that reconciliation. In this portrait of MI's economy, scientific products are exchanged with a spirit of generosity that expresses and continually strengthens communal bonds. As Moyers framed it:

> One of the things I learned from Bill was a model of thinking about the world in a *very generous way*. When you are the recipient of that sort of generosity, you—you are *transformed* by it. I acquired this model of the— of the *intellectual* world being very abundant and a sense that you—you, you, mustn't hoard. And that you really are [5 second pause] *obligated* to give away as much of your intellectual capital as you can. And that . . . *fears* of doing that—are artificial and, and stunting.

This "model of thinking about the world" stands in remarkable contrast to Rollnick's portrait of scientific profiteers. As Moyers understands it, the "*intellectual* world" of American MI is one in which the receipt of a gift transforms into an "*obligation*" to give that gift away. The refusal to do so— particularly amid "great abundance"— is not only a matter of individual greed among those inclined to hoard (intellectual) capital; it is also stunting of an (intellectual) "world."

This very same "model" appears in MINT's 2007 organizational survey of "MINT Values." The survey, "What Does It Mean to Be a MINTie?" asked members to complete the sentence: "being a MINTie means . . ." The top five responses, as reported by the *MINT Bulletin*, include: "Sharing of ideas, information, resources and experiences" (no. 1);. "Becoming a bee rather than a fly" (no. 3); and "Demonstrating generosity of spirit in communications" (no. 5). And while Moyers says this spirit of generosity is a "*direct* legacy of Bill," she did not forget his younger brother across the pond. "And I think it comes directly from Steve—from Bill *and* Steve. Steve, Steve as well, is the kind of person who believes in giving things away and *not* hoarding them and . . . you know . . . has a really egalitarian approach to the dissemination of MI."

It is hard to know the extent to which Moyers is aware of Rollnick's criticism of American MI, not to mention how much he implicates specific US-based researchers in his critical portraiture. But, however much it might frustrate Rollnick, Moyers effectively refuses a distinction between the profits generated from MI research and training, and generosity as pinnacle expression of MI spirit. More remarkable still, by discursively infusing free-dom and generosity into product and profits, Moyers deftly unites the di-vergent political and economic stances of Miller and Rollnick. In doing so, she shows us again how even the most potentially divisive lines in MI are troubled as soon as they are drawn.

. .

As Mauss (2016) long ago taught us, gifts are never simply freely given. What we might readily interpret as the "spirit" of the gift-giver instead resides in the "spirit" or "hau" of *gift given*, which is ultimately what bonds the per-son who gives and the one who receives. Gifts must therefore be returned or passed along in recognizable ways in order to continue to preserve the spirit that resides within the gift itself, which also reinforces and possibly extends the circuit of gift exchange. Generosity is thus always also a matter of economy: solidifying and expanding the relations of exchange. This is not to diminish my own impression, which is that, alongside Moyers's far longer and more proximate experience in the world of North American MI, generosity is highly valued among MINTies. I witnessed, firsthand, how generosity is enacted by way of shared PowerPoint slides, tips on potential training contracts, and lengthy responses to questions or quandaries posed on the MINT listserv; I myself rarely had an email that was not promptly returned or a request for an interview that was denied. That said, the value of generosity is always economic as well as affective and spiritual. I have no doubt that both Miller and Moyers—if not Rollnick—would agree.

Indeed, as gift-givers have long realized, perhaps from the beginning of what anthropologists call "culture," generosity is a necessary ingredient in any economy, including economies characterized by radical inequality. And, as readers may by now predict, MI's spirit of generosity includes refusing the normative distinctions that elevate some forms of knowledge over others and that symbolically differentiate classes of professionals accordingly.

TOTAL QUALITY MI: BRIDGING THE
PRACTICE-RESEARCH DIVIDE

Moyers understands that her devotion to preserving "the essence" of MI as it is disseminated across an increasingly populous and expansive pro-fessional terrain is a potentially fraught line of business. For one thing, her work is undeniably evaluative. As she put it, "in some ways, [my work] *is* a quality control." While these bald commercial terms didn't seem to faze Moyers, she was quick to add a pregnant clarification: "I mean, I wouldn't call [myself] the *police*." This suggests that if there is one lexicon that Moyers is intent to avoid, it is a carceral one.

Moyers's qualification recalls a comment made by Norman, equipped as he was with one of the quality control instruments Moyers has worked so hard to develop. "MINTies don't like policing people," Norman once told me, as he recounted his struggles with his role as a MI coder and therefore MINT gatekeeper. Like police, who guard the state and private property against deviant behavior among those cast as outsiders by that very defense, Norman prevents some professionals' entry into the ranks of MINT, by designating whether or not they are "MI-competent." That irony was very probably not lost on him, as a former/reformed parole officer himself.

However, as we have seen over the course of this book, evaluation—in and of itself—is hardly perceived as problematic in the world of MI. Becoming a MINTie requires not only that one become acutely reflexive, but also that one be open to the surveillance of others. Indeed, well after they pass through coders' gates, MINTies continue to monitor each other's behavior. The TNT and MINT Forum offer plenty of opportunities for more role-plays and real-plays, with participants offering up their skills and spirit to their colleagues' evaluations.

That said, Moyers surely knows that she conducts her assessments in a professionally variegated field, composed of university-based researchers, MINT trainers, aspiring MINT trainers, and practitioners of various stripes (from doctors and clinical psychologists to nurses and social workers). She is likely also keenly aware that the EBP movement has heightened sensitivities about the research-practice divide, with critics charging that researchers are lording their knowledge over practitioners and working to direct them accordingly.[21] This includes Steve Rollnick, who worried aloud in his interview with me that MI, particularly *North American* MI, assigns researchers and practitioners to structurally unequal positions. Such divisions pose a threat to MI's self-image as a quintessentially egalitarian practice, as well as to its "both/and" ethos.

As it turns out, just as North American MI is intent to symbolically level unequal relations between professional interviewers and client interviewees, it strives to defuse perceived class differences among MINTed professionals. One such strategy is presaged by Moyers's characterization of her work as "quality control"—a marketized term that at once confirms Rollnick's political economic critique of North American MI and intriguingly complicates it. Notably, over the last forty years, American ideas about quality control have been influenced by Total Quality Management (TQM), an outgrowth of Taylorism that originated in the American Navy in the early 1980s, contemporaneous with the rise of MI.

While I certainly have no reason to believe that Moyers, Miller, or other prominent US-based MINTies draw directly from TQM, their organizing principles, logics, and ideological effects are strikingly similar. TQM's central idea is that everyone involved in production should devote themselves to their product, not just by preserving its quality but by continually improving it based on the vagaries of consumer demand. Responsibility for the quality of a product, then, is widely distributed and shared, ideologically if not practically, among workers, without obviating specialized roles in production. As Elizabeth Dunn (2004) has argued, in fostering identification with a product no matter one's actual role in the production or profit of it, TQM can both maintain and efface structural inequities between workers.[22]

As in the US-owned Polish factories that Dunn studied, MI has been remarkably successful in stimulating uniform investment in the "essence" of MI across elite university labs, posh private practices, and those who train MI in the trenches of social work, nursing, or corrections. And whatever the actual division of labor, US-based MINTies generally speak of themselves as working on a nonhierarchical terrain where interdependent specializations in knowledge production and dissemination are functionally necessary rather than reflections of structural inequities, especially given the increasing demand for MI. For instance, when speaking of his training contracts, one MINTie from a small southern state said, "Some of these organizations are expecting hard data now . . . you've got to make the evidence case."

Trainers like this do indeed depend on the labor of MI researchers, if not necessarily in the way that so troubles Rollnick. Rather, MI researchers' work provides material they can use to lace their PowerPoint presentations with "evidence" and even "hard data" that will help ensure that the contracts will keep coming.[23] It is no wonder, then, that across every MI training I studied signs of science are readily apparent. Trainers may project slides in which MI skills and spirit are tidily unpacked into bullet points, as well as slides with inspirational quotes from Pascal, Lao-Tse, Gandhi, or Miller. Other slides have embedded AVI clips of Rounder, Ponytail John, or the "Committed Smoker," and instructions for role-playing exercises. Still others display cartoons or memes that generate laughs, project charisma, and demonstrate sympathy with the challenges their professional audiences face. However, invariably, there are also slides citing recently published studies, summarizing their findings, and displaying percentages, pie charts, and even p-values—the unmistakable signs of science.

An analysis of MINT's communications reveals efforts to calibrate and coordinate MI research, training, and practice, while carefully avoiding projecting that there is anything stratified about this division of labor. Consider, for instance, that the *MINT Bulletin*—an online publication written by and addressed to members, if also publicly available—juxtaposes reports on the latest research studies, reflections on training MI skills and spirit, and bits of whimsy, in no predictable order.[24] In a regular opening feature titled, "From the Desert," Miller offers his thoughts on research, practice, and training as if these activities are not just naturally interrelated, but also equally valuable. Like his public addresses, the column is typically jam-packed with the latest research findings, presented in an easy, highly digestible, conversational register, alongside poetic renderings of MI spirit. In one case, Miller's discussion of horse-whisperer Monty Roberts (with whom he shares an interest in the mystical elements of communication) is immediately followed by news of the latest "significant but modest" meta-analytic research findings on the effect of "one dose" of MI on behavior change.

Another regular feature of the *Bulletin* is a running column titled, "What the Research Says . . ." which is apparently an effort to keep all MINTies abreast of the latest indexes of MI's scientific identity. However, lest an uninitiated trainer-reader think they are in for a lecture, they soon find that MI research "says" precisely what they want to hear, with the sentence completed across issues: "About Training, Part II," "About Change Talk, Part III," and "About the MI 'Spirit' and the 'Competence Worldview.'" Reflective columns on training and practice return the favor, frequently closing with reference lists that include recently published or widely cited MI research articles. These are inscriptions of a familiar ethos: while MINTies may have particular areas of specialization, they share equal interest in and responsibility for the production and dissemination of their method.

Social gatherings of US-based MINTies, whether mediated by listservs and Facebook groups or in person, seem like their PowerPoint presentations brought to life, given their remarkable hybridity. Their conversation is as thick with mention of the latest publications on MI—including the most recent studies in academic journals—as with colorful and sometimes hilarious accounts of people's most recent training endeavors. At the packed and jovial bar scene at the MINT Forum I attended, for instance, those whom I knew to have PhDs and elite university posts engaged in lively exchanges with the full-time trainers, not infrequently toasting to a successful session they had co-led earlier in the day. And though there are high-profile and "cool kid" cliques within the organization, some of which inspire quiet if persistent grumbling, these seem mainly to be formed by the extent rather than the kind of participation in the organization. It is no wonder, then, that a striking number of MINTies identify as *both* researchers *and* practitioners, using terms like "scientist practitioner" to describe themselves.[25] According to a 2007 organizational survey, 61 percent of MINT's membership characterized themselves as "involved in research," and 100 percent identified as practitioners.[26] It is as if the cultural and institutional division of "research" and "practice" simply dissolves in the displayed sociality and identity of MINTies.

Nonetheless, there are sometimes disparaging whispers about MINT's "inner circle," whose members tend to be those with PhDs if not with active research careers. But all seem to agree that refusing the antinomy of research and practice, and the division of researchers and practitioners, ultimately benefits everyone. After all, MI trainers exponentially expand MI researchers' audiences, as they display their latest findings to the legions of helping professionals they train. In turn, MI researchers provide MI trainers with signs of scientific authority and the credibility they need to maintain an entrepreneurial living, including those who have been left stranded by the advent of the evidence-based practice. Among the stranded are the many humanist psychologists within MINT, who once struggled mightily to relay authoritative knowledge, and now find their humanism empowered by MI science.

HUMANISM'S EVIDENCE-BASE

In 1959, the British novelist and chemist C. P. Snow famously lamented that the "two cultures" of science and humanism had become so bounded, so circumscribed in their intellectual concerns, so orthodox in their epistemological commitments and methods of engagement, that even his most learned colleagues could not find a way to communicate across them. In the US context as well, the "two cultures" problem is readily evident in the way American higher education and academic disciplines have been organized and institutionalized.[27] Professions, and the helping professions more particularly, reflect this division. Yet, while Snow's main goal was to encourage interdisciplinarity, he also worried that scientific reasoning might be getting short shrift.

The current state of American psychology—in its academic if not its professional manifestation—suggests just the opposite. As a discipline, American psychology was once identified with philosophy and even mysticism (as evidenced by the prominence of William James), and humanistic psychologies enjoyed significant prominence in the mid- to late twentieth century, as epitomized by Carl Rogers. At the same time, US-based MINTies train in a time when scientific reasoning enjoys far more authoritative status, institutional stability, and economic rewards than humanism, as a more proximate critic has recently bemoaned.[28] Indeed, recall that Rollnick worries not only about the marketization of MI by way of the evidence-based practice movement, but about its *dehumanization* as well. For him, contemporary American psychology is as "deluded" by science as it is driven by profit.

In the meantime, Moyers, as one of MI's best known American psychologists and research scientists, explains the method's successful dissemination, first and foremost, in terms of its humanistic qualities rather than its scientific efficacy. She even concedes that there are some things about MI that are probably "just not measurable." Interested in my question of why MI has spread the way it has, Moyers explained with much animation, even hitting the table we were sitting at for emphasis: "I really think that's what has made MI so—so *attractive* and so *sexy* to people is that it's . . . *permission* to *explicitly* focus on what is really tremendously fundamental . . . just to pay attention to the relationship and the experience the person's having when they're with you."

In so saying, Moyers rips a page right out of the humanistic tradition of American psychology, grounded in the work of Rogers and concertedly developed by MI (see chapter 1). Particularly in the evidence-based era, the ability of MI's proponents to accommodate both science and humanism surely accounts for the sizeable number of US-based MINTies who were trained in the humanist tradition. What is more, these MINTies gladly adopt MI's scientific identity as an EBP *so as to* bolster and even propel their humanism.

Consider Vernon, a long-time devotee of Carl Rogers who worked as a lead staff psychologist at a large VA hospital, when I met him at the 2014 MINT Forum. After my plenary address, he approached me to say he thought MI's pragmatism more akin to the work of Peirce and Dewey than indebted to William James, whose picture I'd displayed on a slide as I offered an early version of my thinking about MI's vernacular pragmatism (see chapter 5).[29] Intrigued by this comments, we agreed to meet for an interview the next day—an engagement that ended up having little to do with Peirce and Dewey, but nevertheless proved to be most enlightening.

If clearly more of a pragmatist than a positivist, Vernon began by telling me that not long after the "evidence-based" paradigm found its way from British medicine into social services in the United States, he recognized that his colleagues—especially the young interns he trained—were increasingly questioning his Rogers-informed, humanist leanings. This was in large part because those leanings were hard to quantify. By the early 2000s, the concerted demand for an "evidence-base" of practice convinced Vernon that he was losing professional standing. As he put it in our interview: "research-

driven therapists don't really admit that there's anything of value in anything which is not research-driven," resulting in "whole areas [of practice]
that, kind of, have gotten eliminated."

Yet Vernon eventually found his professional standing rehabilitated. This
occurred when EBP morphed from a model of expert decision-making that
asked practitioners to search through the "best available evidence" to in-
form their clinical decisions, into a complex system of legitimation that
designates particular methods and, by extension, their practitioners *as*
"evidence-based." Luckily for Vernon, and as we know, one such method
was MI, and his sense of gratitude was unmistakable. For if he was not
nearly as spiritually enchanted with MI as Norman or Susan, he felt philosophically rescued and resuscitated by the method. Vernon now simply
calls his Rogerian-informed practice "MI," thereby legitimating his work
and his professional standing accordingly. As he put it:

> I feel like MI let me reclaim some of the humanistic parts of myself and I
> can couch it in the s— the spirit of research and empiricism. I could say
> [to colleagues and interns]: "this is an *evidence-based treatment* that I do."
> You know: "if you want to learn it, you can. It's *evidence-based*." And so,
> to me, [MI] meets this need for being able to teach humanistic values and
> methods without, um, being thought of as a weirdo.

Vernon's commentary is striking for several reasons. First, it suggests that
the evidence-based paradigm opens up rather than forecloses discretion in
his own practice and in his training of other professionals. This runs counter
to critics who charge that EBP eclipses the practice knowledge of helping
professionals and their organizations—curtailing professional autonomy,
however unevenly.[30] Vernon also proposes that some might find themselves
legitimated and empowered by EBP's hierarchy of evidence, which many
critics charge is itself exclusionary.[31]

Second, Vernon's comments underscore that EBP is a *legitimizing* discourse. As he makes clear, it is MI's status as *"evidence-based practice"*
that turns "weirdos" into experts and empiricizes humanistic values and
methods (see Storeng & Béhague 2014). Vernon recognizes, along with
Sandra Tanenbaum, that EBP is a "public idea" (Tanenbaum 2005) with
considerable rhetorical strength, its political power outweighing "its improvement of mental [and behavioral] health practice" (Tanenbaum 2003,
287). Vernon, after all, did not change his practice but rather changed how
he frames it, since "the cause of science is widely meaningful and easy to
adopt" (Tanenbaum 2003, 296).[32] Vernon is one of countless MI trainers for
whom the term "evidence" has offered compelling new ways to frame their

labor, legitimize their expertise, and even expand their professional jurisdiction.

The ways that political and economic discourses bolster a scientific one
in the public framing of EBP are also not lost on Vernon. He presciently
noted: "I think that the rhetoric of science, ya know, you declare that MI
is an EBP and then and then . . . 'Wait a minute! It's even *cheap* to do and
doesn't take much time.' It's like, you know, everybody wants to get on
board." By this account, if government bureaucracies register cost-effective
treatments as evidence-based ones, Vernon is just one of many who benefit
from the state's economic calculus.

Vernon is hardly the only MINTie who sees the multiple values in "the
rhetoric of science," if critiquing its underpinnings in the meantime. As
another proud adherent of the humanist tradition of American psychotherapy, Rex, the clinical psychologist and former chair of MINT whom we
met in the last chapter, provided a science-laced historical account of MI's
ascendance. By Rex's account, while "psychology as a discipline is often
caught in the identity of whether we are science or whether we are art," the
latter side had started losing significant ground by the "late nineties, [when]
the evidence-based movement was—you know—*taking over* psychology."
During the same period, Rex—like Vernon—also found *himself* losing professional credibility in an increasingly scientized field. "Here I was doing
kinds of therapy that were increasingly being, if not marginalized, were
being threatened with marginalization," Rex explained, "because they had
no evidence-base . . . blah, blah, blah." And in case I had missed the dismis-
sive tone in which he animated the scientific colleagues who marginalized
him, he added: "My view at that time was, empirical quantitative research
tells us absolutely nothing. That it's a whole bunch of crap."

As we have learned, such starkly partisan views have little room in
MI, and once Rex was thoroughly socialized as a MINTie, he came to
see the value of what he once dismissed as "crap." As he explained, "I was
mostly talking about, you know, empathy"—a classic humanistic topic in
psychology—"but [now] I could also have [PowerPoint] slides showing,
you know, '*differential* efficacy' that I knew, you know, would make it impossible for people to just dismiss it. That was incredibly empowering." By
"empowering," Rex not only meant more training contracts, higher professional status, and a dramatically enlarged professional community in which
he was widely considered a leader. The rhetoric of science, and more specially of EBP, also potently reframed and legitimated what he was already
primed to practice and train, mobilizing his longstanding intellectual and
philosophical commitments to humanist ideals.

Note that Rex did not become any less of a humanist or any more of a scientist through his affiliation with MI. Rather, MI propelled him forward by allowing him to combine what he—like legions of his fellow American psychologists—once held apart. As with the method itself, MINTies like Vernon and Rex discover the generative energy of defusing cultural opposition, answering "both/and" to "either/or." And, by his own description, it is precisely in his embrace of MI as *both* humanistic *and* scientific that Rex "matured" as a MINTie: "I've become a lot less 'anti' *everything* over the years."

Still, it was apparent that Rex remained relatively uninterested in the substance of MI intervention research. Like Vernon and many of his other fellow MINTies, he took the most important question to be not what the evidence for MI *is*, but rather what the "evidence" *can do*, finding the latter well worth defending. As chair of MINT, he also became a master of rhetorically bundling and therefore bolstering MI's evidence-base. So, if Rex first proposed in our 2014 interview that "I think if you can demonstrate that MI is better than nothing; is better than a placebo kind of intervention and that it's as good as another, you know, evidence . . . to me that should be plenty," he quickly and enthusiastically acknowledged that more legitimation was always needed. In a kind of call and response, using those legitimating terms that I had—at that late date in the study—heard dozens of times, Rex and I recited:

> REX: If it's briefer . . .
> ESC: and more *efficient* . . .
> REX: Then that's/
> ESC: and more *cost* effective!
> REX: Right!
> ESC: Then . . .
> REX: Then it's a good argument.

From this exchange, one might hastily conclude that Rex has become living proof of Steve Rollnick's worries, with which this chapter opened. After all, in this especially candid account—one that Rollnick would surely call very *American*—valuable therapeutic qualities or "common factors," like empathy, are seemingly left in the dust as researchers demonstrate that MI is "better than nothing," which is cast as "plenty." In our exchange, Rex is not troubled that MI's status as "evidence-based" is only tangentially related to science, depending instead on the method's efficiency and cost-effectiveness, with economics the basis of a "good argument." For in addition to its more tangible gains, MI science allows MI humanism to move forward, and this is arguably enough to compel some US-based MINTies to embrace it.

Rex ended our scaffolding of evidence to brevity, efficiency, and cost-effectiveness with a declaration: "clearly" all of this is "an important part of why MI has, you know, disseminated so fast." Given the plasticity of MI's "evidence-base," it is no wonder so many MI trainers reference it during their training regardless of their own affinities. Casting their practice as "evidence-based" can powerfully extend their discretion and bolster their expertise, regardless of what they actually do in practice. Indeed, those who participated in this study before 2016 had plenty of reason to feel that the legitimation of evidence was working as it should, including on behalf of professional trainers and proponents of MI.

Notably, however, the antiscience sentiments of the Trump administration and the public he roused led to the freezing, defunding, and suspension of the NREPP during his first year in office. Soon after it was dismantled by the Trump administration in January 2018, the NREPP found a new home at the Pew Foundation, where it is now archived. And while the future of EBP will need to be tracked (see Carr & Norwood 2022), new actors and institutions will doubtlessly continue to emerge, and that relations and rhetoric will adjust accordingly, so as to (re)legitimate the evidence of evidence-based practice.

CONCLUSION: INTERNAL CRITIQUE
AND ITS CRITICAL DEFUSAL

Some might say that William Miller himself is a study in contradictions. Considering the lack of tension in his self-presentation, he is better characterized as a personification of radical nonpartisanship. His own long and prolific career as a research scientist, whose work is guided by positivist reasoning, has done nothing to quell his enduring mystical sensibilities, penned in his ample writings on horse-whispering, Christian spirituality, and "quantum change." And it is not just across his voluminous writings, but also within his best-known work on motivational interviewing, that one finds the marriage of mystical and humanistic with scientific thinking. With evident relish, he describes himself in turn as a "dustbowl empiricist," a "humanist," and a "mystic."

This way of being and doing many things at once allows MINTies of various stripes and proclivities to be moved by Miller. For instance, I spoke to MI researchers—some of them former students of Miller—who are appreciative of and indebted to his empiricism. They respect him as a "vocal proponent of meta-analytic science" who is nevertheless intent to keep their eyes on the way the "real world works." And then there were those like Vernon, who described Miller as "like this heroic figure that battles the forces of the rigid empiricism." What is more, both parties appreciated that there is more to Miller than the qualities that personally and professionally drew them to him. Indeed, Vernon was quick to qualify his knight-in-armor rendering: "Now I think [Miller is] very, very identified with the values of rigid empiricism, but, but, but . . . I do think that [his humanism] is a really central thing about him to me. He makes [it] possible to be humanist in a way that's acceptable." Miller, like his method, is insistently "both/and," a quality that clearly resonates with his acolytes.

While Miller himself embodies the nonpartisan sensibility of MI, attracting and mobilizing a wide range of North American professionals accordingly, his two primary interlocutors up the ante of MI's "both/and" way of moving through the world. After all, it was Rollnick who coined the term "spirit," only to worry aloud that it has emboldened MI's most ruthless American profiteers. And if Rollnick launches trenchant critiques of MI's productization in the hands of American intervention scientists, Moyers, as MI's most productive American intervention scientist, counters that MI is free because of the "spirit" in which it is given, a spirit that is modeled. What is more, she specifically attributes MI's model of generosity to the man who insists that American market interests are infecting MI's integrity, with researchers (like her?) knee-deep in the corruption. And while Rollnick airs his attempts to save MI from American capitalism, Miller professes that these profits are born of the faith of MI's proponents and are therefore yet another sign of the method's abiding spirit. Nonetheless, the three continue to write, train, and interact with one another.

Faith and what the MI faithful call "spirit" insistently accompany skepticism and science in North American MI, understandably befuddling and raising the suspicions of outside observers, who sometimes have good reason to cling to their convictions. Here again, we are confronted with the conservatism of MI's defusal of ideological opposition. After all, Miller's insistent refusal to take sides, and remarkable ability to enjoy some culturally troubling opposition both ways at once, stands in marked contrast to Rollnick's strident critique. And whether or not one agrees with Rollnick's charge or is inclined to challenge its premise or even quibble with its factual details, there is something to be said (if not always lauded) for taking a side in a charged political debate. The loaded politics and economics of North American intervention science and its shaping of social and behavioral service provision are certainly no exception.

Inviting the loyalty of some and raising the suspicions of others, parti-

sanship gains little traction in MI. Its values, ideals, and modes of authority paradoxically blend, remaining elusive to well-trodden lines of critique,
even those that are launched from within the method's highest ranks. While
we might understandably worry about what happens when a critical and
oppositional stance is defused, the following chapter addresses the philosophy of knowledge that allows paradox to thrive, and which cultivates another kind of critical sensibility—one that is rigorously and unrelentingly
pragmatic and refuses final answers to difficult questions.

CHAPTER 5

American Pragmatism

Learning to Work the Difference
(Or, the Life and Death of MI)

Since education is not a means to living, but is identical with the operation of living a life which is fruitful and inherently significant, the only ultimate value which can be set up is just the process of living itself. And this is not an end to which studies and activities are subordinate means; it is the whole of which they are ingredients.

JOHN DEWEY, *Democracy and Education* (1922, 281)

Having announced by way of a group email nine days earlier that he was moving across the country to deal with pressing family affairs, Ki prepared for what would be his last meeting with his U-Haven apprentices. I sat with him in his spacious if decidedly unglamorous third-floor office as he sifted through large stacks of files and greeted devastated-looking colleagues who stopped by for brief visits, having heard news of his resignation. Ki acknowledged more than once how difficult it was to leave his job as a clinical supervisor at U-Haven. He was also clearly distressed to let go of the advanced MI training that he had instituted and that I had been studying at U-Haven. The training was nine months into its planned full-year course. He wondered aloud whether to extend the last session an additional hour, finally deciding that it would only prolong the inevitable transition, which promised to be "painful" for all involved.

Since the preceding October, Ki had met monthly for two-hour training sessions with U-Haven apprentices, all of whom he had carefully selected from a pool of almost three times as many applicants. No matter the various reasons for joining the training, they had all shown significant investment—though to varying degrees—in the array of training activities that Ki planned for them. And while on the first day of the training, most had expressed their interest in MI as a sharpened if not entirely new instrument in their proverbial professional "toolkit" (see chapter 2), six months in, some were professing a decidedly noninstrumentalist trust in the method. For instance, even before she started her coaching with Norman (see chapter 3), Libby lauded MI as "just a whole new way of thinking" that made her feel "hopeful" about the future of her labor, even if she did not feel remarkably more equipped with new tools or tricks of the trade.

As Ki knew well, having faith in any method is not easy at U-Haven, where the problems with which professionals are charged are so severe that they both demand and elude ready resolution. Most pressingly, U-Haven is a site of life and death, where professionals, including those in Ki's training, feel both desperate to succeed and sometimes destined to fail. Working in the harm-reduction/housing-first model meant that while the dangers of open-air drug use could be mitigated to a great extent, overdoses—including fatal ones—sometimes occurred within the physical and proverbial walls of the organization. As for more routine matters, on the last Friday of every month, U-Haven workers who served as "representative payees" held their breath as they handed over SSI checks, waiting to see if the recipients made it back to U-Haven sites having exchanged rent and food money for goods and services that could do serious harm to themselves or others.[1] Common, too, was professional consternation about having the same conversation with the same clients for months on end—practically begging one to see a doctor for an obviously worsening health condition, while beseeching another to visit the Social Security office to register for due benefits—without resolution and with no immediate consequences to impose. And then there were the bedbugs that, no matter what protocols and instructions U-Haven professionals issued to client residents, seemed to come from everywhere and have nowhere else to go (see Carr 2015).

If these problems have radically different stakes and consequences, they have two qualities in common: they have no clearly discernible cause and seemingly have no discrete end. Even the death of one client by overdose, suicide, or an untreated medical illness was a reminder that others would follow. Thus, to sustain their work, U-Haven professionals had to refocus the ethos of doing *good*, with "good" understood as a discrete goal to which professional action is intentionally directed. They had to invest instead in the *media res* of practice—or, *doing* good—which meant actively abiding by the principle that "an end . . . is nothing but the interaction of the conditions that bring it to pass" (Dewey 2008, 216). And while environmental conditions themselves socialized U-Haven professionals to focus on the means rather than the ends of the work, Ki's training helped facilitate this "whole new way of thinking," as Libby puts it above.

None of the twelve U-Haven apprentices became spiritually invested in MI the way that so many US-based MINTies do. Instead, for them, MI offered a way to rethink the ethical implications of their interactions with clients and, more generally, their work as helping professionals. Thus, while chapter 3 addressed how some advanced trainees come to embody the "spirit" of MI and join the ranks of the most faithful (that is, MINT), this chapter demonstrates the pragmatic effects of MI on its average students. I argue that MI training reframed and ultimately revived U-Haven apprentices' relationship to their work not by pretending to offer them a perfect communication device, but rather by helping them see that there is no such thing (see the prologue). More broadly, this chapter demonstrates that MI inculcates the principles of practice once elaborated by American pragmatist philosophers John Dewey, William James, and Charles Sanders Peirce. And while MI does so with little to no explicit reference to this philosophical tradition, I nevertheless argue that to be trained in MI is to be trained in American pragmatism.[2]

As this chapter highlights, the pragmatism that infuses advanced MI training requires apprentices to resist extracontextual explanations, forestall definitive conclusions, adopt an experimental mindset, and welcome surprise. In this sense, MI is not just a method for producing speech in interaction (see chapter 2); it is also a method of *studying speech as interaction*. Indeed, in the latter stages of training, MI asks its apprentices to jettison diagnostic logics that typologize clients and their problems, and instead become students of their own interactions. Even ambivalence is pragmatized in practice. Rather than assuming ambivalence is a psychic state, inherent to the client, it is instead approached as a supposition or mid-level hypotheses that suggests the next step in a professional interaction (see Miller & Rollnick 2013, 247, also 243–54; Carr 2021).

At U-Haven, we will also learn that advanced training in MI means accepting that knowledge-claims about the nature, source, or content of a problem are not just irrelevant but are also potentially dangerous, short-circuiting the process of learning and—by extension—the helpfulness of the actions that follow. So, while the immediate end of the training, as anticipated in Ki's office that overcast spring day, proved to be painful, its lessons were primed to live on, tethered as they were to a pragmatic philosophy of knowledge.

Taking U-Haven's training as its ethnographic ground, this chapter explores how the central methodological principles of American pragmatism—if understood and learned *as* MI—take root among a group of contemporary US-based helping professionals. More specifically, I will show how training MI inculcates (1) a steadfast focus on the immediate consequences of one's acts rather than floating or abstract conceptions of the true, the good, or the right; and (2) an investment in a highly reflexive mode of knowledge acquisition, which relinquishes the certainty of positivist explanations. By way of these pragmatic principles—which proponents of MI take to be simultaneously ethical and technical—MI offers an alternative to a deductive logic, which finds the roots of problems and (therefore) cues for solutions in the interiors of suffering people, and the focus on measurable "clinical outcomes," now so concertedly embedded in the contemporary culture of behavioral health and social service provision in the United States.

As we will see, training in MI—and by extension, American pragmatism—succeeds to the extent that it cultivates an irreverence toward stabilized and disciplined forms of knowledge, if risking the stabilized and disciplined professional identity entailed therein. To be sure, there are costs of trading definitive knowledge for doubt for helping professionals themselves, like those at U-Haven, who are not widely recognized as experts from the start. Moreover, there is the pressing question of what MI's pragmatic focus on the present and the immediate future may render less professionally visible and perhaps also less actionable, including the historical inequities that shape helping professionals' everyday work and their clients' everyday worlds. With this in mind, I raise questions about the political and professional limits, as well as the promises and possibilities, of MI's vernacular pragmatism, including what it means for "working the difference."[3]

RESISTING ENDS: TRAINING IN
VERNACULAR PRAGMATISM

On the day of U-Haven's final training session, apprentices' faces were noticeably long, as expected, despite the first rays of spring filtering through the large, soot-caked windows of their training room. Ki's characteristic beam was also noticeably dimmed as he assumed his usual spot at the head of the room, hands folded solemnly, almost as if in prayer. With typical morning banter now but a murmur, the bus traffic at the busy intersection five floors down seemed all the louder. Those gathered stared at the wall clock as it crept toward the 9:00 a.m. starting time or studied Ki's furrowed brow as he gathered himself to begin his training's end.

Ki's plan for the session was to solidify the skill of "rolling with resistance" (see chapter 1, note 40) having already firmly established MI's conception of "resistance" as the outcome of unproductive interactions rather than the psychic property of people. Before diving in, Ki broached the thorny issue of how the training would proceed in his absence. Despite the looming disruption, Ki's initiative at U-Haven was on course for a state-of-the-art MI training. His departure happened to coincide with the normal transition point from the didactic and communal portion of the training—which had consisted of a combination of PowerPoint presentations, demonstration films, and various role-playing exercises—to more applied, individualized practice.

With this in mind, Ki had spent the previous week arranging for his replacements; identifying Norman, who would spend the next several months coding the apprentices' recordings; holding one-on-one meetings to discuss their abysmally low scores; and encouraging them to continue their practice (see chapter 3). Ki also made plans for his former grad school mentor, Fred, to lead "group processing sessions" so that the monthly meetings could continue through the planned full-year course. Fred's ample training experience and familiarity with the agency, including an advisory role in its training department, allowed Ki to announce the plan for the remaining training with confidence. That said, Ki's attempts to get past apprentices' initial assent to continue and conjure a sense of productive transition that morning proved challenging. His disciples were intent on a dirge.

Perhaps it should have come as no surprise that, on this particular day, apprentices' attention was trained on death. There was, most immediately, the impending loss of their beloved trainer to mourn. After all, Ki's relationship with most of them extended well beyond the training room, whether he served as their actual supervisor, a less formal mentor, or—as in most cases—a professional model to admire, even adore, from a relative distance. One of the pleasures of the training, several apprentices told me, was to watch and listen to the inspirational Ki in action: role-playing an MI-infused interaction with a recognizably difficult client, underscoring the ethics of their work at U-Haven in moving and eloquent terms, and nodding in deep sympathy as they reported everyday professional struggles. They hated to see him go.

There was also a rash of actual deaths of program clients (often referred to as "participants" at U-Haven). The deaths began in January and built, in tragic crescendo, over the spring. Apprentices and their colleagues found it increasingly difficult to make sense of it all, as they discovered the bodies of longtime clients, dead from overdoses and untreated illnesses. For some, the rash of deaths was like a radical test case for the harm-reduction modality to which U-Haven was committed. As we have seen, while U-Haven offers an impressive variety of treatment options—including individual counseling, group therapy, and referrals to inpatient and detox programs— professionals have little leverage in populating these services, one of the primary reasons they wanted to "better engage" clients through further training in MI. Client deaths, a few dared to quietly worry, might indicate that U-Haven professionals had not only failed to reduce harm but had also perhaps facilitated it.

These simmering concerns notwithstanding, it came as a shock when, during that mournful last gathering with Ki, one of the apprentices implied that the confluence of the trainees' increasing use of MI and the recent deaths of clients was no mere coincidence. Among training participants, news had quickly spread that one of those who had died had recorded an MI practice session with Derrek—a young, white case manager who was widely respected by colleagues and clients alike—just days before. What was more, the recorded session had focused precisely on the drug habit that was suspected of killing the well-known client. So, when Ki began his final training as planned, focusing on how to operationalize the concept of "rolling with resistance," Marcus abruptly interrupted him by wondering aloud whether the communication style Ki had been teaching them might—in fact—be fatal.

KI: I do want to leave us with some ideas about *resistance* in addition to those we're now discussing. To really play the tape out.

M: Roll with it. I just want to say something, [Ki].

KI: Speaking of resistance. [*room laughs*]

M: There have been . . . several deaths of participants that I've had where they contacted me. And I have practiced motivational interviewing in, uh, these interactions with these participants and they *died*.

KI: Yes.

M: And it's like . . . When do we leave it alone? When do you . . . look at what you're doing wrong? Is there . . . and I know I'm not God, but . . . I do believe in those interactions there are some points where it could make a difference. But the resistance is always there, I mean . . .

KI: "The resistance is always there." What do you mean?

M: And just rolling with it? The nonjudgmental approach. And, you know, it's . . . [*trailing off*]

KI: It's not easy. It's not easy. Okay? Simple, not easy. Okay? There's nothing easy.

This was likely not the first time Ki had been accused of teaching a method that leads to, if not directly causes, people's death, and does so precisely because it "rolls with" rather than directly confronts clients' putative "resistance." Several other MI trainers I worked with shared anecdotes of troubled and sometimes hostile trainees, usually at introductory staff trainings, who would raise angry hands, write scathing post-training emails, or use training breaks to personally relay, without mincing words, that MI *could kill people* by not offering direct and forceful verbal counters to participants' self-destructive behaviors and their resistance to change.[4] And, while Ki stumbled a bit in responding to Marcus, resorting to a common MI refrain ("simple, not easy"), he soon regained his composure, offering up a bouquet of pragmatic principles, as filtered through MI, to deal with the death thrust before him.

Significantly, Ki did not hesitate to acknowledge the dead body brought to life in the training room, as well as the resulting horror of U-Haven professionals. Yet he also seized upon the opportunity to connect ontological matters (that is, the death) to methodological questions (that is, the professional interactions that may or may not have contributed to it), with a clear emphasis on the latter. His challenge was to accept that MI, like any other professional intervention, might be somehow implicated in the death, while inspiring continued faith in the method. Ki also was intent on practicing the MI-specific skill on the agenda for that day. Accordingly, Ki remarked: "So [Derrek] did a recording. His recording with someone. And one of the behaviors that they were looking at was one of the behaviors that was probably a contributing factor to this gentleman's death. And so you're right, [Marcus]." In so saying, Ki managed both to model the skill he wanted to impart to Marcus and his fellow trainees, and used it on them *as if they were clients*. After all, by providing an "amplified reflection" of what Marcus had just said (see also chapter 1, p. 73–77), repeating it in somewhat exaggerated terms, Ki demonstrated how to "roll with resistance" even though the resistance was brewing among professionals rather than their clients, in this instance.

In affirming and asking Marcus to clarify his statement that "resistance is always there," Ki focused on another critical disjuncture between what he had been teaching and Marcus's last-ditch challenge. In the pragmatism of MI, the salient question is not whether some quality, such as resistance or ambivalence, already exists. Rather, inquiry is focused on the proximate conditions that could interactionally heighten, lessen, or even manufacture it. Accordingly, Ki not only relocated the deadly entity in question— *resistance*—from inside the client to inside the professionally led conversation; he also explained that resistance is not a stabilized essence, but rather a variable product of interaction:

> If the therapist genuinely has no investment in the outcome, then resistance does not exist. [In MI] the paradox is . . . the more we impinge, the more we intrude, people are even *less* likely to pursue . . . change. And that the less . . . we intrude and are intrusive, the more likely, the more free people are, the more free people are to explore and examine and pursue change, the more likely they are to do so.

Given the references to individual freedom, Ki's explanation may at first appear to be an expression of an ethical commitment to (neo)liberal self-determination. After all, he seems to suggest that people will naturally pursue change if unfettered by external expectations and directives. Yet to read Ki's statement this way would be to obscure its emphasis on a pragmatic method, which trains apprentices' focus on the process rather than the "outcomes" of their work. After all, the "freedom" to which Ki refers is the freedom afforded by the skillful and process-focused therapeutic dialogue—the idea that participants will *verbally* "explore and examine and pursue change" if the conditions to do so are provided within the properly crafted interview. At the same time, MI-trained practitioners use those verbal explorations as evidential fodder—as cues about what to say and do next. This rigorous, reflexive attention to the process of interaction is central to American pragmatism and lies at the heart of MI training.

INSTRUCTION IN ABDUCTION: REHABITUATING PROFESSIONAL PRACTICE

In Ki's comments above, readers will discern—as U-Haven apprentices did—that therapeutic goals are hardly abandoned in MI. As Ki regularly conceded throughout the training, "therapeutic neutrality is a myth." Nevertheless, Ki and his fellow MINTies offer little positive theory in such refusals' stead. Rather, MI trainers ask apprentices to abandon generic theses about who people are and why they suffer, so as to decipher the specific demands of presenting interactions and improvise accordingly. They do so by regearing professional attention from *how and why things are or should be* (for clients) toward *how to effectively act* (as professionals) based upon what has been learned by way of proximate interactions.

In previous chapters we have seen that, in line with the frequent reminders that "clients are the best teachers," MI trainers focus apprentices' attention on the immediate effects of their words on the here and now of the dyadic exchange. In observing role-plays and real-plays, we have also gathered how apprentices learn to calibrate not just *what* they say but also *how* and *when* they say it, in accordance with the speech of the individual who sits before them. Now, we will turn to how apprentices *learn to learn* and, more specifically, how they develop the ability to constantly adjust, refine, or revise what is known by way of their painstaking exchanges. We will find apprentices in the sometimes painful (if ultimately productive) process of realizing that the knowledge gained from practice is radically unstable, always dependent on what happens next, which frequently exceeds expectations. Accordingly, they learn to constantly adjust, refine, or revise what is known in reference to what is gathered through their interviews. In this sense, MI training is *instruction in abduction*—that mode of practical reasoning and reasoning practice most closely associated with progenitor of American pragmatism, Charles Sanders Peirce.

Formally speaking, abduction is inference built from an observed body of data to a working hypothesis, which provides guidelines for further action and investigation (see also Carr 2015; Carr & Fisher 2016; cf. Helmreich 2007, 2009). In practice, abduction requires the inquiring subject to engage in an ongoing process of organizing what they have learned into a provisional guess or supposition that, in turn, organizes how to take the next step of meaningful action. Thus, abduction is a habit of thought that concertedly resists the seduction of definitive answers; instead, abduction necessitates holding meaning in suspense. As Dewey put it, "we stop and think, we *de-fer* conclusion in order to *in-fer* more thoroughly. In this process of being only conditionally accepted, accepted only for examination, meanings become ideas" (1997, 108). Rather than holding firm to meaning, we "tentatively entertain" and evaluate it "*with reference to its fitness to decide a perplexing situation*" (108, emphasis in original). In the context of the motivational interview, then, abduction means treating clients' statements not as referential signs of who they are, what they feel, or how they suffer (see Carr 2011), but rather as "ideas" (in Dewey's sense) that signal how the interview—as a kind of investigation—is going, and how to practically proceed.

The "reflection" is the key to MI abduction. In the early months of the training, Ki explained to U-Haven apprentices that a reflection is "rephrasing what you think you heard." Now, later in the training, the trainer elaborated that a reflection is also "making a guess at what the client means; it's a hypothesis." In line with Dewey's suggested habit of thought, the client response to the interviewer's reflection serves as a *provisional clue for the professional about what to say and do next*. Note that definitive truth is not the goal of the successful reflection. Instead, in MI, the reflection both generates difference between what is said and what was previously known, and temporarily resolves that difference so as to move forward. Thus, we can now fully appreciate Ki's instructions: "So as, as long as the reflection, right or wrong, leads us further down the path, then that's okay. Sometimes getting it wrong gives us as much information as it does to get it right" (see chapter 2, p. 72).

With abduction in mind, let us home in on how MI apprentices are taught to observe, as well as to speak and act, during role-playing exercises. Consider the common exercise "Out of the Woods," which begins with a preface: "Everyone makes mistakes and when you do, it is quickly apparent in your client's response." Assigned observers monitor a role-played interview, discerning the difference between every defensive, resistant, or disinterested client-actor response relative to specific statements made by the acting interviewer, with critical observations shared aloud at the end of the exercise. Eventually, it is expected that apprentices will learn to get "out of the woods" on their own, analyzing and readjusting the interviews they conduct in real time, without their colleagues' assistance. This near-constant, highly analytical reflection on and attendant retooling of what one says and does in relation to the mercurial conditions of interaction is the key to the method, for in MI, as in American pragmatism, "to act intelligently and to see intelligently become at bottom one" (Peirce 1974, 652).

The pragmatism of MI, then, involved sensitizing apprentices to the unpredictable differences between what was (tentatively) known and what might arise, differences that continually arise in everyday practice. Accordingly, when U-Haven apprentices played out the frustrations of seemingly irresolute clients with apparently intractable problems, Ki—like many pragmatists before him—worked intently to reorient his apprentices' attention from the nature of the person or problem at hand to the ethical question of what to do next (see Dewey 1972, 67).[5] Understandably, U-Haven apprentices sometimes yearned for general propositions that could guide their practice, or decision trees that could naturalize and depersonalize their courses of action. Not infrequently, U-Haven apprentices expressed doubt that even the most technically sophisticated and spirit-infused motivational interview would be effective in addressing the grave problems they faced in their daily work. They longed for a perfect communication device.

Significantly, Ki stimulated rather than quelled their doubt that the problems they faced could ever be fully understood and definitively resolved by way of any method, including MI. And so, when Ki was confronted with Marcus's radical questioning of MI, his goal was not to squelch that doubt, but rather to motivate it and render it productive—to *direct* it. Thus, when another apprentice—one who had earned a master's degree in social theory before becoming a case manager at U-Haven—responded to Ki's comment on the dynamics of resistance by saying: "it's almost like a Western arrogance . . . that the individual is actually in control," the trainer both agreed and delicately redirected that comment from theory to method:

I think Western arrogance is . . . is an appropriate way in which to think about it sometimes. And I think in terms of our work with participants, I think we sometimes we really need to *play the tape out*. I think we get these ideas in our head that there are things that we're not doing or that we *could* do to somehow . . . have more control or manipulate the outcome. I have . . . often walked out of those situations feeling what could I have done differently? Should I have pushed harder? Should I have . . . is there something wrong with my practice that it wasn't working or it didn't work as well? Where does my responsibility begin and end? Those are all really good and important questions. At the same time, I am also of the opinion that we do the best we can. And we continue to *learn* and we continue to *practice* and we continue to offer anything and everything that we can to the people with whom we work.

"Play the tape out" is a common therapeutic idiom in the United States, one with which many in the room that day were likely familiar. Encapsulated in the phrase is the idea that those prone to behavioral problems should think ahead about how one (negative) action could lead to another. In Alcoholics Anonymous, for instance, the expression serves as a mnemonic device, reminding the sober alcoholic to anticipate the likely series of events that would unfold if they were to make the decision to have a drink, like a kind of negative forecasting. In MI, as we have seen, the interviewer strives to create the dialogic conditions for the client to verbalize such forecasts aloud so that they might talk themselves out of the verbalized behavior before engaging in it.

However and more significantly, when Ki speaks of "playing the tape out," he is urging *professionals* to engage in this forecasting. Ki thereby reveals that *to abduct* requires the professional to proceed attentively, with readiness to adjust to what they learn along the way, without assuming trajectories based on what happened in the past. In essence, he tries to shorten the time horizon of the professional's reflexive inquiries. In this vein, MI trainers commonly urge apprentices to "slow down" (or, in Dewey's terms, *de-fer*) so as to pay attention to the immediate effects of their practices. For instance, Ki once instructed: "I do think there's value in slowing down sometimes. And so that we can pay attention and really . . . and *also* sometimes it's being comfortable [. . .] with being uncomfortable."

The idea of slowing down may at first seem ironic given that at U-Haven, as in many sites where MI is practiced, interactions with clients are far more likely to occur in time-pressured exchanges in a crowded corridor or an elevator ride between floors than in a cozy office with a timer set to fifty minutes. Yet, as Ki makes clear, the rapid pace of what actually happens is no excuse for being seduced by the expediency of certainty, which only truncates the abductive process. "Slowing down," then, is a mode of attention that allows trained practitioners to both "pay attention" to the verbal data of the interview and make use of them even in the most time-constrained circumstances. Ki, like the other MI trainers I studied, beseeches trainees, if not in these same words, to "consider what effects, that might conceivably have practical bearings, we conceive the object of our conception to have. Then, our conception of these effects is the whole of our conception of the object" (Peirce 1974, 258). This is the pragmatic maxim.

The term "maxim" is often interpreted as a principle or rule that lacks flexibility. The pragmatic maxim, however, is a principle of *conduct* that sensitizes those who follow it to a world of possibilities in which their own actions are always necessarily implicated. In other words, a pragmatic habit of mind anchors interpretive possibilities to the situation at hand, if only long enough to chart the next course of action. It was with these highly reflexive demands of the pragmatic maxim in mind, hoping for a better understanding, that I asked Ki to clarify what he meant by "playing the tape out," long after that last training session. In an emailed response, he distilled what I came to understand as the fundamental pragmatism of MI.

> Too often we think of these aphorisms—and the suggestions/advice contained therein—as applying only to the people with whom we work. they can also be useful for practitioners, if not in our personal lives perhaps in our professional lives. *when faced with a possible course of action or a decision-making point* over the course of our work with someone, i find it useful to "play the tape out" before acting—*we conjure up ideas (fantasies?) about what we can or should (or are expected to) do and anticipated/ expected outcomes (often implicit) when the actual outcomes are often unknown if not unanticipated. we need to see beyond the immediate moment— even in the midst of so-called "crises"—and consider not only the short-term implications/impact, also the long-term. lots of (hopefully) collaborative/ shared decision-making, experimentation, and evaluation.* (original punctuation and capitalization; emphasis added)

Here, Ki clarifies how implicated MI professionals are—and should recognize themselves to be—in the habitual work of producing knowledge for practice. Furthermore, by this explanation, reflexivity is far more than the general reversal of the clinical lens to focus on "practitioners" rather than "the people with whom [they] work." In quintessentially pragmatic terms, Ki explains that reflexivity also entails relentlessly tracking the differences between how one's premises play out in practice, as well as how one's own actions help change conditions that were previously known, shaping further inquiry and action accordingly. Figuring out what to do, then, means pausing, reflecting, and then letting the "tape play out."[6]

To engage in this sort of abductive process is to implicitly embrace the idea that knowledge acquisition is never passive or impartial. Along these lines, Ki's reference to MI as "experimentation" is particularly compelling. He frames proper practice as the manipulation of reality, which harnesses doubt and moves carefully toward more assured belief, which itself survives only as long as it takes to make the next decision. In the meantime, he dismisses the idea that certain means will naturally lead to expected outcomes as "fantast[ic]." For Ki, as for other American pragmatists, observation is always necessarily also about ongoing decision and is therefore always an active process.

Furthermore, note that in Ki's explanation, as in Peirce's, possible courses of action are also constantly *evaluated* for their effects, in both the short and long term.[7] Like his fellow MINTies, Ki's guiding principle—or maxim—is to never determine the end in advance but rather to arrive at the next "incomplete" or "problematic" situation in which something must be done (Dewey 1922, 161, 177–78). Arguably, this is a way of both tightening the connection of means and ends, and suggesting that there are no final answers in inquiry, no solutions that would totally absolve one from further action. And since the problems of practice persist, Ki encouraged his apprentices to keep experimenting and analyzing, whether skipped medications, ignored treatment plans, shared needles, unpaid rents, or bedbugs were at hand.

From this perspective, there is nothing fatalistic about applying the same ideas to the deaths of clients, for as Ki said on that last day of training, "people are going to die no matter what we do." Rather than simply condemning what all in the room already thought to be wrong (death by drugs), Ki tried to clinch what he'd been working at all along—an ethical recalibration by way of MI. More specifically, he reorients the harrowing dilemma away from the acting subject (the professional who prevents an individual's death by an act of intervention) to the abductive interactant (the practitioner who prevents harm *in the long run*, if not in every case, by way of continual reflection and direction). He thereby works to instill in his crestfallen apprentices the belief that knowledge and practice, if properly and rigorously habituated, can live on in the service of others.

Thus, before his own departure, Ki imparted a vital message in clear and moving terms: there are *no ends* to helping professionals' work, whether philosophically, practically, or ethically. For even in the face of physical and material ends—whether the death of clients or the evaporation of service funding—those faithful to their pragmatic training persistently situate themselves in the midst of their practice *as apprentices*. That is, they are always poised to learn in an unfolding world of which they are intrinsically a part, rather than to know in a stabilized world that offers an objective remove from which to claim certain, enduring knowledge (see Lave

& Wenger 1991). When following Ki's directive to "continue to *learn*, continue to *practice*," which echoes Dewey's counsel that "education is not a means to living, but is identical with the operation of living a life" (1922, 281), U-Haven trainees rigorously attended to what just happened so as to move forward with the pressing question of what to do next.

TRAINING IN TRANSITION AND
THE SEDUCTION OF DEDUCTION

At least half of U-Haven trainees were already familiar with Fred by the time he took the reins of the MI training. He was, after all, one of the most experienced clinical trainers in the city and surrounding suburbs. He also taught at a prestigious local university where several of the training participants had received advanced degrees, and had planned or held trainings on various topics at U-Haven in the past. As a trainer, Fred was widely known for the depth of his practical experience, his diverse knowledge base, and his gregarious personality, which played well among the dedicated if often depleted groups of social workers, dieticians, doctors, and program administrators he trained throughout the city. And while he clearly admired and appreciated MI, having trained it alongside other methods since the mid-1990s, he also firmly believed that clinical approaches should be applied relative to pathologies, as diagnosed by practitioners and in accordance with the established "evidence-base" (see chapter 4). Given that MI is considered an evidence-based practice in the fields in which Fred typically trained—addictions, behavioral health, veterans' affairs, and clinical social work—he spent a good portion of his time training MI. Otherwise, Fred was a devout eclecticist who averred that diagnoses should determine which methods professionals adopt and, only when necessary, adapt.

This helps explain why, despite his ample training experience and glowing reputation (including among several local MINTies), Fred never went through the rather byzantine process of being MINTed, as his former student, Ki, had done. Alongside his packed graduate courses on adult psychopathology, he taught a class on spirituality in practice, which inclined him toward the idea of MI spirit, though he did not find it especially unique or unusual as some of his MINTie colleagues did. While Fred could spontaneously produce a dazzling motivational interview on command, he never sent in tapes to be coded, never attended MINT's official Training New Trainers (TNT), and never frequented the populated MINT listserv. And though his lack of formal socialization in MI—as a community of practice if not a practice method—was not obvious in how he demonstrated and spoke about the method, two things became painfully clear as he took over

Ki's training: Fred did not think of diagnosis as a "trap" (Miller & Rollnick 2013, 42–45), and he brought a deductive, rather than pragmatic, style of reasoning to the training room.

Fred's initial training session at U-Haven went quite well, especially considering the dirge that preceded it with Ki's departure the month before. In attendance were ten of the twelve trainees—one having left the agency completely and the other having dropped out for lack of interest after she took on a more administrative position in one of U-Haven's offshoot programs. As soon as the awkwardness of the obligatory round of self-introductions faded, Fred effortlessly eased the group into role-playing, a practice they had once dreaded. Fred was particularly keen to reenact scenes from the trainees' recent practice encounters. While the significance was not yet clear, Fred called these role-plays "case presentations." Asking for volunteers, Fred quickly seized upon the frustrating scenario recounted by Hector, a seasoned professional who had been an increasingly engaged participant in the training leading up to Ki's departure.

By his own account, Hector was troubled not only, or even primarily, with a client who had again blown his SSI check just ten days into the month, leaving him with no money to pay his subsidized rent and other expenses. Hector was moreover disappointed *with himself*, reporting that during a freighted encounter with the client that very morning, he had failed to apply the lessons of his MI training to date. Remarking that talking about money "is always sensitive," Hector confessed: "I have these motivational interviewing ideas in the back of my head, and sort of have them ready to use when I feel that I can use them or need to use them. And this morning it just kind of got, you know . . . again the money situation. So, kind of, just got out of hand more quickly than I, we had anticipated." In so saying, Hector seemed to retrospectively apply Ki's counsel to "slow down" and bemoan his failure to do so. In including his client in what might have been "anticipated" and de-ferred, in Dewey's sense, Hector suggests that he should have used the exchange as a chance to abduct. Instead, he resorted to the speed of deduction, letting the well-worn "sensitive" topic of money get "out of hand."

It was a great opportunity to reinforce the lessons of the training to date, and all seemed eager to do so. With Hector cast now as his own client, Fred performed a virtuosic motivational interview, though in a style that was faster paced, sharper in tone, and slightly more formulaic than Ki's graceful, unhurried approach. The trainees recognized and appreciated Fred's fluent incorporation of open questions, affirmations, reflections, and summaries—the requisite building blocks of the motivational interview. And if startled by Fred's rattling post–role-play synopsis, in which he stated

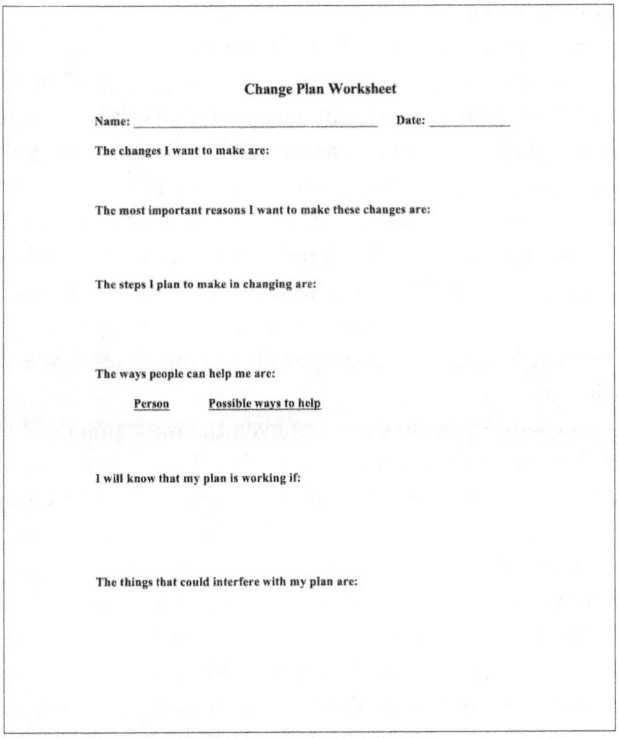

Change Plan Worksheet

Name: _____ Date: _____

The changes I want to make are:

The most important reasons I want to make these changes are:

The steps I plan to make in changing are:

The ways people can help me are:

Person   Possible ways to help

I will know that my plan is working if:

The things that could interfere with my plan are:

Figure 5.1. "Change Plan Worksheet" distributed by Fred to
U-Haven trainees.

that if the client in focus could succeed in even "the simplest management task," it would be "huge because for somebody who has probably never planned anything in his life, that kind of cognitively is, like, a big step," apprentices nevertheless appeared quite impressed. After all, by the end of the role-play, Fred had secured a "change statement," or promise to act, not just from the client as role-played by Hector, but also from Hector himself, as an apparently rejuvenated professional re-equipped to intervene.

Indeed, Hector seemed eager to apply what had just been demonstrated and left the training room with the stated intent to use a "Change Plan Worksheet," which Fred distributed while the trainees were packing up to proceed with their day's work (see figure 5.1). As Fred explained in the final minutes of the session, the worksheet would inscribe and therefore solidify the verbal work of the motivational interview—functioning like a contract to which the client would commit. Hector glanced at the worksheet, folding it in half to place in his well-worn backpack, while nodding at Fred's closing words, promising once again to give it a try.

The training took a decidedly awkward turn during the subsequent session, less than one month later. When prompted by the expectant Fred, Hector nonchalantly reported that he had *not* engaged his client in the discussion that they had role-played. When asked what had happened, Hector explained that the client's imminent financial crisis had been avoided, but that was due to random circumstances—a stroke of luck—rather than to any more or less skillful professional intervention on his or his colleagues' part. When further questioned by Fred, Hector responded without a hint of shame or regret: He had not used the Change Plan Worksheet, nor did he think that the document would be "useful anytime in the future."[8] Professional resistance had again reared its head, and this time, Ki was not there to "roll with" it.

Given how hard it was to carry out even the most practiced interventions at U-Haven, what was more surprising than Hector's recalcitrance was Fred's response to it. Having witnessed similar situations in other MI trainings I studied, I expected Fred to elicit Hector's explanations for why he did not follow through, and to suggest how he might proceed given the stated reasons—that is, I expected Fred to conduct an in vivo *real-play* with the goal of getting Hector to effectively use his MI skills, if not the Change Plan Worksheet, no matter how difficult the circumstances. Yet, rather than maintaining the apprentices' analytic attention on what Hector had said or might say to his client, what effects those statements made or could make, and how he might accordingly readjust—as the deeply pragmatic Ki surely would—Fred regrounded the questions of what happened and what to do next in the inferred psychic qualities of Hector's *client*, John.

Presumably seizing upon Hector's offhand comment that John "worries about everything," which he had made in passing during the previous session, Fred offered that John's distress would only build if Hector avoided talking about money. Offering up a diagnosis, Fred elaborated: "For people with OCD [obsessive-compulsive disorder], the motivational issue is often being willing to do the exposure and response prevention . . . because it's really distressing for them to talk about it. So this is something that's real important for you to decrease."

For a moment it seemed like the training had stopped dead in its tracks. The trainees fell silent. A few went slack-jawed and stared at Fred, perhaps awaiting some corrective. As the silence continued, it appeared that everyone in the training room was at a loss for how to proceed in the face of Fred's diagnostics. After all, with Fred's advice, U-Haven trainees faced a new ontology, and with it, a new set of epistemological assumptions about how to know and treat a problem—assumptions that made infinite sense to Fred as well as to countless other US-based clinicians, but had become foreign, even taboo, to U-Haven apprentices over their nine-month training by

Table 5.1. Modes of (clinical) reasoning

	Deductive Reasoning	Abductive Reasoning
Site of investigation	· Interiority · An origin	· Interaction · In the middle
Organization of inquiry	· Problem > solution · Ideally discrete · Quest for certainty	· Doubt <> action <> effect · Ideally ongoing · Quest for knowledge/doubt
Ontology	· Positivist · Truth is a thing in itself, and can be en- countered as such · Truth is	· Fallibilist · Truth is where we arrive at a juncture in our inquiry, which itself has no end · Truth works (James 1909)
Role of practitioner/ analyst	· Passive. A discoverer, who happens upon the truth	· Active. An experimenter, who changes the conditions being examined through their inquiry and is therefore impli- cated in the knowledge production process

Ki. Once parsed, Fred's analytic turn shares many features of the "diagnosis trap" to which MI, definitionally, is fiercely opposed (see table 5.1).

First, note that Hector's client, John, has now been cast as representative of "people with OCD," a token of a clinical type. Remarkably, Fred's conclusion had not been induced from his own examination of the client, of whom he had no firsthand knowledge. Instead, it had been derived from Hector's decidedly nonclinical characterization of his client. Furthermore, motivation—or lack thereof—is now cast as a symptom of the client with OCD rather than a potential product of an interaction or history of inter- actions. One might even argue that Fred transformed an especially brutal economic difference in a class-segregated society into a clinical category: a meager SSI check on which to live becomes a case of OCD.

The point is not to dwell on some shortcoming with or insensitivity of Fred in particular. Rather, I mean to elaborate the kind of explanatory power diagnostic categories carry, power that apparently reached its limit after nine months of MI training. After all, the authority of diagnosis comes, in part, from a scientific *elsewhere*. This effectively frees the professional to categorize their client as the type of person-with-X-pathology, rather than to attend to context-specific elements of the professional-client interaction. Most important, in this case, this diagnostic logic couched Hector's continued inability to have a successful motivational interview with John in a general theory of how people with OCD *typically* respond to potentially distressing topics.

Consider, too, the "if/then" construction embedded in Fred's instructions, as in: *if* the client has OCD, *then* it is "real important for [Hector] to decrease" potentially distressing talk about the focus of their obsession. It is almost as if Fred falls right into the "expert trap," as Miller once explained it to me, animating a wrongheaded clinician in unabashedly facetious terms: "if I just ask enough questions . . . and get the diagnosis we'll know how to fix the person." In other words, the diagnostic logic that entered the training room with Fred seeks not only to explain problems by way of imputed psychic essences, but also to prescribe a professional course of action accordingly. By this logic, almost as soon as the typification of the client problem is established, the fate of professional interventions, past, present, and future is determined as well. And indeed, as Fred continued to advise what topics would and would not be distressing for someone, like John, "with OCD," he effectively prescribed a course of professional action without reflecting on what Hector did or didn't do.[9] From a pragmatic point of view, this kind of deduction is dangerous, not least because the professional is absolved of responsibility beyond the question of whether the problem, already constituted within the client, has been correctly identified and treated.

Whether or not Hector and his colleagues would articulate the disjuncture they felt in these terms, their ongoing silence made clear that something had gone seriously awry. Perhaps thinking that an extension of his diagnosis from John to potential others might rekindle the conversation, a rather flustered Fred continued: "Have any of the rest of you had participants with OCD that you've had that kind of problem with?" When greeted with yet more silence, Fred responded, "That's not too much who you get in the program here," a conclusion that clearly missed the point. Indeed, under Ki's pragmatic tutelage, U-Haven apprentices were now primed to dismiss the common idea that a course of practice can be causally charted by answering the question: what kind of psychological problem or person do I have before me? They invested instead in the ongoing, grounded investigation based on an omnipresent question: what do I do now based on what I learned from the results of my previous actions? And so, not surprisingly, Fred's second training session came to an early, uncomfortable close with his own deflated concession that the opportunity to learn had clearly "stalled out."

Both Fred and Ki were highly skilled clinicians and talented trainers, dedicated to the helping professionals they taught. Yet, as their respective approaches to the U-Haven training exemplify, there were keen and consequential differences in how Ki and Fred thought about knowledge acquisition in relation to clinical practice. The philosophical assumptions that undergird the distinctive approaches of Ki and his former teacher and mentor, Fred, can be largely attributed to the former's socialization into the vernacular pragmatism of MI. After all, when it came to MI, Fred was self-taught. And although he was perhaps just the kind of professional reader that Miller and Rollnick hoped to reach, he had never been MINTed, or *trained to train* the method, thus escaping the MI quality control recounted by Moyers in the previous chapter. By contrast, as a MINTie, Ki had been socialized to embrace fallibilism, not positivism. Accordingly, he trained his apprentices to thrive on doubt rather than seek certainty. And whereas Fred was intent on helping the helping professionals to land on answers that could provide direction for ameliorative actions, and could be applied across cases of similar kind so as to ease their labor, Ki resolutely refocused his trainees' attention, again and again, to the critical questions of what might have been done differently and what could be learned moving forward. As he left his trainees, Ki told them that there was *always* more to learn.

As compelling as the pragmatism of MI was for U-Haven trainees, it was continually challenged by contrary ways of thinking about the problems and people that professionals faced. After all, outside the training room, trainees consulted on a regular basis with U-Haven's staff psychiatrist, whose ability to prescribe medications depended on achieving as much diagnostic clarity as possible. And it is not especially surprising that, as Fred's portion of the U-Haven training continued, there were signs of diagnostic logic making headway. Though the number of attendees had dwindled to six, the next meeting featured another troubling case, which became the subject of an especially revealing pedagogical exchange. It was presented by a young white trainee named Austin, who had recently graduated with an MSW from the university where Fred taught and whose perfectly tanned face bore no signs of stress, unlike those of his colleagues. Austin apparently came ready to share the saga of a U-Haven client whom he could not "seem to get through to." Rather than role-playing and thereby working through what had been done or not done in the reported exchanges, as MI trainers are almost invariably inclined to do, Fred instead initiated a time-consuming diagnostic query. Fred rattled off a list of questions with apparent excitement: "Does [your client] have AIDS-related dementia? Does he have any cognitive impairment from the AIDS? How does that affect his thinking and behavior?"

Austin, who had been notably quiet through most of the U-Haven training, now appeared quite willing to engage. He nodded along with his new trainer's impressive, off-the-cuff lecture on AIDS-related impairments, perhaps in part because it let his own less-than-engaged practice off the hook. In reflecting on why his client had left a drug treatment program despite his professional efforts, Austin now concluded: "It seems the choices that he makes, he doesn't weigh the consequences, he decides to leave treatment, or it is like the obsession or the urge, he'll just . . . [the] impulse control is not there." With Fred's nodding head greeting Austin's diagnosis, it appeared to me that something dramatic was underfoot, something I later understood as the fate of the pragmatism that Ki—and MI—had worked so hard to instill.

THE DEATH OF DIAGNOSIS AND PRAGMATISM'S REVIVAL

When it comes to *diagnosis*, the paradox-loving William R. Miller does something that he almost never does. He draws a stark line in the proverbial sand and puts himself—and the method that he has done so much to develop and scale—on one side of it. Indeed, Miller and his longtime co-author repeatedly warn their textbook readers against diagnostic routines, suggesting it is one of the main triggers of the "expert trap" (see Miller & Rollnick 2013, 20, 42–45, 136, 409; Miller & Rollnick 2002, 60). As one such reader, I asked him about this prominent, if unusually partisan, theme when I interviewed him. In response, Miller confirmed that the characteristically accommodating MI has no place for diagnosis. As if both the style and the spirit of the method were at stake, Miller was notably adamant when he stated: "It is such an expert trap to say if I just . . . ask enough questions and give enough instruments and get the diagnosis, then we'll know how to fix the person. And that's *not* MI."

Tellingly, MI's foundational textbook frames the dangers of diagnosis in temporal terms. Specifically, Miller and Rollnick (2013, 16, also 42–43) describe diagnosis as a "reflex" driven by both expectation of expediency (or "promptness") and the finality of certitude ("the right answer"). Accordingly, MINTies commonly explain their trainees' occasional recalcitrance in these terms as well, with more or less sympathetic accounts of everyday conditions of the helping professionals they train—including stuffed caseloads, the overwhelming paperwork that comes with audit culture, and the regular need to triage, not to mention the deeply felt sense of responsibility for a long-term client on verge of an overdose. Take the veteran MI trainer whom I visited in the Southwest on one of my trips to see Miller. While she spoke at length about the contagious nature of MI spirit, she conceded that MI "just didn't click for some people" precisely because "they lose that sense of, you know, just wanting to learn about the person, be in the process, and instead just want to immediately problem solve."[10]

For Miller and his apprentices, diagnosis is an "expert trap" not only because it seeks *immediate* knowledge of problems, but also because it claims *unmediated* knowledge of them. That is, diagnosis ensnares because it assumes that knowledge acquisition is a matter of fact finding or fishing, as if problems are things radically separate from the practitioner's attempts to understand or treat them. Miller explained to me that while diagnosis is "the right model when you go to your primary care provider with an infection," it is nonsense to believe, when it comes to the business of behavior change, the presumption that one can "ask a series of questions" and "at the end . . . have an answer for you. A prescription."[11]

Let us pause to consider the epistemological premises of Miller's objections. Diagnosis, Miller implies, may work well when there is a preexisting entity at hand: a thing (like an infection) that can be positively identified as such, treated, and eliminated. In this case, he conceded, there is a "need to know." Otherwise, professional knowledge acquisition should be undertaken quite differently, and not only because behavior is an ongoing process rather than a stabilized thing. In line with MI's pragmatic investment in examining the context of practice, Miller further suggests that professionals are quite mistaken if they think they can find certain answers—and therefore "prescriptions" for definitive solutions—in people's psychic interiors.

Through the pragmatic lens of MI, diagnosis is a style of reasoning that hurriedly, even fatalistically, seeks ends, without due concern for side effects. After all, diagnosis pursues (if arguably rarely achieves) total certainty: a problem that *is*, which radically sidelines and renders symptomatic other ways of defining and knowing it, if not trying to eliminate that inquiry from the start. Because it points to a cause meant to stimulate a general course of ameliorative action, diagnosis can understandably appear as a salve for those who abide by it, particularly those in the crush of daily face-to-face crisis. By contrast, pragmatists—whether MINTies like Ki and Vernon or philosophers like Dewey and Peirce—warn that the ascription of certainty terminates the process of inquiry. They accordingly train others to respect and follow a process that calibrates the immediate past and present to the future, and to examine the present conditions of their practice for data on what to do next (see Peirce 1974, 258).

If never identified as such, the pragmatic orientation to the problems encountered in practice was the primary focus of the vast majority of trainings I studied and was sometimes charmingly laced with memorable bits of MI humor. Take our old friend, the veteran trainer Norman, who impressed the pragmatic principle of "investing in *having the conversation*," rather than focusing on the outcome of that conversation, with a favorite joke:

Uh . . . you know, I go home and my wife, uh, just wants to me listen to how her day was. Uh, I get up and, um, she says, "Where are you going?" I say, "I'm going to go get my gun and kill your problem." [*pause*] All she wants me to do is listen.

Here, the idea of shooting a problem dead is recognized as ridiculous, a "fantasy," to translate it into Ki's previous and more serious terms. And just like the child welfare workers, clinical social workers, and corrections officers that Norman trained, the apprentices at U-Haven were acutely aware that the problems their clients faced were too complex, too opaque in their causes, and too structurally imbricated to enjoy ready resolution, regardless of the technical sophistication, spirit, or delicacy with which they were professionally greeted. This meant that rather than investing in an outcome, which would likely never come, MI apprentices "invest in the conversation," and therefore also in the ongoing present of working with clients. This is both a way to gather more knowledge with which to work and an ethical practice in and of itself.

∴

Of course, all pedagogical programs encounter challenges, including the need to appease students when their attention to and faith in their lessons waver. Such was the case at U-Haven, in apprentices' final months of training, in that spring session with Fred, with diagnostic reasoning rearing its familiar head. Yet it would not go on for long, with a dramatic resuscitation of MI's pragmatism. Maybe it was because the pragmatic Norman had already begun his coaching when Austin's client was diagnosed, by fiat, with AIDS-related cognitive impairment. Maybe it was because Ki's lessons had already become integral to at least some of the twelve apprentices' ways of thinking about and doing their work. Maybe it was because a pragmatic approach to work in sites like U-Haven is the only sustainable way of working in a field notorious for burnout and turnover. Or, maybe it was because the man who spoke up that day had learned to be pragmatic—in both the formal and informal senses of the term—long before he began training with Ki, with whom he apparently shared a deep affection.

But what I observed on that fateful day at U-Haven was this: Jamal, whose brawny frame matched Fred's, wore his usual faint smile along with one of his signature geometric acrylic sweaters. Jamal was seated near the whiteboard—where Fred was pacing while providing impressively information-packed explanations of the cognitive correlates of AIDS— and diagonal to the chisel-faced Austin, whose Oxford-clothed arms were folded in front of him as he nodded slowly at the mini-lecture. Over the course of the training, Jamal had said next to nothing unless called upon to do so. But on this particular day, remaining silent meant acquiescing to the mounting conclusion that the problem at hand was the client's cognitive condition, rather than the qualities of Austin's professional engagement with him. As if channeling Ki, and certainly MI, Jamal raised his hand and began to speak before he was called on. Looking squarely at Austin, whose reflections on his practice were about to be killed by diagnosis, he gently if pointedly posed an open question: "And so, what did *you* learn from [the conversations you had with your client]?" Without that kind of learning, how would the young Austin ever figure out what to actually and ethically do?

If MI training succeeds in its most immediate aims, problems and people are not categorized into types but are approached as unique puzzles that encourage those who encounter them to try again, experiment anew, rigorously reflect, and extend the life of their practice accordingly. MI trains its apprentices to think with difference always in mind: how one problem, person, and interaction is different from the next, how what happens is different from what is anticipated, how difference can be made and managed through the course of any situation. While not all professionals "get it," the pragmatic sensibility that MI training seeks to pass along to its apprentices is experienced by many, like Jamal and Libby, as deeply rewarding and, indeed, reviving. They relinquish the desperate search for definite solutions to indefinite problems; they reflect on their own practice rather than try to peer into the opaque interiors of clients for signs of their own success; and they feel buoyed by —and sometimes feel a deep kinship with—the idea there is always something good to learn, even in the bare face of human finitude.

HAPPILY EVER APPRENTICES: (NO) CONCLUSIONS, PRAGMATISM, AND THE PRESENCE OF HISTORY

> The consequences of a belief upon other beliefs and upon behavior may be so important, then, that men are forced to consider the grounds or reasons of their beliefs and its logical consequences. This means reflective thought—though in its eulogistic and emphatic sense.
>
> JOHN DEWEY, *How We Think* (1997, 5)

Consider the affinities of American pragmatism, as a philosophical program in focus in this chapter, and American behaviorism, as a scientific one, distilled in chapter 1. Note first that they are similarly attuned to the practical analysis of difference. Indeed, both are disciplined programs of reflexively

tracking what happens by way of certain acts and adjusting one's own behavior accordingly. They train professional attention on the difference between expectation and what actually happens, which produces yet another
situation for analysis and action. No wonder that both programs have little
patience for analyses that assume answers are found in essences, including
the notion that observable human behavior can be satisfyingly explained
by putatively co-present and/or causal, if opaque, mental states. As Dewey
insisted, significance lies in "the act of seeing" rather than in some knowledge revealed through the experience "of light" (1972, 97).

Though MI quietly concedes its roots in American behaviorism, as we
know from chapter 1, its pragmatism—as a vernacular—only became clear
to me once I observed the transition from Ki's training to Fred's. Then, I
began to see signs of it all over MI—in exercises like "Out of the Woods"
and "Observer Tracking," in trainers' gentle but insistent admonishments,
in between the lines of the "MI Bible." I also began to appreciate what a
pragmatic mindset could do for the helping professionals whom I, as an
anthropologist, have long taken as my primary interlocutors. This was
made particularly clear in the penultimate meeting with Fred at U-Haven,
when Jamal effectively reframed—or, *repragmatized*—the problem at hand.
Let us briefly play out what might have happened if not for his intervention. Austin could feel himself the recipient of knowledge, having inherited it from Fred, like a chunk of expertise. He could then use this thing-
like knowledge to make sense of everything his client might say and do in
the future, all reduced to predictable signs of AIDS-related dementia and
treated by prescription. With the problem and the client typified, even fro-
zen, Austin would effectively be released from engaging with and learning
from his interlocutor.

Jamal, and the vernacular pragmatism of MI he expresses, radically dis-
rupts this all-too-common practice. He encourages Austin to be an apprentice who learns from his clients rather than a professional who already
knows them. This means relinquishing certainty, "eulogizing" knowledge
as the potentially dangerous sedimentation of "belief upon other beliefs"
(Dewey 1997, 5), so one can continue to engage in and learn from a conversation, always in search of signs for what to do next. This also means taking
one's interlocutor seriously, always looking to their descriptions for courses
of action. As Jamal put it in an interview, "What I try to do is . . . honestly
listen to [clients] . . . and, and help them to meet their needs and . . . if they
don't have any pressing needs at that at a particular time, my responsibility
is to keep . . . the rapport open so that if a need becomes available, they'll
feel comfortable in describing that need to me, and then seeing if I can help
them meet that need."

However, pragmatism is not a panacea, as Jamal—a Black man, with his own history of poverty and homelessness—surely knows from personal experience. After all, before he was a professional at U-Haven, he was a client there. Working now with an encampment of chronically homeless individuals, many of whom had no form of documentation and whose days were filled with violence, trauma, and multifaceted suffering, he can understand how lived histories of difference shaped professional interactions from the start, repeatedly landing some people and not others in the role of interviewee. And while MI's vernacular presentism sensitized U-Haven professionals to their interactions, including what they could learn and do in the present so as to shape the future, it may not be especially well equipped to help them satisfactorily reckon with how enduring social inequities repeatedly and predictably set the stage for their engagements. If we are to accept the pragmatic premise that what we can see and what can we do are entwined, expanding the scope of professional vision would allow for more radical and just interventions.[12]

Arguably, such a charge is well beyond the reach of what any single helping professional can reasonably be expected to do. That does not mean we should not worry that while MI allows professionals to "work the difference" in one way—by dislodging authoritative knowledge, more closely attending to what clients say, and opening up the question of what to do next—it may encourage them to deny difference in another, a dynamic to which we will return in the conclusion. To be sure, reflective listening should include listening carefully for history in the present, adjusting what is known, and figuring out what to do, even if one's contribution to social justice work is undertaken one dyad at a time.

Whereas in chapter 1, we learned that the "expert trap" is problematic because it undemocratically elevates the knowledge of the practitioner above the client, in this chapter we learned that a particular kind of expertise—one that treats knowledge as something one has rather than something one does—is a threat to MI's vernacular pragmatism (see Carr 2010a). That said, it is worth mentioning that Fred's approach to knowledge, along with the features of his own social history, has garnered recognition and respect as an expert, and the professional stability that goes along with that. Perhaps predictably, when asked to conduct an advanced training in MI at a local university months later, he chose Austin and not Jamal to train alongside him. And while it is easier for some to perform expertise, and costs less for others to relinquish it, enacting (in)expertise has different costs for differently positioned professionals—a dynamic MI's proponents would do well to openly acknowledge, given their general appreciation that what we can see and hear is so closely correlated with what we can do.

Dealing with Difference and the Movement of Method

I recently started a new research project on the rise and spread of canine-assisted therapy (CAT) in the United States. Just the other day, at my current field site, where a full-time working dog accompanies abused children through medical exams, forensic interviews, therapy sessions, and waiting rooms, I listened to a clinical supervisor review the case notes of an intern, who is pursuing a professional master's degree in Child Life. The supervisor gently if insistently questioned the intern about whether knowledge of a child's diagnosis with a disability affected various, and seemingly unsupported, conclusions in the case notes. She read passages aloud in order to show the intern how her notes were beset by mid-level theories about *who* the child *is*, rather than observed details about what the child *had said or done* (when, where, and in reaction to what). Though I am paraphrasing here, which I am generally reluctant to do, I am confident that the revealing tutelage went something like this:

> Here, you write: "The boy is confident despite his situation." What did he do to make you say "he's confident"? And here: you shouldn't say, he was "happy" or "excited." Write down exactly what made you think that . . . like, "his face lit up," or "he jumped up and ran over," or something like that. You say that "he wanted to go to garden." Has he been here before? How did he know about the garden? Did you suggest the garden to him? It's totally fine if you did, but that's something also to note down.

This was hardly the first time I recognized something of myself in the helping professionals I study. This time I heard echoes of my ethnography course, during those lessons in which I try to relay the mode of attention and documentation that makes for rich fieldnotes. As the supervisor warned her intern against all the important matters missed when one resorts to typification, I was also reminded of my affinity with the helping professionals I met researching this book, including Ki, Norman, Libby, and Jamal. As I argued in chapter 5, these professionals practice pragmatism under the name of MI, and some train others in it. And when Ki tells his apprentices—and Jamal later reminds Austin—to slow down, to reflect, to attend to the significant details that others overlook, to learn from them rather than dismiss what doesn't fit into expectations, I understand that I practice pragmatism under the name of anthropology. Indeed, the lessons Ki underscored on his last day at U-Haven significantly overlap with what I think, at least ideally, distinguishes my own profession from neighboring social sciences.

My continued engagement with helping professionals is fueled as much by persistent puzzles as it is by these affinities and sympathies, including my wonder about how people sustain themselves in this line of work. In my early twenties, I thought I might want to be a social worker myself, and earned an MSW on my way to a PhD. But it didn't take me long to realize, if with a rightful bit of shame, that I probably could never last as a social worker and really wouldn't want to if I could. From my first internship through every social service setting I've since studied, I have watched helping professionals struggling with their charge to find solutions to endlessly complex if not irresolvable problems no matter how paltry the resources at hand. It's almost as if they are always being asked to build that perfect communication device from old soup cans and faded manuals, as evoked in the prologue. And if such a task is not frustrating enough, they are repeatedly told that their charge is urgent and their failure might result in dire consequences: the continued abuse of the child they just treated; an overdose death of a longtime client who recently celebrated thirty days of sobriety; the deportation of the immigrant family of four for whom they finally found decent housing; and so on and on. Hence my respect for those being asked to take ethnographic-style fieldnotes in a compressed and pressurized context, one to which my own circumstances as an academic hardly compare.

As much as helping professionals want to, and work to, solve the problems they encounter each day, they typically only have recourse to applying some patch or another, then hoping it holds. Their proximity to systemic failure and the suffering it causes is not just first-row, but also frontline. This, by the way, is precisely why it irks—and sometimes even infuriates—me when anthropologists interested in social suffering caricature or simply overlook the professionals within their fields of study. How else could they imply the unparalleled intimacy, sensitivity, and that depth of analysis achieved through their anthropological labor? What irony from a discipline that has actively questioned sovereign vision for at least the last fifty years!

Both despite and in light of these qualms, I ended up pursuing anthropology—and more particularly, the anthropology of social work and other helping professions. Over twenty-five years of research, I have never lost my amazement that so many people voluntarily tolerate work like those in this book's opening thought experiment, let alone those I followed at U-Haven and now study at a Children's Advocacy Center. This means that I also readily understand the notoriously high rates of burnout and turnover, particularly on the mean corners and in the menacing episodes of late capitalism (see Graeber 2018).[1] So while some appear aghast when I relay that MI is first and foremost a treatment for helping professionals themselves, rather than their clients, I very much appreciate the effort to revive and revitalize those driven and drained by such a challenging professional mission. It is sorely needed, along with significant pay raises, more training and resources with which to work, and the solidarity that comes with unionization and job security. And while I certainly don't think MI is equipped to resolve these myriad issues, I have nevertheless witnessed how the method can reinvigorate helping professionals' ways of seeing problems and acting accordingly, thus leading them to reinvest in otherwise draining work.

However, as the preceding chapters have shown, MI does not just revive helping professionals in social service organizations like U-Haven so that they can devote fresh energy to their established line of work. Some professionals become MI revivalists (or MINTies) themselves, leaving their posts to go off and train the method to others, thereby reproducing it. Given this phenomenon, onlookers might readily recognize the pyramidic qualities of MI's dissemination (see introduction, pp. 18–19) and think that an economic explanation would suffice. For example, some may focus on how MI launches once trapped and poorly paid social workers as entrepreneurs who travel the country, and sometimes the world, leaving behind the dismal conditions of windowless rooms, paltry remuneration, and impossible caseloads. Others may feel satiated by an examination of the economics of behavioral health and social service provision in the United States, and its scientization, assuming MI spreads precisely to the extent it is considered and adopted as a reimbursable "evidence-based practice" (chapter 4). Others still might propose, more or less cynically, that MI proponents have simply found a way to most attractively package ideas about "helpfulness" or "good practice" that have been around for decades.

With increased proximity to the world of MI, the more ephemeral aspects of its dissemination inevitably capture one's attention. Recall that insiders claim that it is MI spirit that calls them, mobilizes them, and thereby moves the method (chapter 3); they even occasionally imply that the spirit has the power to spread the method on its own. In response, outsiders raise suspicious eyebrows, wondering if MI is something of a cult. Once learning that MI spirit both depends on, and exceeds, MI techniques, requiring that the method be modeled and transmitted in face-to-face training, some might suggest that claims of spirit are just another canny way that proponents market MI, assuring that capital continually flows through professional chains of distribution. In the meantime, the anthropologist in the crowd might point out that MI promises a quintessentially democratic practice to the professionals it trains (chapter 1); offers them ways to channel sincerity and generate charisma when they speak (chapter 2); and liberally draws on established North American psychologies, while vernacularizing and operationalizing a prominent strain of American philosophy (chapter 5).

As I trust this book has by now demonstrated, quite aside from the relative merits of each of these arguments, none of them alone is sufficient to explain MI's impressive travels across professional fields. Indeed, the case of MI teaches us that innovation must make itself legible and demonstrate its value to a wide variety of audiences if it hopes to extend its reach. Part of this work involves tapping into, and resonating with, rather than simply claiming to improve or displace, that which is already widely appreciated, firmly established, and institutionally entrenched—whether as science, as religion, as politics, as profession, as an effective way of talking, or as an ethical way of being. However, the study of MI also reveals that crafting a method that is culturally resonant and recognizable is not nearly enough. If we are to understand how novel cultural forms transcend the sites of their birth and baptism, leaving their more parochial brethren behind, we must examine the ways they must continually enact their value, to show that they can produce new ways of thinking about, seeing, and acting upon old and stubborn problems.

Anthropologists, among others, have effectively shown how things that appear to simply "flow" through the world require significant labor. And while this often involves a variety of actors working together to create a sense of constancy through transformations so that things on the move may discovered again and again as coherently the same across contexts, MI sheds light on how a method moves—and even becomes a movement—by actively highlighting, defusing, and draining conflict out of what it identifies as potentially troubling sites of *difference*. In the end, the study of MI suggests that an innovation's ability to cross institutional lines may depend, more than we may have imagined, on the careful and highly selective management of normative oppositions.

This book has focused on MI's uncanny ability to manage ideological difference. As we have seen, sometimes this involves combining what appears to be theoretically or epistemologically incompatible ideas, such as Miller's insistence that motivation is *both* an unalienable psychic property of persons *and* an engineerable product of social interaction. This paradoxical proposal entails defying the disciplines and schools of thought that have historically organized these ideas as opposing ones. For instance, in line with the example above, we can recall MI's assertion that there is no need to choose between the client-centered tradition and the behaviorist/directive one, because MI is both at the same time. Furthermore, MI proponents take pleasure in rejecting distinctions between science and spirit, calling and capital accumulation, positivism and humanism, as many of their nonpartisan brethren and forebears have done before. Yet, in MI, we also see real ingenuity in practically stitching together competing ideals, as with the professional direction of those whom they insistently recognize as autonomous (chapter 1) or with the crafting of a conversation style, replete with rhetorical technique, that sounds simply like sincere self-expression (chapter 2).

Depending on one's perspective, MI's facility for turning partisanship into paradox, soothing ideological rifts, and refusing tired oppositions has some obvious practical benefits. While we have noted the material barriers to MI training and MINT membership, the method spreads a "big tent" in another important sense. MI, as movement, makes room for fierce empiricists with research agendas and university posts (like David) to rub elbows with spiritualists who crisscross the country training MI (like Melony) and devout humanists who take cover under MI's status as an EBP as they supervise their in-house clinical staff (like Vernon); it further assures them there is no need to take (familiar) sides. As I heard repeatedly over the course of my research, this bounteous and concertedly nonpartisan communal engagement, alone, invigorates participants in the world of MI training.

In addition, given the various professional backgrounds, locales, and proclivities of those called and collectivized by MI, MINTies have diverse networks. In this sense, MI training is more than simply pyramidic. MI trainers act as tentacles, moving MI into expanding fields of practice and "astonishing" and delighting William Miller as they go. Indeed, the American Miller commonly tells his audiences, "I can't keep track of the places that [MI] keeps popping up," not only in terms of the method's growing professional applications, but also in its expanding international presence.

As indicated in the introduction, if I think of MI as an American movement, Miller insists that the method has been transnational—or, more particularly, has *transcended* the national—from the start. To be sure, MI has always had a strong presence in Britain and Scandinavia, and MINT clearly characterizes itself as a culturally diverse organization by way of its international membership. For instance, the organization states on its website that since its founding in 1997, MINT "has since grown to represent 35 countries and more than 20 different languages." In very similar terms, in a presentation of MI's "current status" in 2014, Miller not only highlighted the remarkable scholarly focus on MI, but also emphasized the countries and languages in which MI is now trained and practiced. "Whole states and whole *nations* are implementing motivational interviewing in the corrections system or mental health system or whatever, so I'm just astonished," Miller proclaimed in showing the slide, shaking his lowered head with marked humility before adding, "It has just taken off like a rocket."

While these portrayals of MI's international spread make prominent use of impressive numbers, the global distribution of MINT trainers shows distinct if unsurprising patterns. Consider an interactive map posted on the MINT website that uses color-coded signposts to mark the number of MINT trainers residing in various countries, except for the United States, where individual states and territories are given their very own markers. Off the bat, one sees the dramatic concentration of MI trainers in the Global North. Observing further, one realizes that without the color-coding, the map would be unreadable, given the density of MI trainers in relatively small countries in Northern Europe. A more detailed reading of the map reveals yet another intriguing pattern: those countries with the most MI trainers are majority Protestant ones (with the interesting exception of Japan).

Recall when I discussed MI's global distribution with Miller, mentioning its relative prevalence in Protestant countries, he demurred, suggesting instead that more "authoritarian cultures" would naturally resist MI, given its democratic aspirations (see chapter 1). Aside from this quiet qualification, Miller not only regularly counts the countries where MI is trained and the languages that trainers use when doing so—much as he tallies RCTs—he also repeatedly cites what he apparently takes to be an awe-inspiring limit-case. In a 2009 address at a health disparities conference held at Columbia Teacher's College, available now on YouTube, Miller used that case to offer a theory of MI's cross-cultural appeal:

> Motivational interviewing seems to cross cultures pretty well. And *why* is that? *Why* has it been adopted *all over the world,* long before there was evidence, long before there were local trainers, people were picking it up, using it in the African *bush* to promote water purification technologies so that babies don't die of diarrhea . . . just *astonishing* things that I would have never bet on . . . And it appears to require, from my expe-

rience around the world, relatively little adaptation to use in different cultures; the doggone thing seems to *communicate* and *take root* without needing to be very different . . . It seems to be very much the *same heart.*[2]

If "same heart" sounds familiar, it is because it is precisely the term Miller used to describe his first chance encounter with Rollnick, whose Australian role-play evinced "exactly the same heart" as his own Norwegian demonstrations did (see introduction, p. 15). And whereas he joked then that his South African co-author is a *bushman,* he provides a more literal reference to the African "bush" as he highlights MI's global reach to an academic audience interested in health disparities. Because he has referenced it before, including formal citations in MI's foundational textbook, I know that Miller is drawing on the published work of Angelica Thevos, who conducted two intervention studies with Zambian public health workers (Thevos et al. 2000; Thevos et al. 2002). However, note that the American-based Thevos is stricken from this public account of MI's ability to save African babies. Miller even oddly claims that "long before there were local trainers" and "long before there was evidence," those dwelling in the African *bush* were "picking [MI] up," to his astonishment.

On other occasions, the generous Miller has credited Thevos's work on water sanitation in Zambia. I also expect that if he had done so here, he would have elaborated on a theme we have seen repeatedly in Miller's mystical account of MI's spread. In the same way that MI spirit used Miller as a "scribe," he implies that whatever training Thevos's team provided was simply building on what people already knew, at least in their "heart." That it is the *same heart* is also crucial, implying that there is something essentially human about MI that not only "communicates" across cultural difference, but seems to erase that difference, or at least render it meaningless: "the doggone thing seems to communicate and take root without needing to be very different." Indeed, in Miller's account here and elsewhere, difference is collapsed into the idea of a single, universal "heart" from which and to which MI knows how to "*communicate,*" whatever language is used.

Notice, too, Miller's use of organic imagery of MI "taking root," which is consistent with his claim that MI—replete as it is with Anglo-American rhetorical devices—is a "natural language" (Miller & Rollnick 2013, 4), an aspirational claim that also has a long American history. When I interviewed US-based MINTies who trained internationally, they often echoed these official portraits, suggesting that MI is a way of being and speaking that communicates across cultural difference. At the same time, they also sometimes betrayed that the circulation of MI "across cultures" is not nearly as easy as it seems when portrayed in Miller's account, instead requiring significant and often stressful translational work.

Consider Travis. Within a minute of my sitting down with him in a room filled with tropical plants in a northeastern American city where he conducts men's therapy groups, Travis told me that he trains MI "150 to 160 days a year" and that he "travels the world" doing so: China, Sweden, Hawaii, a weekend in "Jersey." In case I had any lingering question about how far and wide Travis moved MI, he offered: "You know, I guess what I would say is that I've probably seen every population, done every group, um . . . from corrections to adult corrections to medication resistance to drug . . . drug addictions to therapy communities. The list goes on."[3]

As I had done with all the other MINTies I interviewed, I asked Travis to share his own theory about why MI has spread the way it has. In terms I had heard many times before, he responded that MI spreads because it is "*soooo* culture friendly" and because the method is "*natural . . . it touches* people; it *touches* people, it *touches* practitioners, it *touches* . . ." Saturated with such responses, I wondered if there was a way to elicit from Travis something novel. Tearing a page out of my interlocutors' book, I replaced a probing question with an amplified reflection, stating: "So there's something fundamental about, sort of, how MI hooks up with human nature that allows it to be applied in China or Tanzania or the US or Stockholm." As paltry as my MI skills are, they paid some interesting dividends. I was stunned when Travis responded, apparently triggered by one of the nation-states on my list. "I had a *horrible* time in China," he declared.

Now staring down at the floor as if reliving some trauma, Travis went on to explain his "turmoil" while training MI to Chinese doctors working in the field of smoking cessation. By his own account, once in Shanghai, Travis asked himself repeatedly what he was doing and why he was even there. "I can't even *listen* to them because I don't know any Chinese," Travis recounted. This questioning was compounded by the fact that he was "riddled" with "American guilt," given "that US tobacco companies are responsible for *80 percent* of Chinese male smokers and the consequent cancer deaths." As if he were now talking to himself rather than to an anthropologist with a recording device, Travis—with his forearms resting on his bent knees and shoulder-length gray hair hanging over the sides of his bowed head—murmured: "I mean I . . . I . . . What am I *doing* sitting with *doctors*? I'm not a doctor. I'm talking to them about *smoking*? I don't know *anything* about China."

As we know from previous chapters, (MI) faith and (MI) science both thrive on doubt, and just as quickly as Travis's account of a quintessentially culture-friendly MI had turned into a horror story, he reverted to a familiar refrain. Looking up now and locking eyes with me, Travis dramatically continued: "So you know what happened to me? [*2 second pause*] I had to *trust* that this was a *human* interaction, not a procedure, but a *human* interaction." With this assertion of MI's ability to cut through cultural and linguistic difference by tapping into the universal human, Travis was narratively released, if not from his material labor, then from the psychic burden that once stymied his efforts. "I could finally get to train them and just let them be. Let them talk and let them do it themselves," he told me. And indeed, Travis continued his work in China, returning to the country four times. He even produced a demonstration film of himself motivationally interviewing an American smoker, to which Chinese subtitles were added. Weeks after our visit, I received a copy of the DVD in the mail, with a handwritten notecard that reminded me, "We listen to people."

∴

At about the same time that Miller was questioning his training in American psychology, American anthropology began a trenchant self-accounting, commonly glossed as the "reflexive turn." While this spawned an array of disciplinary experiments, they were united by a single question: how can the (North American/Western European/British) anthropologist really learn anything about difference if they refuse to interrogate the position from which they observe and "listen to people"?

One common response in US anthropology was to "repatriate," taking one's presumed homeland as the only ethical ground of study (Marcus & Fisher 1986). This move was readily recognized by some as thoroughly beset with its own problems, such as who can call what ground "home," and by what historical reasoning, especially in a settler-colonial state built in part by enslaved persons (see, for example, Mohanty 1984; Ong 1988). Many began to wonder just how productive "the turn" had really been, and for whom, including a whole host of feminist anthropologists, who rightly claimed they had been inquiring about the representational politics and practices of "writing culture" well before Clifford and Marcus (1986) began (see Behar & Gordon 1996). More recently, a similarly trenchant line of questioning has led some to the provocative suggestion that perhaps it is time to let American anthropology "burn," along with the rest of the planet (see Jobson 2020).

In the 1970s, the most prominent North American anthropologists who were publicly working out which way, and how, to "turn" were white men, if only because they largely ignored the contemporaneous anthropological work of women and scholars of color. It was legal anthropologist Laura Nader who broke through the ironic silencing by famously calling on anthropologists to "study *up*" (1972; emphasis added), thereby giving rise to a large and rich anthropological literature on elites, professionals, and experts of various stripes, which continues to grow today.[4]

Yet as this book shows, when one "repatriates" and "studies up," one frequently encounters ways of dealing with difference that are similar, sometimes even identical, to those that anthropologists have long worked to leave behind. This raises critical dilemmas. For however relatively enlightened the North American anthropologist might want to believe herself to be, and however quickly she might point to the hubris built into Travis's and Miller's accounts, she should first remember why, despite fifty years of disciplinary reflection, the radically disappointing results have some colleagues and compatriots calling to *burn it down*. Difference is hard to deal with, and my own profession and I myself have not always done such a good job of it.

Furthermore, as an *American* method and movement, MI has much proximate company. As Savannah Shange (2019) has recently demonstrated, even earnest attempts to deal with racial difference in the United States are plagued by white progressives' stubborn blindness to the institutional perches from which they see and act, perches that are anti-Black from start to finish. In addition to progressive schooling, we could list many institutional forms in the United States that have a fractal relationship with whiteness, which would then require us to foreground questions like: who can make universal claims about what a "natural language" is? Who identifies the *same heart*? From what position does MI "listen to people," and who is the "we" that purportedly listens? Who can affordably deny expertise? Who gets to recognize whom?

These kinds of questions are not new, and they are not ones to which US-based MINTies should be solely charged with the responsibility of providing more satisfactory answers. They are ones I try to ask myself, my students, and my fellow anthropologists, because the failure to adeptly deal with sociological differences—that is, inequities—and the suffering they cause should press upon us all here and now. Indeed, if I have not yet sufficiently convinced my readers that MI is American—and American democracy, American rhetoric, American spirit, American science, and American pragmatism, more specifically—I will give it one last try, coming from another angle: MI is American to the extent that it fails to *historically situate itself* and its ways of seeing and speaking to others.

∴

It will, by now, come as no surprise to readers that MI has more than one way of dealing with what it calls "cultural difference." With this in mind, and with our end in sight, let us briefly consider three especially curious pages that appear late in MI-3, the 2013 edition of the MI Bible. According to the book's index, these pages (348–51) address "cultural issues, in MI applications." In those pages, one finds a dissonant rendering of MI's take on the matter, one that is apparently directed to critics who charge—much as I have done—that MI is a culturally specific communication style that may not enjoy universal resonance. After several hundred pages of warm welcome, Miller and Rollnick now warn that such critics are relativists, united by "frustration or skepticism that MI might not work with a particular subgroup" (Miller & Rollnick 2013, 348). Interestingly, they promptly turn the tables, writing: "the idea that all members of a particular group require or prefer one communication style underestimates within-group heterogeneity and itself smacks of stereotype" (349). Thus, if Miller tells his live audience that MI "appears to require, from my experience around the world, relatively little adaptation to use in different cultures," he and his co-author write instead: "MI adapts to differences rather than assuming them" (349).

This can be read as a classically pragmatic statement, of course, reflective of MI's commitment to anti-essentialism. Under some circumstances, I am quite sympathetic to this view.[5] That said, it can also be read as a refusal to situate the position from which one makes an audacious claim: that MI can accommodate difference wherever it discovers it. The refusal to "assume" population-specific and other demographic differences crops up elsewhere in MI's foundational text. For instance, if one combs its long index, as I have done many times, one finds some telling omissions in otherwise content-packed, nine-point font. Although at page 475 the index gives 56 lines of text devoted to "Engagement," "Equipoise," and "Evoking change talk," there is no entry for "Ethnicity." Turning the page, one finds no "Gender" entry wedged between "Gandhi, Mathatma, 352," and "Generalizability, 402." And if looking for MI's take on "Race" or "Racism," one will come up empty again. (No need to search further for "Sexual orientation," it is safe to presume, nor to flip back to the letter C in search of "Class").

This whitewashed index recalls the demographics of MI's most widely circulating training films, as discussed in the introduction. There, I noted—as MI trainees sometimes did—that almost all of the actors in these films are white, whether playing the role of professional or client. While representative of MINT membership in the United States (which was, by my best estimation, approximately 80–85 percent white during the period of this study), these prominent portrayals of the method stand in stark contrast to the demographics of US-based helping professionals trained in MI and even more dramatically to those professionals' clientele (see figure 0.2). Of course, it is hard to know, and rather beside the point, how intentional this casting and staging may have been. As I offered in an earlier chapter, given that Miller and Moyers play the therapists in these films, it is safe to bet that casting women and/or people of color as client actors might foreground the inequities that MI, with its democratic aspirations, is intent on transcending.

Staging the demographic difference in a way that accurately reflects social service and behavioral health interventions in the United States could further highlight the directive qualities of the motivational interview, which—as we know from chapters 1 and 2—MI's trainees learn to rhetorically downplay. Indeed, some of Miller's and Moyers's brilliant maneuvers to subtly direct Ponytail John and Rounder into change statements might seem more obvious, and perhaps more problematic, had a nonwhite actor been sitting across from them. After all, to mark particular "kinds" of people would suggest that demographic barriers could hinder, if not halt, the circulation of the method—a suggestion that purveyors of the method have many reasons to want to avoid. To not do so, however, is to allow white American men to continue their starring role as universal subjects, who stand for everything and nothing (in particular). And while I do not doubt for a moment Miller's earnest belief in the universal humanism he espouses, the spread of MI is certainly facilitated by the figure of the undifferentiated human with the "same heart" through which MI can simply flow.

So despite MI's impressive, even inspiring, agility in managing differences in other ways, the method is hardly innovative when it comes to demographic difference—whether in the United States or abroad. Nevertheless, I continue to think that within MI (and within anthropology) there may be some promise of a more productive way to "turn." With that in mind, I will conclude by letting Ki explain what can and should matter about MI, well outside training rooms, once again.

· ·

Before the U-Haven training started, Ki told me that in 2005 he took a contract with the US State Department to train MI to Iraqi Kurds. Specifically, his task was to teach MI to community mental health workers who had the complex and highly fraught task of identifying and treating victims of "state torture." By the time I began talking with Ki about his work in the war-torn, US-occupied country, he had been to northern Iraq seven times, training workers with the idea that MI would help engage and retain torture survivors in "a form of a treatment that they might not be ready, willing, or able to accept or participate in," given their political as well as psychological circumstances. Ki eventually instituted a "train-the-trainer" model—much like MINT's, if on a much smaller scale—so that MI training could continue in between and well after his visits.

Ki clearly understood that his work as an American in Iraq was freighted in many ways, which probably explains why he never brought it up over the previous nine months of the U-Haven training. And although Ki told me, "the people of Iraq have a very special place in my heart," he was also quick to concede: "It's hard enough to train motivational interviewing in English. It was very hard to train it across . . . cultures and across language." Ki described the disorienting and sometimes excruciating process of working with the most "well-meaning" of interpreters, particularly in circumstances that he keenly understood could not be more politically loaded. That said, Ki's solution was very different from that of his fellow MINTie, Travis. Rather than taking relief in a universalist narrative, he stayed true to MI's pragmatism, and accordingly asked himself a set of trenchant questions about the very categories he was trying to translate.

For instance, Ki realized that more than "linguistic difference" stood in the way of training MI when he and the interpreter were looking for the right Kurdish word for "empathy." And if beset by the American guilt that Travis felt in Shanghai, Ki began to wonder about the idea of empathy itself. When we spoke, Ki was still turning questions about empathy over in his head: "It's hard enough. I mean, what *is* empathy? You know? How do you understand it? How do you know you're doing it? What *is* it?"

If such questions sound familiar to readers, it is because they are the ones that North American MINTies and North American anthropologists—having both had large doses of pragmatism injected into their training—are supposed to continually ask themselves. Note that Ki doesn't question whether Iraqi Kurds have, know, or value empathy, as if empathy can be taken as a given. Nor does Ki's inquiry leave the definition of empathy—one of MI's foundational principles of practice—unquestioned, as if it were the stable ground from which to measure his Kurdish trainees' response. Indeed, notice the deictic play of the pronoun "you" in Ki's report above, which points at once to himself, to the Kurds with whom he interacted, to me, and implicitly and critically to a universal absence that can never answer the question. As a good pragmatist, Ki not only asks what empathy *is*, he also actively wonders aloud: "how do you know you're doing it?" folding the mystery of empathy back onto itself and, by extension, himself as the person trying to understand it even as he teaches it.

As enlivening as it is frustrating, Ki's line of inquiry is an exemplar of the pragmatic method. Like Peirce and Dewey, if through MI, Ki understands that his work must keep questions alive, always with the understanding that immediate answers are only temporary, best guesses. Those guesses themselves should derive from situated experience and specific interactions, which are never complete and should therefore never be generalized. Furthermore, as Dewey once advised, the "consequences of a belief upon other beliefs and upon behavior may be so important" that we are "forced to consider the grounds or reasons of [our] beliefs" (1997, 5). This is a pragmatism endowed with a reflexivity that historically situates itself, asking what of the past we can see in the present and why, as well as what we need to dislodge in the immediate present to keep learning and growing in the future. Ki honed if not acquired this way of thinking as he learned how to do a motivational interview. It revitalized his own work and revived those he taught.

How, then, might we bring these pragmatic sensibilities in MI to scale? With that question in mind, I must now humbly ask MI—as well-trained motivational interviewers regularly ask their clients—for "permission to give some advice" (Miller & Rollnick 2013, 141).

MI needs more paradox, not less. Over so many generous engagements, MINTies like Ki have convinced me that something—whether in principle, practice, or fact—can be simultaneously known and unknown, deeply felt and expressly fictional, a falsehood and a truth. Along with my anthropological training, MI has further taught me that paradox is not a logical contradiction immune to history; rather, paradox is what Greg Urban (2001) calls *metaculture*, a way that people stimulate ideas, beliefs, and practices by combining, reflecting on, and puzzling over what they would otherwise assume to be categorical oppositions. After all these years, the study of MI has helped me realize that what I, with all my equivocations and disciplinary qualifications, call "culture" depends less on what people hold in common than on how people cope with what is normatively held apart.

So, with the closing of this study of helping professionals, which has inspired the beginning of my next one, I've come to believe that the best of North American MI is like the best of North American anthropology. If we share shortcomings, we also share great promise: reflecting on our own as well as others' native categories and concepts, remembering always to take these categories as hypotheticals rather than essences, and experimenting with what one can think and do with them. And while the clinical supervisor at my new field site suggests neither course of training is necessary to develop such sensibilities, I can say with confidence: it certainly helps a lot.

Acknowledgments

There are many people without whom this book would not have been possible, and to whom I am profoundly grateful. This begins with my interlocutors in the field, from MI's developers and lead proponents to the trainers and trainees whose work I observed over an extended period. In addition to those like "Ki" and "Libby," who allowed me to shadow them for months on end, there were many who—as relative strangers—offered insights during interviews and more informal exchanges. Indeed, MINTies almost unfailingly responded affirmatively to my cold-call requests for interviews, often following up with me over email, sometimes just checking in to see how my slow-going writing was coming along. Those who participated in this study demonstrated an abiding interest and investment in getting an outside perspective on their practice, which precipitated two invitations to speak at the annual MINT Forum—in 2014 and 2022—when I was showered with thoughtful questions as well as new angles and ideas to consider. Even those who contribute to MI by studying it, using very different methods than my own, welcomed another (and very different) way to examine MI. I am especially thankful that William R. Miller reached out in the very beginning stages of my research, invited me to speak with him on numerous occasions, and was always quick to share thoughtful and often intriguing responses to my publications. I wish I could name all the others who also generously participated in this research, but I trust you know who you are!

Back on my own professional home front: there is no shortage of people to learn from and laugh with at the University of Chicago. This begins with my trusty writing group, consisting of three dear colleagues and friends: Julie Chu, Jennifer Cole, and Constantine Nakassis. We began writing together in 2012, and since that time, each one has taken great pains to read chapter drafts while pretending that it was a pleasure to do so.

There are many other colleagues, past and present, at the University of Chicago who have supported this project along the way. I am especially indebted to Susan Gal, who has been a sage mentor and friend, and who has offered excellent guidance on this project at several critical junctures. I am also profoundly appreciative of Joseph Masco's steady encouragement and incisive feedback. His ability to gently direct while seeming to fully recognize my struggles made me sometimes wonder if he himself was a closet motivational interviewer. Many thanks are owed to Bill Sites, who tolerated my griping and provided words of wisdom when I found myself stuck. My late colleagues—Michael Silverstein and Michael Sosin—helped inspire and cultivate my early work on this project, if in very different ways.

With the support of the Center of International Social Science Research, led by Jenny Trinatapoli, I was able to convene a book workshop consisting of Charles Briggs, Michael Lempert, Danilyn Rutherford, and Gregory Urban. Each brought their special brand of brilliance to bear on very early drafts of the chapters that became this book. As I revised, I often looked back on the notes from that workshop taken by then second-year doctoral student, Hannah Obertino Norwood. I am profoundly indebted to their early interventions. For supporting my field research, I am grateful for funding I received from the University of Chicago's Crown Family School of Social Work, Policy and Practice and the Center for Health Administration Studies, as well as an outside grant from the Fahs-Beck Foundation.

Many other university infrastructures helped foster this project, including the US Locations Workshop, the Semiotics Workshop, and the Medicine, Body, Practice Workshop—all of which invited me to present draft chapters. I thank Nicholas Harkness, Jenny Hua, and Lily Ye for their insightful discussions of early versions of chapters 2, 3, and 1, respectively. This book developed under the influence of the interinstitutional gem known as "Michicagoan"—consisting of linguistic and semiotic anthropologists (mostly) housed at the University of Michigan and the University of Chicago. Brilliance abounds within Michicagoan, and I thank Susan Gal, Judith Irvine, Alaina Lemon, Bruce Mannheim, Barbra Meek, Costas Nakassis, Susan Philips, Justin Richland, the late Michael Silverstein, and Kristina Wirtz for their comments on this work. Special thanks are owed to Michicagoan members Richard Bauman, Matt Hull, and Michael Lempert, all of whom offered discussant remarks on chapters at different stages of development and all of whom happen to be especially brilliant fellows that I am lucky enough to count as friends. Webb Keane, with whom I worked in graduate school, continued to offer his encouragement, feedback, and inspiration while this project was underway, in part through his participation in the Michicagoan group.

In addition to those mentioned above, I am grateful for the camaraderie and collegiality of fellow UChicago faculty members, past and present. In addition to those named above, special thanks are owed to Hussein Agrama,

Bill Borden, Evelyn Brodkin, Sean Brotherton, Jessica Cattelino, Robert Fairbanks, Judith Farquhar, Julie Henly, Don Kulick, Zhiying Ma, Patchen Markell, Stan McCracken, Virginia Parks, Eugene Raikhel, Danilyn Rutherford, and Tina Rzepnicki. Over my years at the university, I have crossed paths with so many stellar scholars, several of whom I came to know as trusted colleagues and supportive friends, including Amahl Bishara, Hilary Parsons Dick, Paja Faudree, Ilana Gershon, Greg Matoesian, Elizabeth Mertz, Susan Philips, and Ben Smith.

I have also been blessed with a wonderful group of doctoral students over the years of this study. From the outset of my research to the completion of this book, I watched with delight my first set of PhD students graduate and take their own faculty posts, while continuing to introduce scores of professional students to an anthropological sensibility to carry into their practice. Yvonne Smith and Marianne Brennan helped me collect data at U-Haven, and Gregory Thompson provided critical assistance with technological matters. Gregory "Duff" Morton, Aaron Seaman, and Matthew Spitzmueller assisted with interviewing U-Haven training participants, and Patricia Round transcribed many of these interviews. Duff also conducted background research on the economics of MI training. Hilary Agro collected work on charisma for me, which ended up shaping my thinking with material in chapter 3. My former student, Katie Gibson, proofread and offered cover-to-cover editorial comments on the entire manuscript during the summer of 2021. Hannah Obertino Norwood played an especially substantial role in the development of this book, proofreading early chapter drafts and collecting substantial background research on chapter 4, which also led to our recent co-authored paper in *Social Science & Medicine*.

For their invitations to present or publish parts of this work, and their feedback on it, I am grateful to Regina Bendix, Susan Blum, Donald Brenneis, Charles Briggs, Paul Brodwin, Matei Candea, Jessica Cattelino, James Costa, Gil Eyal, Paja Faudree, William Garriott, Andrew Graan, Elina Hartikainen, John Mathias, Thomas Medvetz, Morten Nissen, Dorothy Noyes, Eugene Raikhel, Jurgen Spitzmueller, Matilda Stubbs, and Fiona Wright. Along the way, I received especially generative feedback from Asif Agha, Niels Åkerstrøm Andersen, Lynnette Arnold, Georgina Born, Dominic Boyer, Marcy Brink-Denton, Nancy Campbell, Cecile Canut, James Clark, James Faubion, Mi-Cha Flubacher, Ilana Gershon, Jonas Hassamer, Graham Jones, Hanna Knudsen, Don Kulick, Tess Lea, Aliana Lemon, Michael Oldani, David Prescott, Natacha Schull, Shalini Shankar, Sandra Tanenbaum, Anna Weichselbraun, and Alan Young.

Parts of this book have been previously published in different form. Small sections of chapter 2 and chapter 5 appear in my 2021 paper, "Learning How Not to Know: Pragmatism, (In)expertise, and the Training of American Helping Professionals," *American Anthropologist* 123 (3): 526–38. The final sections of chapter 2 overlap with the 2014 paper, "The Poetics of Therapeutic Practice: Motivational Interviewing and the Powers of Pause," *Culture, Medicine & Psychiatry* 37 (1): 83–114, co-authored with Yvonne Smith. Sections of chapter 4 have been published in the 2022 paper, "Legitimizing Evidence: The Trans-institutional Life of Evidence-based Practice," *Social Science & Medicine* 310: 115130, co-authored with Hannah Obertino-Norwood. Parts of of chapter 1 have been revised and accepted for publication by Oxford University Press in *The Oxford Handbook of Expertise and Democratic Politics*, edited by Gil Eyal and Thomas Medvetz, due to appear in 2023.

I am thankful to the University of Chicago Press, and especially for the guidance, kindness, and reliability of Kyle Wagner who—even though he inherited this project after Priya Nelson left—has been invested and unfailingly responsive. I am grateful to Priya for her early interest and work on this book, and to my previous editor at Princeton, Fred Appel, with whom I've had many fruitful conversations about this project over the years. Thank you to UCP's Kristin Rawlings for her good spirits, sharp eye, and patient help with figures and permissions, and to Lys Weiss of Post Hoc Academic Publishing Services who copyedited this manuscript. During a busy spring, Bob Offer-Westort industriously produced the index for the book. And, last but not least, I was lucky to be able to count on senior production editor Caterina MacLean, who gracefully kept press matters moving forward.

Life had much in store for me over the course of this study: I was awarded tenure. I had a baby and watched him grow into a twelve-year-old, Armand, delighting in his sensitive and joyful ways of engaging the world. I lost my mother to a difficult battle with brain cancer. My family moved, COVID-19 hit, and we adopted Clyde, who helped inspire my current study of canine-assisted therapies and who has since sustained me with walks and cuddles. Through it all, there has been Daniel. Patient. Steadfast. (Almost) always willing to be pulled away from engaging with his own carefully curated pile of books or podcasts to hear of my latest conundrum, whether born of this project or of my take on the life that swirled around it. Ready with a characteristically brilliant intervention when asked if an idea or interpretation made sense. Sending relevant passages from his own reading along whenever he sensed my enervation. All while doing so much to keep our household running and as happy as could be. I'm not sure how this book or its author would have persevered without my love, Daniel Brian Listoe. I dedicate this book to him.

Appendix

Some Notes on the Study of (In)experts

In the United States, social scientists are among the many professionals who tend to privately presume if not publicly pronounce, with obvious investment and perhaps a bit of conceit, that expertise is something the expert *has*, a hard-won property of intellect. My research to date has convinced me instead that expertise is something one *does*, and must continuously do, in order to be realized and recognized as expert (Carr 2010a). That is to say, expertise is always an interactional process, even when it is cast and consumed as intellectual product.

Among the many things my MI interlocutors taught me: *(in)expertise* is also a matter of ongoing enactment. As we have seen in the preceding pages, MINTies view themselves as lifelong apprentices—or what Lave and Wenger (1991) would call "situated learners"— who continuously engage and learn from the world, rather than as established experts who know and deploy that knowledge (see also, Lave 2011). MI insiders also assume, as I do as an anthropologist, that communication is a kind of interaction that is especially vital to generating knowledge, and that each communicative event offers up the opportunity to learn, not only from one's interlocutors, but from the reflexive evaluation of interaction in real time. After all, people often emerge as more or less expert not in unmediated relationships to the objects they evaluate—whether genes, germs or gems—but rather through the processes of representing those objects in language (Carr 2010a; but see also Briggs 1986; Lave 2011). MINTies' pragmatic attitude was deeply appealing to me as a scholar, and one whose insatiable drive to keep learning regularly competes with my own and others' expectation that I *know*.

Over the course of my research, I also came to realize that one of many reasons MI spreads across an ever growing range of professional fields is because its participants refuse to identify as accomplished experts, in the sense of possessing stable knowledge, and instead continually reinvest in the ongoing work of training themselves and others. In this and other ways, MI raises new and exciting challenges in the social scientific study of expertise, which has typically looked to the ways that would-be experts project authoritative, definitive knowledge (e.g., Bosk 2003; Carr 2010a; Cicourel 1995, 2001; Craciun 2018; Eyal 2013, 2019; Goodwin 1994, 1996; Jones 2011; Mertz 2007; Saunders 2008; Sheehan 2022; Silverstein 2016; see also Bergmann 1992). MI required me to look for far less obvious reasons why some professional practices take institutional form, including the ways that practitioners *work difference.*

Given the in vivo observation that ethnography typically entails, anthropologists are particularly well positioned to illuminate the social dynamics of expertise, whether by documenting how apprentices are socialized, examining how institutions authorize experts, or tracking how expertise is received and engaged by clients and laypersons. However, existing ethnographies of experts and professionals tend to focus on expertise that is already publicly recognized as such, often with a special interest in its travels. If expertise is what people do rather than what they have, we should recognize that even the most authoritative and well-institutionalized expertise has inherent instabilities, and accordingly we should attend to the ways of acting and speaking that are selectively cultivated and recognized *as expertise.* The study of MI training enriches the social scientific literature on expertise by documenting and analyzing the intensively interactive social processes required to generate, and continuously regenerate, (in)expertise.

Professional training is ethnographically alluring, in part, because it so often hosts explicit discourse about the distinguishing features of a particular form of knowledge (for instance, Chumley 2016; Goodwin 1994, 1996; Jacobs-Huey 2003; Mertz 2007; Cicourel 1995; Lave & Wenger 1991; Luhrmann 2000; Saunders 2008; Wilf 2014; cf. Briggs 1986; Lave 2011). When we observe professionals in action, we are left to deduce much of what is often plainly articulated in training, such as theoretical foundations, epistemic bases, genealogies, operational instructions, practical challenges, or anticipated lessons. Furthermore, in the life of a training, wherein apprentices and trainers interact with PowerPoint slides, manuals, tests, instruments, and practice proxies of all sorts, we find abundant doubt, ambivalence, anxiety, and critical questioning alongside explicit rationalizations, justifications, and carefully drawn definitions of what makes some form of knowledge or expertise useful and unique. At the same time, thanks to their bountiful self-descriptions, trainings invite observing anthropologists to connect what is professionally defined and bounded with the broader cultural principles and practices from which trainers more implicitly draw and contribute (see Carr 2021).

For me, MI training was an especially revelatory experience because it is the site where cultural principles and paradoxes are articulated, unpacked into rationales, and experimented with in practice. Luckily enough, in MI, I discovered a professional community who were not just tolerant of an interloping anthropologist, but welcomed me with an interest and investment in getting an outside perspective on their practice.

· ·

Given the way it is disseminated, MI required me to undertake what Hugh Gusterson calls "polymorphous engagement"—that is, "interacting with informants across a number of dispersed sites, not just in local communities, and sometimes in virtual form" as well as "collecting data eclectically from a disparate array of sources in many different ways" (1997, 116). Between 2009 and 2015, I conducted hundreds of hours of ethnographic fieldwork on MI training, including fourteen consecutive months as a participant-observer of an advanced MI training at a large urban social service agency (U-Haven). I observed, as well as audio- and video-recorded all group training sessions at U-Haven, as well as individualized coaching sessions, in which apprentices worked with a contracted coach and coder to review their audio-recorded practice MI sessions, which I also collected. While most of these coaching sessions took place in person, some were conducted over Skype. With the help of two PhD students, I shadowed the twelve U-Haven apprentices in their daily work, with an interest in whether and how they were applying what they learned in training, and conducted formal interviews with all participants before, after, and in the midst of the training.

In addition to this intensive ethnographic work at U-Haven, I observed fourteen MI trainings, which ranged in length from several hours to several days, and which varied in number and professional background of participants, and in institutional and geographic location. I audio-recorded and/or video-recorded approximately half of these trainings, amassing a large archive of verbatim transcripts. My observations included a daylong advanced training, which was co-conducted by U-Haven's trainer ("Ki") and William Miller himself.

I not only observed scores of professionals being trained in MI, but also observed people being *trained to train* MI. In 2014, in conjunction with the talk I delivered at the MINT Forum, I negotiated to participant-observe and audio-record the MINT Training New Trainers (TNT)—at once an intensive training and a rite of passage into MINT membership that directly precedes the forum. One must apply to attend the TNT, showing an extensive record of previous training, coaching, and threshold scores on the MITI—an MI-specific fidelity instrument. If the TNT is the pinnacle training experience, it is usually not the final one. It not only establishes professionals as MINT trainers and, in line with the ethos of this professional community, it also initiates many as lifelong apprentices. By the time I studied the TNT, I had completed most of my fieldwork. Still, I marveled that the same anxieties accompanied the excitement that MINT initiates brought to three days of intensive workshops, which included the usual mix of role-playing, breakout groups, and didactic lectures, run by well-known MINTies. A visit from Miller was among the highlights of TNT by most of the participants' reports.

In addition to the fieldnotes and transcripts from my observations, I collected and analyzed the copious textual material MI trainings generate. This includes trainers' PowerPoint presentations, exercise descriptions, poster paper on which breakout groups tracked their progress on exercises, binders full of MI literature collated by trainers and distributed to apprentices, and training evaluations. To complement this training-specific archive, I collected MINT newsletters and other organization-specific material, trainer websites, and training demonstration films. Though it proved a near impossible task, I attempted to track the ever growing research literature on MI, which now boasts almost 2000 control trials and thousands of articles on the method and its training, along with one lonely ethnographic study.

Interviewing experts on interviewing proved a challenging if rewarding aspect of my fieldwork. Alongside the countless informal, unrecorded exchanges with training participants, I conducted dozens of recorded interviews with participants in MI training, from newcomers to the method's most prominent trainers and proponents. These included interviews with MI's lead proponents and figureheads—William Miller; Stephen Rollnick; and MI researcher, trainer, and star of many MI training films, Theresa Moyers—all of whom are publicly recognized to the degree that I could not afford them the confidentiality granted to my other informants (who are anonymized with pseudonyms). Miller was an especially generous and informative interlocutor, throughout the study, and the series of interviews I did with him in 2010 and 2017 have been invaluable to my understanding of the social significance of MI.

∴

"Studying up" (Nader 1972) and "across" (Gusterson 1997) means that those whom one studies also end up as part of one's audience, once observations are put to ink. This is just one reason that I audio- and video-recorded all of my formal interviews, as well as many of the informal conversations I report in this book. Likewise, in the "naturally occurring" discourse that I present here—from the trainings I studied or my shadowing of trainers and trainees, I rely on a combination of audio- and video-recordings and field-notes. I recorded all of the trainings and coaching sessions I attended at U-Haven (chapters 2, 3, and 5); the training Miller co-led featured in chapter 1; Norman's advanced training group, addressed mostly in the same chapter; as well as the training sessions at MINT's annual TNT. Throughout the text, when reporting on the elicited speech of another, I am careful to mark when I am directly quoting, when I am paraphrasing based on re-corded data, and the relatively rare occasion when I am paraphrasing an-other's words from my fieldnotes. I wish all anthropologists would provide these qualifications, whether or not they are studying elite actors who are likely to read their books.

Further, I acknowledge that my approach to documentation was initially amplified by my knowledge that I was studying a formidable professional movement, if made up of especially generous and engaging individuals, and one that is far more unified than my own professional community. That said, over the course of my engagement with the world of MI, as it became increasingly clear that my account would be laced with some points of af-finity, as well as respect, I have been edified that I could re-present my MI interlocutors with maximum fidelity if sometimes respectfully offering crit-ical perspectives on their work. I feel sure they will return the favor.

· .·

It is a truism in anthropology that encountering a different way of concep-tualizing the world allows one to reflect upon the cultural and historical contingency of one's own analytics (see Strathern 1988). This approach is no less valuable when studying close to home, whether geographically or ideologically, if decidedly more difficult to undertake. Whereas anthropol-ogy has traditionally been a mode of making difference intelligible if not familiar, being an Americanist anthropologist means distancing oneself and many of one's readers from familiar formulations, making the familiar strange so as to examine and analyze it, and then reengaging it. And while the differences in our respective ideas and interests were clear from my first encounters with MI proponents, it was equally apparent that the difference was valued and embraced as the way to deepen understanding of our own habits of thinking by trying to understand those of others. This book would not be what it is without that engagement.

Notes

1. MI training films—such as Miller, Rollnick & Moyers (1998)—have also been used to develop guidelines for the correct use of the Motivational Interviewing Treatment Integrity Code (MITI), which specially trained coders and coaches use to evaluate trainees' developing "skills" and "spirit" (see chapter 3). MITI-coded transcripts of the films have been made available online by the instrument's developers and can therefore be considered authoritative native analytics. The MITI coded transcript marks the passage cited above as "complex reflection (added meaning: escape responsibility)," thereby acknowledging the way the interviewer has "added" a culturally pejorative "meaning" to the interviewee's statement in reflecting it.

2. Professional actors have long played roles as simulated clients in psychotherapy demonstration films, as well as in classroom and training settings in which role-playing is a central part of clinical training. In MI training films, there is a mix of professional and nonprofessional actors, with the client role as well as the therapist role sometimes played by MI proponents.

3. Goffman's (1981) participation framework reminds us to sort out the roles that are collapsed into the normative model of the individual speaker. The *author*, as the one who selects the ideas and sentiments expressed, can be distinguished from the *animator*, as the one who actually utters those ideas and sentiments. Neither of these is necessarily commensurate with the *principal*—that is, the one whose beliefs are being represented in the expression. As we explore MI in more detail, we will see how the ideological conflation of these three roles into a singular autonomous speaker is productively exploited.

4. In the first part of the interview, one hears the lengths to which Miller goes to construe his client as rightfully autonomous and free from external authorities. Interestingly, later in the interview, Miller exploits the same ideals in his suggestion that while Ponytail John is *free* (to use drugs) he is *escaping responsibility* by doing so.

5. Translated more directly into Austin's terms, client statements are thought to have both *illocutionary force* (they are behaviors in their own right) and *perlocutionary force* (they precipitate other behaviors).

6. Those training in MI eventually learn to qualify the "strength" of change talk and work accordingly. More generally, as MI has developed, it has grown MI-specific metalinguistic terms to denote the technicalities of the conversation style (see chapter 2).

These terms are often represented by acronyms that both serve as mnemonic devices for interviewers and arguably make the method more portable.

7. I follow Silverstein's (1996, 126; 2023) definition of a speech community as an organization of people by way of regularities in the way language is actually used, as opposed to a language community, which is, by contrast, organized relative to structural norms for denotational coding, such as a grammar.

8. However, as we will see in chapters 2 and 5, ambivalence is pragmatized in practice. Rather than being theorized as an ontological state, inherent to the client, ambivalence is instead a property of interaction, which can be amplified or lessened by the conversation style that is MI. In Star and Griesemer's terms (1989), we might say that ambivalence is MI's "boundary object." That is, framed as inherently plastic and shaped by perspective and situated practice, ambivalence convenes a wide variety of professionals and welcomes their engagement.

9. Even discussion of moving "toward a theory of motivational interviewing"—the title of a 2009 paper penned by Miller and Gary Rose—is notably circumspect. The authors conclude that "after three decades of research, motivational interviewing is a psychotherapeutic method that is evidence-based, relatively brief, specifiable, applicable across a wide variety of problem areas, complementary to other active treatment methods, and learnable by a broad range of helping professionals. A testable theory of its mechanisms of action is emerging, with measurable components that are both relational and technical" (Miller & Rose 2009, 535).

10. Research that focuses on treatment efficacy specifically includes examinations of MI in substance abuse treatment (e.g., Burke et al. 2004; Carroll et al. 2006; Csillik, Meyer & Osin, 2022; Hettema et al. 2005; Miller, Benefield & Tonigan 1993; Miller et al. 2004; Walker et al. 2017), mental health counseling (e.g., Angus & Kagan 2009; Dean et al. 2016; McCabe et al. 2019), health care and primary care medicine (e.g., Emmons & Rollnick 2001; Frost et al. 2018; Ghizzardi et al. 2022; Resnicow et al. 2015; Rollnick, Miller & Butler 2012), intimate partner violence and couples counseling (e.g., Cordova et al. 2001; Kistenmacher & Weiss 2008; Musser & Murphy 2009), corrections and parole (e.g., McMurran 2009), and HIV risk prevention in the United States (Picciano et al. 2001; Grodensky et al. 2017), Northern Europe (e.g., Baker et al. 1994), and sub-Saharan Africa (e.g., Cornman et al. 2008), smoking cessation with Chinese Americans (e.g., Wu et al. 2009), and water purification interventions in Zambia (e.g., Thevos et al. 2000; Thevos et al. 2002).

11. As is ethnographic custom, I use pseudonyms for all individuals who participated in my research throughout the text, with three important exceptions: William Miller and his two closest colleagues, Stephen Rollnick and Theresa Moyers, all of whom are prominent figures whose identities it would be impossible to disguise even outside the MI community. Accordingly, they participated in my research with consent to be named. "U-Haven" is also pseudonymized to further protect the identities of the individuals I engaged there.

12. Chapter 3 will elaborate on MI-as-vocation, working with and extending Weber's classic formulation, with neighboring ethnographic cases also in mind (see, for instance, Bialecki 2017; Coleman 2004; Harding 2001; Klassen 2011; Stromberg 1993).

13. I make this argument alongside—rather in contrast to—other scholars who have studied behavioral and psychotherapeutic forms in particular contexts, by elaborating their cultural character rather than simply seeing them as straightforward expressions (see especially Brotherton 2020; Davis 2012; Kitanaka 2011; Marsilli-Vargas 2022;

Raikhel 2015; Zhang 2020). Despite my keen interest in the aforementioned scholar-ship, across this book, I painstakingly work to show that MI is "made in/of America," without regular resort to cross-cultural comparison.

14. For ethnographies of professional training, see Ahmed (2012), Brada (2022), Chumley (2016), Cicourel (1995), Gershon (2017), Goodwin (1994), Jacobs-Huey (2003), Jones (2011), Lave (2011), Luhrmann (2000), Mertz (2007), Saunders (2008), Wendland (2010), and Wilf (2014). For studies of professionalism, see Bishara (2013), Boyer (2013), Brenneis (2006), Goodwin (1996), Gusterson (2004), Hull (2012), Lea (2008), Masco (2006), Mason (2019), Matoesian (2008), Philips (1998), Raikhel (2015).

15. "Helping professionals" is a term of art, which euphemistically refers to those—like social workers, counseling psychologists, nurses, teachers, and dieticians—whose jobs are devoted, by definition, to caring for others. However, as I have addressed elsewhere (see Carr 2015), and as the decades-long literature on burnout readily sug-gests (e.g., Cherniss 1980, 1995; Morse et al. 2012; Savicki & Cooley 1983; Skovholt & Trotter-Mathison 2016; Söderfeldt, Söderfeldt & Warg 1995), helping professionals are especially prone to feel overwhelmed by their work. This is not only because their work involves "control" as much as "care," or even because they are commonly charged with solving complex problems that defy ready and clear solutions, but also because they typically lack resources—from their own time to concrete services—relative to cli-ent demand for them (see DuBois 2010; Hardesty 2015; Lipsky 1980; Smith & Donovan 2003; Sosin 2002). Given that US-based helping professionals are affected by the vaga-ries of state budget cuts, which typically mean less staff and therefore even larger case-loads, their experience of precarity and uncertainty is structured by macroeconomic forces, contributing to their sense and experience of inefficacy.

16. For example, licensed clinical social workers in the state in which I currently reside (Illinois) must receive 3,000 hours of supervised practice if they hold an MSW and 2,000 hours if they hold a PhD, as well as 30 hours of continuing education (CE) every two years.

17. When attending to my own or my family members' health care, I have frequent occasion to conduct a revealing breach experiment. Knowing the register well, I re-mark to professionals using it: "Oh, I see you've been trained in MI!" This invariably stops them in their tracks.

18. Given that more than half of the US population is female by birth, it is especially remarkable that women were almost never cast as client-interviewees in the first gen-eration of MI films, produced in the late 1990s. One might also imagine that the reluc-tance to cast white women, and people of color, across from white professional-class men stemmed from MI's insistence on framing MI as an exchange between equals and the reluctance to highlight directive elements of the practice (see chapter 1). In 2013, new demonstration films were released, with more women playing clients—including two white women interviewed by Miller and Rollnick, respectively—and an appar-ently Latinx client actor interviewed by a well-known MI proponent, Theresa Moyers. Moyers conducted what is arguably the most popular of all of the original MI films, called *Rounder*, a rough-talking cowboy. One might guess that whereas the highly ed-ucated Miller may come off as high-handed with Rounder, the female Moyers was able to split the loaded difference.

19. "Analytic" here is shorthand for "psychoanalytic," which in the United States by the 1970s had already suffered serious blows with the rise of self-help, on the one hand, and the medicalization of psychological problems, on the other. Rising anti-

authoritarianism and feminist critiques of Freud added fuel to the fire, as laypeople joined professionals in problematizing psychoanalysis. For excellent ethnohistorical studies of Freudianism in the United States, see Burnham (2012) and Schecter (2014). The imbrication of post–Cold War politics and professional psychology in the United States, particularly as related to the development of MI, is addressed at length in chapter 1.

20. Role-playing is an indispensable part of MI training and is common in professional clinical training more generally. Role-plays are reenactments of client-professional encounters, in which trainees and trainers rotate playing the roles of clients, professionals, and observers. As I argue in chapter 2, these exercises are inherently pragmatic, in that they allow trainees to anticipate, revise, and generally practice methods of engagement, with the idea that they will continuously learn from each role they play.

21. Miller and Rollnick (2013) take pains to differentiate this approach from what is most popularly known as "reverse psychology" and has been taken up by some clinicians—particularly in the family systems tradition that grew out of Bateson's 1972 work on the double-bind—as "therapeutic paradox." They write: "Although this method fits well with the ambivalence model . . . we confess some serious discomfort with the ways in which therapeutic paradox has sometimes been described. There is often the sense of paradox being a clever way of duping people into doing things for their own good. In some writings on paradox, one senses almost a glee in finding innovative ways to trick people without their realizing what is happening. Such cleverness lacks the respectful and collaborative tone that we understand to be fundamental to the dialectical process of motivational interviewing" (2002, 107). For classic writing on therapeutic paradox, see, for example, Frankl 1960; Feldman 1976; and Watzlawick et al. 1967.

22. Notably, since at least the late 1960s, American counseling psychology has become much more eclectic—or, as most prefer, "integrative"—with practitioners drawing from any number of ostensibly discrete traditions. In 1967, Arnold Lazarus coined the term "technical eclecticism" to refer to the use of techniques from various schools or traditions without changing the theoretical orientation of one's own practice. As Goldfried, Pachankis, and Bell (2005) explain, by the 1980s the integrative or eclectic approach had become a "movement." These circumstances lend themselves to the integration of plastic methods like MI, though we will explore in chapter 1 why MI might represent American psychotherapy as more bifurcated than it is.

23. Culture has long been both the central and most dubious of all of anthropology's interests, whether approached as object, heuristic, keyword, problematic, phantasm, and/or foundation. For decades, "culture" in anthropology has come with scare quotes (see Engelke 2018) and the insistence that "it" radically depends on the ideological, material, and historical sedimentation of practice. Along with those who have famously argued that culture is a verb (e.g., Ortner 1984; Williams 1986), pioneering anthropologists have highlighted the inequities of who and what is recognized as involved in the ongoing work of doing and producing culture (e.g., Ginsburg & Tsing 1990; Trouillot 1995; Weiner 1993) and have helped inspire, shape, and provide critical fodder for so many contemporary anthropologies accordingly.

24. Some claim that intervention science is "contempor[aneous] with the genesis of modern science" (Soydan 2013, 536). However, contemporary intervention science would be unthinkable without the dramatic growth of the RCT as a scientific modality

from the 1960s through the early 1980s. The increasing reliance on political bureaucracies to filter and designate evidence, and the growing tendency for public and private funders to make program decisions accordingly, suggests that the current form of intervention research emerged in tandem with the EBP movement.

25. For instance, dialectical behavioral therapy (DBT), a prominent contemporaneous behavioral therapy, has been manualized, allowing individuals and institutions to anticipate and control the costs of training and lessening the need for ongoing human labor.

26. MINT serves fundamental bureaucratic functions of authorizing trainers, assuring the quality of the method, and organizing the dissemination of the method. The organization's website describes MINT as "an international organization of trainers in motivational interviewing, incorporated as a 501(c)(3) tax-exempt non-profit charitable organization in the state of Virginia, USA. The trainers come from diverse backgrounds and apply MI in a variety of settings. Their central interest is to improve the quality and effectiveness of counseling and consultations with clients about behavior change. Started in 1997 by a small group of trainers trained by Miller and Rollnick, the organization has since grown to represent 35 countries and more than 20 different languages." https://motivationalinterviewing.org/about_mint.

27. Based on conversations and other available data, I estimate that about 3,000 people have been inducted into MINT, though not all keep their membership active. At the time of this writing, the number of MI trainers with *active* MINT membership stands at 1712 trainers worldwide, according to the chair of the MINT board of directors, with about two-thirds (65–70%) of the membership being citizens of North American nations. These estimates do not include MINTies who are not currently paying membership dues to MINT (about $130 per year at standard rate), and the many professionals who have received extensive training in MI and now train MI themselves but who have never gone through the formal process of being inducted into MINT.

28. Four-to-six-hour in vivo trainings—whether introductory, intermediate, or advanced—typically cost $100–$125 per person; more intensive, two-to-three-day trainings can cost up to $600 per person; and online classes vary in cost, averaging about $79 per participant. Coding and coaching, which is discussed in detail in chapter 3, are also lucrative activities, with MINTies typically charging by the recorded minute to transcribe and code practice sessions, and, for coaching services, by the hour.

29. Since the number of MINT members alone has more than doubled since the date of Miller and Rollnick's calculation, this growth strategy appears to be working.

30. Note that this account was published in a journal in which MI proponents have frequently written and which they have studiously read and cited for three decades. It might therefore be (loosely) considered an insider account in contrast to Miller's public lectures, which tend to be meant for a broader audience.

31. The book has been so influential that many applied organizational sociologists, psychologists, and economists have adopted the acronym of the book's title, "DOI," to refer to the dissemination of innovations. The fifth edition (Rogers 2003) includes an explanation of the influence of the internet on the dissemination of innovations, which garnered criticism, though the influence of the text holds.

32. See, for instance, Appadurai (1988), Chu (2010), Dick (2018), Kelty (2008, 2019), Larkin (2013), Lempert (2012), Lévi-Strauss (2016), Mauss (2016), Munn (1986), Tsing (2004, 2015), Urban (2001), Weiner (1993), Wolf (1982), Zhan (2009).

33. See, for example, Bauman & Briggs (1990), Carr & Lempert (2016), Gal (2015, 2016), Hull (2012), Inoue (2018), Nakassis (2016), Silverstein & Urban (1996), Silverstein (2004, 2016).

34. Readers may find parallels between MI and AA, particularly in their explicitly "anti-expert" stance and their popular uptake, as well as in their emphasis on the formative powers of speech, despite the many differences in the organization of their paradigmatic verbal practices. More important, however, is the epistemological and ideological disjuncture between AA and MI. Whereas addicts, in an idealized AA (see Bateson 1972), are freed and communally accepted once they speak who they putatively really are (see Carr 2011), MI is not primarily concerned with acts of inner reference. As chapter 5 highlights, rather than investing in revelation of subject positions or identitarian stances, MI dissolves difference by its radically pragmatic (if also, often, socially conservative) focus on what can be practically achieved by what is actually said.

35. The eight-minute rule temporally organizes how some service providers can bill Medicare (providers must provide eight minutes of care to earn one billable unit).

36. As chapter 2 details, MI's ideas about interviewing, and the ideas about language that underlie them, are no less paradoxical.

37. Consider Annette Weiner's (1993) meditation on inalienable possessions—paradoxical things that circulate widely while remaining intrinsically identified with their owners. As Weiner writes: "The paradoxical tension created by keeping-while-giving exists at the root of all attempts to avoid loss. To overcome the destructiveness of loss, individuals and groups devise myriad ways of disguising the impermanence of social life" (10).

38. Inspired by Weiner's feminist revision of gift-giving, I agree and work to substantiate here that the practice of paradox is risk-laden work and, accordingly, "the power that [paradox] generates is sought after, yet submerged, proclaimed yet disguised, nurtured yet defeated" (Weiner 1993, 151).

CHAPTER 1

1. I typically introduce myself to other professionals as a social work scholar and anthropologist who works between cultural, linguistic, and medical subfields. Tellingly, most MI proponents picked up on the "linguistic" part of this self-description when I engaged them, suggesting a shared interest in language.

2. This statement is indicative of the vernacular pragmatism of MI, in which the possibility of definitive conclusions is eschewed and exchanged for always and evermore learning. While this chapter focuses on (in)expertise, and relevant questions of therapeutic and democratic governance, chapter 5 will revisit the pragmatism of MI (see also Carr 2021).

3. Chapter 5 will discuss how MI apprentices exchange diagnostic reasoning, and the mode of expertise it indexes, for a more abductive approach to knowledge acquisition.

4. The public mistrust of experts must be considered alongside their recruitment as those who "check and balance" democratic governance (see Collins & Evans 2019). Indeed, in terms of the official workings of the federal government, experts have long enjoyed the status of the fifth branch (Jasanoff 1990), if sometimes with considerable controversy (see, for example, Carr & Norwood 2022).

5. In this sense, recognition appears to be the antidote to expertise. Unlike exper-

tise, which specifies knowledge, authorizes particular individuals, and erects institutional boundaries, MI repeatedly signals the *recognition of* others as equally knowing subjects, thereby vivifying an American democratic ideal.

6. Fraser writes: "Folk paradigms of justice do not express the perspective of any determinate set of social subjects. Nor do they belong exclusively to any one societal domain. Rather they are transpersonal normative discourses that are widely diffused throughout democratic societies, permeating not only political public spheres, but also workplaces, households, and civil-society associations. Thus, they constitute a *moral grammar* that social actors can (and do) draw on in any sphere to evaluate social arrangements" (2003, 208, emphasis added).

7. Nicholas Rose (1998; 1999) has written far more generally about how psychology, writ large, has historically struggled to produce counseling styles consistent with the production of free, democratic participants. However, not all psychotherapeutic interventions invite the participation of *knowledgeable* subjects, which suggests the need for more critical scrutiny on questions of transparency in addition to Rose's focus on the therapeutic governance of the will.

8. The full interview is posted on Miller's website and was published in abbreviated form in *Addiction* 104, no. 6: 883–93. No individual is identified as the interviewer.

9. In his exploration of "signs of recognition," Webb Keane begins with the "ordinary" sense of recognition as the perception of something as a repetition of something already known, a token of a type (1996, 14). As he points out, to recognize, in this sense, is already fraught with risk (as the dynamics of typification are unstable across contexts of interpretation), but nevertheless carries authorizing potential. The dynamics of authoritative recognition, and particularly the attempt to deny the authority of recognition, which has been fruitfully explored by other anthropologists (see Povinelli 2002), are of central interest in this chapter.

10. "To recognize," in these terms, is to both identify and see beyond particular circumstances of others—to treat everyone as if they were both different and the same. Consider, for instance, the influential work of feminist scholar Iris Marion Young (1990) on this front, who proposed that the paradigm of recognition could revive American feminism, which, in its second wave, was notoriously guilty of failing to *recognize* difference among women. Accordingly, she offered the movement's "third wave" the metaphor of a city capable of endlessly accommodating difference and the "being together of strangers" (318). In contrast, Nancy Fraser (2008) has consistently argued that redistribution rather than recognition should be the primary basis of feminism and social justice.

11. Interestingly, Fanon was broached in a sidebar conversation I had with a white New Zealander in his sixties at a MINT meeting. He relayed his belief that MI is the only just way of intervening in Indigenous communities, which he—as a public health specialist—had been doing for most of his career. His explanation hinged on the idea of recognition as antidote to expertise, saying: "We don't buy into that expertise rubbish . . . We see people for who they are." Here, Elizabeth Povinelli's (1998, 2002) notion of the cunning of recognition comes to mind: the ability to accommodate racism to the extent that one refuses to acknowledge the authoritative traces that extend from a way of seeing. And while MI is an intensively reflexive practice, as I will argue in chapter 2, what is concertedly left unexamined in its self-reflections is its own authoritative dynamics.

12. Consider the resonances with Charles Taylor's account as well. He writes that

"non-recognition or misrecognition can inflict harm, can be a form of oppression, imprisoning someone in a false, distorted, reduced form of being" (1994, 25).

13. Here, we may consider Markell's call to inquire if and how a politics of recognition can become "a medium of injustice" (2003, 3) in its own right.

14. "Third wave" behavioral therapies have enjoyed tremendous success, having been widely institutionalized and trained, though they typically restore some notion of a willful interiority—"cognitively" or otherwise—that radical behaviorists were criticized for largely evacuating. On this and other grounds, adherents of CBT, for instance, may argue that it is ethically preferable to Rogerian therapy.

15. The air crib was enclosed with three opaque sides and a glass front that allowed the baby visual stimulation but also provided light, temperature, and sound control. Equipped with a rotating linen-like plastic sheet, the crib also diminished the amount of laundry generated and therefore the extent of maternal labor required (Nye 1992). Although critics charged that the "baby box" (as the title of the *Ladies Home Journal* article dubbed it) was simply a larger version of the box Skinner had created for his pigeons (see Bjork 1997), the air crib was undoubtedly also controversial for drawing attention to existing conventions of infant control, implicitly questioning their efficacy, and for easing maternal labor. See Skinner (1945). Skinner's use of the word "experiment" in the article drew especially vitriolic commentary because it suggested that he had turned his own daughter into an object of his expertise and that human babies, like any other animal, could be positively conditioned given an ideal environment. As the vaguely understood nature of Skinner's scientific program of behaviorism coalesced with the public focus on the externally uninhibited cultivation of open American minds, the explicitly directive (and arguably feminist!) nature of Skinner's child-rearing, labor-saving device was considered problematic while Dr. Spock's paternalistic pointers on child rearing remained implicit and normatively acceptable. For a fuller discussion of Skinner's program in the context of the Rogers-Skinner debate, see Carr (forthcoming).

16. As Rutherford (2006, 2009) adroitly explains, this criticism coexisted with ample application of Skinnerian ideas about behavior modification across numerous fields. And while third-wave behavioral therapies like CBT have enjoyed tremendous success, in part because of their relative efficiency and cost-effectiveness, they have been cleansed of the most politically problematic implications of Skinner's radicalism, most centrally his displacement of an internal motor of human action (that is, autonomy).

17. In his 1963 paper on "operant behavior," Skinner provides a brief history of the study of "the relation between behavior and its consequences," emphasizing the role of reinforcement in producing behaviors. Though behavior had frequently been studied as a product of an organism's motivation or purpose, the study of these "inner processes," Skinner argued, failed to account for the role of external "contingencies" in shaping the course and consequences of behavior. He thus asserted that the study of behavior requires close attention to the set of reinforcements an organism encounters in its environment.

18. As an assistant professor at MIT, Chomsky clearly had other axes to grind with Skinner as well (see Chomsky 1967). After all, Skinner understood speech as "behavior reinforced through the mediation of other persons" (1957, 2), which could deal a substantial blow to the young linguist's emerging theory of universal grammar. Skinner's *Verbal Behavior* was interested in the conditions, including community-specific norms

as well as speech of other speakers, that shape the actual production of verbal behavior (all familiar fodder for linguistic anthropologists). The book can also be read as a sustained attack on mentalist views of language, including Chomsky's formal theories of universal grammar (which Skinner never explicitly addressed). After all, *Verbal Behavior* refuses the idea that the speaking subject is simply spilling grammatical rules, stored in the mind, out into the world. Skinner insisted that, like any other behavior, speech was subject to environmental conditioning, past and present, including, of course, *language socialization* (see Schiefflein 1986). For a more extensive discussion of how Chomsky's critique played into the famous debates between Rogers and Skinner, see Carr (forthcoming).

19. According to Rutherford (2006), Agnew's speech was originally delivered at the Farm Bureau of Chicago and reprinted later in *Psychology Today*. (See Agnew 1972).

20. Both Rogers and Skinner ran active research labs and did not hesitate to generalize their findings to actual practice (Kirschenbaum & Henderson 1989). Skinner, unlike Rogers, was not a practicing psychotherapist; he nevertheless was keenly interested in the practical implications of his theory of behavior, especially in the field of education. As with the psychotherapist and the client, Skinner argued, the teacher's job is "to implant or shape behavior—to build it up and strengthen it, rather than to find it already in the student and draw it out [as Rogers claims]" (Kirschenbaum & Henderson 1989, 118).

21. For instance, Skinner certainly would have objected to the idea that his lab experiments were mediated by politics as much as Rogers declined to see the directive elements of his therapeutic style.

22. Rogers later added another ruthless personal dig at his opponent, stating: "some of the most pathetic individuals I know are those who continually attempt to understand and predict their behavior objectively" (Kirschenbaum & Henderson 1989, 86). Not surprisingly, Skinner declined to take it personally. Skinner did not exempt himself from behaviorist principles, and accordingly refused to attribute his scholarship to his own mental attributes, despite his critics' frequent baiting. When asked during a video-recorded interview in his office at Harvard, the then eighty-four-year-old Skinner (1988) went on to detail the operant conditions that allowed him to be productive as a scholar—the arrangement of his desk, the time of day in which he set to work, the presence or absence of others—suggesting that all those conditions were as much responsible for scholarly production as he, as an individual organism, was himself.

23. Against more or less subtle charges of nihilism, Skinner repeatedly clarified his thesis that, while inner states do indeed exist, they do not make significant contributions to behavior. In other words, he refused to grant the inner epistemological primacy, if consistently underscoring what he saw as the uniquely human capacity for self-reflection.

24. As a devout empiricist, Skinner eschewed all attempts to find causes within the black box of individual psyches, instead seeking explanations for behavior in the observable history of interaction. And Skinner differentiated human beings from other species, such as the pigeons he trained, by way of reflexive capacities in environmental learning. More specifically, he believed human beings can observe the consequences of our own responses to stimuli and, when these provoke unpleasant or harmful responses in others, reorient and anticipate how to respond differently in the future.

25. See Carr (forthcoming) for further discussion. The behaviorist focused on engineering ideal, even utopian, environments, where speech and other behavior was

valued for the quality of associations and interactions it helped forge—or, for what speech communally produced rather than what it individually expressed. In contrast, client-centered psychotherapy was premised on the idea that the professional, as an external authority, should minimally influence what clients say so as to understand their speech as free.

26. For a particularly elegant examination of relevant questions about Rogers's psychotherapeutic/speech style, see Benjamin Smith (2005), who details "Rogers's unwillingness to create . . . his 'own denotational material'" (269).

27. Furthermore, MI is a "brief intervention," most often used in conjunction with other therapies. In practice, this means clients' self-actualization is not the aim of the MI session, even if proponents would hardly eschew this goal in principle. Instead, the motivational interview is behaviorally targeted: cutting back on drink, brushing and flossing teeth, boiling river water, taking prescribed medications.

28. Note the relative lack of interest in the hermeneutics of *why*—arguably one important commonality between radical behaviorism and Rogerian therapy, both of which roundly rejected psychoanalytic approaches, if for rather different reasons. While Skinner was deeply invested in questions of causality, he maintained a disciplined focus on observable stimuli. Rogers's hostility to psychoanalysis was born from the idea that people simply need recognition and listening, rather than analysis, to fully self-actualize.

29. Colloquially, the term "interview" can imply a kind of investigation, in which authority is unevenly distributed between participants (as in the "job interview" or the "medical interview"). Yet "interviewing" can also connote an interactional routine in which those who question learn from those who answer, affording respect and accruing knowledge. (This, of course, is how many anthropologists think about the "ethnographic interview"). More specifically, approaches to interviewing are shaped by culturally specific beliefs about what we can learn and know from elicited speech; the degree to which one person's speech is shaped and mediated by convention, context, and the dynamics of interaction; the ability of language to create and produce as well as denote; and the relationship of language and the inner states of speakers (see also Briggs 1986, 2007; Carr 2010b). Furthermore, the interview form as a communicative technology is organized by implicit ideas about language and its functions—what linguistic anthropologists call *language ideology*—that is, value-laden presuppositions about speech (and speakers), including ideas about how language should function, which are regularly enacted and produce social effects (see Bauman and Briggs 2003; Carr 2011; Gal 1991; Gal & Irvine 1995, 2019; Irvine & Gal 2000; Kroskrity 2000; Philips 1998; Silverstein 1977, 1985, 2004; Woolard 1998). As I have argued elsewhere, while language ideologies organize people's default assumptions about the nature and function of speech, they are hardly impervious to critical assessment and creative mobilization by speakers who appear to simply abide by them (see Carr 2011).

30. Chomsky's disgust with Skinner was likely spawned in large part by their competing theories of language, and well before his attempt to take down Skinner's *Beyond Freedom and Dignity*, Chomsky (1959) wrote a scathing review of the behaviorist's 1957 book, *Verbal Behavior*. After all, Skinner's refusal to accept mentalist explanations of language challenged not only Chomsky's cognitivist theory of universal grammar, but also the portrait of the (political) subject on which that theory relied.

31. Additionally, as MI has spread, it has encountered stark differences in professional authority among its trainees. For instance, bald directiveness is generally ac-

ceptable and even expected from white male doctors but tends to be more fraught for social workers who are female and/or persons of color. While some helping professionals are afforded expert status by their clients and general public, others never have had the opportunity—let alone the inclination—to become ensnared in the "expert trap" (Miller & Rollnick 2013, 409), which suggests that the risks and rewards of (in)expertise are stratified.

32. On the ethics of MI, see especially Miller (1994, 1995).

33. Of the seventy participants in the university training, almost 67% had earned master's degrees and 22% held PhDs, PsyDs, or MDs.

34. Regardless of the impetus, developments in an already popular method, once branded as such, are economically lucrative for authors, publishees, and trainers of MI. After all, each new edition of *Motivational Interviewing* means new definitions, mnemonic devices, and practical understandings that those already familiar with previous editions will have to learn. The second edition now stands as outmoded in the implicit shadow of its successor, as do readers who are not keen to learn new terminology, despite the relatively minor adjustments to the substance of the method. According to Miller's 2022 address to MINT, the same holds true for the forthcoming fourth edition, slated for publication in summer of 2023.

35. Aside from a penchant for shades of purple and gold, Miller commonly uses his own photographs of southwestern landscapes, which also adorn his home's entryway, in his PowerPoint presentations. In addition to his talents as a photographer, Miller composes choral music, dabbles in landscape architecture, and—as an ordained minister—has served as a deacon of his Albuquerque congregation.

36. Interestingly enough, MI-3 has calibrated its self-definitions to different audiences, with a particularly client-centered framing of the method for "laypeople": "Motivational interviewing is a collaborative conversation style for strengthening a person's own motivation and commitment to change" (Miller & Rollnick 2013, 29).

37. As explained in the training, "equipoise" means that the MI practitioner remains attuned to their own ethical stances so that they might exercise control of those stances in the interview. Note that while these stances are to be reflexively monitored by the professional, they are to be only very selectively shared with and transparent to the client.

38. Li Zhang's *Anxious China* (2020) stands as a fascinating counterpoint, describing as it does the influence of Carl Rogers in Chinese psychology relative to the unabashedly "directive" and "authoritative" quality of the Chinese talk therapy sessions she observed. While both settings share what she calls the "contradiction" of a simultaneously client-centered and directive approach, it suggests that part of what is particularly American in the case of MI is the need to disguise the latter aspect. In another interesting example of the hybridity of therapeutic forms, see also Raikhel 2015.

39. The fascinating dynamics of real-plays, from their bootstrapping quality to the semiotics of participant roles, will be discussed at more length in the following chapter.

40. In more technical terms, to "roll with resistance" means to offer verbal supports rather than counters to what clients say, regardless of the interviewer's evaluation of or investment in that statement. For instance, if an interviewee with a few months of hard-won sobriety says: "At this point, I think I can manage having a drink now and then," the interviewer "rolls with resistance" when responding with statements like: "It's not like before. You can handle alcohol now." Rolling with resistance is risky work, and technically difficult to pull off. After all, the client could simply take the interviewer

at her word. Yet the rewards, as Norman and other MI proponents emphasized, are ample. As a (false) hypothesis, the amplified reflection invites clients' verbal corrections, both increasing the likelihood that clients would "talk *themselves* into [positive] change" (Miller & Rollnick 2013, 159), while providing more fodder with which professionals can learn and act in the meantime.

41. Or, as I've described in other work, "flipping the script"—that is, discerning what the professional wants to hear and felicitously articulating those expectations as one's own without investment or intention of follow-through (Carr 2011).

CHAPTER 2

1. I employ the term "apprentice" in lieu of "trainee" or "training participant" in the case of U-Haven not simply to indicate the relatively long-term and intensive nature of their engagement with MI, but more specifically because their training took place within what Lave and Wenger (1991) would call an "activity system" in which they could become more or less "peripheral participants" in the everyday practice of MI, given that they all worked in proximity to each other and to their trainer.

2. Both the *Rhetorica ad Herennium* (Cicero [attrib.] 1954), formerly attributed to the Roman orator Cicero, and Cicero's own rhetorical manual *De Inventione* (Cicero 1949), present five categories or canons of rhetoric. He describes them in the latter as follows: "Invention is the discovery of valid or seemingly valid arguments to render one's cause plausible. Arrangement is the distribution of arguments thus discovered in the proper order. Expression is the fitting of the proper language to the invented matter. Memory is the firm mental grasp of matter and words. Delivery is the control of the voice and body in a manner suitable to the dignity of the subject matter and the style" (1949, I.vii.9).

3. In the psychotherapy research literature, the term "active ingredient" generally refers to actions by the therapist that are believed to affect the outcome of an intervention (see, for example, Elkin et al. 1988). A growing literature addresses the extent to which the unique, hallmark actions characteristic of a particular intervention or "common factors" across many interventions are responsible for client outcomes (see Ahn & Wampold, 2001). I use the term "active ingredient" somewhat differently here, to point to the way therapy-specific poetics—including the uses of pause—actively shape how helping professionals and institutions perceive a therapy as more or less effective.

4. Keith Sawyer's ethnography of improv theater in Chicago is relevant here, not only given his general attention to the semiotics of improvised action, but more particularly in his description of "offers," which require a reflexive attention to other actors as well as an overall attention to the emergent frame of the event (see, in particular, Sawyer 2002, 74, 124).

5. More specifically, in the pragmatic mode, one learns by (role-)playing, and (role-)playing is learning. Consider here that John Dewey (1913) distinguished play (from work) by the absence of a goal exterior to the activity itself. In MI training, MI role-plays are not only the central way apprentices learn the method and its inherent techniques, but are also the means of continually refining those techniques, with no promise of mastery ever offered.

6. It is common for MINTies to evoke Miller and MINT in this way. This works at once to both authorize and generalize the task at hand. Indeed, these citational practices are important ways, in and of themselves if not by speaker intent, to scale the method.

7. Note, particularly in line with chapter 1, that the rotating ritual of role-play is itself democratic, as all apprentices serve to check and balance each other, ostensibly leveling the interaction and power dynamics of the role-played exchanges.

8. The concept of reflexability builds on linguistic anthropological work on reflexive language and metapragmatics (Lucy 1993; Silverstein 1977, 1993) and on work that attends to circumstances of performance, in which (social) actors learn to read discursive context so as to build upon and direct it (Duranti and Goodwin 1992; Sawyer 2002; Silverstein 2001). Whereas I have written previously on how people, particularly in high-stakes circumstances, develop such keen metapragmatic awareness that they can anticipate and "flip" authoritative scripts (Carr 2011), MI training provides the chance to show one way that this ability is cultivated.

9. This is consistent with the current process research on MI, which suggests that reflections facilitate more change talk (Catley et al. 2006), which is in turn associated with changed behavior (Amrhein et al. 2003; Moyers et al. 2007).

10. Notice the behaviorism implicit in this approach: in MI, a good reflection is not so much oriented to *who the client really is* but is rather a process of helping to shape what the client should say and therefore do.

11. See Miller and Rollnick's discussion of reflections as "guesses" (2002, 69), which is quite consistent with Ki's remarks here.

12. Emphasis added for the amplified reflections in bold; change talk underlined; italics in original.

13. Suboxone, a combination of buprenorphine and naloxone, is an opioid-based prescription drug used to treat opioid addiction (SUBOXONE® [Buprenorphine and Naloxone] Sublingual Film [CIII] 2016). It is similar to methadone, though the Controlled Substances Act designates methadone a Level II controlled substance—indicating that it is more addictive—compared to Suboxone's Level III (Drug Enforcement Administration 2013). Though Suboxone is used to treat opioid addiction because of its ability to reduce cravings without generating a high, users of Suboxone can reportedly get high if they inject or snort the drug. Suboxone is considered by some to be addictive, and there is debate over its role as a drug that improves outcomes and is safer than many alternatives, compared to its frequent abuse and presence in unregulated markets (Macy 2018).

14. Conversation analysts regard pause as an interactional resource (Jaffe & Feldstein 1970; Levinson 1983; Sacks, Schegloff & Jefferson 1974; Watts 1997), suggesting that pause—depending on its length and position in an ongoing verbal exchange—is one of the many features of conversation that help participants interpret what has already been said and decide how to respond in turn. Taking the pair-structure of dialogue as the unit of analysis, conversation analysis (CA) is particularly useful in understanding American therapeutic genres, in which both participants are highly attuned to the meaningfulness of the exchange (see, for example, Peräkylä 1995). However, as critics of CA have argued, due to CA's tendency to isolate conversation as a unit of analysis, the social and institutional genealogy of the linguistic resources that people bring to interactions is unclear. For example, CA does not offer a way to systematically understand how people's conversations—particularly professional conversations—are often intensively rehearsed before they are actually performed, including just when and how to pause.

15. Jefferson was apparently deeply frustrated by his own oratorical failures, especially given his love of music, in comparison to the mesmerizingly rhythmic speech

of his rival. As Fliegelman notes, "Patrick Henry played by ear; Jefferson couldn't" (1993, 196).

16. Fliegelman (1993) identifies the mid-eighteenth century as a period in which matters of American democracy hinged on changing standards and expectations of rhetorical performance, and particularly the emerging demand that politicians speak "natural" language and authentically presence themselves through their speech (see also Bauman & Briggs 2003). As we will see in chapter 3, the paradoxical demand for "natural theatricality" (1993), in which the performer works to seemingly spontaneously presence themselves through highly stylized rhetorical techniques, is one with which MI apprentices also contend.

17. Relative to everyday discourse, many American psychotherapeutic registers have a high tolerance for pause both within a single speaker's statements and between speakers' turns at talk. That said, there are discernible stylistic differences among schools of psychotherapy, particularly between the directive and client-centered modalities that MI integrates, including the degree to which they incorporate pause. Most obviously, the overall ratio of client-to-therapist talk tends to differ dramatically between directive and client-centered therapy, with the former entailing far less silence and much more verbal intervention on the part of the therapist. Whereas Albert Ellis, for instance, allows for little to no pauses throughout the session, Carl Rogers sustains lengthy silence between turns at talk and punctuates his own turns at talk with micropauses, if not in the patterned fashion found in MI (see Carr & Smith 2014).

18. Functionally, if not formally speaking, this kind of tag question is not "closed" because it conventionally calls for a correction and potentially an elaboration, rather than a simple yes or no. It is thus an example of how an open question and a reflection can produce the same results, depending on their ordering relative to other speech acts, stylization, and overall delivery.

19. Other than its role in these turn-taking sequences, SAE speakers tend to avoid silence in everyday conversation (see Levinson 1983; Jaworski 1993; Schegloff 2007, 21; Scollon 1985; Tannen 1985), by using "ums," "ahs," and other "verbal fillers." These are precisely the conventions that the poetics of MI both references and manipulates, leaving fascinating questions about how these pauses are understood by practitioners and clients outside mainstream institutions in the United States.

20. Psycholinguists have looked at pauses as cognitive devices that allow a speaker to plan what to say next. Within this tradition, some have argued that while speakers may plan when they pause at clause boundaries, randomly occurring pauses do not necessarily allow for this planning work (Ferreira 1993; Goldman-Eisler 1968; Krivokapic 2007). According to this theory, pauses in therapeutic discourse create junctures that afford practitioners time to carefully craft questions and responses to their clients. Though it is certainly conceivable that pauses can sometimes function in this way in therapeutic exchange, it is unclear why pauses would be *patterned* as they are in MI and why practitioners would be trained to employ these patterns, suggesting that something conventional as well as cognitive is at play. By contrast, linguistic anthropologists have shown that silence is a complex discursive resource with a wide variety of context-specific functions and values. As Keith Basso explains, "Although the form of silence is always the same, the function of a specific act of silence—that is, its interpretation by and effect upon other people will vary according to the social context in which it occurs" (1970, 215). Anthropologists have shown how linguistic practices and proclivities, including patterns of pause, are institutionally as well as socially me-

diated. For instance, challenging the standard feminist thesis that women's silence is always and everywhere a sign of male oppression, Susan Gal (1991) points out that when institutions *require* self-exposure, "it is the silent listener who judges and who thereby exerts power over the one who speaks" (175). Linguistic anthropologists have further demonstrated that silence can be a central defining feature of specific genres and registers of speech. For example, Richard Bauman's classic work on the Quakers (1983) demonstrates that silence is a particularly potent communicative act within this speech community, both epitomizing and performing the very experience of Quaker spirituality.

21. For a more extensive analysis of the poetics of pause in MI, see Carr and Smith (2014).

22. Sacks, Schegloff, and Jefferson (1974) demonstrate that pauses at what they call "transition-relevance places" (TRPs) tend to be closely monitored for their length, with interlocutors generally regarding pauses at these junctures as signs that the speaker is ceding their turn at talk. Thus, speakers tend to allow little to no pause at such junctures if they want to hold the floor. Notably, in the other turn-relevant places—for instance, between "in with them" and "around to what extent" and "and I get this" and "am I understanding"—Ki does not pause. The rhetorical attention here is apparently between being "open" (pauses) and also controlling (that is, not pausing in places where he would be giving up the floor). One should acknowledge that in the context of a therapeutic encounter, the turn-taking system is already skewed toward Ki as the professional, which shapes how, when, and to what extent the client, as the other part of the conversational pair, jumps in.

23. As Roman Jakobson once famously explained, poetics distinguishes or "estranges" texts, whether written or spoken, from everyday discourse, thereby serving as an index of a register and shaping its social effects accordingly (1960; see also Shklovsky 2015). While underscoring that poetics influences the ways spoken and written texts operate in social worlds, including what they are understood to mean, Jakobson described the poetic function of language as *autotelic*—that is, as having no *necessary* function other than itself. Students of Jakobson and, most notably, Michael Silverstein (2023) brought these insights to linguistic anthropology, allowing the subfield to demonstrate how frequently and in how many realms of social practice poetics enjoys prominent social functions. For example, see Bauman (2023); Bauman & Briggs (1990), Bate (2002, 2009), and Silverstein (2005) on the poetics of political communication; Carr & Smith (2014), Labov & Fanshel (1977), Marsilli-Vargas (2022), and Peräkylä (1995) on the poetics of therapy; Matoesian (2001) and Mertz (1994) on the poetics of legal texts; Nakassis (2019, 2023) on the poetics of "cine-politics"; and Wilce (1998) on the poetics of complaint.

24. By my own experience and by my informants' reports, Miller fastidiously tracks the ballooning literature on MI, and not infrequently writes directly to authors with a combination of praise, correctives, and general feedback.

25. As Miller once explained to a highly amused audience at an advanced training in MI-3, you "don't go to the marriage altar and say, 'I'm willing to . . .'" Those familiar with speech act philosophy will recognize the twist on the classic Austinian example of the performative "I do." In Austin (1962), the phrase is understood to be a conventional way of *doing* something (that is, marrying), as well as of saying something, equivalent to naming a ship with the ceremonial breaking of a bottle over the bow. It is the sociological rather than the psychological force that is at stake for Austin, whereas Miller—

in line with Amrhein—evaluates *the strength* of the commitment of the individuals involved in such contracts.

26. Amrhein has published theoretical papers on lexical meaning (1992), as well as his MI-specific work on "client talk" (for instance, 2004). He has also published numerous co-authored papers, including many with lead MI proponents, like Miller and Moyers (see, for example, Amrhein, et al. 2003).

27. This is not unusual in psychotherapy process research, particularly for those who study behavioral therapies. Researchers of behavioral interventions tend to view therapist language as a series of speech acts, such as questions, reflections, or advisements (for example, Stiles, Shapiro & Firth-Cozens 1988) or "speech content" (see Luborsky et al. 1982) to the exclusion of the poetic features of therapist language. For an interesting exception, see Elkin et al.'s (2013) measure of "therapist responsiveness" in CBT and interpersonal psychotherapy.

28. Thus, the MITI can be seen as an index of the evolving nature of the native view of MI. Indeed, a substantial portion of the 2014 MINT Forum I attended was devoted to explaining the latest developments in the MITI.

29. MITI scoring is undertaken in two passes: the coder first engages in behavior counts, "which requires the coder to tally and code instances of particular interviewer behaviors," and then determines "global scores" that are "meant to capture the rater's global impression or overall judgment about the dimension, sometimes called the 'gestalt'" (https://casaa.unm.edu/download/miti4_1.pdf). According to the MITI manual, transcribed session segments should be broken into "volleys," which are defined as "uninterrupted segments of clinician speech," for analysis. The manual also offers many examples of types of statements, along with "decision rules" to help coders decide how to qualify and quantify them.

30. Although, of course, the "how" and the "what" of speech acts are inseparably entwined when making meaning in the world.

31. As I have argued elsewhere, there are ample reasons to avoid conflating what speakers know about their speech (metalinguistic awareness) and what they say about it during an ethnographic encounter (metalinguistic description), including the strategic reasons why speakers fail to explicate what they (mean to) do with their words (Carr 2011, 196).

32. MI's lead proponents have put much thought into how to disseminate and train their method to other professionals, and scores of research studies on how to best teach MI have been published over the past two decades. The most cited of this line of MI research includes Miller et al. (2004), Miller & Mount (2001), and Madson, Loignan & Lane (2009), and Madson et al. (2019).

33. Tethering novice practitioners to more experienced ones is the primary if not exclusive way of distributing the profits of MI. Indeed, while versions of the MITI are available online and the third edition of *Motivational Interviewing* is just an Amazon click away for $72 (with more than 425,000 copies in print), the demonstration films in which MI's poetics are on full display, if not with attendant explication, are also expensive. I recently paid $180 for a streaming version, which included oldies but goodies like "Ponytail John," "Rounder," and "The Silent Man," as well as newer demonstrations like "The Committed Smoker."

34. Poetics is not only a way that psychotherapists of all stripes realize their therapeutic principles and agenda; it is also an opportunity to distinguish or brand their respective approaches. Like all brands, MI must be on the lookout for counterfeits if not

competitors. Thus, we might conjecture that MI's under-specification of poetics plays an important role in branding the method as well.

35. For some apprentices, who engaged in one-on-one coaching, the U-Haven training continued for a full year after Ki's unexpected departure, when he was compelled to move out of state to handle pressing family matters. The transition to a new trainer, and the lessons it revealed about the principles of practice MI instills, will be addressed in chapter 5.

36. Interestingly, this apprentice added that this reflexivity was sometimes "to the detriment of the client"—who he worried had sometimes slipped from his view. This was one of several instances in which apprentices questioned the wisdom of redistributing attention between the client and the professional as Ki regularly urged them to do.

37. See Miller & Rollnick 2013, 323–24, 330, 343.

38. Among MINTies, some recorded interviews have gained reputations as "masterpieces"—with Irish MINTie and once widely known (now retired) MI trainer, Jeff Allison, frequently cited as having produced, as one of my informants put it, "the most beautiful recorded motivational interview of all time." In line with the dance metaphors reviewed in the conclusion of this chapter, the home page of Allison's website features a couple performing ballroom dancing (http://www.jeffallison.co .uk/history/).

39. Thanks to Daniel Listoe for elaborating these points.

40. This is particularly true of the client-centered tradition, from which MI draws. As touched upon in the previous chapter, Carl Rogers was insistent that the language used in his therapeutic approach was virtually transparent, with words operating as windows into the inner selves of client and therapist alike.

41. As John Jackson (2005, 14) argued in his work on what "Real Black" requires of residents in Harlem, and as I have elaborated in the context of mainstream American drug treatment (Carr 2011), Americans who understand performance as the way to sincerely connect with others are often judged by others as being inauthentic, given the cultural proclivity to judge the ethical value of an act by its relation to preexisting truths. Accordingly, Jackson elaborates sincerity and authenticity as competing, if entwined, folk theories.

CHAPTER 3

1. The U-Haven study design included interviews with all trainees before, during, and immediately after the training. With the help of two doctoral students, I also began shadowing training participants in their daily work at the six-month mark of the training, work that carried on for approximately five months. We also observed and recorded posttraining coaching and supervision, in which the original trainees participated to varying degrees.

2. Because these observations were conducted well after the MI training commenced, it is impossible to know to what extent these qualities of Libby's practice were MI-trained or otherwise acquired.

3. As will be discussed in chapter 5, Ki resigned his position at U-Haven and moved out of state nine months into the advanced training. Though he had started some MITI coding before his departure, it was with some apparent trepidation, as he did not have extensive training in how to use the instrument. He was intent to find an experienced coder and coach to assume this work. While Ki hand-picked a former professor to run

the remaining group sessions, he sought my and others' advice about local MI coders and coaches, with Norman garnering several recommendations, including mine. Norman was contracted by U-Haven and traveled to the city on four occasions to coach U-Haven apprentices; he also conducted coaching sessions on Skype.

4. Quite aside from apprentices' attitudinal reticence, it was difficult and awkward to get clients to agree to be recorded, and the equipment to do so was cumbersome in bags already crammed with paperwork, med bottles, and the other professional accoutrements. Recording at least twenty successive minutes of client interaction, which was required by the MITI, was especially difficult at U-Haven, where many contacts with clients were spontaneous or brief.

5. We might recall, from chapter 1, that Norman was particularly well known for real-plays. One of Norman's longtime apprentices once told me: "His PowerPoints are a mess, and he goes off on tangents, so he really doesn't have a glossy shtick like some others. But man does he know how to real-play."

6. As elaborated further in this chapter, the distinction between "spirit" and "technique" is a defining feature of (American) Protestantism. For instance, in his work on Dutch Calvinist missionaries, Keane (2002, 2007) describes efforts to divert attention from rituals and relics, and especially the materiality of language, so as to create the effect of an unmediated channel between the responsible and sincere subject and the divine.

7. As Marilyn Strathern beautifully puts it: "Anthropological exegesis must be taken for what it is: an effort to create a world parallel to the perceived world in an expressive medium (writing) that sets down its own conditions of intelligibility" (1988, 17). This holds true, and may be all the more challenging, when one studies interlocutors who are close to home and/or when the native anthropologist's investments in the categories and practices are at stake, which may make it all the more difficult not to collapse or caricature the differences in perception.

8. There are multiple striking connections between twentieth-century liberal Protestant participation in medicine and healing, as documented by Pamela Klassen (2011), and the work of MINTies: the simultaneous embrace of science and spirit, the welcoming of religious difference from a firmly planted Protestant position, and the notably enchanted quality of Protestant healers, by way of what Klassen calls "supernatural liberalism."

9. Consider Richard Bauman's (2016, 2023) account of the late nineteenth-century orator and populist politician William Jennings Bryan, who attentively cultivated his oratorical skills from childhood; however, his charismatic appeal, or aura, rested on the reception of these cultivated speaking skills as the raw expression of Bryan's persona and populism. In US politics, eloquence of any sort is typically considered suspicious, itself a sign of insincerity, and disfluent political speech reigns, as Michael Silverstein's diagnosis of former president George W. Bush's style of speech amusingly demonstrates (2003; see also Lempert & Silverstein 2012). Studies such as these suggest that the persuasive American speaker is one who can naturalize the cultivation of their speech, so that it seems innate or gifted, and therefore *sincere*.

10. From the liberalizing reforms of Vatican II that hoped to reinvigorate the practice of Catholicism worldwide (see Carr 2013) to the rise of American Evangelicalism, we find concerted attempts to free the pious voice from worldly authorities, so that congregants' speech appears to be the unmediated expression of the divinely inspired will. The concern with mediation is especially pervasive in American Protestant tradi-

tions, with the most valued speech typically being that which bears the least obvious sign of social authority (see Harding 2001; Yelle 2012), sometimes including intelligibility (Bialecki 2017). For instance, in American Quakerism, silence reigns until congregants are "moved" to speak, with elegant soliloquies understood as spontaneous expressions of inner light (see Bauman 1983).

11. Tellingly, Susan commented on the circumstances of her initial training: "This is certainly *not* the model [of learning MI] that I would recommend." Further into my research, I found that it was common among MINTies, whose initial exposure to MI was institutionally driven or mandated, to reframe their relationship to the method in terms of spirit rather than instrumentalism.

12. And still believes, judging from her attendance at the 2022 MINT Forum and enthusiasm when I spoke with her.

13. Alongside his books on MI, addictions, addiction treatment, and psychotherapy, Miller is the author of *Living As If: How Positive Faith Can Change Your Life* (1985); the edited volume, *Integrating Spirituality into Treatment: Resources for Practitioners* (1999); a co-edited volume, *Judeo-Christian Perspectives on Psychology: Human Nature, Motivation, and Change* (2005); two editions of a book on pastoral counseling co-authored with his wife, Kathy Jackson (1985); and his more recent, pamphlet-sized book, *Lovingkindness: Realizing and Practicing Your True Self* (2017).

14. On conversion narratives in other settings, see Engelke (2004), Greil & Rudy (1983), Keane (2007), Stromberg (1993).

15. As Paul Reitter and Chad Wellmon (Weber 2020) put it in the introduction to an edited collection of the *Vocation Lectures*, Weber originally defined charisma, in the religious sphere, as a "gift of grace," only to extend it later to theorize political charisma. While of enchanted origin and dependent on others' devotion, political charisma "can neither be taught like a technical skill nor entirely robbed by rational structures" (xix).

16. It is typical to distinguish evangelical Protestants from mainline ones by the former group's emphasis on conversion, awakening, and being "born again." As we will see in the following section, mainline Protestants tend to privilege spiritual realization through work rather than the experience of conversion per se.

17. Sinatra fans will know that "dobedobedo" is a play on "doobydoobydoo," prominent lyrics in his song, "Strangers in the Night."

18. Theresa Moyers is well known within and beyond the MI community given both the nature and extent of her publication record and her starring roles in MI training films—like "Rounder" (Miller, Rollnick & Moyers 1998) and "The Committed Smoker"—which is why she is one of three MI proponents whose identity I could not, and did not promise to, protect, unlike my other informants.

19. Bellah famously posited that the "dual emphasis on the individual and on society can be traced in the dialectic of conversion and covenant that was continuously worked over in the colonial Protestant Churches and came to provide a series of feelings, images, and concepts that would help shape the meaning of the new republic" (1975, 18). Though for early Puritan colonists, conversion was experienced as deeply personal and understood to be an individual experience, their churches required and evaluated a public accounting of this experience (18).

20. One might also interpret this as a way of countering an evangelical reading of MI by grounding the method in a mainline one. Indeed, in mainline traditions, the goal of proselytizing goes well beyond conversion to include economic assistance, for instance. Another distinction between mainline and evangelical Protestantism is the

relationship to the "word" itself, with the former encouraging an interpretive reading of the Bible as a historical if highly significant document.

21. In one of their more prominent evocations of American folk heroes, Miller and his co-authors have repeatedly grounded one of MI's signature techniques—the decisional balance—in their interpretation of Franklin's accounting system (Miller & Rollnick 2013; Miller & Rose 2015).

22. A sociolinguistic analysis of the pronounced deictics of this exchange further supports this interpretation. Note that Miller repeatedly marks a normative American Protestant perspective as his own—"I" and "to me"—which arguably both situates his perspective and circumvents its cultural dominance.

23. Such comments, which some may understandably find orientalist, are not only common in MI training, but—accordingly to Pamela Klassen— have been part and parcel of an "undercurrent" in contemporary liberal Protestantism that "welcomes this interreligious transformation as an authentic, faithful path" (2011, 174).

24. Rogers was a graduate of the Union Theological Seminary and later declared himself an atheist.

25. It is not uncommon for MINTies to harbor rather obscure interests in Anglo-American philosophy, particularly relative to questions of language. In this case, it was hard to know whether the lecture itself, which inspired many suppressed yawns in the audience and a fluctuating brow on an observing anthropologist, was for my benefit, given that it was long established that I would be observing this particular trainer's TNT group. That said, I often joked with linguistic anthropological colleagues that MI was the behavioral therapeutic realization of J. L Austin's speech act theory, which the American Searle spent his career developing.

26. The gift logic of MI will be explored at greater length in the following chapter.

27. In fact, Norman himself, who personified MI spirit in so many eyes, had been publicly accused of careerism by another well-known MINTie who trained in the same regional market. It was 2009, and Norman was participating in the heavily trafficked MINT listserv, responding to a thread on the downturn in the economy. MINTies were collectively bemoaning that fewer and fewer agencies could afford to hire MI trainers and strategizing about how to respond to shifting economic circumstances. By Norman's telling, his accuser intervened in an otherwise civil conversation, writing that "it was about time" that Norman started "doing some pro bono work." Norman clearly felt both wronged and hurt, telling me, months afterward: "It was like, Wow! I do *a lot* of pro bono work." A wave of MINTies, armed with keyboards, came to Norman's defense. As the accuser later told me, these defenses were "*ferocious,*" and she was effectively "beaten down." The exculpated Norman said: "We didn't hear from her for a couple of months," though he later invited the very same woman to participate in his coding listserv—what many saw as a restorative act of MI spirit.

28. The story included a long and remarkable account of a former client who had been so transformed by Melony's professional presence that she named her first-born child after the MINTie.

29. Talk of the cliquishness of MINT, with particular attention to its social center and peripheries, was not entirely new to me, though the opportunity to see for myself evidence of these institutional patterns and stratifications, whether formal or informal, was.

30. Linguistic anthropologists emphasize how these kinds of citational practices generate authority and create or reinforce institutional continuities, and many of them

apply here. See, in particular, Silverstein and Urban's 1996 edited volume, *Natural Histories of Discourse*, as well as Bauman and Briggs's 1990 paper, recontextualized now in countless linguistic anthropological accounts. See also Nakassis (2013).

31. This resonates with Fritz Ringer's reading of Weber's 1915 essay "Intermediate Reflection," which points out: "both prophetic and priestly religions again and again seek relationships with rational intellectualism" and particularly with empirical science (2004, 158) so as not to be destroyed by the historical tide of rational authority. This, as Pamela Klassen (2011) elaborates, is certainly the case for liberal North American Protestantism.

CHAPTER 4

1. In one recent conversation, Miller told me that, while responsible for the term "spirit," Steve Rollnick is "not religious in any sense—he's sorta sorry he did it [i.e., coined the term] in some ways, because it [i.e., the term "spirit"] makes him nervous." My interview with Rollnick, along with his reported conversation with Rex in chapter 3, suggests that the religious uptake of MI "spirit" per se is not nearly as concerning for Rollnick as the way spirit is used to frame and fuel MI's marketization.

2. It is somewhat ironic, considering Rollnick's charge, that the evidence-based movement is of *British* origin, though arguably it has come to dominate, some might even say colonize, professional fields in the United States in recent years. Of particular significance to evidence-based medicine (EBM) was the British-based Cochrane Collaboration, named after epidemiologist and randomized controlled trial (RCT) advocate Archie Cochrane, who published the book *Effectiveness and Efficiency: Random Reflections on Health Services* (1972). The Cochrane Collaboration website today describes its mission "to promote evidence-informed health decision-making by producing high-quality, relevant, accessible systematic reviews and other synthesized research evidence" (Cochrane.org 2020). These ideas have since made widespread inroads into the United States and into domains far beyond medicine—what Bell (2012) calls the "creep" of evidence-based medicine into behavioral health. The Campbell Collaboration, established in 2000, exemplifies EBP's movement into behavioral science, bringing the systematic, review-based approach of the Cochrane Collaboration to social service and behavioral health interventions.

3. Consider Sackett's seminal article on EBM, which he defines as "the conscientious, explicit and judicious use of *current best evidence* in making decisions about the care of individual patients" (1997, 3, emphasis added), which is widely cited by EBP advocates. I will delve further into the question of EBP's epistemic virtues, including what it counts as "best evidence" and the best ways to procure it, later in the chapter.

4. As noted above, the common factors approach suggests that different practices and therapies share features that underlie the effectiveness of treatment, pushing back against the idea that what makes different therapies effective are unique and distinct features or "specific factors" (Drisko 2013). This thinking supports the integration of different psychotherapies in practice and in research. By contrast to the evidence-based practice movement, research motivated by a common factors approach has instead identified features shared across different psychotherapies and asks whether there are meaningful differences in results between different psychotherapies studied.

5. In his early works, Latour argues that politics and society should not be considered as outside science, as a kind of external pressure, but as already within and integral to it. Politics is "science's blood flow," Latour proposes, in a chapter of that title in

Pandora's Hope (1999), rather than a force to which either science succumbs or resists. Latour's later and clearly connected claim that everything interesting and important in (never yet) modern science happens in the "middle kingdom" where hybridization happens despite efforts to purify science (1993) is borne out in MI, if with politics working more like a force with which to bond than a threat against which to guard.

6. See also Zhang on what she calls "a 'double aura' of making scientific claims and promising magical effects" (2020, 5) in the case of "anxious China."

7. This shift ushered in new institutional players, such as the Campbell Collaboration in EBP, whose central charge was to produce this "filtering information."

8. Though some organizations may consult the APA-12, a list of psychological treatments that the American Psychological Association has identified as associated with the "best research evidence," most US-based organizations and professionals considering the adoption of MI would probably consult the NREPP. It is important to note, however, that there are multiple registries that differ in terms of how they are funded— from federal and state-specific registries to those funded by philanthropic and international organizations—and in the specificity of their focus. For a comprehensive review, see Burkhardt et al. 2015.

9. Here, it is important to note the relative humility with which the NREPP explicitly presents itself—that is, as a "repository" aimed at increasing access to "reliable information" about programs and interventions, and assisting in "an informed decision-making process" (NREPP 2017), rather than designating and authorizing particular methods as EBPs. That does not prevent it, however, from being used as a definitive list of EBPs—not just by trainers like Susan, but by the agencies that hire them and the insurers that reimburse those agencies. And while the registry insists that the "review of interventions and their inclusion on the NREPP website do not constitute an endorsement, promotion, or approval of the interventions by NREPP or SAMHSA" (NREPP 2017), for many who consult it, it undoubtedly does.

10. Oregon has a long history of concern about cost-effective treatments, but nevertheless serves as a telling example of how states engage in the rhetorical marrying of scientific and economic discourses to justify the (re)distribution of social service funding. More generally, the Oregon case highlights modes of legitimation that happen far from the labs of intervention scientists, providing a powerful example that EBP is as much a political movement as a scientific one (see Carr & Norwood 2022).

11. Rollnick is not alone in casting EBP as a neoliberal strategy that drives helping professionals into private entrepreneurialism (see, for example, Butler 2019; Kerrigan & Johnson 2018; Snell-Rood et al. 2020; Standring 2017).

12. One might investigate how the social science of economics fits into this picture, given so much reliance on the "invisible hand." Interestingly, commentators with very different agendas have associated Keynes with "magical thinking" (for instance, Drucker 1946; see also Harries 2000).

13. Many scholars have offered ample criticism of EBP's narrow definition of evidence, which elevates RCTs as the best if not only way to produce "definitive" evidence. Unfortunately, far fewer scholars have explored the black-boxed and byzantine regulatory apparatus by which evidence is evaluated and ultimately confirmed in the evidence-based era—but for notable exceptions, see Bell & Ristovski-Slijepcevic (2015), Cambrosio et al. (2006, 2009), Carr & Norwood (2022), Hogle (2009), Knappen (2013).

14. Remarkably, while interest in comparative research has found other institutional homes (see, for example, PCORI 2010), this is true for all twenty of the EBP registries

reviewed by Burkhardt et al., who report that "no register offered any sense of comparative standards, which in effect makes all evidence-based interventions equal" (2015, 97; see also Means et al. 2015).

15. As discussed in a co-authored paper (Carr & Norwood 2022), the disjuncture between the bureaucracies that authorize practices and programs as evidence-based, on the one hand, and the organizations, professionals, funders, and insurers that adopt them as such, on the other, raises some obvious concerns. These concerns may have prompted the NREPP's 2015 revision and relatively transparent rendering of program descriptions (if not its own review practices)—after all, registries too must work continually to demonstrate expertise and maintain legitimacy. If one delved past "the list" itself, linked program descriptions became more legible, as were the NREPP's evaluations. This is in large part because of "program snapshots" that rated select outcomes—though not the program itself—as "effective," "promising," or "ineffective." Nevertheless, the NREPP's inclusion/exclusion criteria still meant programs could be listed, and thus legitimated as "evidence-based," even if not a single study showed a positive behavioral outcome, so long as they had been studied in a particular way and been reported transparently (see Knaapen 2013), with the claim of transparency arguably being yet another legitimating device.

16. A 2007 multisite trial conducted by Ball et al. showed that while, as Miller put it, MI "worked at certain sites . . . [these effects] kind of wash out when you average them all together."

17. For instance, Carroll et al. (2001), Carroll et al. (2006), Miller et al. (2003).

18. Indeed, the MITI itself has been researched for reliability and validity (Bennett et al. 2007; Moyers et al. 2005; Pierson et al. 2007; Moyers et al. 2016) and used in MI training and dissemination studies (Bennett et al. 2007; Hartzler et al. 2007; Smith et al. 2007).

19. In addition to continual refinement of the instrument itself, including its recent renaming as CLEAR (Glynn & Moyers 2012), the MISC has also been the subject of scholarly articles on fidelity and coding (Lord et al. 2015; Moyers et al. 2003).

20. These include SCOPE (Sequential Code for Observing Process Exchanges); MICA (Motivational Interviewing Competency Assessment); MITS (MI Target Scheme); VASE-R (Video Assessment of Simulated Encounters—Revised); BECCI (Behaviour Change Counselling Index); AMIGOS v1.2 (Assessment of MI Groups—Observer Scales).

21. US-based EBP advocates have indeed implied, and not uncommonly outright stated, that practitioners' go-to ideas about what helps clients tend to be problematically "intuitive" (for example, Gaudiano, Brown & Miller 2011), "biased" (for example, Gibbs & Gambrill 2002), and tethered to "traditional" sources of institutional authority (for example, Gambrill 1999; Gibbs & Gambrill 2002), and therefore highly unreliable. These characterizations justify researchers prescribing steps for practitioners' consumption and application of evidence, effectively claiming jurisdiction over their work by scientizing it. Others have accordingly objected that EBP diminishes the knowledge and expertise of practitioners and curtails their discretionary capacities in their everyday work with clients (Haynes et al. 2002; Van de Luitgaarden 2009; Webb 2001).

22. Interestingly, Dunn also shows that self-auditing is a key technology of TQM, which asks workers to continually reflect on their own contributions to the total quality of a product.

23. Aside from assisting in the now normative practice of "visual learning," Power-

Point is an indispensable technology of MI training because the projected slides serve as cue cards for trainers, helping to assure that the trainer's lessons sound authentic rather than scripted (see chapter 2). Though MINTies strive to personalize their PowerPoint presentations and the pedagogical performance that accompanies them, the visual representation of MI in training is definitely genred. Use of Tahoma font, background screens in shades of purple, and photographs of quintessentially American landscapes (especially mountain-filled ones) are favored aesthetic modalities with which to present definitions from the MI Bible, usually with Miller and Rollnick cited.

24. According to the MINT website, "The MINT Bulletin replaced the Motivational Interviewing Newsletter: Updates, Education and Training (MINUET), which was the MINT newsletter from 1994 through 2004. The MINUET served as the primary vehicle for communication among MINT trainers until the establishment of a restricted MINT list-serve in 1999. After that time, the MINUET continued to serve as a vehicle for distributing conceptual articles, international updates, and 'distilled' summaries of some of the topics discussed on the list-serve" (https://motivationalinterviewing.org/bulletin). In 2012, the *Bulletin* was replaced by another publication called *MI-TRIP: MI Training, Research, Implementation and Practice*. Though the publication's title again underscores the stringing together of activities that so many others hold apart, its formatting and content made it virtually indistinguishable from an academic journal.

25. Moyers specifically said that she was trained as a "scientist practitioner," and was therefore dedicated to a "model in which clinical practice ought to be informed by science." She made clear that her dedication to research was nurtured by William Miller, who was the chair of her dissertation committee and introduced her to MI. At the same time, she underscored that it was when she became a clinician, working at a VA hospital, that she really learned MI—more evidence of the MINTie adage that "we learn MI from our clients."

26. Zuckoff et al. (2007, 10).

27. For a critical extension of Snow's classic paper, see chapter 5 in Barbara Herrnstein-Smith's *Scandalous Knowledge* (2005).

28. Although James, sometimes called the father of American psychology, was also a philosopher and a mystic, there is now little tolerance for the kinds of inquiries and interests that drove William James's career in mainstream psychology. Yet even James, in the opening lines of his University of Edinburgh lectures (which later became *The Varieties of Religious Experience* [1902]), admits some trepidation in approaching the question of mystical experience by way of psychology and neurology—not only because the science of the day failed to consider religious experience a properly scientific subject, but also because there were those who wanted to protect the realm of the sublime from systematic inquiry.

29. As the next chapter makes clear, I wholeheartedly agree and had only used James's figure thinking he would be more recognizable to my audience.

30. See for example, Mosley, Marwell & Ybarra (2019); Van de Luitgaarden (2009); Webb (2001). Note that critics sometimes assume conformity between mandate and implementation. By contrast, Yvonne Smith (2014) studies professionals in a residential treatment center, finding that despite formal training in a specific EBP method of crisis intervention, workers rarely follow the step-by-step decision-making guidelines the intervention prescribes, even while using some of the techniques learned through the

curriculum. This raises questions about the ways in which EBP decision-making models are or can be successfully implemented in practice (see also Smith 2017). Empirical studies of evidence-based medicine (EBM) have also cautioned that practitioner expertise is not simply overpowered or replaced by scientizing logics or standardization, and that the resulting professional power dynamics and decision-making practices merit empirical investigation (Timmermans & Berg 2003). Looking at EBM in the field of transgender medicine, where uncertainty is prevalent, Shuster finds that providers use the rhetoric of EBM toward different ends, some to contain uncertainty and others to embrace it (2016). Thus, EBM guidelines can help some providers reaffirm their claims to expertise, in a field where there is limited evidence.

31. See, for example, Butler (2019), Lambert (2006), Padgett (2016, 9–10), Standring (2017). Compare to Juul Jensen (2007), Morse (2006).

32. One might add that in addition to being "widely meaningful and easy to adopt" (Tanenbaum 2003, 296), EBP, like other successful policy framings, is highly ambiguous (Brodkin 1991).

CHAPTER 5

1. Representative payees legally act on behalf of people who both receive government benefits, such as SSI, and are deemed legally incompetent to manage their income. Representative payees can be individuals, typically family members or friends of the beneficiary, or organizations, when a family member or friend is not able to act in the role, or in the case of inpatient treatment centers (Social Security Administration, n.d.). The Social Security Administration's messaging of how to be a proper representative payee emphasizes using "best judgment" to determine and meet the "immediate needs" of a beneficiary, then allowing them a small amount of spending money if there is any left over, and saving any additional money in an account (Social Security Administration 2018). Although individuals are prohibited from charging for their services as a representative payee, organizations that act as representative payees can solicit a small fee for the service (Social Security Act 1982).

2. Consider, for instance, the implications of Dewey's formulation of the relationship among habit, action, and belief: "Thoughts that result in belief have an importance attached to them which leads to reflective thought, to conscious inquiry into the nature, conditions and bearing of the belief" (1997, 5).

3. Aside from a few passing references to William James, among many others, there is no mention in the voluminous MI literature of the relationship between MI and American pragmatism. James is cited in the MI-3 (Miller & Rollnick 2013), in an epilogue to chapter 25, "Applying Motivational Interviewing." There, James's pragmatism is colloquially mobilized in the short quote: "Act as if what you do makes a difference. It does." Though Miller and Rollnick do not attribute it to any particular writing, the quote originates in James's *Principles of Psychology* (1890) and is quite widely used in American new age and inspirational texts. Accordingly, I use the term "vernacular" here to suggest that the pragmatism of MI is experienced by those who adopt it as second nature, like a "native tongue," and is therefore the subject of little explicit commentary.

4. Among other things, we see the tension here between MI and the traditional, mainstream approach to addiction treatment, which confronts rather than "rolls" with resistance, with resistance conceived as an acquired attribute of the addicted person (see Carr 2011, chap. 3). As a participant-client in AA, as well as participant-trainee in

MI, Marcus was working—as were several of his colleagues—between these two ways of thinking about resistance (or "denial").

5. In his elaboration of experiential learning, Dewey underscored that the "object or event" never be considered in isolation because any "object or event is always a special part, phase, or aspect, of an environing, experienced world—a situation" (2008, 67).

6. This could be considered an alternative way to understand the poetics of pause described in chapter 2. Specifically, pauses at the planning junctures that semanticists identify are exploitable, allowing interviewers not only to "slow down" to ascertain what has happened but also to anticipate what to say next. As with so much else about MI, I suspect it's both/and.

7. As in: "consider what effects, that might conceivably have practical bearings, we conceive the object of our conception to have . . ." (Peirce 1974, 402).

8. It is worth noting here that the worksheet seems to assume that a client "I" will either fill out the worksheet, or sit down long enough with a U-Haven professional so that their responses could be transcribed. Having shadowed the apprentices for months, I knew this was highly unlikely in the crunch of everyday practice. This is therefore likely yet another, and perhaps even a main, factor in Hector's resistance.

9. It is important to underscore that Fred's approach to knowledge production in no way means that he thought clients could be *reduced* to their diagnoses. In an interview Fred explained: "your job no matter what the client does, no matter how crazy it seems to you, your job is figure out how it makes sense, because if you cannot do that, you won't be able to help."

10. Given my research at U-Haven, I couldn't help but wonder just what persons and problems she had in mind. I knew, as a textbook reader, that Miller and Rollnick are certainly not opposed to "saving time." A closer read reveals that they simultaneously advocate "listening" along with a "few well-chosen words" to lead to clients who "feel understood" while assuring the especially time-pressed professional that there may be "little need to explore further" (2013: 56).

11. One might also see this as a kind of exemption for the medical profession into which MI has made significant inroads.

12. In his classic paper on professional vision, Charles Goodwin incisively notes: "Discursive practices are used by members of a profession to shape events in the domains subject to their professional scrutiny. The shaping process creates objects of knowledge that become the insignia of a profession's craft: The theories, artifacts, and bodies of expertise that distinguish it from other professions" (1994: 606). These are precisely the interpretive frameworks that allow, for instance, testifying police to expertly transform the brutal beating of Rodney King into discrete "professional responses" (i.e., kicks, clubbings, punches), or archaeologists to determine the color of the artifacts they retrieve in line with the categories provided by Munsell—two types of professional vision that Goodwin brilliantly addresses. This kind of analysis suggests that institutional contexts (like courtrooms) and professional affiliations (like "doctor" and "lawyer") do not automatically confer expert status onto their inhabitants. Arguably, it is only when we rigorously attend to real-time semiotic interaction—where struggles of law, science, magic, and medicine play out in improvisational and contingent if always already conventionally controlled ways—that we can also discern just what role institutions have in the organization, authorization, and enactment of expertise. (See Carr 2009, 2010, 2011; Collins 2008; Goodwin 1994; Matoesian 2008; Mehan 1996; Mertz 2007; Silverstein 2004, 2006; Wilf 2014.)

CONCLUSION

1. Indeed, there is plenty of reason to question David Graeber's contention that helping professionals do not suffer the contemporary labor condition he calls "bullshit jobs" (2018). As he defines them, bullshit jobs are those that—even for those who hold them—lack meaning, utility, and purpose, if also requiring the job holders to pretend otherwise. In the helping professions, Graeber finds a kind of labor endowed with the nobility of care, perhaps precisely because he overlooks the myriad conditions (such as the chronic lack of resources relative to demand for services), ambiguous goals (such as the charge to implement state policy and soften the effects of policy on citizens), and ethical dilemmas (such as the competing demands to direct and control as well as care and advocate for client base) that those closer to this line of work have documented for decades. Indeed, the bullshit factor is arguably multiplied for those whose labor is widely expected to be "noble" and productive of extramonetary value, but who continuously encounter the structural frustration of these ideals.

2. The address was entitled, "Motivational Interviewing: Facilitating Change across Boundaries," and was given as part of the Fourth American Health Disparities Conference on October 22, 2009.

3. Though a longtime MINTie, Travis did not share the pronounced humility of most of his colleagues, at least when speaking to me. Consider what he told me, early in our interview: "I think what I do is bring the *spirit* of MI to a much more vivid process. That's what I'm *known* for. That's probably what [*sic*] you got my *name*."

4. This includes Don Brenneis's sage guidance (2004, 2009) for anthropologists to study *each other*, applying what we have learned about forms of evaluation and expertise by studying other professional elites. Indeed, Brenneis reminds us that, however much we'd like to idealize our professional perches as sites of critique rather than complicity, anthropologists increasingly find ourselves entangled in metrics-based managerialism and the marketization of higher education. He therefore urges anthropologists to always recognize and actively manage our complicity in systems, and never write ourselves out of critique.

5. For one thing, tailoring an intervention to a particular population, considering intergroup heterogeneity and intersectional identities, we can easily run into the problem of infinite regress (see Alcoff 1991).

Works Cited

Abbott, Andrew. 1995. "Boundaries of Social Work or Social Work of Boundaries?" *Social Service Review* 69 (4): 545–62.

Agnew, Spiro T. 1972. "Agnew's Blast at Behaviorism." *Psychology Today* 4: 84–87.

Ahmed, Sara. 2012. *On Being Included: Racism and Diversity in Institutional Life.* Durham, NC: Duke University Press.

Ahn, Hyun-nie, and Bruce E. Wampold. 2001. "Where Oh Where Are the Specific Ingredients? A Meta-analysis of Component Studies in Counseling and Psychotherapy." *Journal of Counseling Psychology* 48 (3): 251–57.

Alcoff, Linda. 1991. "The Problem of Speaking for Others." *Cultural Critique* 20: 5–32.

Amrhein, Paul C. 1992. "The Comprehension of Quasi-performance Verbs in Verbal Commitments: New Evidence for Componential Theories of Lexical Meaning." *Journal of Memory and Language* 31 (6): 756–84.

Amrhein, Paul C. 2004. "How Does Motivational Interviewing Work? What Client Talk Reveals." *Journal of Cognitive Psychotherapy* 18 (40): 323–36.

Amrhein, Paul C., William R. Miller, Carolina E. Yahne, Aimee Knupsky, and D. Hochstein. 2004. "Strength of Client Commitment Language Improves with Therapist Training in Motivational Interviewing." *Alcoholism: Clinical and Experimental Research* 28 (5): 74A.

Amrhein, Paul C., William R. Miller, Carolina E. Yahne, Michael Palmer, and Laura Fulcher. 2003. "Client Commitment Language during Motivational Interviewing Predicts Drug Use Outcomes." *Journal of Consulting and Clinical Psychology* 71 (5): 862–77.

Angus, Lynne, and Fern Kagan. 2009. "Therapist Empathy and Client Anxiety Reduction in Motivational Interviewing: 'She Carries With Me, the Experience.'" *Journal of Clinical Psychology* 65 (11): 1156–67.

Appadurai, Arjun. 1986. "Commodities and the Politics of Value." In Arjun Appadurai, ed., *The Social Life of Things: Commodities in Cultural Perspective*, 3–63. Cambridge: Cambridge University Press.

Appadurai, Arjun. 2015. *Banking on Words: The Failure of Language in the Age of Derivative Finance.* Chicago: University of Chicago Press.

Arkowitz, Hal, and William R. Miller. 2008. "Learning, Applying, and Extending Motivational Interviewing." In Hal Arkowitz, Henny A. Westra, William R. Miller, and Stephen Rollnick, eds., *Motivational Interviewing in the Treatment of Psychological Problems*, 1–25. New York: Guilford Press.

Austin, John L. 1962. *How to Do Things with Words.* Cambridge, MA: Harvard University Press.

Baker, Amanda, Nicole Kochan, F. Dixon, Nick Heather, and A. Woadk. 1994. "Controlled Evaluation of a Brief Intervention of HIV Prevention among Injecting Drug Users Not in Treatment." *AIDS Care* 6 (5): 559–70.

Bakhtin, Mikhail M. 1981. *The Dialogic Imagination.* Austin: University of Texas Press.

Bakhtin, Mikhail M. 1990. *Art and Answerability: Early Philosophical Essays by M. M. Bakhtin.* Trans. V. Liapuv. Austin: University of Texas Press.

Ball, Samuel, Steve Martino, Charla Nich, Tami Frankforter, Deborah Van Horn, Paul Crits-Cristoph, et al. 2007. "Site Matters: Multisite Randomized Trial of Motivational Enhancement Therapy in Community Drug Abuse Clinics." *Journal of Consulting and Clinical Psychology* 75 (4): 556–67.

Basso, Keith H. 1970. "To Give Up on Words: Silence in the Western Apache Culture." *South Western Journal of Anthropology* 26 (3): 213–30.

Bate, John Bernard. 2002. "Political Praise in Tamil Newspapers: The Poetry and Iconography of Democratic Power." In Diane P. Mines and Sarah Lamb, eds., *Everyday Life in South Asia*, 308–25. Bloomington: Indiana University Press.

Bate, John Bernard. 2009. *Tamil Modern and the Dravidian Aesthetic: Democratic Practice in South India.* New York: Columbia University Press.

Bateson, Gregory. 1972. *Steps to an Ecology of Mind.* Chicago: University of Chicago Press.

Bauman, Richard. 1983. *Let Your Words Be Few: Symbolism of Speaking and Silence among Seventeenth-Century Quakers.* Cambridge: Cambridge University Press.

Bauman, Richard. 2016. "Projecting Presence: Aura and Oratory in William Jennings Bryan Presidential Races." In E. Summerson Carr and Michael Lempert, eds., *Scale: Discourse and Dimensions of Social Life*, 25–51. Oakland: University of California Press.

Bauman, Richard. 2023. *A Most Valuable Medium: The Remediation of Oral Performance on Early Commercial Recordings.* Bloomington: Indiana University Press.

Bauman, Richard, and Charles L. Briggs. 2003. *Voices of Modernity: Language Ideology and the Politics of Inequality.* New York: Cambridge University Press.

Behar, Ruth, and Deborah Gordon, eds. 1996. *Women Writing Culture.* Berkeley: University of California Press.

Bell, Kirsten. 2012. "Cochrane Reviews and the Behavioural Turn in Evidence-based Medicine." *Health Sociology Review* 21 (3): 313–21.

Bell, Kirsten, and Svetlana Ristovski-Slijepcevic. 2015. "Communicating 'Evidence': Lifestyle, Cancer, and the Promise of a Disease-free Future." *Medical Anthropology Quarterly* 29 (2): 216–36.

Bellah, Robert N. 1975. *The Broken Covenant: American Civil Religion in Time of Trial.* New York: Seabury Press.

Bem, Daryl J. 1967. "Self-perception: An Alternative Interpretation of Cognitive Dissonance Phenomena." *Psychological Review* 74 (3): 183–200.

Bem, Daryl J. 1972. *Self-perception Theory.* New York: Academic Press.

Bennett, Gerald A., Julie Moore, Tina Vaughan, Lindsey Rouse, Jood A. Gibbins, Peter Thomas, Kay James, and Phil Gower. 2007. "Strengthening Motivational Interviewing Skills Following Initial Training: A Randomized Trial of Workplace-based Reflective Practice." *Addictive Behaviors* 32 (12): 2963–75.

Bergmann, Jörg R. 1992. "Veiled Morality: Notes on Discretion in Psychiatry." In Paul

Drew and John Heritage, eds., *Talk at Work: Interaction in Institutional Settings*, 137–62. Cambridge: Cambridge University Press.

Bialecki, Jon. 2017. *A Diagram for Fire: Miracles and Variation in an American Charismatic Movement*. Berkeley: University of California Press.

Bishara, Amahl. 2013. *Back Stories: U.S. News Production and Palestinian Politics*. Durham, NC: Duke University Press.

Bjork, Daniel W. 1997. *B. F. Skinner: A Life*. Washington, DC: American Psychological Association.

Bosk, Charles. 2003. *Forgive and Remember*. Chicago: University of Chicago Press.

Boyer, Dominic. 2013. *The Life Informatic: Newsmaking in the Digital Age*. Ithaca: Cornell University Press.

Brada, Betsey. 2022. *Learning to Save the World: Global Health Pedagogies and Fantasies of Transformation in Botswana*. Ithaca: Cornell University Press.

Brenneis, Donald. 2004. "A Partial View of Contemporary Anthropology." *American Anthropologist* 106 (3): 580–88.

Brenneis, Donald. 2006. "Reforming Promise." In Annalise Riles, ed., *Documents: Artifacts of Modern Knowledge*, 41–70. Ann Arbor: University of Michigan Press.

Briggs, Charles. 1986. *Learning How to Ask: A Sociolinguistic Appraisal of the Role of the Interview in Social Science Research*. New York: Cambridge University Press.

Briggs, Charles. 2007. "Anthropology, Interviewing, and Communicability in Contemporary Society." *Current Anthropology* 48 (4): 551–80.

Brodkin, Evelyn Z. 1990. "Implementation as Policy Politics." In Dennis Palumbo and Donald Calista, eds., *Implementation and the Policy Process: Opening up the Black Box*, 107–18. Westport, CT: Greenwood Press.

Brotherton, Sean. 2020. "Armed against Unhappiness: Psychoanalytic Grammars in Buenos Aires." *Medical Anthropology Quarterly* 34 (1): 99–118.

Brown, Janice M., and William R. Miller. 1993. "Impact of Motivational Interviewing on Participation and Outcome in Residential Alcoholism Treatment." *Psychology of Addictive Behaviors* 7 (4): 211–18.

Burke, Brian L., Christopher W. Dunn, David C. Atkins, and Jerry S. Phelps. 2004. "The Emerging Evidence Base for Motivational Interviewing: A Meta-analytic and Qualitative Inquiry." *Journal of Cognitive Psychotherapy* 18 (4): 309–22.

Burkhardt, Jason T., Daniela C. Schröter, Stephen Magura, Stephanie N. Means, and Chris L. Coryn. 2015. "An Overview of Evidence-based Program Registers (EBPRs) for Behavioral Health." *Evaluation Programming and Planning* 48: 92–99.

Burnham, John, ed. 2012. *After Freud Left: A Century of Psychoanalysis in America*. Chicago: University of Chicago Press.

Butler, Claire. 2019. "Working the 'Wise' in Speech and Language Therapy: Evidence-based Practice, Biopolitics and 'Pastoral Labour.'" *Social Science & Medicine* 230: 1–8.

Cambrosio, Alberto, Peter Keating, Thomas Schlich, and George Weisz. 2006. "Regulatory Objectivity and the Generation and Management of Evidence in Medicine." *Social Science & Medicine* 63: 189–99.

Cambrosio, Alberto, Peter Keating, Thomas Schlich, and George Weisz. 2009. "Biomedical Conventions and Regulatory Objectivity: A Few Introductory Remarks." *Social Studies of Science* 39 (5): 651–64.

Cannell, Fenella. 2006. *The Anthropology of Chiristianity*. Durham, NC: Duke University Press.

Carr, E. Summerson. 2006. "Secrets Keep You Sick: Metalinguistic Labor in a Drug Treatment Program for Homeless Women." *Language in Society* 35 (5): 631–53.

Carr, E. Summerson. 2009. "Anticipating and Inhabiting Institutional Identities." *American Ethnologist* 36 (2): 317–36.

Carr, E. Summerson. 2010a. "Enactments of Expertise." *Annual Review of Anthropology* 39: 17–32.

Carr, E. Summerson. 2010b. "Qualifying the Qualitative Social Work Interview: A Linguistic Anthropological Approach." *Qualitative Social Work* 10 (1): 123–43.

Carr, E. Summerson. 2011. *Scripting Addiction: The Politics of Therapeutic Talk and American Sobriety*. Princeton: Princeton University Press.

Carr, E. Summerson. 2013. "Signs of Sobriety: Rescripting American Addiction Counseling." In Eugene Raikhel and William Garriott, eds., *Addiction Trajectories*, 160–87. Durham, NC: Duke University Press.

Carr, E. Summerson. 2015. "Occupation Bedbug: Or, the Urgency and Agency of Professional Pragmatism." *Cultural Anthropology* 30 (2): 257–85.

Carr, E. Summerson. 2021. "Learning How Not to Know: Pragmatism, (In)expertise, and the Training of American Helping Professionals." *American Anthropologist* 123 (3): 526–38.

Carr, E. Summerson. 2023. "(In)expertise and the Paradox of Therapeutic Governance." In Gil Eyal and Thomas Medvetz, eds., *The Oxford Handbook of Expertise and Democratic Politics*. New York: Oxford University Press.

Carr, E. Summerson. Forthcoming. "An American Canard: Carl Rogers, B. F. Skinner, and the Freedom of (Therapeutic) Speech." In Matei Candea, ed., *Anthropologies of Free Speech: Language, Ethics and Power in Comparative Perspective*. Toronto: University of Toronto Press.

Carr, E. Summerson, and Brooke A. Fisher. 2016. "Interscaling Awe, De-escalating Disaster." In Carr and Michael Lempert, eds., *Scale: Discourse and Dimensions of Social Life*, 133–58. Berkeley: University of California Press.

Carr, E. Summerson, and Michael Lempert. 2016. "The Pragmatics of Scale." In Carr and Michael Lempert, eds., *Scale: Discourse and Dimensions of Social Life*, 1–24. Berkeley: University of California Press.

Carr, E. Summerson, and Hannah Obertino-Norwood. "Legitimizing Evidence: The Trans-institutional Life of Evidence-based Practice." *Social Science & Medicine* 310: 115130.

Carr, E. Summerson, and Yvonne Smith. 2014. "The Poetics of Therapeutic Practice: Motivational Interviewing and the Powers of Pause." *Culture, Medicine & Psychiatry* 37 (1): 83–114.

Carroll, Kathleen M., Samuel A. Ball, Charla Nich, Steve Martino, Tami Frankforter, Christiane Farentinos, et al. 2006. "Motivational Interviewing to Improve Treatment Engagement and Outcome in Individuals Seeking Treatment for Substance Abuse: A Multisite Effectiveness Study." *Drug and Alcohol Dependence* 81: 301–12.

Carroll, Kathleen M., Bryce Libby, Joseph Sheehan, and Nancy Hyland. 2001. "Motivational Interviewing to Enhance Treatment Initiation in Substance Abusers: An Effectiveness Study." *American Journal on Addictions* 10 (4): 335–39.

Carton, Tony. 2014. "The Spirit of Motivational Interviewing as an Apparatus of Governmentality: An Analysis of Reading Materials Used in the Training of Substance Abuse Clinicians." *Sociology Mind* 4 (2): 192–205.

Catley, Delwyn, Kari Jo Harris, Matthew S. Mayo, S. Sandra Hall, Kolawole S. Okuyemi, Thuy Boardman, and Jasjit S. Ahluwalia. 2006. "Adherence to Principles of Motivational Interviewing and Client Within-session Behavior." *Behavioral and Cognitive Psychotherapy* 34 (1): 43–56.

Cherniss, Cary. 1980. *Staff Burnout: Job Stress in the Human Services.* Beverly Hills, CA: Sage.

Cherniss, Cary. 1995. *Beyond Burnout: Helping Teachers, Nurses, Therapists and Lawyers Recover from Stress and Disillusionment.* New York: Taylor Francis.

Chomsky, Noam. 1967. "A Review of B. F. Skinner's *Verbal Behavior.*" In Leon A. Jakobovits and Murray S. Miron, eds., *Readings in the Psychology of Language*, 142–43. Hoboken, NJ: Prentice-Hall.

Chomsky, Noam. 1971. "The Case against B. F. Skinner: Review of *Beyond Freedom and Dignity* by B. F. Skinner." *New York Review of Books*, January 30, 1971, 18–24.

Chu, Julie. 2010. *Cosmologies of Credit: Transnational Mobility and the Politics of Destination in China.* Durham, NC: Duke University Press.

Chumley, Lily. 2016. *Creativity Class: Art School and Culture Work in Post-socialist China.* Princeton: Princeton University Press.

Cicero. 1949. *On Invention; The Best Kind of Orator; Topics.* Trans. H. M. Hubbell. Cambridge, MA: Harvard University Press.

Cicero (attrib.). 1954. *Ad C. Herennium. De Ratione Dicendi (Rhetorica ad Herennium).* Trans. Harry Caplan. Cambridge, MA: Harvard University Press.

Cicourel, Aaron. 1995. "Medical Speech Events as Resources for Inferring Differences in Expert-novice Diagnostic Reasoning." In Uta M. Quasthoff, ed., *Aspects of Oral Communication*, 364–87. New York: Walter de Gruyter.

Cicourel, Aaron. 2001. "Expert." In Alessandro Duranti, ed., *Key Terms in Language and Culture*, 67–70. Malden, MA: Blackwell Press.

Clifford, James, and George E. Marcus, eds. 1986. *Writing Culture: The Poetics and Politics of Ethnography.* Berkeley: University of California Press.

Coalition for Evidence-Based Policy. n.d. "Our Mission." http://coalition4evidence .org/. Accessed August 30, 2017.

Cochrane, Archibald L. 1972. *Effectiveness and Efficiency: Random Reflections on Health Services.* London: Nuffield Trust.

Cochrane.org. 2020. "About Us" page. https://www.cochrane.org/about-us.

Cohen-Cole, Jamie. 2014. *The Open Mind: Cold War Politics and the Sciences of Human Nature.* Chicago: University of Chicago Press.

Coleman, Simon. 2004. "The Charismatic Gift." *Journal of the Royal Anthropological Institute* 10 (2): 421–42.

Collins, Harry, and Robert Evans. 2019. "Populism and Science." *Epistemology & Philosophy of Science* 56 (4): 200–218.

Collins, James. 2008. "'You Don't Know What They Translate': Language Contact, Institutional Procedure, and Literacy Practice in Neighborhood Health Clinics in Urban Flanders." *Journal of Linguistic Anthropology* 16 (2): 249–68.

Community Care of North Carolina. 2017. "CCNC: A History of CCNC." https://www .communitycarenc.org/about-us/history-ccnc-rev/. Accessed July 2017.

Cordova, James V., Lisa Z. Warren, and Christina B. Gee. 2001. "Motivational Interviewing as an Intervention for At-risk Couples." *Journal of Marital and Family Therapy* 27 (3): 315–26.

Cornman, Deborah H., Susan M. Kieve, Sarah Christie, William A. Fishcer, Paul A. Shiper, Sany Pillay, Gerald H. Friedland, Cyril Monty Thomas, Linda Lodge, and

Jeffrey D. Fisher. 2008. "Clinic-based Intervention Reduces Unprotected Sexual Behavior among HIV-infected Patients in KwaZulu-Natal, South Africa: Results of a Pilot Study." *Journal of Acquired Immune Deficiency Syndrome* 48 (5): 553–67.

Craciun, Marianna. 2018. "Emotions and Knowledge in Expert Work: A Comparison of Two Psychotherapies." *American Journal of Sociology* 123 (4): 959–1003.

Csillik, Antonia, Thierry Meyer, and Evgeny Osin. 2022. "Comparative Evaluation of Motivational Interviewing Components in Alcohol Treatment." *Journal of Contemporary Psychotherapy* 52: 55–65.

Daston, Lorraine, and Peter Galison. 2010. *Objectivity*. New York: Zone Books.

Davis, Elizabeth. 2012. *Bad Souls: Madness and Responsibility in Modern Greece*. Durham, NC: Duke University Press.

Dean, Sarah, E. Britt, James Stanley, and Sunny Collings. 2016. "Motivational Interviewing to Enhance Adolescent Mental Health Treatment Engagement: A Randomized Clinical Trial." *Psychological Medicine* 46 (9): 1961–69.

De Souza Leão, Luciana, and Gil Eyal. 2019. "The Rise of Randomized Controlled Trials (RCTs) in International Development in Historical Perspective." *Theory and Society* 48 (3): 383–418.

Dewey, John. 1913. "Play." In *The Encyclopedia of Education*. New York: Macmillan.

Dewey, John. 1922. *Democracy and Education*. New York: Macmillan.

Dewey, John. 1972. *The Early Works of John Dewey, Vol. 5: 1882–1898*. Carbondale: Southern Illinois University Press.

Dewey, John. 1997. *How We Think*. Mineola, NY: Dover Press.

Dewey, John. 2008. *The Late Works of John Dewey, Vol. 13: 1925–1953*. Carbondale: Southern Illinois University Press.

Dick, Hilary Parsons. 2018. *Words of Passage: National Longing and the Imagined Lives of Mexican Migrants*. Austin: University of Texas Press.

Dickens, Regina Schaaf, Kelly Crosbie, and Michael S. Lancaster. 2012. "Primary Care/Behavioral Health Integration Efforts in North Carolina." *North Carolina Medical Journal* 73 (3): 204–8.

Drisko, James W. 2013. "Common Factors in Psychotherapy." In *Encyclopedia of Social Work*. New York: NASW Press.

Drucker, Peter F. 1946. "Keynes: Economics as a Magical System." *Virginia Quarterly Review* 22 (4): 532–46.

Drug Enforcement Administration 2013. Title 21 United States Code [USC] Controlled Substances Act—Section 812 2017.

DuBois, Vincent. 2010. *The Bureaucrat and the Poor: Encounters in French Welfare Offices*. Farnham, Surrey, UK: Ashgate Publishing.

Dunn, Elizabeth. 2004. *Privatizing Poland: Baby Food, Big Business and the Remaking of Labor*. Ithaca: Cornell University Press.

Duranti, Alessandro and Charles Goodwin, eds. 1992. *Rethinking Context: Language as an Interactive Phenomenon*. New York: Cambridge.

Elkin, Irene, Lydia Falconnier, Yvonne Smith, Kelli Canada, Chad Henderson, Eric Brown, and Benjamin McKay. 2013. "Therapist Responsiveness and Patient Engagement in Therapy." *Psychotherapy Research* 24 (1): 52–66.

Elkin, Irene, Paul A. Pilkonis, John P. Docherty, and Stuart M. Sotsky. 1988. "Conceptual and Methodological Issues in Comparative Studies of Psychotherapy and Pharmacotherapy: I. Active Ingredients and Mechanisms of Change." *American Journal of Psychiatry* 145 (8): 909–17.

Emmons, Karen M., and Stephen Rollnick. 2001. "Motivational Interviewing in Health Care Settings: Opportunities and Limitations." *American Journal of Preventive Medicine* 20 (1): 68–74.

Engelke, Matthew. 2004. "Discontinuity and the Discourse of Conversion." *Journal of Religion in Africa* 34 (1–2): 82–109.

Engelke, Matthew. 2007. *A Problem of Presence: Beyond Scripture in an African Church.* Berkeley: University of California Press.

Engelke, Matthew. 2018. *How to Think Like an Anthropologist.* Princeton: Princeton University Press.

Eyal, Gil. 2013. "For a Sociology of Expertise: The Social Origins of the Autism Epidemic." *American Journal of Sociology* 118 (4): 863–907.

Eyal, Gil. 2019. *The Crisis of Expertise.* Cambridge: Polity Press.

Feldman, Larry B. 1976. "Strategies and Techniques of Family Therapy." *American Journal of Psychotherapy* 30 (1):14–28.

Ferreira, Fernanda. 1993. "Creation of Prosody during Sentence Production." *Psychological Review* 100 (2): 233–53.

Fliegelman, Jay. 1993. *Declaring Independence: Jefferson, Natural Language, and the Culture of Performance.* Palo Alto, CA: Stanford University Press.

Frankl, Victor. 1960. "Paradoxical Intention: A Logotherapeutic Technique." *American Journal of Psychotherapy* 14 (3): 520–35.

Fraser, Nancy. 2008. *Adding Insult to Injury: Nancy Fraser Debates Her Critics.* Ed. Keven Olson. New York: Verso.

Fraser, Nancy, and Alex Honneth. 2003. *Redistribution or Recognition? A Philosophical Exchange.* Trans. Joel Golb, James Ingram, and Christiane Wilke. London: Verso Books.

Frost, Helen, Pauline Campbell, Margaret Maxwell, Ronan E. O'Carroll, Stephan U. Dombrowski, Brian Williams, Helen Cheyne, Emma Coles, and Alex Pollock. 2018. "Effectiveness of Motivational Interviewing on Adult Behavior Change in Health and Social Care Settings." *PLoS One* 13 (10).

Gal, Susan. 1991. "Between Speech and Silence: The Problematics of Research on Language and Gender." In Michaela di Leonardo, ed., *Gender at the Crossroads of Knowledge: Feminist Anthropology in the Postmodern Era*, 175–203. Berkeley: University of California Press.

Gal, Susan. 2015. "Politics of Translation." *Annual Review of Anthropology* 44: 225–40.

Gal, Susan. 2016. "Registers in Circulation: The Social Organization of Interdiscursivity." *Signs and Society* 6 (1): 1–24.

Gal, Susan, and Judith T. Irvine. 1995. "The Boundaries of Languages and Disciplines: How Ideologies Construct Difference." *Social Research* 62 (4): 967–1001.

Gal, Susan, and Judith T. Irvine. 2019. *Signs of Difference: Language and Ideology in Social Life.* New York: Cambridge University Press.

Gambrill, Eileen. 1999. "Evidence-Based Practice: An Alternative to Authority-Based Practice." *Families in Society* 80 (4): 341–50.

Gaudiano, Brandon, Liliana Brown, and Ivan Miller. 2011. "Let Your Intuition Be Your Guide? Individual Differences in the Evidence-based Practice Attitudes of Psychotherapists." *Journal of Evaluation in Clinical Practice* 17 (4): 628–34.

Gershon, Ilana. 2017. *Down and Out in the New Economy: How People Find (or Don't Find) Work Today.* Chicago: University of Chicago Press.

Ghizzardi, Greta, Cristina Arrigoni, Frederica Dellafiore, Ercole Vellone, and Rosario

Caruso. 2022. "Efficacy of Motivational Interviewing on Enhancing Self-care Behaviors among Patients with Chronic Heart Failure: A Systematic Review and Meta-analysis of Randomized Controlled Trials." *Heart Failure Review* 27: 1029–41.

Gibbs, Leon, and Eileen Gambrill. 2002. "Evidence-based Practice: Counterarguments to Objections." *Research on Social Work Practice* 12 (3): 452–76.

Ginsburg, Faye, and Anna Lowenhaupt Tsing. 1991. *Uncertain Terms: Negotiating Gender in American Culture*. Boston: Beacon Press.

Glasner-Edwards, Suzette, and Richard Rawson. 2010. "Evidence-based Practices in Addiction Treatment: Review and Recommendations for Public Policy." *Health Policy* 97 (2–3): 93–104.

Glynn, Lisa H., and Theresa Moyers. 2012. "Chasing Change Talk: The Clinician's Role in Evoking Client Language about Change." *Journal of Substance Abuse Treatment* 39 (1): 65–70.

Goffman, Erving. 1981. *Forms of Talk*. Philadelphia: University of Pennsylvania Press.

Goldfried, Marvin, John E. Pachankis, and Alyssa C. Bell. 2005. "A History of Psychotherapy Integration." In John C. Norcross and Marvin R. Goldfried, eds., *Handbook of Psychotherapy Integration*, 24–60. New York: Oxford University Press.

Goldman-Eisler, Frieda. 1968. *Psycholinguistics: Experiments in Spontaneous Speech*. London: Academic Press.

Goodwin, Charles. 1994. "Professional Vision." *American Anthropologist* 96 (3): 606–33.

Goodwin, Charles. 1996. "Transparent Vision." In Elinor Ochs, Emanuel A. Schegloff, and Sandra A. Thompson, eds., *Interaction and Grammar*, 370–404. Cambridge: Cambridge University Press.

Graeber, David. 2018. *Bullshit Jobs*. New York: Simon & Shuster.

Grasso, Christopher. 2002. "Skepticism and American Faith: Infidels, Converts, and Religious Doubt in the Early Nineteenth Century." *Journal of the Early Republic* 22 (3): 465–508.

Grasso, Christopher. 2018. *Skepticism and American Faith: From the Revolution to the Civil War*. Oxford: Oxford University Press.

Green-Hennessy, Sharon. 2018. "Suspension of the National Registry of Evidence-Based Programs and Practices: The Importance of Adhering to the Evidence." *Substance Abuse: Treatment, Prevention, and Policy* 13 (26).

Greil, Arthur L., and David R. Rudy. 1983. "Conversion to the World View of Alcoholics Anonymous: A Refinement of Conversion Theory." *Qualitative Sociology* 6 (1): 5–28.

Grodensky, Catherine, Carol Golin, Megha A. Parikh, Rebecca Ochtera, Carlye Kincaid, Jennifer Groves, Laura Wildman, Chirayath Suchindran, Camille McGirt, Kemi Amola, and Steven Bradley-Bull. 2017. "Does the Quality of Safetalk Motivational Interviewing Counseling Predict Sexual Behavior Outcomes among People Living with HIV?" *Patient Education and Counseling* 100 (1): 147–53.

Gusterson, Hugh. 1997. "Studying Up, Revisited." *Political and Legal Anthropology Review* 20 (1): 114–19.

Gusterson, Hugh. 2004. *People of the Bomb: Portraits of America's Nuclear Complex*. Minneapolis: University of Minnesota Press.

Hardesty, Melissa. 2015. "Epistemological Binds and Ethical Dilemmas in Frontline Child Welfare Practice." *Social Service Review* 89 (3): 455–98.

Harding, Susan. 2001. *The Book of Jerry Falwell: Fundamentalist Language and Politics*. Princeton: Princeton University Press.

Harries, Martin. 2000. *Scare Quotes from Shakespeare: Marx, Keynes, and the Language of Reenchantment*. Palo Alto, CA: Stanford University Press.

Hartzler, Bryan, John S. Baer, Chris Dunn, Dave B. Rosengren, and Elizabeth Wells. 2007. "What Is Seen through the Looking Glass: The Impact of Training on Practitioner Self-rating of Motivational Interviewing Skills." *Behavioural and Cognitive Psychotherapy* 35 (4): 431–45.

Haynes, R. Brian, P. J. Devereaux, and Gordon Guyatt. 2002. "Clinical Expertise in the Era of Evidence-based Medicine and Patient Choice." *Evidence-Based Medicine* 7 (2): 36–38.

Helmreich, Stefan. 2007. "Induction, Deduction, Abduction and the Logics of Race and Kinship." *American Ethnologist* 34 (2): 230–32.

Helmreich, Stefan. 2009. *Alien Oceans: Anthropological Voyages on Microbial Seas*. Berkeley: University of California Press.

Herrnstein-Smith, Barbara. 2005. *Scandalous Knowledge: Science, Truth and the Human*. Durham, NC: Duke University Press.

Hettema, Jennifer, Julie Steele, and William R. Miller. 2005. "Motivational Interviewing." *Annual Review of Clinical Psychology* 1: 91–111.

Hill, Jane. 2000. "Read My Article: Ideological Complexity and the Overdetermination of Promising in American Presidential Politics." In Paul Kroskrity, ed., *Regimes of Language*, 259–91. Sante Fe, NM: School of American Research Press.

Hogle, Linda. 2009. "Pragmatic Objectivity and the Standardization of Engineered Tissues." *Social Studies of Science* 39 (5): 717–42.

Honneth, Axel. 2003. "Redistribution as Recognition: A Response to Nancy Fraser." In Nancy Fraser and Axel Honneth, eds., *Redistribution or Recognition? A Philosophical Exchange*. Trans. Joel Golb, James Ingram, and Christiane Wilke. London: Verso Books.

Hull, Matthew. 2010. "Democratic Technologies of Speech: From WWII America to Postcolonial Delhi." *Journal of Linguistic Anthropology* 20 (2): 257–82.

Hull, Matthew. 2012. *Government of Paper: The Materiality of Bureaucracy in Urban Pakistan*. Berkeley: University of California Press.

Inoue, Miyako. 2018. "Word for Word: Verbatim as Political Technologies." *Annual Review of Anthropology* 47: 217–32.

Irani, Lilly. 2019. *Chasing Innovation: Making Entrepreneurial Citizens in Modern India*. Princeton: Princeton University Press.

Irvine, Judith T., and Susan Gal. 2000. "Language Ideology and Linguistic Differentiation." In Paul V. Kroskrity, ed., *Regimes of Language: Ideologies, Polities, and Identities*. Santa Fe, NM: School of American Research Press.

Jackson, John. 2005. *Real Black: Adventures in Racial Sincerity*. Chicago: University of Chicago Press.

Jacobs-Huey, Lanita. 2003. "Ladies Are Seen, Not Heard: Language Socialization in a Southern, African American Cosmetology School." *Anthropology of Education Quarterly* 34 (3): 277–99.

Jaffe, Joseph, and Stanley Feldstein. 1970. *Rhythms of Dialogue*. New York: Academic Press.

Jakobson, Roman. 1960. *Language and Poetics*. Cambridge, MA: MIT Press.

James, William. 1890. *Principles of Psychology*. New York: Henry Holt & Co.

James, William. 1902. *The Varieties of Religious Experience*. London: Longmans, Green & Co.

James, William. 1909. *The Meaning of Truth*. London: Longmans, Green & Co.

Jasanoff, Sheila. 1990. *The Fifth Branch: Science Advisers as Policymakers*. Cambridge, MA: Harvard University Press.

Jaworski, Adam. 1993. *The Power of Silence: Social and Pragmatic Perspectives*. Thousand Oaks, CA: Sage.

Jobson, Ryan C. 2020. "The Case for Letting Anthropology Burn: Sociocultural Anthropology in 2019." *American Anthropologist* 122 (2): 259–71.

Jones, Graham. 2011. *The Trade of the Tricks: Inside the Magician's Craft*. Chicago: University of Chicago Press.

Juul Jensen, Uffe. 2007. "The Struggle for Clinical Authority: Shifting Ontologies and the Politics of Evidence." *BioSocieties* 2 (1): 101–14.

Keane, Webb. 1996. *Signs of Recognition*. Berkeley: University of California Press.

Keane, Webb. 2002. "Sincerity, 'Modernity,' and the Protestants." *Cultural Anthropology* 17 (1): 65–92.

Keane, Webb. 2007. *Christian Moderns: Freedom and Fetish in the Mission Encounter*. Berkeley: University of California Press.

Kelty, Christopher. 2008. *Two Bits: The Cultural Significance of Free Software*. Durham, NC: Duke University Press.

Kelty, Christopher. 2019. *The Participant: A Century of Participation in Four Stories*. Chicago: University of Chicago Press.

Kerrigan Monica R., and Ane T. Johnson. 2019. "Qualitative Approaches to Policy Research in Education: Contesting the Evidence-Based, Neoliberal Regime." *American Behavioral Scientist* 63 (3): 287–95.

Kierkegaard, Søren. 1985. *Philosophical Fragments, Johannes Climacus*. Ed. and trans. Edna H. Hong and Howard V. Hong. *Kierkegaard's Writings VII*, Vol. 7. Princeton: Princeton University Press.

Kirschenbaum, Howard, and Valerie Land Henderson, eds. 1989. *Carl Rogers, Dialogues: Conversations with Martin Buber, Paul Tillich, B. F. Skinner, Gregory Bateson, Michael Polanyi, Rollo May, et al.* Boston: Houghton, Mifflin.

Kistenmacher, Barbara R., and Robert L. Weiss. "Motivational Interviewing as a Mechanism for Change in Men Who Batter: A Randomized Controlled Trial." *Violence and Victims* 23 (5): 558–70.

Kitanaka, Junko. 2011. *Depression in Japan: Psychiatric Cures for a Society in Distress*. Princeton: Princeton University Press.

Klassen, Pamela E. 2011. *Spirits of Protestantism: Medicine, Healing, and Liberal Christianity*. Berkeley: University of California Press.

Knaapen, Loes. 2013. "Being 'Evidence-based' in the Absence of Evidence: The Management of Non-evidence in Guideline Development." *Social Studies of Science* 43 (5): 681–706.

Krivokapic, Jelena. 2007. "Prosodic Planning: Effects of Phrasal Length and Complexity on Pause Duration." *Journal of Phonetics* 35 (2): 162–79.

Kroskrity, Paul. 2000. "Regimenting Languages: Language Ideological Perspectives." In Kroskrity, ed., *Regimes of Language: Ideologies, Polities, and Identities*, 1–34. Santa Fe, NM: School of American Research Press.

Labov, William, and David Fanshel. 1977. *Therapeutic Discourse: Psychotherapy as Conversation*. New York: Academic Press.

Lambert, Helen. 2006. Accounting or EBM: Notions of Evidence in Medicine. *Social Science & Medicine* 62 (2): 63–645.

Larkin, Brian. 2013. "Making Equivalence Happen: Commensuration and the Grounds of Circulation." In Patricia Spyer and Mary Steedly, eds., *Images without Borders*. Santa Fe, NM: SAR Press.

Latour, Bruno. 1988. *Science in Action*. Cambridge, MA: Harvard University Press.

Latour, Bruno. 1993. *We Have Never Been Modern*. Cambridge, MA: Harvard University Press.

Latour, Bruno. 1999. *Pandora's Hope: Essays on the Reality of Science Studies*. Cambridge, MA: Harvard University Press.

Latour, Bruno. 2007. *Reassembling the Social*. New York: Oxford University Press.

Lave, Jean. 2011. *Apprenticeship in Critical Ethnographic Practice*. Chicago: University of Chicago Press.

Lave, Jean, and Etienne Wenger. 1991. *Situated Learning: Legitimate Peripheral Participation*. Cambridge: Cambridge University Press.

Lea, Tess. 2008. *Bureaucrats and Bleeding Hearts: Indigenous Health in Northern Australia*. Randwick: University of South Wales Press.

Lempert, Michael. 2012. *Discipline and Debate: The Language of Violence in a Tibetan Buddhist Monastery*. Berkeley: University of California Press.

Lempert, Michael, and Michael Silverstein. 2012. *Creatures of Politics: Media, Message, and the American Presidency*. Bloomington: Indiana University Press.

Levinson, Stephen C. 1983. *Pragmatics*. Cambridge: Cambridge University Press.

Lévi-Strauss, Claude. 2016. *Elementary Structures of Kinship*. Boston: Beacon Press.

Lipsky, Michael. 1980. *Street-level Bureaucracy: Dilemmas of the Individual in Public Services*. New York: Russell Sage Foundation.

Lord, Sarah P., Dogan Can, Michael Yi, Rebeca Marin, Christopher W. Dunn, Zac E. Imel, Panayiotis Georgiou, Shrikanth Narayanan, Mark Steyvers, and Davic C. Atkins. 2015. "Advancing Methods for Reliably Assessing Motivational Interviewing Fidelity using the Motivational Interviewing Skills Code." *Journal of Substance Abuse Treatment* 49: 50–57.

Luborsky, Lester, George E. Woody, A. Thomas McLellan, Charles P. O'Brien, and Jerry Rosenzweig. 1982. "Can Independent Judges Recognize Different Psychotherapies? An Experience with Manual-guided Therapies." *Journal of Consulting and Clinical Psychology* 50 (1): 49–62.

Lucy, John A. 1993. *Reflexive Language: Reported Speech and Metapragmatics*. New York: Cambridge University Press.

Luhrmann, Tanya. 2000. *Of Two Minds: An Anthropologist Looks at American Psychiatry*. New York: Knopf.

Maclochlainn, Scott. 2022. *The Copy Generic: How the Nonspecific Makes Our Social Worlds*. Chicago: University of Chicago Press.

Macy, Beth. 2018. *Dopesick: Dealers, Doctors, and the Drug Company That Addicted America*. Boston: Little, Brown.

Madson, Michael B., Andrew C. Loignan, and Claire Lane. 2009. "Training in Motivational Interviewing: A Systematic Review." *Journal of Substance Abuse Treatment* 36 (1): 101–9.

Madson, Michael B., Margo C. Villarosa-Hurlocker, Julie A. Schumacher, and Jami A. Gauthier. 2019. "Motivational Interviewing Training of Substance Abuse Professionals: A Systematic Review." *Substance Abuse* 40 (1): 43–51.

Mann, Geoff. 2017. *In the Long Run We Are All Dead: Keynseianism, Political Economy, and Revolution*. New York: Verso Books.

Mannheim, Bruce. 1986. "Popular Song and Popular Grammar: Poetry and Metalanguage." *Word* 37 (1–2): 45–75.

Marcus, George E., and Michael M. J. Fischer. 1986. *Anthropology as Cultural Critique*. Chicago: University of Chicago Press.

Markell, Patchen. 2003. *Bound by Recognition*. Princeton: Princeton University Press.

Marsilli-Vargas, Xochitl. 2022. *Genres of Listening: An Ethnography of Listening in Buenos Aires*. Durham, NC: Duke University Press.

Masco, Joseph. 2006. *The Nuclear Borderlands: The Manhattan Project in Post Cold-War New Mexico*. Princeton: Princeton University Press.

Mason, Arthur. 2019. "Consulting Virtue: From Judgement to Decision-making in the Natural Gas Industry." *Journal of the Royal Anthropological Institute* 25 (S1): 124–39.

Matoesian, Gregory M. 2001. *Law and the Language of Identity: Discourse in the William Kennedy Smith Rape Trial*. New York: Oxford University Press.

Matoesian, Gregory M. 2008. "Role Conflict as an Interactional Resource in the Multimodal Emergence of Expert Identity." *Semiotica* 171 (1): 15–49.

Mauss, Marcel. 2016. *The Gift*. Expanded ed. Chicago: University of Chicago Press.

McAuley, Janet. 2015. "Guidelines and Value-based Decision Making: An Evolving Role for Payers." *North Carolina Medical Journal* 76 (4): 243–46.

McCabe, Randi E., Karen Rowa, Nicholas R. Farrell, Lisa Young, Richard P. Swinson, and Martin M. Anthony. 2019. "Improving Treatment Outcome in Obsessive-compulsive Disorder: Does Motivational Interviewing Boost Efficacy." *Journal of Obsessive Compulsive Disorder* 22: 100446.

McLoughlin, William G. 1978. *Revivals, Awakenings, and Reform*. Chicago: University of Chicago Press.

McMurran, Mary. 2009. "Motivational Interviewing with Offenders: A Systematic Review." *Legal and Criminological Psychology* 14 (1): 83–100.

Mehan, Hugh. 1996. "The Construction of an LD Student: A Case Study in the Politics of Representation." In Michael Silverstein and Greg Urban, eds., *Natural Histories of Discourse*, 253–76. Chicago: University of Chicago Press.

Mertz, Elizabeth. 1994. "Legal Language: Pragmatics, Poetics, and Social Power." *Annual Review of Anthropology* 23 (1): 435–55.

Mertz, Elizabeth. 2007. *The Language of Law School: Learning to "Think Like a Lawyer."* New York: Oxford University Press.

Miller, William R. 1983. "Motivational Interviewing with Problem Drinkers." *Behavioral Psychotherapy* 11 (2): 147–72.

Miller, William R. 1985. *Living As If: How Positive Faith Can Change Your Life*. Philadelphia: Westminster Press.

Miller, William R. 1994. "Motivational Interviewing: III. On the Ethics of Motivational Interviewing." *Behavioral and Cognitive Psychotherapy* 22 (2): 111–23.

Miller, William R. 1995. "The Ethics of Motivational Interviewing Revisited." *Behavioral and Cognitive Psychotherapy* 23 (4): 345–48.

Miller, William R., ed. 1999. *Integrating Spirituality into Treatment: Resources for Practitioners*. Washington, DC: American Psychological Association.

Miller, William R. 2009. "Conversation with William R. Miller." *Addiction* 104 (6): 883–93.

Miller, William R. 2017. *Lovingkindness: Realizing and Practicing Your True Self*. Eugene, OR: Cascade Books (Wipf & Stock).

Miller, William R., R. Gayle Benefield, and J. Scott Tonigan. 1993. "Enhancing Motivation for Change in Problem Drinking: A Controlled Comparison of Two Therapist Styles." *Journal of Consulting and Clinical Psychology* 61 (3): 455–61.

Miller, William R., and Janet C' de Baca. 2001. *Quantum Change: When Epiphanies and Sudden Insights Transform Our Ordinary Lives*. New York: Guilford Press.

Miller, William R., and Harold D. Delaney, eds. 2005. *Judeo-Christian Perspectives on Psychology: Human Nature, Motivation, and Change*. Washington, DC: American Psychological Association.

Miller, William R., and Kathleen A. Jackson. 1985. *Practical Psychology for Pastors: Toward More Effective Counseling*. Englewood Cliffs, NJ: Prentice-Hall.

Miller William R., and Kathy A. Mount. 2001. "A Small Study of Trainings in Motivational Interviewing: Does One Workshop Change Clinician and Client Behavior?" *Behavioural and Cognitive Psychotherapy* 29 (4): 457–71.

Miller, William R., and Theresa B. Moyers. 2006. "Eight Stages in Learning Motivational Interviewing." *Journal of Teaching in the Addictions* 5 (1): 3–17.

Miller, William R., and Stephen Rollnick. 1992. *Motivational Interviewing: Preparing People to Change Addictive Behaviors*. New York: Guilford Press.

Miller, William R., and Stephen Rollnick. 2002. *Motivational Interviewing: Preparing People for Change*. New York: Guilford Press.

Miller, William R., and Stephen Rollnick. 2009. "Ten Things That MI Is Not." *Behavioural and Cognitive Psychotherapy* 37 (2): 129–40.

Miller, William R., and Stephen Rollnick. 2013. *Motivational Interviewing: Helping People Change*. New York: Guilford Press.

Miller, William R., Stephen Rollnick, and Theresa B. Moyers. 1998. *Motivational Interviewing Professional Training VHS Videotape Series*. Albuquerque: University of New Mexico.

Miller, William R., and Gary Rose. 2009. "Toward a Theory of Motivational Interviewing." *American Psychologist* 64 (6): 527–37.

Miller, William R., and Gary Rose. 2015. "Motivational Interviewing and the Decisional Balance: Contrasting Responses to Client Ambivalence." *Behavioural and Cognitive Psychotherapy* 43 (2): 129–41.

Miller, William, Carol Yahne, Theresa Moyers, Jennifer Martinez and M. Pirritano. 2004. "A Randomized Control Trial of Methods to Help Clinicians Learn Motivational Interviewing." *Journal of Consulting and Clinical Psychology* 72 (6): 1050–62.

Miller, William, Carol Yahne, and J. Scott Tonigan. 2003. "Motivational Interviewing in Drug Abuse Services: A Randomized Trial." *Journal of Consulting and Clinical Psychology* 71 (4): 754–63.

Mohanty, Chandra Talpade. 1984. "Under Western Eyes: Feminist Scholarship and Colonial Discourses." *boundary 2* 12 (3): 333–58.

Morse, Gary, Michelle P. Salyers, Angela L. Rollins, and Maria Monroe-DeVita. 2012. "Burnout in Mental Health Services: A Review of the Problem and Its Remediation." *Administration and Policy in Mental Health and Mental Health Services Research* 39 (5): 341–52.

Morse, Janice M. 2006. "The Politics of Evidence." *Qualitative Health Research* 16 (3): 395–404.

Mosley, Jennifer, Nicole Marwell, and Marci Ybarra. 2019. "How the 'What Works'

Movement Is Failing Human Service Organizations, and What Social Work Can Do to Fix It." *Human Service Organizations: Management, Leadership & Governance* 43 (4): 326–35.

Moyers, Theresa, Jennifer Manuel, and Denise Ernst. 2014. "Motivational Interviewing Treatment Integrity Coding Manual 4.1." Unpublished manual.

Moyers, Theresa B., Timothy Martin, Delwyn Catley, Kari Jo Harris, and Jasjit S. Ahluwalia. 2003. "Assessing the Integrity of the Motivational Interventions: Reliability of the Motivational Interviewing Skills Score." *Behavioural and Cognitive Psychotherapy* 31: 177–84.

Moyers, Theresa B., Tim Martin, Paulette J. Christopher, J. Scott Tonigan, and Paul C. Amrhein. 2007. "Client Language as a Mediator of Motivational Interviewing Efficacy: Where Is the Evidence?" *Alcoholism: Clinical and Experimental Research* 31 (3): 40s–47s.

Moyers, Theresa B., Timothy Martin, Jennifer Manuel, Stacey Hendrickson, and William R. Miller. 2005. "Assessing Competence in the Use of Motivational Interviewing." *Journal of Substance Abuse Treatment* 28 (1): 19–26.

Moyers, Theresa, Timothy Martin, Jennifer Manuel, William Miller, and Denise Ernst. 2009. "Revised Global Scales: Motivational Interviewing Treatment Integrity 3.1." Albuquerque: University of New Mexico Center on Alcoholism, Substance Abuse and Addictions.

Moyers, Theresa, L. N. Rowel, Jennifer Manuel, Denise Ernst, and Jon M. Houck. 2016. "The Motivational Interviewing Treatment Integrity Code (MITI 4): Rationale, Preliminary Reliability and Validity." *Journal of Substance Abuse Treatment* 65: 36–42.

Munn, Nancy. 1986. *The Fame of Gawa*. Durham, NC: Duke University Press.

Musser, Peter H., and Christopher M. Murphy. 2009. "Motivational Interviewing with Perpetrators of Intimate Partner Abuse." *Journal of Clinical Psychology* 65 (11): 1218–31.

Nader, Laura. 1972. "Up the Anthropologist—Perspectives Gained from Studying Up." In Dell Hymes, ed., *Reinventing Anthropology*, 284–311. New York: Vintage Books.

Nakassis, Constantine. 2013. "Citation and Citationality." *Signs and Society* 1 (1): 51–78.

Nakassis, Constantine. 2016. "Scaling Red and the Horror of Trademark." In E. Summerson Carr and Michael Lempert, eds., *Scale: Discourse and Dimensions of Social Life*, 159–84. Berkeley: University of California Press.

Nakassis, Constantine. 2019. "Poetics of Praise and Image-texts of Cinematic Encompassment." *Journal of Linguistic Anthropology* 29 (1): 69–94.

Nakassis, Constantine. 2023. *Onscreen/Offscreen*. Toronto: University of Toronto Press.

Nichols, Thomas. 2017. *The Death of Expertise: The Campaign against Established Knowledge and Why It Matters*. New York: Oxford.

North Carolina Department of Health and Human Services. 2016. North Carolina Medicaid and NC Health Choice Section 1115 Demonstration Waiver Application. Raleigh: North Carolina Health and Human Services.

NREPP. 2017. National Registry of Evidence-Based Programs and Practices. https:// nrepp.samhsa.gov/about.aspx. Accessed August 4, 2017.

Nye, Robert D. 1992. *The Legacy of B. F. Skinner*. New York: Brooks/Cole.

Ong, Aihwa. 1988. "Colonialism and Modernity: Feminist Re-presentations of Women in Non-Western Societies." *Inscriptions: Journal for the Critique of Colonial Discourse* 3–4: 79–93.

Oregon Health Authority Behavioral Health Services. N.d. Approved Evidence-based Practices. https://www.oregon.gov/oha/HSD/AMH/Pages/EBP-Practices.aspx. Accessed July 8, 2017.

Oregon Senate Bill 267. 2003. Chapter 669 Oregon Laws Sections 3 and 7. https://www.oregonlegislature.gov/bills_laws/lawsstatutes/2003orLaw0669ses.html. Accessed July 8, 2017.

Ortner, Sherry. 1984. "Theory in Anthropology since the Sixties." *Comparative Studies in Society and History* 26 (1): 126–66.

Padgett, Deborah. 2016. *Qualitative Methods in Social Work Research*. 3rd ed. Thousand Oaks, CA: Sage.

PCORI. 2022. About PCORI. https://www.pcori.org/about/about-pcori. Accessed March 2022.

Peirce, Charles Sanders. 1974. *The Collected Papers of Charles Sanders Peirce*. Cambridge, MA: Harvard University Press.

Peräkylä, Anssi. 1995. *AIDS Counseling: Institutional Interaction and Clinical Practice*. New York: Cambridge University Press.

Philips, Susan U. 1998. *Ideology in the Language of Judges: How Judges Practice Law, Politics, and Courtroom Control*. New York: Oxford University Press.

Philips, Susan U. 2016. "Balancing the Scales of Justice in Tonga." In E. Summerson Carr and Michael Lempert, eds., *Scale: Discourse and Dimensions of Social Life*, 112–32. Oakland: University of California Press.

Picciano, Joseph, Roger A. Roffman, Seth C. Kalichman, Scott E. Rutledge, and James P. Berghuis. 2001. "A Telephone-Based Brief Intervention Using Motivational Enhancement to Facilitate HIV Risk Reduction Among MSM: A Pilot Study." *AIDS and Behavior* 5: 251–62.

Pierson, Heather M., Steven C. Hayes, Elizabeth V. Gifford, Nancy Roget, Michelle Padilla, Richard Bissett, Kristen Berry, Barbara Kohlenberg, Robert Rhode, and Gary Fisher. 2007. "An Examination of the Motivational Interviewing Treatment Integrity Code." *Journal of Substance Abuse Treatment* 32 (1): 11–17.

Povinelli, Elizabeth A. 1998. "The State of Shame: Australian Multiculturalism and the Crisis of Indigenous Citizenship." *Critical Inquiry* 24 (2): 575–610.

Povinelli, Elizabeth A. 2002. *The Cunning of Recognition: Indigenous Alterities and the Making of Australian Multiculturalism*. Durham, NC: Duke University Press.

Pressman, Jon F. 1994. "Pragmatics in the Late Twentieth Century: Countering Recent Historiographic Neglect." *Pragmatics* 4 (4): 461–89.

Raikhel, Eugene. 2015. *Governing Habits: Treating Alcoholism in the Post-Soviet Clinic*. Ithaca: Cornell University Press.

Resnicow, Kenneth, Fiona McHaster, Alison Bocian, Donna Harris, Yan Zhou, Linda Snetselaar, Robert Schwartz, Esther Myers, Jaquelin Gotlieb, Jan Foster, Donna Hollinger, Karen Smith, Susan Woolford, Dru Mueller, and Richard C. Wasserman. 2015."Motivational Interviewing and Dietary Counseling for Obesity in Primary Care: An RCT." *Pediatrics* 135 (4): 649–57.

Results First Clearinghouse Database. 2020. https://www.pewtrusts.org/en/research-and-analysis/data-visualizations/2015/results-first-clearinghouse-database. Accessed October 2020.

Richelle, Marc. 1993. *B. F. Skinner: A Reappraisal*. Hillsdale, NJ: Erlbaum.

Ringer, Fritz. 2004. *Max Weber: An Intellectual Biography*. Chicago: University of Chicago Press.

Robbins, Joel. 2004. *Becoming Sinners: Christianity and Moral Torment in a Papua New Guinea Society*. Berkeley: University of California Press.

Rogers, Carl. 1946. "Significant Aspects of Client-centered Therapy." *American Psychologist* 1 (10): 415–22.

Rogers, Carl. 1947. "Some Observations on the Organization of Personality." *American Psychologist* 2 (9): 358–68.

Rogers, Carl. 1951. *Client-centered Therapy: Its Current Practice, Implications, and Theory*. London: Constable.

Rogers, Carl. 1961. *On Becoming a Person: A Therapist's View of Psychotherapy*. London: Constable.

Rogers, Carl. 1980. *A Way of Being*. New York: Houghton Mifflin.

Rogers, Carl. 1986. "Reflections of Feelings." *Person-Centered Review* (4): 125–40.

Rogers, Carl, Frederick S. Perls, Albert Ellis, and Everett L. Shostrom. 1965. *Three Approaches to Psychotherapy*. Film. Corona Del Mar, CA: Psychological and Educational Films.

Rogers, Everett. 2003. *Diffusion of Innovations*. 5th ed. New York: Free Press.

Roitman, Janet. 2013. *Anti-crisis*. Durham, NC: Duke University Press.

Rollnick, Stephen, William R. Miller, and Christopher C. Butler. 2012. *Motivational Interviewing in Health Care: Helping Patients Change*. New York: Guilford Press.

Rosaldo, Michelle. 1982. "The Things We Do with Words: Ilongot Speech Acts and Speech Act Theory in Philosophy." *Language in Society* 11 (2): 203-37.

Rose, Nikolas. 1998. *Inventing Our Selves: Psychology, Power, and Personhood*. New York: Cambridge University Press.

Rose, Nikolas. 1999. *Governing the Soul*. New York: Free Association Books.

Rutherford, Alexandra. 2006. "The Social Control of Behavior Control: Behavior Modification, Individual Rights, and Research Ethics in America, 1971–1979." *Journal of the History of the Behavioral Sciences* 42 (3): 203–20.

Rutherford, Alexandra. 2009. *Beyond the Box: B. F. Skinner's Technology of Behaviour from the Laboratory to Life, 1950s–1970s*. Toronto: University of Toronto Press.

Sackett, David L. 1997. Evidence-based Medicine. *Seminars in Perinatology* 21 (1): 3–5.

Sacks, Harvey, Emanuel A. Schegloff, and Gail Jefferson. 1974. "A Simplest Systematics for the Organization of Turn Taking for Conversation." *Language* 50 (4): 696–735.

Saunders, Barry. 2008. *CT Suite: The Work of Diagnosis in the Age of Noninvasive Cutting*. Durham, NC: Duke University Press.

Savicki, Victor, and Eric Cooley. 1983. "Theoretical and Research Considerations of Burnout." *Children and Youth Services Review* 5 (3): 227–38.

Sawyer, Keith. 2002. *Improvised Dialogues: Emergence and Creativity in Conversation*. New York: Praeger.

Schechter, Kate. 2014. *Illusions of a Future: Psychoanalysis and the Biopolitics of Desire*. Durham, NC: Duke University Press.

Schegloff, Emanuel A. 2007. *Sequence Organization in Interaction: A Primer in Conversation Analysis I*. New York: Cambridge University Press.

Schieffelen, Bambi. 1986. "Language Socialization." *Annual Review of Anthropology* 12: 163–91.

Scollon, Ron. 1985. "The Machine Stops: Silence in the Metaphor of Malfunction." In Deborah Tannen and Muriel Saville-Troike, eds., *Perspectives on Silence*, 21–30. Norwood, NJ: Ablex Publishing.

Searle, John. 1969. *Speech Acts: An Essay in the Philosophy of Language*. Cambridge: Cambridge University Press.

Shange, Savannah. 2019. *Progressive Dystopia: Abolition, Antiblackness, and Schooling in San Francisco*. Durham, NC: Duke University Press.

Sheehan, Patrick. 2022. "The Paradox of Self-help Expertise: How Unemployed Workers Become Professional Career Coaches." *American Journal of Sociology* 127 (4): 1151–82.

Sheridan, Thomas. 1968. *A Course of Lectures on Elocution, 1762*. New York: B. Blom.

Shklovsky, Viktor. 2015. "Art, as Device." *Poetics Today* 36 (3): 151–74.

Shuster, Stef M. 2016. "Uncertain Expertise and the Limitations of Clinical Guidelines in Transgender Healthcare." *Journal of Health and Social Behavior* 57 (3): 319–32.

Silverstein, Michael. 1977. "Language Structure and Linguistic Ideology." In Paul R. Cline, William F. Hanks, and Carol Hofbauer, eds., *The Elements: A Parasession on Linguistic Units and Levels*, 193–247. Chicago: Chicago Linguistic Society.

Silverstein, Michael. 1993. "Metapragmatic Discourse and Metapragmatic Function." In John Lucy, ed., *Reflexive Language: Reported Speech and Metapragmatics*, 33–58. New York: Cambridge University Press.

Silverstein, Michael. 1996. "Encountering Language and Languages of Encounter in North American Ethnohistory." *Journal of Linguistic Anthropology* 6 (2): 126–44.

Silverstein, Michael. 2001. "The Limits of Awareness." In Alessandro Duranti, *Linguistic Anthropology: A Reader*, 382–401. New York: Blackwell.

Silverstein, Michael. 2003. *Talking Politics: The Substance of Style from Abe to "W."* Chicago: Prickly Paradigm Press.

Silverstein, Michael. 2004. "'Cultural' Concepts and the Language-Culture Nexus." *Current Anthropology* 45 (5): 621–52.

Silverstein, Michael. 2005. "The Poetics of Politics: 'Theirs' and 'Ours.'" *Journal of Anthropological Research* 61 (1): 1–24.

Silverstein, Michael. 2016. "Semiotic Vinification and the Scaling of Taste." In E. Summerson Carr and Michael Lempert, eds., *Scale: Discourse and Dimensions of Social Life*, 185–212. Berkeley: University of California Press.

Silverstein, Michael, and Greg Urban. 1996. "The Natural History of Discourse." In M. Silverstein and G. Urban, eds., *Natural Histories of Discourse*, 1–19. Chicago: University of Chicago Press.

Simmel, Georg. 1978. *The Philosophy of Money*. Trans. T. Bottimore and D. Frisby. London: Routledge & Kegan Paul.

Skinner, B. F. 1945. "Baby in a Box—Introduction to the Mechanical Baby-tender. *Ladies Home Journal* 62: 30–31, 135-6, 138.

Skinner, B. F. 1948. *Walden Two*. New York: Macmillan.

Skinner, B. F. 1953. *Science and Human Behavior*. New York: Macmillan.

Skinner, B. F. 1957. *Verbal Behavior*. New York: Prentice Hall.

Skinner, B. F. 1963. "Operant Behavior." *American Psychologist* 18 (8): 503–15.

Skinner, B. F. 1971. *Beyond Freedom and Dignity*. New York: Knopf.

Skinner, B. F. 1988. "Philosophy of Behaviorism." Interview conducted by Eve Segal. https://www.youtube.com/watch?v=NpDmRc8-pyU.

Skovholt, Thomas M., and Michelle Trotter-Mathison. 2016. *The Resilient Practitioner: Burnout and Compassion Fatigue Prevention and Self-care Strategies for the Helping Professions*. New York: Routledge.

Smith, Benjamin. 2005. "Ideologies of the Speaking Subject in the Psychotherapeutic Theory and Practice of Carl Rogers." *Journal of Linguistic Anthropology* 15 (20): 258–72.

Smith, Brenda, and Stella E. F. Donovan. 2003. "Child Welfare Practice in Organizational and Institutional Context." *Social Service Review* 77 (4): 541–63.

Smith, Jennifer L., Paul C. Amrhein, Adam C. Brooks, Kenneth M. Carpenter, Deborah Levin, and Elizabeth A. Schreiber. 2007. "Providing Live Supervision via Teleconferencing Improves Acquisition of Motivational Interviewing Skills after Workshop Attendance." *American Journal of Drug and Alcohol Abuse* 33 (1): 163–68.

Smith, Yvonne. 2014. "Rethinking Decision Making: An Ethnographic Study of Worker Agency in Crisis Intervention." *Social Service Review* 88 (3): 407–42.

Smith, Yvonne. 2017. "Beyond 'Common Sense': The Role of Local Knowledge in Youth Residential Treatment." *Social Work Research* 41 (4): 221–34.

Snell-Rood Claire, Elise T. Jaramillo, Lara Gunderson, Sarah Hagadone, Danielle Fettes, Gregory A. Aarons, and Cathleen Willging. 2020. "Enacting Competition, Capacity and Collaboration: Performing Neoliberalism in the U.S. in the Era of Evidence-based Interventions." *Critical Public Health* (online).

Social Security Act. 1982. Vol. 47 FR 30475 §416.601. July 14, 1982.

Social Security Administration. 2018. "A Guide for Representative Payees." Publication No. 05-10076. https://www.ssa.gov/pubs/EN-05-10076.pdf.

Social Security Administration. n.d. "Representative Payee Program: FAQs for Representative Payees." Social Security Administration. https://www.ssa.gov/payee/faqrep.htm. Accessed March 29, 2017.

Söderfeldt, Marie, Bjorn Söderfeldt, and Lars-Erik Warg. 1995. "Burnout in Social Work." *Social Work* 40 (5): 638–46.

Sosin, Michael R. 2002. "Negotiating Case Decisions in Substance Abuse Managed Care." *Journal of Health and Social Behavior* 43 (3): 277–95.

Soydan, Haluk. 2013. "Intervention Science." In *Encyclopedia of Social Work*. New York: NASW Press.

Standring, Adam. 2017. "Evidence-based Practice and the Politics of Neoliberal Reason." *Critical Policy Studies* 11 (2): 227–34.

Star, Susan L., and James R. Griesemer. 1989. "Institutional Ecology, 'Translations' and Boundary Objects: Amateurs and Professionals in Berkeley's Museum of Vertebrate Zoology, 1907–39." *Social Studies of Science* 19 (3): 387–420.

Stiles, William B., David A. Shapiro, and Jenny A. Firth-Cozens. 1988. "Verbal Response Mode Use in Contrasting Psychotherapies: A Within-subjects Comparison." *Journal of Consulting and Clinical Psychology* 56 (5): 727–33.

Storeng, Katerini T., and Dominique P. Béhague. 2014. "'Playing the Numbers Game': Evidence-based Advocacy and the Technocratic Narrowing of the Safe Motherhood Initiative." *Medical Anthropology Quarterly* 28 (2): 260–79.

Strathern, Marilyn. 1988. *The Gender of the Gift*. Berkeley: University of California Press.

Stromberg, Peter. 1993. *Language and Self-transformation: A Study of the Christian Conversion Narrative*. Cambridge: Cambridge University Press.

Tambiah, Stanley. 1973. "Form and Meaning of Magical Acts: A Point of View." In Robin Horton and Ruth Finnegan, eds., *Modes of Thought: Essays on Thinking in Western and Non-Western Societies*. London: Faber & Faber.

Tambiah, Stanley. 1990. *Magic, Science, Religion and the Scope of Rationality*. Cambridge: Cambridge University Press.

Tanenbaum, Sandra J. 2003. "Evidence-based Practice in Mental Health: Practical Weaknesses Meet Political Strengths." *Journal of Evaluation in Clinical Practice* 9 (2): 287–301.

Tanenbaum, Sandra J. 2005. "Evidence-based Practice as Mental Health Policy: Three Controversies and a Caveat." *Health Affairs (Project Hope)* 24 (1): 163–73.

Tannen, Deborah. 1985. "Silence: Anything But." In Tannen and Muriel Saville-Troike, eds., *Perspectives on Silence*, 93–111. Norwood, NJ: Ablex.

Taylor, Charles. 1994. "The Politics of Recognition." In Amy Gutmann, ed., *Multiculturalism: Examining the Politics of Recognition*. Princeton: Princeton University Press.

Thevos, Angelica K., Sonja J. Olsen, Josefa M. Rangel, Fred A. Kaona, Mathias Tembo, and Robert E. Quick. 2002. "Social Marketing and Motivational Interviewing as Community Interventions for Safe Water Behaviors: Follow-up Surveys in Zambia." *International Quarterly of Community Health Education* 21 (1): 51–65.

Thevos, Angelica K., Robert E. Quirk, and Violet Yanduli. 2000. "Motivational Interviewing Enhances the Adoption of Water Disinfection Practices in Zambia. *Health Promotion International* 15 (3): 207–14.

Timmermans, Stefan, and Marc Berg. 2003. *The Gold Standard: The Challenge of Evidence-based Medicine*. Philadelphia: Temple University Press.

Traux, Charles B. 1966. "Reinforcement and Non-reinforcement in Rogerian Psychotherapy." *Journal of Abnormal Psychology* 71 (1): 1–9.

Traux, Charles B., and Robert R. Carkhuff. 1967. *Toward Effective Counseling and Psychotherapy*. Chicago: Aldine.

Trouillot, Michel-Rolph. 1995. *Silencing the Past: Power and the Production of History*. Boston: Beacon Press.

Tsing, Anna L. 2004. *Friction: An Ethnography of Global Connection*. Princeton: Princeton University Press.

Tsing, Anna L. 2015. *The Mushroom at the End of the World: On the Possibility of Life in Capitalist Ruins*. Princeton: Princeton University Press.

Urban, Greg. 2001. *Metaculture: How Culture Moves through the World*. Minneapolis: University of Minnesota Press.

Van de Luitgaarden, Guido M. 2009. "Evidence-based Practice in Social Work: Lessons from Judgment and Decision-making Theory." *British Journal of Social Work* 39(2): 243–60.

Walker, Denise D., Thomas O. Walton, Clayton Neighbors, Deborah Kaysen, Lyungai Mbilinyi, Jolee Darnell, Lindsey Rodriguez, and Roger A. Roffman. 2017. "Randomized Trial of Motivational Interviewing Plus Feedback for Soldiers with Untreated Alcohol Abuse." *Journal of Consulting and Clinical Psychology* 85 (2): 99–110.

Watts, Richard J. 1997. "Silence and the Acquisition of Status in Verbal Interaction." In Adam Jaworski, ed., *Silence: Interdisciplinary Perspectives*, 87–116. Berlin: Mouton de Gruyter.

Watzlawick, Paul, Janet B. Beavin, and Don D. Jackson. 1967. *Pragmatics of Human Communication: A Study of Interactional Patterns, Pathologies, and Paradoxes*. New York: W. W. Norton.

Webb, Stephen. 2001. "Some Considerations on the Validity of Evidence-based Practice in Social Work." *British Journal of Social Work* 31 (1): 57–79.

Weber, Max. 1952. *The Protestant Ethic and the Spirit of Capitalism*. Trans. Talcott Parsons. New York: Charles Scribner's Sons.

Weber, Max. 1968. *On Charisma and Institution Building*. Chicago: University of Chicago Press.

Weber, Max. 2020. *Charisma and Disenchantment: The Vocation Lectures*. New York: New York Review Books Classics.

Weiner, Annette B. 1993. *Inalienable Possessions: The Paradox of Keeping While Giving*. Berkeley: University of California Press.

Wilce, James. 1998. *Eloquence in Trouble: The Poetics and Politics of Complaint in Rural Bangladesh*. New York: Oxford University Press.

Wilf, Eitan Y. 2014. *School for Cool: The Academic Jazz Program and the Paradox of Institutionalized Creativity*. Chicago: University of Chicago Press.

Williams, Raymond. 1986. *Keywords: A Vocabulary of Culture and Society*. New York: Oxford University Press.

Wirt, William. 1816. *Sketches of the Life and Character of Patrick Henry*. Philadelphia: Webster.

Wolf, Eric. 1982. *Europe and the People without History*. Berkeley: University of California Press.

Woolard, Kathryn A. 1998. "Introduction: Language Ideology as a Field of Inquiry." In Bambi B. Schieffelin, Katheryn A. Woolard, and Paul V. Kroskrity, eds., *Language Ideologies: Practice and Theory*, 3–47. New York: Oxford University Press.

Wright, James. 1987. "B. F. Skinner: The Pragmatist Humanist." In Sohan Modgil and Celia Modgil, eds., *B. F. Skinner: Consensus and Controversy*, 85–92. New York: Routledge.

Wu, Dunli, Grace X. Ma, Kathy Zhou, Dinglun Zhou, Andy Lin, and Adrienne N. Poon. 2009. "The Effect of a Culturally Tailored Smoking Cessation for Chinese American Smokers." *Nicotine and Tobacco Research* 11 (2): 1448–57.

Wyatt, W. Joseph. 2000. "Behavioral Science in the Crosshairs: The FBI File on B. F. Skinner." *Social and Behavioral Issues* 10 (1): 101–9.

Yelle, Robert. 2012. *Sovereignty and the Sacred: Secularism and the Political Economy of Religion*. Chicago: University of Chicago Press.

Young, Iris Marion. 1990. "The Ideal of Community and the Politics of Difference." In Linda Nicholson, ed., *Feminism/Postmodernism*, 300–323. New York: Routledge.

Zhan, Mei. 2009. *Other-Worldly: Making Chinese Medicine through Transnational Frames*. Durham, NC: Duke University Press.

Zhang, Li. 2020. *Anxious China: Inner Revolution and the Politics of Psychotherapy*. Berkeley: University of California Press.

Žižek, Slavoj. 2006. *The Parallax View*. Cambridge, MA: MIT Press.

Zuckerman, Charles H. P., and N. J. Enfield. N.d. "Limits of Thematizability." Unpublished manuscript.

Zuckoff, Allan, Judith Carpenter, Jacque Elder, and Tim Van Loo. 2007. "How I Learned MI: A Qualitative Inquiry." *MINT Bulletin* 14 (1): 14–15.

Index

abduction, 7, 17; contrasted with deduction, 178, 181, 183–84, 220n3; definition, 172; MI as training in, 166, 171–77, 203; reflection as, 67, 72, 74–5, 226n40, 227n11. *See also* de-ferral; Dewey, John; Peirce, Charles Sanders

abstinence. *See* contingency-based programs

acceptance, 16, 37, 115, 122

accountability. *See* responsibility

active ingredient, 62, 83, 88, 148, 150; definition, 226n3

addiction, drug: ideologies concerning, 33, 35

addiction treatment and counseling, 1–4, 7, 10, 15, 22, 28, 34, 46, 57, 59, 75, 132, 143, 145, 165, 169, 176, 177, 184, 197, 215n4, 227n13, 231n41, 233n13, 239n4. *See also* alcoholism

advice, 230n27; and expertise, 34–5, 105; MI perspective on, 66, 68–70, 97, 139; requesting permission to give, 98, 203

aesthetics: speech, 61, 63, 89, 92 (*see also* poetics); visual, 48, 238n23

affirmation, 54, 66; definition, 67; tone of, 76. *See also* OARS

Africa, 15, 195–96, 216

AIDS-related dementia, 183, 186, 188

Albuquerque, 13, 32–33, 48, 56, 107, 142, 225n35

Alcoholics Anonymous (AA), 22, 112, 174, 220n34, 239n4

alcoholism, 5, 6, 12–13, 33–35, 50, 59, 81, 83, 97, 174, 224n27, 225n40. *See also* addiction, drug; Alcoholics Anonymous

ambivalence, 166, 170, 210, 216n8, 218n21; and change talk, 74; definition of, 5; developing, 76; in interviews, 6; MI addressing, 5, 74, 98, 216n8; MI understanding of, 73–76, 166, 170; pragmatic approach to, 166, 170, 216n8; and therapeutic paradox, 218n21; in training, 210

American: ahistoricism, 199–201; anthropology, 198–99, 202, 213; authoritarianism, 56, 57; capitalism, 8, 100, 110, 114, 117, 124, 129, 131, 140, 162; character, 16, 31, 222n15, 231n41; democracy and democratic ideals, 16, 32, 40, 47, 53, 56, 57, 102, 199, 221n5, 228n16; discourses, 20, 35, 140; expertise, 57; folk heroes, 234n21; governance and government, 31; guilt, 197, 202; individualism, 41; innovation, 8 (*see also* Motivational Interviewing: innovativeness of); market, 131; motivating Americans, 12; philosophy (*see* pragmatism; speech act theory); pragmatism, 17, 166–67, 171, 172, 173, 176, 187, 199, 239n3; professional culture, 128, 162; Protestantism, 20, 21, 35, 99, 102, 109, 110, 114–16, 124, 140, 147, 232n6, 232n10, 232n22, 235n31; psychology, psychotherapy, and counseling, 16, 24, 26, 32, 43, 93, 102, 156–57, 160, 193, 198, 218n22, 227n14, 228n17, 238n28; rhetoric, 62–63, 81, 89, 92, 93, 102, 196, 199, 232n9; science, 17, 162, 199

evidence, 129, 138, 141–46, 154, 158, 160–
61, 195–96, 236n13; best, 131–32, 135,
158, 235n3; hierarchy of, 135–36, 143,
158
evidence-based practice, 129, 131–33, 136–
47, 154, 156–61, 177, 192, 194, 236n7,
236n9, 236n14, 237n21, 239n30; am-
biguousness of, 239n32; definition of
evidence, 236n13; and efficacy, 145;
and entrepreneurship, 236n11; MI's
designation as, 5, 7, 16, 18, 19, 22, 100,
106, 129, 131–37, 145–47, 177, 192,
216n9; movement, 123, 135, 141, 145,
153, 157, 159, 219n24, 235n2, 235n3,
235n4, 236n7; registry of, 18, 136–38,
143–45; state support, 135, 137–41,
143, 236n10, 237n15; utility of designation for professionals, 140, 156–61
experimentation, 166, 175–76, 181, 187,
203, 211. See also abduction
expertise, 6, 8, 23, 26, 36, 50, 119, 167, 199;
anthropology of, 9, 210, 241n4 (see
also training, professional); as authority, 32, 57, 66; of client, 13, 30, 34, 44,
48, 53, 57, 63, 72, 171, 188, 191, 237n21;
and democracy, 53; distrust of, 31, 32,
57, 220n4; as interactional process,
209; of practitioners, 237n21; and professional distinction, 240n12; and recognition, 220n5; of registries, 237n15;
as trick, 95. See also expert trap;
(in)expertise
expert trap, 30–31, 45, 50, 57, 71, 182, 184–
85, 189, 225n31. See also diagnosis

Facebook, 126–27, 155
faith: in American ideals, 124; and doubt,
141–45, 147, 197; in MI, 21, 59, 104,
106, 134, 146, 147, 162, 165–66, 170,
186. See also spirit, MI
fallibilism, 181, 183
family systems, 218n21
Fanon, Frantz, 35, 37, 221n11
feedback, 66, 70. See also evaluation;
scoring
"feeling heard," xi, 62, 70, 74, 78. See also
recognition

feminism, 198, 218n19, 220n38, 221n10,
222n15, 229n20
fidelity instruments, 86, 111, 147–48, 150,
211, 237n19, 237n20. See also Motivational Interviewing Treatment Integrity scale
film, demonstration or training, 1–4, 10,
11, 60–62, 81–82, 88, 101, 150, 198,
215n1, 230n33; demographic composi-
tion of actors, 60, 91, 200, 217n18
Fliegelman, Jay, 77, 92, 228n15, 228n16
flipping the script, 226n41, 227n8
"flow," 20, 22, 115, 116, 123, 193, 201. See
also diffusion; dissemination
fluency, 76, 81, 91, 101, 103. See also disfluency; natural: language
fractal recursion, 66, 199
Franklin, Benjamin, 114, 234n21
Fraser, Nancy, 32, 36, 37, 56, 221n6, 221n10
"Fred," 168, 177–84, 186, 188–89, 240n9
freedom, 32, 46, 128, 150–52, 171; and behaviorism, 38, 40–41; in/of speech,
47, 71, 171
Freud, Sigmund, 41, 218n19. See also psychoanalysis

Gal, Susan, 23, 66, 220n33, 224n29,
229n20
gatekeeping, 46, 99, 106, 109, 111, 120, 153
gender, 4, 10, 22, 60, 91, 198–201, 217n18,
221n10, 225n31, 229n20, 239n30
generosity, 115, 122, 151–52, 162, 213
genre, 227n14, 229n20, 238n23
genuineness. See sincerity
gift: in anthropological theory, 151–52,
220n38, 234n26; MI spirit as, 99, 108,
147–52
Goffman, Erving, 215n3
gold standard. See randomized controlled
trials
Goodwin, Charles, 210, 217n14, 227n8,
240n12
Graeber, David, 192, 241n1
guess. See abduction
"guide," 29, 45, 50–51
guru, 15, 126–27, 129
Gusterson, Hugh, 211, 212, 217n14

practitioner, 52, 112, 117, 155, 174, 182, 184, 188, 199

reverse psychology, 218n21

revival: professional, xii, 6, 20, 100, 113, 165, 192, 203; religious, 21; Second Great Awakening, 113

"Rex," 116–17, 123, 125, 159–61, 235n1, 238n24

rhetoric: Anglo-American, 16, 196, 232n9; classical, 226n2, 228n16; and MI spirit, 101, 103; of Motivational Interviewing, 62, 69, 74, 92, 98; of science, 159; and sincerity, 194; suspicion of, 92. *See also* pause; reflection; rhythm

rhythm, 15, 77, 80, 86, 90, 227n15

Rogerian therapy. *See* client-centered therapy; Rogers, Carl

Rogers, Carl, 16, 32, 34, 36, 43, 51, 56, 72, 115, 149, 156–57, 158, 219n31, 223n20, 223n21, 224n28, 225n38, 228n17, 234n24; debate with Skinner, 38–41, 45, 56, 135, 222n15, 223n22; opinions on therapeutic interventions, 38, 41. *See also* client-centered therapy

Rogers, Everett, 21, 219n31

role-play, 12, 30, 54, 60, 62, 64–70, 95, 98, 101, 103, 153, 154, 168, 171, 178–80, 183, 212; definition of, 218n20; democratic, 227n7

rolling with resistance, 54–55, 167, 169–70, 180, 225n40. *See also* resistance

Rollnick, Stephen, 141, 216n11; on aims of MI, 20; British healthcare, 131; career history of, 15, 17; on charismatic authority, 126, 130; on collaboration and partnership in MI, 31, 37, 50; collaboration with William Miller (*see* Miller, William R.: collaboration with Steven Stephen); on interview ethics, 47; and MI spirit, 18, 30, 131, 162, 235n1; on threats to MI spirit in US, 16, 123, 125, 131–34, 137, 140, 141, 150–54, 157, 160, 162, 235n2, 236n11 (*see also* branding; careerism; packaging; productization; profit); in training films, 217n18. See also *Motivational Interviewing* (textbook); "Ten Things That MI Is Not"

Rose, Nicholas, 221n7

Rounder, 81–82, 154, 201, 217n18, 230n33, 233n18

sanitation, 5, 17, 32, 195–96, 216n10

Sawyer, Keith, 64, 226n4

scaling, 5, 8, 9, 12, 18, 19, 21, 35, 37, 62, 87, 203, 226n6. *See also* dissemination

Scandinavia, 15, 123, 194. *See also* Norway

science, MI, 13, 147–56; efficacy and, 146–48; and humanism, 156–61; and magic, 100, 129, 134, 142, 236n6, 240n12; and politics, 133, 134 (*see also* evidence-based practice: state support); and spirit, 111, 134, 142

Science and Technology Studies (STS), 22, 134, 137

scientist practitioner, 156, 238n25

scientization, 18, 132, 159, 192, 237n21, 239n30

scoring, 99, 103, 104, 109, 118, 168. *See also* coding

Searle, John, 4, 118, 234n25. *See also* speech act theory

secularism, secularization. *See under* Protestantism

self-actualization, 36, 41, 224n27, 224n28. *See also* client-centered therapy

self-determination. *See* autonomy

self-direction. *See* autonomy

self-help, 10, 217n19

self-perception theory, 43. *See also* Bem, Daryl

semantics, 76, 84–89; semantic slope, 85

sexual orientation, 200

silence, 228n20; and Quakerism, 233n10; about silence, 85; in Standard American English, 79–80, 228n19. *See also* pause

Silent Man, 60, 81, 92, 230n33

Silverstein, Michael, 83, 84, 86, 89, 92, 102, 210, 216n7, 220n33, 224n29, 227n8, 229n23, 232n9, 235n30, 240n12

Simmel, Georg, 150

sincerity, 13, 63, 76, 89, 92–94, 98, 102, 103, 104, 106, 193, 194; and divine will, 102. *See also* authenticity

skepticism: of business and marketing, 123–24; of experts, 30–31, 38; and